MW01194659

CINEMA
ALCHEMIST

CINEMA ALCHEMIST

HOW I BUILT THE LIGHTSABER AND WON AN OSCAR

DESIGNING STAR WARS & ALIEN

A MEMOIR
ROGER CHRISTIAN

TITAN BOOKS

Cinema Alchemist
ISBN 9781783299003
eBook ISBN 9781785650857

Published by Titan Books
A division of Titan Publishing Group Ltd.
144 Southwark Street, London SE1 0UP
United Kingdom

First edition: July 2016
2 4 6 8 10 9 7 5 3 1

Did you enjoy this book? We love to hear from our readers. Please e-mail us at:
readerfeedback@titanemail.com or write to **Reader Feedback** at the above address.

To receive advance information, news, competitions, and exclusive offers online,
please sign up for the Titan newsletter on our website: www.titanbooks.com

A CIP catalogue record for this title is available from the British Library.

Printed in the US

CONTENTS

FOREWORD
BY J.W. RINZLER

O nce upon a time, while doing research in the Lucasfilm Image Archives, I came across a mysterious photograph. At first I didn't know who the five people in it were, but there was an unmistakable aura about the group. Sometimes an energy is present when a photo is taken that can make itself felt many years later, even a century beyond its time. In this case it was about thirty years later and the group soon revealed itself to be the English art department core of the first *Star Wars* film: production designer John Barry, art directors Norman Reynolds and Les Dilley, construction supervisor Bill Welch—and one long-haired twenty-something, who looked like he might be a visiting rock star: Roger Christian, set dresser and provocateur.

For it was Roger, in league with John Barry, who hit upon the idea of a used universe.

This greasy, worn out world became, in late 1975, the ingenious answer to multiple questions at the time. The big quandary had been, How on earth would the art department build the multi-set visionary worlds George Lucas had dreamt up, given their tiny budget? Linked to that question was another: How would they differentiate *Star Wars* from its low-rent trashy sci-fi cousins? (*2001* excepted, but that was an art film.)

To make things that much harder, just before principal photography was to begin, Twentieth Century Fox, their very reluctant studio backer, had slashed their budget from $8.2 to $7.5 million, ten percent of which reduction came directly out of the art department's coffers. Christian's work-around brainstorm, based on years of experience under several genial mentors, was to source a cheap supply of odd materials, consisting of pre-fabricated realistic shapes, forms, and ideas; junk, that is. Lots and lots of junk: airplane junk, washing-machine junk, plumbing junk. He would also sell Lucas on the idea of real, but enhanced, weapons to stand in for the script's blasters and lightsabers.

I've written about some of this in *The Making of Star Wars*; it was while doing research for that book that I found said photo, in an old binder of black-and-white film. That book was the best job I could do as an outsider, decades after the fact (though relying on contemporary interviews). So when Roger told me he was writing his own memoirs, and as I came to appreciate his phenomenal memory for both details and the big picture, I was thrilled. His account would be—and now is—the story of someone who was right there: meeting with George Lucas in Mexico early in preproduction; standing with him as the studio dithered, and then, while prepping the sets, watching Lucas's back in Tunisia and at Elstree Studios. His account of the enormous uphill battles and mind-bending challenges of the shoot are unrivaled.

Afterward Lucas rewarded Christian's ingenuity and loyalty with matched loyalty, helping him become a director, in turn, by backing his live-action short *Black Angel*. That short has recently been revived (a fascinating story) and its influence acclaimed. Roger's account of his low-budget independent filmmaking, as he cobbled together talent and resources to make *Black Angel* a reality, should be required reading for film students.

Roger then returned Lucas's backing, jumping in when needed as second-unit director on *Return of the Jedi* and *The Phantom Menace*. In later conversations Lucas would refer to Christian, Barry, and a paltry few others as those who had saved his quirky little space fantasy from disaster, helping it become the undreamt-of phenomenon it is today (though they did think that it would be successful even at the time).

Yet Roger's is more than a book about *Star Wars*. It is unlike any other film book that I've read in that it presents, unvarnished, the raw emotional world of the craftspeople and artists, the producers, directors, and actors, who often toil in impossible conditions under great duress—long hours, life-threatening illness, and internal foes—because they so love what they are doing.

This is never more evident than in Roger's further adventures during the making of another classic film, the horrifying and beautiful *Alien*, an art-directing job almost immediately after *Star Wars*, on a film that would have almost as great an impact on cinema. The vicissitudes he colorfully describes feel real; his portraits of his contemporaries are insightful and compassionate (although a few receive naught but righteous wrath); and his descriptions of London life during one of its creative peaks, during the 1960s, 70s, and early 80s, is a lot of fun, as he rubs shoulders with the Rolling Stones and other luminaries (the book even has a side of Monty Python's *Life of Brian*).

So if you want to find out how a wily artist matched wits with the likes of George Lucas and Ridley Scott, how integral art departments functioned during a British heyday of film creation on the first *Star Wars* and *Alien*, how an Academy Award–winning director crafted an enigmatic tale from nothing, and how death was defied in devotional service to the silver screen, then, by all means, read on…

J. W. RINZLER

AUTHOR'S NOTE

When I was having my first interview for a job in the film industry as tea boy to the art department on *Oliver!*, production designer John Box gave me this advice:

> "You are alone in the desert, standing next to a silver airplane with a bottle of green ink in your pocket. A cloud of dust approaches nearer and nearer as the director and producer arrive. The director looks at the plane and says, 'Great, this will work, can you have it red by tomorrow morning?' You either do it or talk your way out of it there and then. That's the film industry."

These wise words have served as my mantra throughout a long career and in no small way came to full force when I was asked to set decorate *Star Wars* on a budget that most people would have said, no; it cannot be done.

PREFACE

T he title for this book came from my coming up with the idea to make all the interiors of the sets and props on *Star Wars* from scrap metal and old airplane parts, and being rewarded with an Academy Award for it. I signed on to set-decorate *Star Wars* in August of 1975 having met George Lucas in Mexico earlier that year while working on *Lucky Lady*. Being asked to come up with props, guns, and robots, new inventions in George's script like a lightsaber, Luke's speeder and a diminutive robot called R2-D2 and the golden C-3PO took a huge leap of faith and confidence. The initial budget at that time was four million dollars and my set-dressing budget a tiny two hundred thousand.

Even in those times this was hardly enough for John Barry, Les Dilley, and me to create this world imagined and beautifully illustrated in Ralph McQuarrie's paintings. My first conversation with George Lucas in Mexico revolved around a common language, that science-fiction films had portrayed unrealistic sets and props that were all new and plastic-looking. We had a common goal—to make a spaceship that looked oily and greasy, and held together like a very used second-hand car. Thus the *Millennium Falcon*, looking like a cross between an old submarine and a used spaceship, came about, a philosophy extending to every detail, including the props and guns and all dressing.

My path to making *Star Wars* and my experiences made it possible to reach far outside the conventional way I was brought up, and prepared me to go out on a limb and suggest to George Lucas new ways to dress the sets, like buying old airplane scrap and breaking it down and using it to create the *Falcon's* interiors. My pet peeve was sci-fi guns that looked and sounded like toys, so I suggested using real guns and adapting their look for *Star Wars*. My luck was having a director who was an independent filmmaker who, having made a very low budget science-fiction film, *THX 1138*, did not flinch when I presented untried solutions to the then insurmountable problem of making all the dressings and props.

Alien was exactly the same, and under director Ridley Scott I was able to take further my ambition to make a spaceship that looked like we had rented an old and used space truck.

This book in some ways illustrates how my independent thinking enabled me to be a part of *Star Wars: A New Hope*, arguably the best-known and most successful film of all time, an enduring classic that deserves its place amongst humanity's great myths and legends, and *Alien*, which has also become a cinema classic, the chestburster scene being recognized as one of the seminal moments of modern cinema.

I think John Barry's speech on accepting the Academy Awards for *Star Wars* says it all.

"We are very pleased to accept this beautiful award on behalf of all our friends and compatriots who worked so hard to make the sets of Star Wars a success. And there's one man whose name should be engraved on this above everybody else and whose name should be on every frame of Star Wars, and that's George Lucas. Thank you, George."

CINEMA
ALCHEMIST

CINEMA ALCHEMY

LUCKY LADY—THE ROAD TO *STAR WARS*

Ring… ring… ring…

The ringing of the phone cut through my apartment. I was watching a tennis match at Wimbledon on the television and wondering, as were the players, if it was going to rain again or even snow as predicted by those illustrious television weathermen. The old fishermen's way to predict the weather was to hang a bunch of seaweed outside the door and simply feel it with their fingers and smell it. They would tell you, in their broad Devon or Cornish accent, exactly what the weather would be and they were almost one hundred per cent accurate.

This serves well as a metaphor for my way of working as a set decorator, art director, and a director. I still use the lowest tech way possible on the shooting floor, which saves money and time, and gives a reality to the images. My effects supervisors all know that I used to minimise motion control from my main unit shoots, for 'watching paint dry' is the correct metaphor for that agonizingly slow process. This came to be the most valuable skill when I was offered *Star Wars* with a tiny budget at the time to make such a cinematic epic.

"Hello, hello, hello?" The voice at the end of the phone was insistent. "Is Roger Christian there? I've been trying to find him."

"Yes, it's me. Who is this?"

"It's Graham Henderson, from Twentieth Century Fox. I've had a call from the production designer, John Barry. He's working on a film called *Lucky Lady* in Mexico. Les Dilley's out there with him. They need another person in the art department urgently, and suggested I call you to see if you are available."

"When would they need me?"

"Can you get on a plane immediately to Mexico?"

"Yes, I could. Where to, and what for?"

"You'll never have heard of this place; it's a small city on the west coast of Mexico called Guaymas."

"Guaymas, funnily enough I have been there. It's stunningly beautiful; I remember the pelicans diving in the bay." I had taken a trip around America with an actor friend of mine, Chris Plume, and we had taken a Mexican bus from San Diego to Guaymas and stayed three nights there in a shack on the beach.

This offer came after a long history of working experience and connections, but it was clearly the moment that the journey to *Star Wars* began.

I read the script of *Lucky Lady* on the plane flying across the Atlantic. It was written by Gloria Katz and Willard Huyck, a married team, and it was one of the best scripts I had read. A fast-paced and original drama set around the illegal rum running that took place between Mexico and America during prohibition, the movie centered on a triangle of characters living in Mexico. A *ménage à trois* composed of a nightclub singer played by Liza Minnelli and two wonderful characters vying for her attention but glued together as best friends played by Gene Hackman and Burt Reynolds. They were huge box office stars at the time, so it was a tantalizing mix.

The movie was an epic production financed by Twentieth Century Fox that was growing in size weekly under director Stanley Donen. They needed another assistant art director to work as set decorator to help the tiny British art department working under production designer John Barry. If I had been asked to make John Barry's tea I would have happily gone. He had designed Stanley Kubrick's *A Clockwork Orange* and was one of the most gifted designers working. Les Dilley, my long-time art-directing partner, was already there and had recommended me to John for this; Norman Reynolds was the other art director. They comprised the entire art department. When one considers this was a period film set in the twenties and involved over fifty ships fighting battles on the ocean between the rum runners and the coast guards, as well as being a movie that required the building of a plethora of sets, it was a very small department to handle it all. Now that the film was running way over schedule and budget, they needed the extra help.

Filming with boats is worse than working with animals and robots! It was a huge endeavor. Anything to do with boats is truly one of the worst situations for any director. Controlling them is so difficult, especially on the ocean, as they constantly move and change position with the tidal movement, so it's really hard just to get them all in place for a shot. If a boat shifts position, it takes ages to move it back to the right spot and by then all the others have shifted. Then, of course, there is the unpredictable weather as well. Fifty boats, one of them a large navy destroyer with weapons and guns fighting huge sea battles as the coast guards tried to apprehend the rum runners, made it all horrendous. And this was only one part of the movie...

The problem with the production running way over schedule, aside from the budget swelling, was twofold: the worst was the heat as it escalated towards mid summer; the second was that the crew was needed to move south to Mexico City to complete the shoot, so a second crew would be left in Guaymas to carry on filming the sea battles. The stars had a contracted number of weeks and going over schedule meant paying huge overages.

I met John Barry and Norman Reynolds and went over what I had to do. John had designed and created wonderful sets in the studios and had also built into existing buildings on location to give them an authenticity. He took me to the nightclub set, which was evocative of the Mexican clubs of the thirties full of color and glitter. They had already filmed part of the sequence here, so it was dressed and lit.

Liza's character was a torch singer, a classic diva, and the set created a perfect atmosphere for her song performance with a wrought-iron staircase dominating the main room for her to descend as she sang.

John quickly fathomed out where I would be most useful and put me in charge of dressing the old rum factories, a salt factory, and a houseboat that was a hippy traveler's boat. This was written in the script as being covered in junk and flowers and plants, and no one knew what to do with it. It played a prominent role in the film, however, so it was important that it looked right.

I needed junk and scrap to dress the sets that were being constructed by our construction manager Bill Welch and his team to make them look authentic, particularly the houseboat. We were in a country where roughly half of the population of Guaymas lived in shanty towns constructed from cardboard boxes, soft drink cans, anything that could be found and used. These shanty towns spread out around Guaymas on every available hillside. Guaymas itself was a prosperous fishing town; the bay was absolutely packed with every variety of fish: the famous red jumbo prawns, sardines, and blue marlin.

Anything that could be caught and eaten was there in huge numbers. The labor for the canning factories, fishing boats, and the luxury hotels dotting the coastline came mainly from the shanty towns. Scrap was therefore just not available; anything of any use whatsoever was recycled and used again.

Somehow through all this we bought enough junk and scrap to dress the sets. I managed to create a wonderful old boat covered in plants, furniture, old bicycles, etc. It was covered from bow to stern in a wonderland of junk that gave it a really strong hippy character. This experience was still fresh in my mind not long afterward when another film came along…

STAR WARS: HOW IT BEGAN

Meeting George Lucas and Gary Kurtz

One really interesting old set I had to get finished and dressed was a salt factory, a beautiful old period set with peeling paint and faded walls. We had to cover all the ground around it with salt where the bags would have been stacked and loaded onto cargo ships. It was built near the ocean so that trucks could transport the sacks of salt for delivery.

That evening at dinner John told us that a producer and director were flying in to meet us the next day and look at the sets. George Lucas and

Gary Kurtz were friends of Gloria Katz and Willard Huyck, who had recommended us for a science-fiction film the director was making. He was looking for the same 'used' style of sets and Twentieth Century Fox had told George Lucas that he could make the film if he made it in the UK for the budget they had allocated. We had become great friends with the Huycks; they were married but kept separate professional writing credits. Gloria and Willard had written the first draft of *Radioland Murders* for George, and had polished and rewritten dialogue for George on the last draft of *Star Wars*. They loved John Barry, not only for his precocious talent as a designer but also for his intelligence and humor.

Next morning I was out in the midday heat shoveling white salt with the prop-dressing gang and our local Mexican crew. It was supposed to be a run-down factory in the script and to stand indistinguishable from a real building that had been there for a good hundred years. We had a sign painted across the wooden front saying SALT FACTORY in faded and peeling letters. I'd had the painters age down the wooden boarding using a technique that John Box had taught me when I started my career on *Oliver*. They used a clear glaze and added in paint colors like old greens that gave it a patina that usually comes only after years of weathering. Then with blowtorches I had them burn the lettering and paint back, as if years of intense heat had dried and cracked it. I dressed suitable carts and an old car around the front to add character. We had a wrecked boat as well, so the set looked absolutely natural and weathered, as if it had been there for years.

The set was almost finished and ready for shooting. We were just adding the final touches when a car arrived and pulled to a stop. Two figures got out looking more like film students than a Hollywood director and producer. George Lucas was in his now familiar plaid shirt, jeans, and sneakers that was his daily wear and still is, and Gary Kurtz in a similar look, I think, with his hat to ward off the relentless sun. George and Gary came across and introduced themselves to me.

George looked at the set and was really surprised to find it was not an old factory but a specially built film set. I took him round the back and showed him what we had built, as behind the ancient façade was nothing but timber scaffolding. George asked a lot about the aging techniques, the salt and the dressings I had carefully placed around. He talked briefly about a science-fiction movie he was about to start and wanted the same patina look and detailing, everything natural and used, not science-fiction designed. We talked about some of my history and working with John Barry. George even helped me with dressing the salt and got stuck in, spreading some around with a shovel as I explained how I saw science-fiction crafts and worlds: old oily ships, distressed from use, somewhat like a mix between a submarine and a bomber cockpit. I disliked the overly designed plastic worlds prevalent in films of that genre, with the toy-like weapons and gray uniform-style costumes based on communist-era dress that they always seemed to have. It all looked totally unnatural to me and unbelievable. George agreed. His vision, he told me, was more of a dusty Western combined with *2001*. I understood immediately.

They went on to meet with Geoffrey Unsworth and I was invited to catch up later with him and Gary at dinner.

That night under the stars in the courtyard of the hotel, a little cooler after the sun had gone down but still incredibly hot, George talked to me and John about his movie at length and his aspirations. George had met and liked Geoffrey, and respected his immense talent. Among many legendary movies he had photographed were *2001* and *Cabaret*. He was a natural choice. *Lucky Lady* was looking a lot like a dusty Western filmed on location. Moreover, John, Gloria, and Willard explained that Geoffrey was a wonderful and talented director of photography, and an enormous help to his directors.

George and Gary left the next day. I found out later, when we were in Los Angeles, that George had hired us for *Star Wars*, or *The Journal of the Whills* as it was called then. I was the third person hired. First was John Barry as production designer, and then Geoffrey Unsworth as director of photography, and third was me as the set decorator (noted in this order in the official book, *The Making of Star Wars*). Fourth was Les Dilley, but, being standby on the shooting floor, he had not managed to meet George on that trip. John's intelligence, his passion for film, and his understanding of what George was looking for visually, had given George the confidence that we could be trusted to create his vision for this space epic.

The heat during the day was becoming intolerable as the movie ran more and more over schedule. It was so intense even the Mexicans were complaining and saying we were crazy to be working such long hours in this heat without the afternoon siesta they were accustomed to. Working at sea most days on the boats, there was nowhere to hide from the fierce sun. Umbrellas did their best to keep the rays off the cameras and crew, but working at a high pace meant ignoring the conditions and getting on with it.

Many of the crew got sick; it was inevitable. We did what we could to try to keep safe, but in the end some form of bacteria will get you. British crews tend to go on working and grin and bear it, unless it's really bad. I was no exception and carried on despite some form of typhoid infection I had obviously contracted. I remember Rudy, the wonderful Mexican assistant assigned to me with a face deeply lined with a life of experience, saying to me one day in late June, that we should not be working in this heat, but I didn't feel I had a choice.

I was carrying on, despite being as sick as a dog. My weight was down to under nine stone. My jeans were falling off me, but being tanned from the relentless sun, the glow of my skin after months in it did not betray how ill I was. The end of the shoot was in sight and I did not want to give up. All I was passing now from my many visits to the Mexican-style toilets was a small amount of thin green liquid. That only happens when the kidneys and liver are near to giving up.

The next morning I awoke feeling really exhausted. I walked out of the house into that wall of heat and felt instantly nauseous and weak. I got into the car and turned on the air full blast to try to cool down, but it was the same futile effort as every other day. I drove to the docks where all the boats were docked every night. I had the local boatman take me in the small motor launch to the boat where the camera crew was setting up for the day's filming. When we arrived I realized as I climbed up the steps to get on board that I had zero energy left. I could barely make it up the ladder to the deck. I felt as if I was about to pass out. I had no liquid with me, and was gasping with thirst. I was so weak I finally succumbed to the realization that I could not carry on any more without seeking help. I talked to the third assistant director and made sure the crew didn't need anything urgently that Les and the standby prop man couldn't deal with, climbed back down the ladder and told the launch driver to take me back to the mainland jetty. We landed and I staggered my way into the shack that was an imitation of a local shop. They had no water; the only liquid available was a can of terrible vegetable juice and, being desperate, I took it and drank it. It made me more nauseous and thirsty. Somehow I drove home feeling quite delirious. Arriving at our house I grabbed some water, drank copiously and, feeling really faint, collapsed on my bed.

Next thing I knew there were scorpions climbing all over the ceiling and the walls. I saw Les standing over me, talking to me, trying to make sense of what I was saying. I was telling him to remove the scorpions and kill them all, and could not understand why he kept asking me what I wanted. Why couldn't he see them? Les told me later that at that moment he thought to himself, this is bad! He explained he was taking me in to the local hospital. It was more like a small clinic and had only about six beds.

I remember trying to answer questions that the doctor asked as he examined me and took blood samples. He took my blood pressure and looked at me seriously, as if the end was nigh! Suddenly I was whisked into a room at the back, which was the equivalent of a ward. I think they moved the patient out who was in there before me, as the bed was still bloodstained. But I really couldn't care by this time where I was or what condition the room was in; I felt like I was about to die. I had relinquished all control over my situation.

I was lying down pondering my fate, passing in and out of consciousness, when a nurse came to see me. I had noticed on the wall next to the bed was a poster of Scotland, which I stared at in slight bewilderment as it seemed so incongruous in this Mexican hospital. I stared at it whilst drip feeds were attached to my arm and needles plunged into various body parts, including my backside. No one spoke a word of English, so I couldn't ask any questions or get any information. I looked again at the poster; it was a stunning vista of the lochs in autumnal colors.

The nurse hooked up an IV drip and then, taking my arm, searched for a suitable vein to attach it to. She pushed the needle into me, hooked up the plastic line and left. My reverie was broken when the door opened and the nurse came back holding an enormous syringe. She silently proceeded to stick the needle into my artery, a really painful procedure. She looked down at me, talking in Spanish, trying to get me to comprehend her flood of unintelligible words. I could speak basic words, count, order food and find my way to the bathroom, but this stream of obvious questions was unfathomable to me. She kept pointing to the syringe full of thick white liquid she was forcing into my tiny vein. I looked confused and could not respond, so she continued to inject. The pain was excruciating. It felt like she was ramming concrete into my arteries. I was grimacing, while she kept taking my silence as a sign that all was fine. So I just stared at the poster and tried to visualize away the pain. Tough one that, though, when it feels like enough concrete to lay the foundations of a house is being pumped into an artery that is way too small to take the thick sludge. She just kept slowly but persistently pumping it into me, and my eyes were watering in pain.

Finally, after an age, it was over. She had had to do it really slowly for obvious reasons. She tapped my arm, pulled out the needle, re-attached the drip feed, and left.

It was then that I noticed the air bubble. It was trapped in the clear plastic tube carrying whatever liquid was being added to my blood by transfusion. It was near the bottle of liquid hanging on the metal arm and making its way slowly down towards my vein. Now I don't know about you, but I have always lived with the belief that if an air bubble enters the bloodstream— that's it, curtains!

I was feeling so ill and weak at this time, the fever was clouding my thoughts somewhat, and I started to think that maybe this was an omen. The mind goes into a different state when the body is closing down and is near the point when the vital organs lose enough chi or fire to keep functioning. I must have been very near that point because it didn't seem such a bad option. It was all so surreal. I watched that bubble as it silently made its way down the transparent tube. In my confused mind was the thought that when that bubble entered my vein, all this feeling of nausea and weakness would finally be over.

The bubble inched its way down the tube towards my arm at a snail's pace. Should I call for help or let destiny decide? I listened but there was no sound of nurses. I called out once but there was silence and the humming of the air conditioning. I was alone. This tiny innocuous bubble got nearer and nearer to the needle stuck in my arm where the tube entered. Everything in the universe came down to this moment. Nothing else had any consequence whatsoever. I do remember my past flashing before my eyes, thinking about moments that came back to me like fragments in time.

I looked again at the poster of the loch in Scotland, where I later filmed *Black Angel*. Something deeply connected there, somewhere at the bottom of the well of my subconscious, where the heart of spirituality lies. Looking at that picture and thinking of Scotland somehow made a connection to an inner knowledge. A resolve to live kicked back in with a force that surprised me. I made a vow to myself that dying here in Mexico on this movie was not an option—I had too much to live for. I became determined to fight this and get well.

The bubble had now reached about three inches from my arm.

Suddenly the door opened, and the nurse walked in. That brought my instinct for life into full adrenal-punching force. I sat up and pointed to the bubble, exclaiming loudly in English, "LOOK!" The nurse did indeed look, laughed, and turned the valve on the drip feed line. The bubble shot like a Ferrari straight into my arm.

I stared wide-eyed and waited for my heart to explode. She was laughing at me and explaining something in Spanish. Nothing happened. My heart stayed beating, very slowly because of my weakness, but soundly beating, so I just lay back and tried to sleep. Apparently it was not my time to go, and a peace descended over me.

Les came to visit the next day with our Mexican interpreter. He explained that the doctor had told him I was very sick and that I'd be there a few days. Les and I had planned to go back to Los Angeles on the way home once shooting was over. We could still do that, depending on my recovery time. Les had called John Barry in Mexico City, who was very concerned and was monitoring the situation. I got the nurse in and asked the translator to ask about the injections. What she had been trying to tell me was if the pain was too much, to say so, and she'd stop and slow down. Ah, the bonus of being able to speak several languages!

They explained that it was a serious infection that could have affected my liver and kidneys, but they thought that because my system was strong, once they had killed the infection I'd recover one hundred percent. I was also chronically dehydrated from the illness, and they were pumping vitamins into me. The shoot was winding down fast so I wasn't missing much. Les had only a few days left to supervise.

I was alone the next day when a production assistant came to see me. He had a proposal from the film's line producer, Arthur Carroll, to put me on the next plane to London, without enquiring as to my medical condition and if I was able to fly over fourteen hours. For that offer he needed me to sign a contract that stated that they had no more responsibility for me. He had presumed that the carrot of putting me on the plane home was the thing I most wanted in the world and that I would just say yes.

Of course I would be well looked after in hospital in Britain, but Carroll had not bothered to come to see me, or inquired how I could travel. The doctors thought that a fourteen- to sixteen-hour plane ride in my condition could have dire consequences.

Even in my weakened condition I refused to sign anything. I knew instinctively that despite this being such a poor facility, it's always best to get treated locally when it's an infection in the stomach or intestines, as they generally know what to do faster than a hospital in London would.

Maybe Carroll presumed that we all felt like him and were desperate to get home to the green hills of safe old Blighty. John Barry had found out the situation and really torn a strip out of Carroll. John had realized very fast what had happened. When someone is sick they are automatically covered under a movie's insurance policies. John had told them that I should stay in the Mexican hospital until they said I was able to travel and then be put in a hospital in Los Angeles, where we were ticketed home from anyway, to get full clearance before being allowed to go on. John had realized they didn't want to bother filling out all the forms at such a late stage of the production.

I was finally told I could leave the hospital and would be sent to Los Angeles, to a hospital in Santa Monica where I would be cleared. I had not been able to enjoy the last days and say goodbye to all the friends I had made there. I did see Rudy and gave him my leather briefcase that he had coveted and a load of unused per diems. Movie crews become like extended families; we work under such stress and heavy workloads that barriers come down and people bond really quickly. I loved Mexico. The people were so generous, filled with warmth and romance, and a true love of life.

I was told in the hospital in Santa Monica that the doctor in Guaymas had in fact cured me, and they confirmed I had had paratyphoid. After a week of recuperation I was discharged to the hotel. Les and I were told to meet John Barry the next day before he flew home. Driving up the coast to Malibu to meet him for lunch was a glorious drive.

I pulled into the parking lot at the end of the Malibu pier, and here stood the famous Alice's Restaurant named after the Arlo Guthrie song and movie. Painted white with large blue letters saying ALICE'S it stood out from the rest of the landmarks there. Built right at the end of the pier it was famous for its all-round views of the ocean, for its seafood and a special cocktail called a B52. It was a known hangout for the in-crowd of the day who would spend a lunch or dinner at the restaurant and then hang out on the beach watching the surfers. This was in the sixties and seventies, the era of the Beach Boys, and Malibu was the Mecca. We parked right next to the Spanish buildings at the roadside end of the pier that used to be a fishing-equipment shop and walked down the wooden planks of the pier to the restaurant. We entered through their famous stained-glass door.

We met John and talked a great deal about *Lucky Lady* and our experiences. We had not seen each other since John had left Guaymas for Mexico City with the first unit, so we had a lot of war stories to recount. Then John made the auspicious announcement: George Lucas had officially asked us to start work in London in August. I was confirmed as set decorator and John said that the budget would be really tight for this type of movie and we only had seven months to prep it, which was just doable if we got everything planned with George in the coming months. The robots and other planned scenes would take the most time. Just the three of us would be working on it at first, as Norman Reynolds had gone back to the UK onto another film.

John had planned that we were to spend the next weeks alone with George to work out the logistics of making the film. This was going to be a challenge. The present budget he had discussed with Gary and George and Fox meant that the sets and construction and dressing and art department costs were well under a million dollars. This would be incredibly tight for the envisioned world we had to create. John told us about the movie, George's aspirations, and what the basic story and premise was. We knew George had liked our sets on *Lucky Lady*. He was determined to make *Star Wars* look as if we had filmed on old locations and create ships as if they existed and were used and real. This was my dream, the way I always wanted to see science-fiction movies made. We celebrated and John told me to rest up and be ready for work in August.

Les and I drove back down the coast and back to the hotel to arrange our own flights home. I was ecstatic—to have another movie with John Barry to go straight onto was obviously a good thing, but to have one that was in a genre that I loved and which were rarely made in Britain was a rare gift. For me that lunch in Alice's Restaurant, now long vanished into local history, is engraved in my memory forever as a truly auspicious moment, a defining moment in my destiny. I was pulling my Excalibur out of the rock and envisaging Luke choosing his as he watched the twin suns of Tatooine…

STAR WARS

B ack in the UK, John, Les, and I were called to Soho Square for a meeting with Peter Beale, the managing director of Twentieth Century Fox in the UK. Peter explained that the budget was really tight. He said that they would allocate around four million dollars to make the film with, so the entire art department budget was just under a million. The budget had come out at eight million dollars to make the movie in America, and Peter had persuaded them that we could make the same film in the UK for half that. So our job now was to prepare a budget for the art department and make it work. We left knowing we had a lot of work to do and a great deal of alternative thinking to make this possible. Time was also short as shooting was destined for March the following year.

Robert Watts was employed as the British line producer to pull the production together for Gary and George. An experienced and wonderfully calm man at the head of a seemingly impossible task, he ended up staying with the team as a producer through the first three movies. Robert and John Barry hired a few rooms for the art department and a small stage at Lee Studios in Kensal Rise, West London. This was a tiny studio owned by Lee Electrics, who were the largest cinema lighting and electrical hire company in the UK. I had worked there several times, including on Ken Russell's movie *Mahler*, which I art-directed; we made all the sets and studio shooting there. Ken Russell liked the studios as they were just a mile from his house, and he also made some of The Who's rock opera *Tommy* there. I made a commercial with David Lean's DP Freddie Young, building a Kensington-style house and garden in the main studio that was famous for its central pillar, which we all had to design around. I turned it into an apple tree on that one.

I signed my letter of agreement for *Star Wars* for the princely sum of one hundred and fifty pounds a week. This was a lower salary than normal, but George Lucas was paying us from his own pocket, and I personally wanted his film to be made. It was a chance to be innovative, and I had ideas brewing in my mind about how to create a revolutionary look for the props and dressing. The money was irrelevant.

I was given a copy of the script to read and had to swear on my life that it was for my eyes only—it was so secret. It was titled *Journal of the Whills* by George Lucas. In fact very few people ever got a script— even the actors only got pages to read—but as set decorator I had to break down every scene and list out every prop and weapon required, and also work out all the dressings needed for each environment. I read the script through quickly to get a sense of the story and atmosphere first, before going back again to study it in detail. I liked it enormously. I immediately connected with it because it felt so familiar, reminding me of the great myths and legends I had grown up with, but set in a totally new way in space. It was full of action and drama and was essentially a Western in space with mythic heroes, good against bad, evil against the forces of light. The lightsabers stood out as an amazing invention and a natural evolution, bringing ancient sword-fighting heroes into a science-fiction setting.

George and Gary came over to work with us and go through aspects of the design and feel for the film. He confirmed that he wanted everything natural and real and made as if it were practical, just as he had outlined to me and John in Mexico. The dusty Western feel he had seen in the sets we had created in Guaymas was a reference point. He wanted nothing that would stand out as being specially made for a science-fiction film, no sets or props should ever be conspicuous as sets or objects designed to attract attention. Hallelujah! I smiled inside; this was music to my ears as this had always been my philosophy. I hated the older science-fiction films where everything looked 'science fiction'.

George had a few paintings by the brilliant concept artist Ralph McQuarrie to show us. Ralph had painted characters and settings, which had been developed whilst George was working on the script. These became our reference point to rely on to create George's vision. R2-D2 was there as a design and character, and C-3PO, a sophisticated droid who carried the story along with R2-D2 on many adventures. They were integral to the movie working, and we had to think of a way to make them real. Also in another painting were Luke and his landspeeder, and other details of the Death Star and characters. Ralph was the unsung hero behind George, creating paintings to illustrate *Star Wars* as George envisioned it. We talked about *Silent Running* and how Douglas Trumbull had built his robots around amputees, and of course we talked about Fritz Lang's great German masterpiece *Metropolis*, unbelievably released in 1927 Klein-Rogge's golden robot inspired our belief that a character could work as a robot if we developed R2-D2 around the right actor. With our small budget and time for preparation pretty tight at this stage, it was agreed that to make R2-D2 work, we would need to experiment with the possibility of building it around a very small person. We were all thinking on the same page.

George had asked Ralph McQuarrie to design C-3PO and R2-D2 to his exact specifications as he worked on the script. The actual inspiration for these two bickering characters came from one of my favorite Kurosawa movies, the wonderful *Hidden Fortress*. George liked the idea of the story being told by the two lowliest characters, and their bickering and arguing made the adventure funny in places and supplied the glue to connect the action and the drama.

Kurosawa has been a major influence on so many filmmakers; he was considered the master by most filmmakers before *Star Wars* came along. Now everyone I meet in the industry says it was *Star Wars* that changed their lives and made them pursue their goals of working in film. When I wrote and directed *Black Angel*, I was influenced by Kurosawa and the idea of the lone samurai. Ideas feed on ideas with artists, and reinterpretations create new and fresh art. C-3PO had one thing in common with the central robot in *Metropolis*: the costume had to fit tightly to an actor. However, we had to create our own iconic character. For us the two robots were the most complicated task in the short timeframe before shooting the following March. George had created interesting robot police for *THX 1138*, so we had his confidence in exploring these ideas. Fortunately for us he had seen the results work using the same techniques with a very low budget already.

Reading the script I recognized the deeply embedded homage to myth and the philosophy of the power of legend, where good triumphs over evil. I reread it several times and then set about doing the very accurate breakdowns I always made, listing everything in the script relating to my task as set decorator and anything I could think of that I needed for dressings. Robert Watts was there with John Barry preparing the budgets with Gary. We took George to Julie's Restaurant in Portland Road on the first day he was there. This restaurant served as our canteen from then on, as he liked it so much. It was one of my favorite restaurants, just off Ladbroke Grove. The restaurant was laid out in individual rooms, each one with its own décor and style. The owner, Julie Hodgess, had found the building and decorated it with an eclectic mix of found bric-a-brac, objects, and furniture. Julie was one of the designers of the famed and legendary fashion house Biba on Kensington High Street. Julie's had beautiful eclectic furnishings like an eastern restaurant. We sat this first day on a richly covered tapestry sofa with a low carved Moroccan coffee table in the middle to eat from, and deep velvet armchairs the other side to sink into. Moroccan lamps hung from the decorated ceilings. George appreciated the atmosphere; it was clearly an influence on our thinking in a way. Not sitting stiffly at a white cloth-covered table in a classical restaurant but in the rather more exotic and bohemian atmosphere the owner had created was certainly more in harmony with our discussions of the muted look of the movie. Julie's has survived and is as trendy as ever, having played host since those early days to so many celebrities, actors, and rock stars, still proving a great place to hang out and relax. Little has changed it seems, from the photographs. I guess it should warrant a small blue plaque now for hosting such auspicious guests for so many months.

Every lunchtime we spoke in detail about the movie and used this time to focus our attention on getting the feel for it exactly right. These early discussions with George and Gary were imperative in getting the world he envisioned unified into our minds. George had spent a lot of time developing the universe, working with Ralph McQuarrie on illustrating the characters and costumes and the look. R2-D2 and C-3PO were the key to this universe and the first characters we see in *Star Wars* (along with Darth Vader). They were the Laurel and Hardy of the movie, whose humor and banter told the story for the audience to key into. Getting these characters right when there were limited special effects in those days was key to the movie being fully realized. So we had to make them work, and create their personalities through their visual appearance. Then there were the sets and the weapons and props. We spent hours and hours discussing it all, so that we were all playing the same violin as it were. Fortunately John Barry and I instinctively understood what George was after and that's essential. I found to my own cost it is impossible to make someone understand, even with visual reference, if they do not get the genre and the rules and regulations one has to adhere to.

When we were creating the first of the trilogy of movies we were literally breaking new ground. We had nothing to fall back on, no prior visual references in any movies to create the worlds that *Star Wars* pioneered. It meant taking a huge leap of faith for George Lucas, John Barry, Les, and me. To find a visual language that we all understood, and all within the tiny budget allocated, seemed a daunting task in those early days.

John Barry stayed busy sketching out ideas for all the sets and trying to find ways with George to cut costs as Gary's budget kept escalating above the eight million dollar mark. John Stears wasn't working on the film at this stage but was doing budgets for Gary and Robert, and his special-effects budget kept ballooning way up. It was made clear to us that Twentieth Century Fox wouldn't commit until the budget was locked and proven, and as George was paying us from his own pocket the pressure was very much focused on our small team.

Instinctively, I knew I could not set-dress this film conventionally. The budget was simply not there to do it that way, and also on my mind was how to achieve the gritty documentary look required for the interiors and exteriors of the ships and sets. We needed to make it as if we had just gone on location and found a spacecraft that was well used and worn for the *Millennium Falcon*, and had rented it for the filming. How to achieve what I had been extolling to George for this look was causing me a lot of angst. Fortunately, George had had the experience of making an experimental science-fiction movie with *THX 1138*. He had created a science-fiction world in real locations with a very limited budget, so he was instinctively able to understand what we had to achieve and what we were up against. This made our small team of five people, comprising John, Les, me, George, and Gary, feel like a small band of unified cinema revolutionaries.

I finished my breakdown of the script, which had taken a few days as it was highly extensive. I first grouped all the scenes in the same settings together. Then, to imagine what the interior or location scenes would look like, I talked with George and John Barry, and carefully studied the sketches of Ralph McQuarrie and John.

On a normal modern-day or period film my breakdown becomes a list of the furniture and dressings that will make the set real. This also includes anything specifically written into the scene, like the owner smashing up the room in anger, or cooks creating a meal in a kitchen, for example. We list out tables and chairs and curtains, carpets, and the main dressings. Then I list out any objects or props utilized in the script, and also anything else I think of that they might need. There may be an object in the next scene or later on in the film that has to be seen for the plot. There is a separate list for weapons, so all guns, knives, sticks—whatever is required—are listed. Animals are another category and vehicles yet another.

On a science-fiction movie there are no reference points to go to, as it is all in the imaginations of the writer and director. All we had to visualize at the start were the few paintings in which Ralph McQuarrie had so beautifully illustrated George's imagination. There were really no reference points as most of the science-fiction movies that had been made were not as oily and real as George envisioned. I had to try to imagine what the interior of Obi-Wan Kenobi's hideaway in the desert would be like, first described in this draft of the script as a much larger complex than the eventual budget cuts would reduce it down to. I had to imagine the contrasting interiors of the specially built Death Star to the used and battered *Millennium Falcon*, and the various exteriors and interiors on Tatooine. One set in particular stood out, the Cantina, and another got me wondering how to dress and make real the garbage compactor.

I stared at my comprehensive list of what was required and tried to estimate the budget to make it all. I had to find a solution to pull this off. When I looked at my list of weapons required as well, my heart sank. All the principals had guns, or lightsabers for the Jedi Knights, including

Obi-Wan. The stormtrooper army alone amounted to nigh-on a hundred weapons. There were the Tusken Raiders and Chewbacca, and of course Darth Vader and his consorts. My budget would never allow for all this if we designed and built them all from scratch. Then there were robots— not just R2-D2 and C-3PO, but all the ones for sale by the Jawas and a load more for the interior of the Sandcrawler, which stood out, filled with junk robots and machinery. Then there were the vehicles like Luke's landspeeder and others outside the Cantina, and various animals too. The *Millennium Falcon* was to be the most densely dressed of the ships judging by the descriptions from George, especially as it was old and banged up. The Death Star had a lot of built-in dressings as it was much cleaner and more *2001*-like, but had areas to create within it like the garbage-disposal room and Darth Vader's conference room.

Then there were all the desert scenes in Tatooine. I knew John was thinking of Morocco or Tunisia for the locations, as both have sand dunes and amazing architectural oddities from the past that are well preserved. I knew Morocco well, having been there many times. I was pondering things like Luke's homestead with his aunt and uncle—as there were domestic scenes written in, like having a meal with blue milk, what would they be eating? There were various scenes around the Sandcrawler and the moisture-collection devices in the desert. The exterior of the Cantina was described as being in the locale of a small township with markets where they went to buy spares for the ship. There was a crashed spaceship described in the script right behind the Cantina entrance. That one gave me food for thought! All of this would require a lot of imagination to create.

I guess I was lucky in that my sensibility towards movies, especially science-fiction ones, was reality-based. I wanted to see environments that were lived in and real, so that I could finally connect to a science-fiction world I believed in, and felt that an audience would, too. George mentioned Westerns a lot, and I understood what he meant. Of course we all loved the Spaghetti Westerns made by Sergio Leone, films like *A Fistful of Dollars*, inspired by *Yojimbo*, another in the collection of masterpieces by Akira Kurosawa. We weren't making a Western but there's a feeling in the look that especially relates to the first *Star Wars*, much more so than in the other films in the *Star Wars* series.

Once Upon a Time in the West, Leone's masterpiece, really set the tone.

The atmosphere is gritty, real and dusty, and everything you see is used and practical. The newer buildings where they are building the town around the railroad seem real, not like a film set—this is the art. There was a propensity in science-fiction films before *Star Wars* to imagine the worlds as clean and spotless that made them somehow devoid of any character. Costumes were often gray and completely characterless, like Russian communism when anything of beauty was regarded as frivolous. It seemed to me that the Indian-style Nehru collar somehow denoted future apparel, as if everyone would be wearing gray, colorless versions of the Indian jacket. Humans simply aren't like this. A ship might be new and shiny when sold, but it is soon dented and rusting and aged with use. Then they get sold and as they go down the market chain, economics means that people start repairing them themselves and fixing things and changing them. This is like Han and the *Millennium Falcon*.

George stated it quite simply. One sets a scene, but not in order to show off the architecture every time. That can happen when filmmakers are given the design of a science-fiction setting; they often feel they have to show the audience, just because it's there and different, and so it introduces an unreality. I was lucky—I understood inherently George's vision and had my personal references: Jean-Luc Godard's *Alphaville*, to me the first graphic novel-style movie, and Tarkovsky's *Solaris*. John Barry personally loved science-fiction films like *Barbarella* and *Flash Gordon* that have fun designs and show them off with full abandon. However, John was a brilliant designer and quickly understood what George was after. George's vision was forming in our collective minds.

I was also a long-time fan of graphic novels and science-fiction artists. I spent a great deal of my time and hard-earned money in Forbidden Planet, the holy grail of shops for sci-fi fans. I spent so much time there researching artists like Frank Frazetta, Moebius, one of my favorite graphic-novel artists Bilal, Chris Foss, and Roger Dean, and I loved the paintings that seemed like real worlds. Forbidden Planet really helped me with my science-fiction education, preparing my path towards working on *Star Wars* and *Alien*.

George and Gary were flying back and forth to Los Angeles, still trying to get Twentieth Century Fox to commit, and to understand that the robots alone required an enormous amount of development time to create. Still reeling under the hugely over-budget *Lucky Lady*, Fox were being very reticent and difficult with Gary Kurtz over the film's estimated cost. To make matters more difficult, John Stears' special-effects budget continued escalating as time to prepare the film diminished. Gary was wrestling with the finished budget like a balloon full of water with holes in it, trying to block the holes with his fingers. Of course, as always, the art department budget was the main target for cuts. Fox decided that the seven and a half million-dollar budget that Gary had completed had to include their overheads, so he was forced to pull six hundred thousand dollars out of it. This was targeted at the construction and art department costs, including my dressing budget.

George and John Barry worked really hard to reduce the art department costs by amalgamating some scenes in different locations into one location, and combining scenes in different sets into one. Even Obi-Wan Kenobi's hideaway went from a complex of different rooms down to a single cave, although in some ways this made him simpler and stronger. The Buddhist-influenced Force meant he was non-attached to material things and here budget restraints created a stronger dynamic for a central character. Sometimes restraints that push one into creative solutions can add to the film, not detract from it. This certainly influenced my thinking later on the dressing for Obi-Wan's cave. When Twentieth Century Fox cut ten percent off the budget, settings, and locations like Alderaan went out the window, those scenes amalgamated by John and George into the Death Star. We were all doing what we could to reduce costs, but John Stears' budget just kept going the other way, which alarmed Fox and Gary Kurtz. We had our own ideas about this, but John Stears was working in his workshops and quite separate from us at this stage until we started in Elstree. John Barry did attempt to intervene and constantly came up with suggestions. Part of the main problem of the budget's escalation was the two main robots and the time to develop and make them. Robots are difficult to categorize, unlike furniture, say, which falls naturally under the art department. Robots are a combination of design, the art department and the special-effects team. John thought that John Stears was allowing more than enough to create fully functional radio-controlled robots, a costly procedure at this stage as they were entirely experimental. So we decided to work on our version of R2-D2.

John Barry and George decided the best way for our small team to proceed was to build mock-ups of R2-D2 and Luke's landspeeder as time was so short. These would take the longest time to develop and were critical to the film, as R2-D2 and C-3PO are the first characters seen in the movie. We decided the best way to gauge the look and the scale of each one was to make rough wood and polystyrene mock-ups. John hired Liz Moore, who was one of the best sculptors working in the film industry, to sculpt clay models of C-3PO's head to allow George to see the design in three dimensions.

R2-D2 was already a comprehensive design painted by Ralph McQuarrie. Looking at his height we needed to make R2-D2 as small as possible. For both R2-D2 and C-3PO the idea of a person inside working the robots seemed the only way to go, but we had to somehow reinvent the wheel and become way more sophisticated in our approach. With a huge budget and a long development time it might have been easier, but all we had was faith in our abilities as a team and to put our ideas into action, and pray they worked. The previous science-fiction robots in film were nothing like the problems we were presented with for R2-D2 and C-3PO in design or concept. R2-D2 and C-3PO were sophisticated and complex robots, each with a strong individual personality and character. They had to be convincing as main characters, and never ever betray that a human was underneath working them. C-3PO was an advanced humanoid-type robot and R2-D2 was a complex engineered astromech droid, who could do many things needed in the script.

Robert Watts set about finding a suitable small person who we could build a mock-up around to see if we could do what we were thinking. He also began the search for a suitable-sized actor who could be inside C-3PO.

I began working on R2-D2 with Les. To get things moving and to build a very rough mock-up in wood we needed a skilled carpenter and prop maker, someone who could join the team and work without complaining about lack of funding or materials. Someone who could create something from nothing, and at the same time construct a simple mock-up of the landspeeder, as we couldn't determine what size would work from the paintings. Someone like Bill Harman.

Bill was the construction head who had created the Everest commercial for me and other sets for commercials where he pulled rabbits out of the hat every time. We always had limited budgets but Bill was brilliant at solving problems. He worked on several of the early Monty Python films as a kind of do-it-all construction head, and had last worked on *Monty Python and the Holy Grail* with them and for Terry Gilliam on *Jabberwocky*. He made many zany props for Gilliam, all with little money or materials, but always came through. With Bill you can throw him an impossible task and he'll find a way to make it happen, and laugh all the way. A far more productive approach than the usual negative grumbling that often occurs, and which simply translates to 'more money please and I'll fix it'.

I suggested we hire him, and when Bill came in to meet John Barry, his obvious experience and willingness to get stuck in on his own, combined with his chirpy personality and humorous approach to life, got him the job. Bill's first task was to make up around a dozen or so wire stands for Liz Moore to sculpt C-3PO's heads in clay, and to start to experiment with the look for Darth Vader's helmet. With these stands built in the small stage at Lee Studios, Liz started sculpting about ten different designs for C-3PO's head to enable George to see how he would look, and also to envision how we could build him around an actor.

We knew for certain that R2-D2 would have to be operated by a small person, but finding the right one was not proving easy. Robert Watts was arranging casting sessions for George to meet any candidates he could find. Les and I went through the requirements with Bill to construct the first wood mock-up of R2-D2 and Bill set about making the prototype. He worked based on the McQuarrie painting, a very rough sketch by George and Bill on Monty Python-headed notepaper, and George's descriptions and rough height measured out by hand against a normal person. He made a plywood cylinder around a frame of ash using seven-eights-thick marine plywood that he had left over at home from an earlier job and kindly donated to us. It was used to skin boats and planes, so it easily bent to shape. The diameter of the body was only two foot six on this one so very small, but it looked too large compared to the painting, so we had to go smaller.

George went down to the stage we had rented to look at Liz's heads one morning, and started talking to Bill as he was fascinated by how the Python movies were made so cheaply yet looked so grand. He asked Bill a lot of questions about them and Bill explained that all he often got from Terry Gilliam were rough sketches done on the spot. George was fascinated and asked to see some. The next day Bill brought in sketches of props and sets to show him, from both *Monty Python and the Holy Grail* and *Jabberwocky*. They were roughly drawn on the back of call sheets by Gilliam, but were very descriptive. Bill described to George how everything was made with absolutely no money, and I think it helped to convince George that our way of making mock-ups and developing things would work. The production values on the Python movies were very high compared to their small budgets, and the sets looked very authentic. Bill still has the coconut shells used when the Pythons realized they couldn't afford horses on *Monty Python and the Holy Grail*.

Looking at Bill's first attempt, the rough wood mock-up of R2-D2, we decided it had to be made smaller. The cylinder was a guide to how it looked in practical terms, and was definitely going to be too big. Bill had roughed in legs and even without the head it looked too clumsy. The problem was still there, and now even more acute: who could we find this small to work it from inside? We pressured Robert to find the smallest person we could as quickly as possible—we really needed to build the next mock-up around that person.

Bill was a massive help. He'd scrounge around at home and in local junkyards to find materials for us to make the mock-up landspeeder and R2-D2, as Robert made it clear he had no budget at this stage to give him. This does require a certain adaptability; many people cannot understand or work that way. Bill had always thought differently to the conventional art department ways, and working on the Monty Python films had really honed this adaptability, requiring props and gags and sets that would have stumped conventional methods. Bill was an ace at this and kept us all laughing with his anecdotes and jokes.

We all bonded quickly, and in the evenings at the end of the workday, George would sometimes bring a 16mm movie to watch. Bill Harman used to go and get a few beers and sandwiches from the pub opposite called the Lads of the Village, and Cokes for Gary and George, who never ever touched alcohol. So we watched films together, basically to try to get ideas for making the look and atmosphere for *Star Wars* work. Everything was geared around finding ideas for producing it. Watching *Forbidden Planet* again, this movie was pretty advanced considering the clean and cheesy science-fiction movies that were made at the time (the 1950s). The important thing was that the robot was a central character in the movie and it worked.

I thought back to the Daleks in the early episodes of *Doctor Who*, obviously operated by smaller people hidden inside them as they rolled around the studio floor on casters. They had really frightened me as a child. It's funny now, looking back. They had what resembled (and most likely was, due to budget constraints) a sink plunger stuck on them for their front probe, but they still scared many children. Illusion—it's all down to a believable character and drama and then audiences accept the world as real. Now, of course, things had become far more sophisticated, and *Star Wars* would be the film to push the envelope way, way further than ever before—we just had to make it happen.

George had us look at Douglas Trumbull's robots in *Silent Running*, Huey, Dewey, and Louie, not for their look (they were very simple affairs that looked like plastic bins dressed with different shapes), but because they were convincing characters. I think their interactions with Bruce Dern, often with a slight humorous edge, allowed the viewer not to question that they were actually just plastic bins dressed up. The legs were simple, designed around the arms of the amputees using plain convoluted plastic tubing to enable them to walk or waddle, and box feet to look like robot shoes. It meant they could move around and the waddle gave them a sympathetic kind of personality. They worked because they became personalities in the movie and one forgave their simplicity. Also Trumbull filmed much of the movie in an old mothballed battleship, which in my opinion gave a credible and authentic atmosphere in general, and helped the viewer believe in the story and the robots' existence.

Could we create the same illusion?

Robert Watts found a cabaret group called The Mini Tones comprising of Kenny Baker and Jack Purvis, and had gone to see them perform. They seemed like they could be potential R2-D2s, so Kenny and Jack and the other small actors went to audition for George at Fox House in Soho Square. George Lucas took one look at Kenny and said, "You are R2-D2." Kenny was by far the smallest person there, and he was correctly proportioned. He came to Lee Studios to meet us, and Les and I had Bill measure him up; he fitted our requirements exactly, being only three feet eight inches high. Kenny also had legs strong enough to make the walking steps that R2-D2 would be required to have. He was very funny— The Mini Tones were a comedy musical act—and we felt his personality would hold up under the difficult conditions we would place him under during filming. We showed him the paintings and talked him through what he would be required to do, and how important R2-D2 was to the movie. He met up with George and John Barry and seemed really excited to come work with us. Kenny was now crucial to making R2-D2, as he was the only person small enough and strong enough that we could find.

The only problem that arose was that Kenny had entered The Mini Tones into Hughie Green's hugely popular TV show, *Opportunity Knocks*. This was a television show in the UK where talent competed to get noticed and win. It was the forerunner to *The X Factor* and *Britain's Got Talent*, and just as popular in its day.

Then came a blow to our plans. The Mini Tones reached the final on *Opportunity Knocks*, and if they won it would elevate their career. Kenny was now concerned about his partner, Jack Purvis, as working with us meant putting The Mini Tones on hold for a while, leaving Jack with no income. Robert Watts and George promised him that Jack would also be hired for the movie, as there were various other roles to be filled that needed someone of his size. After deliberating, and despite this guarantee of Jack working on the film, Kenny turned us down and told us he couldn't do it.

John Barry was really concerned about losing him, so he made Les go to Kenny's house with instructions to persuade him and not to leave until he had. Les lived in the area and drove straight to his home. He found the house all right, but couldn't find the doorknobs or the doorknocker. He looked around, totally confused, not knowing how to let Kenny know he was there. He couldn't find a bell, nothing. Then, glancing down, he realized that they were all placed two feet off the ground, carefully positioned so Kenny and his equally small wife could reach them. Les bent down and knocked and was finally met at the door by Kenny.

After a few hours of persuasion by Les, Kenny finally agreed to work with us. He saw the potential if we could pull R2-D2 off as a major character, and took a gamble. He had always wanted to work in movies. He'd had a long career in show business before this but had never been offered a leading role in a film, and he realized this was a huge opportunity for him and Jack. Trusting Les that we would employ Jack clinched the deal. As it turns out, a wise decision Kenny made…

I got Kenny in for a fitting when I was directing Second Unit on *The Phantom Menace*. Kenny duly arrived and before doing anything he asked me to come outside and see something. There was Kenny's electric-blue Rolls-Royce Corniche, a beautiful Mulliner Park Ward Coupe especially adapted for him to drive. He proudly drove me all around Leavesden Studios. There were miles of road and a long airplane runway; it used to be a Rolls-Royce airplane engine factory. Kenny told me that making appearances at science-fiction events all over the world had bought the 'roller', so it hadn't been a bad decision to come play the little robot.

In Lee Studios, Bill Harman began creating another smaller body frame based around Kenny's measurements. We were able to gauge the proportions and size based on Kenny's height, and by relating these to Ralph's drawings where R2-D2 was shown next to Luke and C-3PO. Bill clad the body using more of the marine plywood bent around the frame.

Having constructed a body, we needed a dome-shaped head. This stymied Bill as it was a convex round shape, and a spherical top was way too costly to make. When I art-directed Ken Russell's film *Mahler* in the same studios and built all the sets there, I had gotten to know it really well. The Lee brothers, who owned the studios, housed all their lamps and electrical equipment in stores out back. I had an intuition I'd find something, and went on a hunt around. In the dump section where they chucked unwanted or broken equipment I uncovered a 1940s P5.2 rifled reflector lamp that had been thrown out.

These were older 1000-watt lamps used to give a deep light on movie sets, and were pretty large. The shape of the lamp housing that held the reflector at the back caught my eye. It looked about the right size and shape to mock up a head for R2-D2. I got Bill over to take a look, and getting out his trusty tape measure, he deemed it perfect with a bit of modification. I left Bill to negotiate a price with the studio manager, Dennis, as I knew, being the set decorator on an American sci-fi picture, the price would be elevated if I tried. Bill negotiated to buy it for ten shillings, or about a dollar in today's money, and we set about making it fit. Bill laughs about it to this day, he still claims he never got his ten shillings back from Robert Watts!

Bill stripped off the metal brackets on the housing to give us a smooth head-shaped dome, and set about making it fit on the wooden cylinder. We were lucky: it was the perfect size.

Cutting away some of the brackets so that it fitted onto the wooden body, we had a robot shape that resembled the painting. Next we needed to mock up legs to match Ralph's illustration. Les still didn't have enough information to make draughtsman's drawings at this stage, so he and John just sketched out ideas for Bill on scrap paper, which Bill kept. George was always involved when he was with us on his trips back from America, making suggestions and following our experimental ways. Bill carefully crafted a mock-up of the legs as they were in the drawing. We made two large cylindrical body pieces where we knew we had to disguise Kenny's legs between the body and the feet. His legs went through the body at an angle and into the bottom part of R2-D2's legs so he could move them— or that was the idea anyway. The legs themselves were bolted with a nut and bolt onto the body at the top, so they could swing backwards and forwards to simulate walking.

We called Kenny back in. He was smaller than our mock-up with the top on when we stood him by it, so with some alterations to the interior structure work we got him inside. Adjusting the wooden frame, we tried Kenny in it for the first time and Bill went to lift Kenny up. He placed his arms round Kenny's chest, but I could see by the bemused look on Kenny's face that something was up. Bill tried to lift Kenny and couldn't get him off the ground, he just went red in the face; all we got was a "Cor blimey, you're heavy." Kenny, laughing his head off, said, "Strong bones..." We helped Bill lift him into the robot. After a lot of shuffling and complaining as bits of timber and metal bolts were digging into him, we made him fit, albeit very tightly. Kenny's face looked up at us, as he kind of sat and crouched into the robot. We had to cut holes and jiggle around the frame to get his legs through the cylinder and into the holes where the legs would be, so Kenny would eventually be able to make R2-D2 walk. It was a bit of a struggle but Kenny's legs and the proportions of his body made him a unique fit, exactly what we required for R2-D2. It looked like it was going to work! Kenny kept complaining that the bolts and wood were biting into his legs, so someone rushed off and found some foam rubber and we packed this in all around him. That alleviated his complaints, temporarily...

Now that R2-D2 was under way and we had a basis to build on, I needed to get some prop pieces to add into him to start mocking up the details we would build onto his frame. He had his central eye and various compartments, and in the drawing were little gadgets all over him, and different vents and arms and robot-type 'greeblies'. 'Greeblies' was the name George came up with one day speaking with me and John Barry. "Stick some greeblies on him". We liked the name, it was so appropriate for what I was doing and as there was no name for this as it was a new invention I had come up with. We christened anything that we stuck onto found objects as greeblies from then on to give them the *Star Wars* natural look, and this is what they came to be known as amongst the art department for the entire movie. Often the call came to me during filming, "Can you bring some greeblies down to the shooting stage and dress into a prop on camera to make it look more authentically functional?"

Poor little R2-D2 looked rather bland in his plywood skin, and Bill Harman had the idea to spray him silver. I rushed down in a panic when I heard the silver paint was out. Bill looked at my panicked face as I told him, "Never, ever paint anything silver, John will go mad!" I also hated that look. John Barry and I had a pact: no silver paint would ever be seen on screen. It reminded me of TV science-fiction films where the answer to anything to make it look more 'spacey' was to spray it silver. Even worse were the silver material space suits. So Bill, being suitably admonished, threw away all the silver spray cans in the workshop.

Peter Dunlop, my art-department production buyer who would eventually come on board full time, drove me to Trading Post. This was the hire company and film-rental facility where you could get all manner of mechanical, scientific and electrical materials, anything from tin mugs and army equipment to radio-station dressings. A wonderland for me as it had things you could never find in the usual prop houses, which specialized in antiques or modern furniture, beautiful objets d'art, fabrics and art. Anything to dress a period film from most eras one could find between the rental houses, but nothing to dress a spaceship, or a Cantina or a Death Star! I spent hours digging around in dusty cardboard boxes and trays of old second-hand mechanical and electrical goodies. Suddenly I came upon a box of 1950s airplane air nozzles and reading lamps. These were the little units placed above each passenger's head; you could swivel them to control the force of a jet of air by turning the wheel-type knob to control the flow from nothing to full blast, and turn on the light and focus it on your book or magazine. Painted in institutional green, there were a dozen in the box that originally came from an old Vickers Viscount turboprop used in the 1950s. I also found a variety of flexible steel pipes and small metal piston-like objects. In another box I found some rectangular grilles, like small air-vent coverings, very similar to Ralph McQuarrie's painting. Looking around I could see the wealth of dressing that could be built into something if I could find a larger source of it.

I drove back with my first treasure trove of old bits of scrap, an auspicious beginning to a journey that was to consume me over the next few months, and like planting an acorn, the germ of an idea of using scrap and junk was developing in my mind as a solution to getting the look I envisaged for *Star Wars*.

Back at Lee Studios I had Bill set about placing some of these onto the robot to give him a personality, and to see how we could begin to make him look like a working, functioning robot, again based on Ralph's painting. The airplane reading lamp was perfect and I set one of them into his head, next to his central seeing eye. We placed a couple more around the back. This little greeblie I added, the first one to go onto the little mock-up robot, has remained as a part of R2-D2's character ever since. It was cast and remade when we starting producing the metal working R2-D2s later in pre-production. I found a junk plastic disc that we inserted to give an idea of his eye. I placed the grilles and other tubes and pistons, emulating Ralph's drawings, to get a feel of what we could do. Each of these additions began to give the little robot a kind of mechanical authenticity. I was fortunate in having experienced this kind of dressing before and I think I inherited an engineering and mechanical leaning from my father, because I understood how technologies worked. This is essential for this type of dressing to have a reality to it. Sticking bits of junk in any random way does not look real; it has to have a very controlled method to it as one is trying to create the illusion of something technical operating under the skin, whether in a robot or a set. John Barry had this creative understanding as well, and George too, so without having to resort to hours of dialogue and explanations we had a shorthand in communication, and this made working like this so easy.

With mock-up legs, a body, and a head we had our first R2-D2 to show to George.

George and Gary came down to inspect our wooden robot. Though primitive indeed, one could use one's imagination and see R2-D2. It was pretty exciting for all of us, as this was the first visible piece of hardware ever made for *Star Wars*. George deemed it would work and the scale was now exactly right. Now we had to see if we could make him walk or waddle with Kenny inside!

Chatting about R2-D2's functions, George said that he envisaged a scene where R2-D2 was in peril and having to hang onto a pole or pipe for dear life. There were two shapes on his front under the head in the McQuarrie painting that could be interpreted as arms folded in, or utensils. George said it was kind of like a spoon and fork that he could unfold and hang onto the pipe with. George used the words as a way of explaining something that was unexplainable. Conventionally if I was following how to do things, I would have noted it down as the director had instructed it and gone away and created a spoon and fork. This is important to mention, as it was the beginning of a way of communicating between us, without needing to go to lengthy explanations. This was how a level of trust was established early on, and making R2-D2 as a wood mock-up began the process—I instinctively knew what he meant. I knew I could not find anything suitable as junk, so I talked it over with Bill Harman. He drew out the two slots in the main body to the shape required, and cut out one of them so that the arm could be made to fit into it. I got him to cut me a piece of curved wood that would fit across his front into the slot. I took this home with me, along with a carving knife, and spent the evening carving out a little arm that would look exactly like what I felt George envisioned. Next morning we fitted it into place and left it so it could open up to show George. These shaped arms have stayed exactly as I carved them in the final design and are still part of R2-D2's anatomy. Making this at home in my spare moments was normal for me. It was fun, and brought back memories of my first position on *Oliver!* when I made Fagin's box by hand.

If you sign on, you do the work one hundred per cent. John Barry always had the same philosophy. Working on *Star Wars* I cannot remember having a day off ever in the year I worked on the film—seven days a week, public holidays or not, I worked. My advice to students at Beaconsfield film school, where I attended later to help my transition into directing, was that one word sums up what you need to survive in the film industry: *tenacity.*

Now all we had to do was turn a plywood mock-up with an old lamp for a head into a movie character that we could actually shoot with.

The next step was to see if Kenny could move the legs and make R2-D2 walk. The interior wood frame was adapted so Kenny could fit correctly with his legs down through the side holes into the feet. This took a lot of adjustments and a lot of sawing and chiseling by Bill, who had to keep cutting pieces of the frame away. Kenny kept complaining that he was getting scratched or cut by the pieces of interior structure. He persevered though, his pain eased by the foam padding we added wherever he was getting pinched. Kenny was a great sport about it. His young son used to come and watch some days, and he towered over his dad sitting in the wooden mock-up.

Kenny kept with the programme despite all the hardship involved; even when The Mini Tones won *Opportunity Knocks* he kept to his agreement to stay with us. Kenny had no idea really at this stage what on earth we were creating; he just kept relishing the fact that he was working on a movie. Never having worked on one before, he had nothing to compare our small art department to, working with virtually no funds. All he had was our inspirational and enthusiastic talk and Ralph's wonderful illustrations to inspire him. We were under huge pressure to get R2-D2 to work as a prototype. John and George knew the time it would take to actually build working models of him and were concerned and so, despite our lack of development funds, we were working as fast as possible. Les worked with Bill to create some new legs in the design of McQuarrie's painting that we could fit Kenny into. We needed to see if the theory was correct and Kenny could actually move the legs through the holes in the cylinders and walk. The swivel joints meant the legs swung freely back and forth, so all we had to do now was let Kenny try to move them on his own in a shuffle-like movement.

Kenny tried. Attempting to swing his legs forward to move the unit's mock-up legs was nigh-on impossible. The wooden structures kept bruising him. We determined it was difficult for him to hold his feet inside the legs and support himself, so we fixed an old pair of his boots inside the legs for his feet to fit into. This way he was attached to the legs and every step they moved with him. He tried to waddle around and to our delight he made the first few faltering steps. That waddling gait of R2-D2's, so familiar now, was there in its primitive infancy as Kenny shuffled along, complaining about the bits of metal and wood that dug in at every bump. When we fitted the lamp top back on we created the first glimpse of what R2-D2 would actually become as Kenny made him shake from side to side.

Kenny's muffled complaints from inside the little chap were duly noted as we asked him to try to swivel the lamp top with his hands, as R2-D2's head was intended to do. Any attempt to turn it was met with cries of anguish from inside. Kenny's flushed red face stared at us when we lifted the head off, and he pointed out the red marks on the back of his neck. The brackets inside the lamp were biting into his flesh. Bill took the top back to the workshops and removed the brackets which would have severely lacerated poor Kenny's head had we really attempted to see if the top would swivel. After removing all such erroneous pieces the head was able to turn when Kenny moved it. Kenny still complained that the bolts dug into his head, and it was tight in there for sure, but we knew we were on the right track. We were becoming a little more convinced that we could make the diminutive robot work. I marked out on his body where the dressings would be, and I began searching for more suitable items to add in and onto his body to create his look.

Finally the day came when we strapped Kenny in and prepared for the first fully dressed walking test. Kenny took a few wobbling steps forward as we watched closely. The little robot staggered a few feet, then started keeling over backwards at a dangerous angle, overbalanced, and fell over onto its back. Stranded like a tortoise upside down, all we could see were Kenny's feet waving around inside the bottom of the plywood tube, and we could hear his muffled cries to get him out of there. We lifted him upright and got a very red-faced and sweaty Kenny out, but he was excited that he'd actually made it walk a few steps. John was really encouraging him, and fortunately Kenny was still very game. He suggested modifications that would alter the balance of the robot frame for him, and to add more foam padding around his thighs as he was getting really chafed. Kenny tried again. He moved the legs and made the little robot walk forward, but it was still really difficult so we thought about some more modifications.

Searching for bits of dressing to mock up Ralph's details on R2-D2's body I had come across some junked fighter pilot's harnesses, used to strap the pilots securely into their seats at massive speeds and altitudes. I thought the harness might be useful and brought it back. We surmised that if Kenny could carry the weight of the body, he would find walking it along easier. Bill Harman fitted the harness inside R2-D2's body and adjusted the straps around Kenny. This way we were able to strap Kenny inside, the weight of the R2-D2 body now supported by his shoulders like a rucksack, taking the weight off his legs. Then we adjusted the height of his old pair of boots inside the legs so that Kenny could maneuver himself into them and move in a waddling walk. After some practice he did it; Kenny waddled around the studios. Finally we had a working mock-up.

Gary and George returned from America and came to look. They waited, and around the corner waddled R2-D2. Watching R2-D2 walk towards them with that funny gait, a result of Kenny's restrictions inside the tiny robot, was a truly inspirational moment. George was smiling. "That'll work," he said immediately. Limited as it was, this simple dummy in plywood, with a lamp top for a head, enabled one to see the little robot come alive. Kenny really got into the spirit of it, and tried to make R2-D2 have some character as he waddled around. He made R2-D2 jump as if frustrated, and swiveling the body forward and backward seemed to be nodding yes and no. We were on the way to solving the first major problem the movie presented us. However primitive the mock-up, and despite being made with a shoestring budget, we had made the first R2-D2.

Bill's jack-of-all-trades abilities had helped enormously. From nothing but a leap of faith and a painting, some scrounged wood and a lamp top, we had built an R2-D2. Making the little robot this small and working to the scale represented in Ralph's painting was going to be possible. The vision of *Star Wars* was now on its tentative way.

As we continued to develop R2-D2, Bill started on a landspeeder mock-up. This was another important piece of *Star Wars* hardware that was required first up on the location shoot. Bill scrounged around for a basis for it, and again did what he could without any petty cash. He began constructing the mock-up to John and Les's rough sizes, with Ralph McQuarrie's painting as a reference and some pencil sketches done by John whilst discussing the mock-up with Bill. He decided to build a wood frame covered in plywood.

Bill had found an old set of wheels at home that came from some wheelbarrows, and a dolly, which he donated for free. When Bill had made enough of a rough shape to look like a speeder, George and John came down and we all judged the outcome. Looking at it in three dimensions in front of us, it was clearly way too big. It looked cumbersome, just not right. This was the only way at the time to really discover how a prop or vehicle can work scale-wise. So building these rough mock-ups out of plywood and cardboard and bits of junk were invaluable testing times for *Star Wars* to start taking shape. Fortunately George was involved enough and understood the process. Many directors would have been insecure at this stage seeing how rough these early mock-ups were, but they were invaluable tools for the designing process. There was a lot of discussion about the scene in the script when Obi-Wan Kenobi travels with Luke, C-3PO, and R2-D2 past the stormtroopers' roadblock. This had determined the size Bill had made it for John Barry, who imagined it more like a four-seater vehicle, based on the scene. George didn't want them all sitting comfortably inside—he didn't mind if they were squeezed in as they might be in a smaller sports car. He explained that Luke would not be able to afford anything more than a small second-hand vehicle, and would be more attracted to a kind of sports-car equivalent, being young and also an excellent pilot. This clearly illustrates how the process works, how being able to stand around a practical example of an object described in a script enables decisions to be made. Any scene can be interpreted in different ways, and in the end the director has to get it as he wants it, to conceive it as it is in his mind. Every detail cannot be written in a script, it would be as long and thick as a book. Also ideas come from discussions, especially so for a sci-fi movie where one is reliant on imagination only.

So we set Bill to work again to create one much smaller. He built this one really quickly. When Bill had knocked it into shape we all gathered on the stage, but again it still seemed too big, and the scale just didn't work. While we were discussing the smaller version a furious tea lady came storming out of the canteen. I could see Bill hiding a smile under his sleeve, and I knew the boys in Lee's had been up to something again. They were always playing practical jokes on people. Seems they had put washing-up liquid in her tea urn, so when she poured the water in to make the tea, soap suds came pouring out all over the kitchen like a foaming monster. This was a recurring joke played on her by the boys, who laughed hysterically of course. This must have been a totally different world for George and Gary, living and working daily in this tiny, damp and smelly studio infested with rats, with working-class technicians who drank copious amounts of tea and did a lot of stupid things to get a laugh. When Gary Kurtz's wife, Meredith, came to see our work she looked around the small old studios at our wooden mock-ups of R2-D2 and the landspeeder, and the tiny band of people developing the movie, and she made a memorable quote which sums it all up really—"*This sure ain't Hollywood.*"

These were invaluable times during this period, to experiment and determine how to create this new world with the director from his original ideas. The time spent making mock-ups and designing the elements that no one was sure would work saved an enormous amount of time and money later when pre-production actually started. John was able to draw ideas for the sets, and working closely with George, homed in on a look for the movie. Also, constantly adjusting the size of the sets and consolidating ideas helped to reduce the costs for the budget. With each budget cut they even went as far as establishing how George would shoot certain sets and John was able to cut down on walls and areas that George wouldn't see, helping to pull the budget down, bit by bit. Again this requires an experienced and understanding director, because many cannot envisage what they require until they see a full-size set and walk around it, necessitating a designer to build a full four-walled set to cover any direction the director might point the cameras.

Going back to my John Box days when he made models of all the sets for the director to see, I saw how invaluable this process is, as it is sometimes hard to judge from a two-dimensional drawing on a drafting board exactly how the scale works and how a set or prop will look. John Barry later made cardboard models of all the sets so that George could really get a sense of what he would be getting on the shooting floor.

Across the ocean in Marin County things were not at all different from our conversations with Gary and George. Joe Johnston was storyboarding, Richard Edlund, John Dykstra and his crew were working in similar conditions in old workshops and garages in Van Nuys. They were trying to work out how on earth to create the special effects required to make the flying sequences work. No, this wasn't Hollywood at all, and that is how and why *Star Wars* got made and broke such new ground. It all came to fruition because of George's faith and trust that somehow it would work. I think that his instinct in choosing the right people to help him pull this off was paramount, and his encouragement to think alternatively and not traditionally made it possible. Thinking outside the box and being inventive requires a leap of faith, and imagination, and George's has changed cinema forever. George never wrote what could be done technically, he wrote what he wanted and made the technology catch up, and in that way he is one of cinema's true pioneers.

Liz Moore had sculpted about ten mock clay models of C-3PO's head by now. She had modeled the different versions, changing the designs slightly on each one, again all based around Ralph McQuarrie's painting of him.

John Barry kept showing George the heads in three dimensions as Liz developed them. They played around with different looks for him; the advantage of the modeling clay was that she could remodel ideas on the spot to see what they looked like. John was always taking into consideration an average human head, as we knew that we had to find an actor to play him and wear the costume. The ridge running around the head was essential, because it had to be cast in two pieces to fit onto an actor. This was tried running across the forehead from front to back for a different look, but seemed a little like a historical costume with a nose piece. It ended up running across the side of the head, as it really looked best that way.

George's detailed descriptions of what he wanted whilst working with her and John improved her evolving designs and kept changing his look. George didn't like the open mouth and at one point stuck coins in the clay to see how they looked for his eyes. With those large eye shapes, there was C-3PO finally complete as a character. We all made comments as the head evolved, and we were all in agreement as C-3PO's look began to emerge with those large eyes and slot mouth. I had found some scrap slotted vent pieces that Liz built into one of the designs, and that idea remained with the character as he was developed further by Norman and John into the final vac-formed suit.

The rats became an increasing problem for Bill. Lee Studios was an old studio complex, sited next to a Victorian canal that used to carry coal and steel when waterways like this covered the British Isles. The studios were taken over by whole families of the rodents. I think they gravitated to the stage as Bill Harman and Liz would eat their morning egg-and-sausage sandwiches there, and buns and cakes for tea, leaving crumbs everywhere. This was Britain in the seventies and breakfast and tea were sacrosanct ceremonies. A tea lady appeared every morning clunking down the corridor outside our rooms, with her creaking trolley laden with warm sausage, egg, and bacon sandwiches and an urn of British tea that was strong enough to age a set with. For a few pence we had a greasy breakfast every day. Even George and Gary succumbed daily to these greasy breakfast rolls.

Bill Harman used to get annoyed with the rats and set traps to catch them if they as much as dared to invade the stages. He kept them in a cardboard box before getting rid of them, much to George's amusement. Every time George came down to see the work on the heads, Bill said he always had a word about them when he saw the box. Giving it a nudge with his foot he used to say, "Grrrr, get out of here." Bill also complained that everyone used to go and visit him to see his work progress before Liz arrived and since she came no one bothered to see him. Liz was not only a superb sculptress but also a very beautiful woman and really warm as a personality. Bill continued to command attention though with jokes and kept everyone laughing. Liz made some amazing mock-ups of the heads and gradually George and John, through discussing each one and having us add our two-cents' worth, narrowed the design down to one that really worked. When created in three dimensions in clay you could really get a feel for the character, and finally C-3PO was born. George signed off on the design and once Norman Reynolds was able to join us, he would begin drawing him up.

During discussions in Lee's with everyone, we had all decided that if we created a three-wheeled chassis as a base for the landspeeder with a single wheel at the front like Mr Bean's Reliant Robin, it would be easier to disguise the wheel for shooting. Three-wheelers were more popular in the seventies than now as they were classed as a motorcycle and so cheaper to insure and run. The single wheel in the front meant that it would be easier to hide and help create the speeder's illusion of riding off the ground on air.

In November, John Stears brought over an old Volkswagen camper van he had lying around in the workshop, the type revered by hippies on the trail to India at the time, and often painted in psychedelic colors and designs. They cut the top off and decided that the chassis was ideal to build the next landspeeder mock-up on, and it was no cost at the time. So John Stears cut the front wheels off and made it into a single front-wheel steering mechanism. This was delivered to Lee's and Bill had to weld the chassis to accommodate the body he was going to assemble to give us a rough idea of the shape and size of the landspeeder. Bill only had this old chassis to work with; we couldn't afford to buy a three-wheeler chassis like a Bond Bug or a Reliant Robin at this stage.

As Bill was welding away, George had gone down to the stage to look at C-3PO's progress with Liz, and stood fascinated at Bill's endeavors. When Bill stopped and looked up at George, George said, "That's the roughest piece of welding I have ever seen!" and laughed. Bill adapted the body he had mocked up and bolted it down onto the chassis to hold it in place. George, John, Les, and I watched as Bruce, one of John Stears' assistants, drove it up and down Lee's small alleyway between the stages. The miracle was that it actually worked at all. He could steer it, albeit with some difficulty, and stop. The important thing we established was that the size was now correct. The third attempt had worked: this landspeeder hit the mark. It was exactly right in scale and size, so George signed off on it.

We set Bill to work to make it a bit more like the drawings, to see how the shape would work. He made plywood and polystyrene engine shapes and other details. Les had mentioned that a Jensen Interceptor rear screen looked about the right size to make a front windscreen. There was a smashed-up one down the road from Lee's. Bill went down and measured it up, did yet another cheap deal for us and bought it. We fitted it onto the landspeeder and indeed it almost fit. Bill fixed it on and plastered in around the bottom so that it looked like part of the body and was held in place. Now we could get a better idea of the design of it. This was the mock-up that went with us to ABPC, now Elstree Studios, when we started prep.

My biggest peeve with science-fiction movies up to then, except perhaps for *Alphaville*, were the weapons. They all seemed to portray the future with little plastic boxes that didn't make sounds or backfire. They just emitted beeps or ray-gun sounds that to me were anything but dangerous or scary, and guns had to be that for the drama to work. They all seemed so consciously 'designed' and made the audience aware of that.

I had created my breakdown with all the weapons required for the movie and studied Ralph's paintings. I knew what I wanted to do which was adapt old weapons, and rather than try to explain myself I thought the best way was to prepare a couple of the guns and show them to George and John. I first wanted to see if the idea I had in mind would work before saying anything to them. George constantly affirmed that he didn't want anything to stand out as if created specifically for a science-fiction movie, and my idea would certainly suit his philosophy for all the props. The way I had envisioned making them was to rent real weapons and change them. This way I knew I could afford it within budget, a serious consideration at that time, the way the budget meetings were going. Also important to me was that the actors could fire the guns on stage with blanks. This would look correct as you get the backfire movement when they shoot. You get a flame, smoke from the barrel, which makes them look real on film, and also a great sound.

Actors handle real guns differently to toy ones or plastic mock-ups, and that is really important in bringing reality to a scene with guns firing in them.

So thinking about all this, inspired by our progress with R2-D2 and feeling that George was now comfortable with us knowing his vision, I took a leap of faith. Trusting my instinct, I went off on my own one day to create what I thought would work for the weapons and hoped that George and John would accept my ideas.

I had Peter Dunlop buy me a roll of rubber t-section material that he told me was used on vehicles and cupboards to keep out drafts; I had seen material like this when I had my Wood and Pickett Mini Cooper repaired at the Rolls-Royce restorers. He bought me a tube of superglue and a couple of Stanley knives.

I then went to Bapty and Co., the gun-hire company in Acton, west London. If you needed a weapon of any kind for a movie, blanks to fire with it and an armorer on set, you went to Bapty's. It was a treasure trove of every weapon you could think of, all housed in a rambling group of older premises. Everything was stacked on shelves, hung on poles or walls, or kept in boxes in a labyrinth of rooms running off each other. Inside some rooms were stacks and stacks of weapons by the hundreds. You could outfit a Robin Hood movie or any medieval battle with archers and spiked poles, outfit a full Crusades battle scene, equipping both sides fully. There were enough rifles and canon for the Charge of the Light Brigade or any Second World War movie with weapons that fired, or dummy weapons for the background. There were even rubber mock-ups for action scenes so the actors would not get hurt when doing stunts. I could go and ask Peter Bapty for a sixteenth-century Japanese sword for a sequence, describe the era and action, and a few minutes later he would turn up with the exact weapon required.

As I knew Peter Bapty well, having rented many weapons over my career as a set decorator, Peter kindly gave me a workshop room to work in and allowed me to spend a day there preparing my designs. I spent a morning prior to this searching through the weapons for suitable models to base my idea on for the stormtroopers, and had settled on a Sterling sub-machine gun. Bapty's had hundreds of these so I was conscious that if my idea worked we had many that we could rent and adapt.

I had decided to start with the stormtroopers' gun, as I had thought of an idea for them after looking again at Ralph's sketches. The Sterling's shape and profile fascinated me and seemed suitable for the stormtroopers. It looks like a really powerful weapon and the size was exactly right. It is an incredible design in itself, and well-known enough to be familiar to audiences. I knew with the few modifications I envisaged I could turn this into something more interesting.

They gave me an older Sterling sub-machine gun to play around with. The exact model is a Sterling Arms Mk4/L2A3 sub-machine gun, according to Bapty's records. I wanted an older, used weapon with scratches and blemishes and tarnished metal. I did not want to present George with a shiny new gun, all specially made and polished to look like a film gun. I wanted a used and innocuous weapon to base my idea on, a gun that was already well worn.

Having broken down the requirements for the film and given them to Peter Bapty for a first look, he realized that we would need a lot of guns for the movie, so it was in his interest to help as much as he could. Carl Schmidt, whom I had worked with on *Lucky Lady*, helped me source the guns and showed me the boxes of spares and scrap items they had bought, and other rescued parts from their spare-parts stores. Once again I began digging around in dusty cardboard boxes and shelves that seemed not to have been touched for years to see what was there.

My main idea was to change the shape of the barrel, to give it a different look. I measured the plastic t-strips to the barrel and cut them to length. Then I rounded off the ends so that they looked like part of the metal of the gun, and carefully stuck the first piece of plastic t-strip into the holes at the ends of the barrel and stuck it down with superglue the length of it. Working my way round the barrel I carefully placed the rest of the strips at equal distance. This change alone completely reshaped the look of the barrel; they looked like some form of cooling fins and fit as if they had always been there. They immediately transformed the look of the Sterling into a different weapon, and gave the gun a better feel for the *Star Wars* world. Looking at that simple modification, my idea was working. Now to give it a more advanced technological feel I wanted to put more greeblies on it.

While digging around in the boxes on Bapty's shelves, where they kept all manner of discarded spares for their weapons, I had seen some interesting-looking telescopic sights. I found the box in question and holding them against the Sterling they fitted exactly on top of the gun. I was told that these were army surplus night sights that had been used in Ireland for night reconnaissance and had been discarded. They appeared the right shape and size, and I liked the technical look of them. They enabled the gunner to see in the dark, apparently, and were fatter than most sights because of the technology inside. Bapty's had bought them as army surplus so we could have them all. I managed to fix one of these on top to look like a kind of targeting device. The weapon looked totally different then. Many questions have been asked about the origins of this scope. This one I used for the prototype was specifically for the army to be able to see at night and definitely used in Ireland during the Troubles there. It was a rangefinder or telescopic scope, so could pinpoint targets at night. I fitted it onto the prototype weapon myself.

I didn't think that the long magazine on the side looked right, so I tried a cut-down version they had that fired about four shots, and that they could easily replicate and make more of. These would hold enough blanks for most of the action and, if required, for machine-gun-like bursts we could revert to the long magazines.

After a few other minor modifications with some greeblies I found in their spare parts boxes, I had a really mean-looking weapon for the stormtroopers. The beauty of this was that the gun could still fire with blanks. This was really important to me. On camera, in action when the stormtroopers were firing them, they would give the flash from the barrel and a puff of smoke, just like in a Western. Also they sounded great; the bang when the blanks fired was really loud and being original Sterlings they could fire in either single-shot mode or automatically, so they would look awesome in battle.

Feeling more confident that my idea was working, I looked through Bapty's collection of pistols and handguns for a gun suitable for Han Solo. Something that a rebel would use and that would look really unique to him, and which I could easily adapt to the *Star Wars* look. I didn't want a revolving-chamber Western pistol used by cowboys, which his character resembled in a way, or a more modern automatic pistol. They were too bland as a shape for what we needed, despite being beautiful in their own way. Even the Eagle, a huge handgun that was an awesome weapon, did not have the unique character I was looking for.

The Mauser DL-44 automatic pistol caught my eye as soon as I saw it. It had a very original look to it, it was unlike any other pistol, and as a bonus it was an automatic so could repeat fire. I loved the fact that it had a wooden handle with its own signature shape to it. I could picture it in Han Solo's hands. It was large enough to be a serious handgun, and the design could easily be altered to make it look like a totally different weapon, but keep the cool nature of the gun. It was a rather beautiful design, and quite different to any other handgun that I had seen.

Once again I rummaged around the boxes of spare parts, and looking through the boxes of rifle sights I found one that was much bigger. This was a German rifle telescopic sight. I placed this on top, next to the barrel, and that worked. It immediately made the weapon look more interesting and changed its profile. I managed to adjust the bolts on the sight, fixed it on top of the Mauser and made it safe. I dug around some more, as I wanted to change the look of the slim barrel, and discovered a flash hider from an aircraft machine gun, used so that the gunner's location was hidden from enemy fighters. As soon as I fitted this onto the end of the barrel it became Han Solo's weapon to me. It gave the gun a totally different look that I thought would suit Harrison Ford's Western-inspired rebel character. I used some blacking marker and aged the brown wooden handle so it looked darker, as this would make it less identifiable and also less noticeable. I added a few more greeblie pieces around the gun to really disguise its origins and decided the time had come to show George. I was a little nervous as this was a novel idea for the weapons and would be a big surprise for them. I hadn't really discussed at all what I was up to. I called John and told him to come over with George.

Entering Bapty's with John, George was fascinated by their massive array of weapons of all kinds. I took him into my room and showed him my creations. George immediately liked the look of the stormtroopers' weapon, and feeling the weight of it, decided it was exactly what he wanted. A huge relief for me, proving I was on the right track, and I think an even bigger relief for him. All of our discussions about weapons that didn't stand out, that simply looked functional but suitable for the *Star Wars* universe, had paid off. George's biggest relief was that I really understood his philosophy. I know myself, from bitter experience as a director and a designer, that sometimes when I explain things I need in detail I am disappointed when presented with something far from what I had envisioned. This is the difficulty of using language when there are no visual references. John Barry was also relieved. The weapons looked used and natural and not designed, but still looked like weapons suitable for a science-fiction movie that was more like a Western in its approach.

I felt safe to bring out Han Solo's weapon. This garnered an even more enthusiastic response and George signed off that one immediately as well. Both weapons had a kickback when fired and sounded like real weapons. Bapty's assistant fired off rounds for George to see what I meant.

Like me, George never liked the plastic look of guns in prior movies and this philosophy of finding objects and dressing them up with scrap or junk set the momentum across the board with all the dressings and weapons. Slowly but surely it gave George the confidence that we were all working towards the same vision, and this is the imperative comfort level for a director, whether dealing with the sets, props or actors. As a major bonus we could afford to make the weapons like this within budget once a deal was struck with Bapty's by the buyer, Peter Dunlop. We could rent the numbers we needed for all the foreground action—these would all be real weapons modified to my prototype—and make fiberglass and rubber duplicates for all the background stormtroopers in the studio for a much lower cost.

It was a huge relief for me. My first problem regarding all the weapons could be solved. I had made my first steps as set decorator and now felt maybe I could climb this mountain before me. George was naturally nervous but he had quickly trusted John Barry who was a remarkably talented designer and his enthusiasm and patience made him a good friend to George. John told me to carry on and sort out all the weapons this way and left to go back to the studio.

George was so interested in my take on the weapons he stayed with me for a few hours. We worked together with scrap and superglue to create Princess Leia's gun. I liked the Vostok Margolin .22LR target pistol as it was small and would fit in Princess Leia's hand. We added a muzzle flash from another gun to change its appearance. Her gun was really one of the only ones I left a little cleaner—she was a princess and would not have recourse to use a weapon very much before the turmoil that was erupting in the story. So I left hers almost as it was. It seemed to work for her character and George and I discussed that when she needed a tougher look in battle after she'd been arrested, she could grab a stormtrooper's weapon and use that.

In case Luke needed a weapon his pistol was made from the same Mauser base as Han's gun, but with different add-on pieces. This was used in *The Empire Strikes Back*. George very much liked the look of the British Lee-Enfield light machine gun, which had a distinctive thick barrel, so we designated this for the stormtroopers as a heavy blaster to be used in certain scenes. I continued over the next few days to search and identify weapons for each character. This way I would be ready for when the movie finally got the green light, and we could begin to rent or mass-produce these weapons for the backgrounds.

Ralph McQuarrie had drawn Chewbacca holding a heavy-duty gun with an open steel butt, so we developed that idea. I had a few guns that were similar in feel to Ralph's painting laid out for George to look at, but I had one secret weapon I kept aside. George looked at them all and we discussed how we could easily modify them to work, but like me I could sense that George wasn't really enamored with them. So I told him that I had found one weapon, that though totally different to the painting, I felt really looked right for his character. Bapty's had an array of ancient and modern crossbows for hire, and one of them, which looked like a Barnett Commando crossbow but has since been established as a Gunmark crossbow made in Winchester, had an iron butt that looked similar in shape to the Ralph McQuarrie painting of Chewbacca. It immediately caught my eye. I really liked the ball-shaped ends of the crossbow part, and that it had a stock that looked more like a gunstock. I brought it out and showed George. I could see from his face that I had struck gold. He worked with me on it, and together we found an interesting-looking rifle telescopic sight. Sticking this onto it with superglue immediately changed its look. I then added two smaller ones either side of it, and these modifications gave it the *Star Wars* 'stamp'. George felt the crossbow idea really suited Chewie better, so that became his weapon and Chewbacca's Bowcaster was born. This is the one seen in an often-used picture of Han Solo and Chewbacca, weapons raised as they charge an enemy. There have been mistaken bloggers and writers of articles saying that George took the idea of Chewbacca and the Bowcaster from another source, but for the weapon this is definitely not so. It was never intended in Ralph's sketches and painting of Chewie; he had a large weapon somewhat like a stormtrooper's weapon. The idea of the Bowcaster came about right here in Bapty's because seeing its shape we thought it interesting enough for Chewie and suitable for his character, and George chose it.

In general with all the weapons, using older, interestingly-shaped guns helped make them look integral to the scenes and blend well with the characters. What was important is that the aged patina of the originals helped to create the right feel to all these weapons, and I was careful to preserve this with the found pieces I was sticking on.

As the Jawas' weapons were different to the more sophisticated Darth Vader's Death Star armies and the rebel forces, I wanted to try to find suitable weapons. If one were making, say, a World War II epic in the desert, the modern armies would have their sophisticated weapons and if there were rebel tribes who lived in the region, their weapons would be antiques or ones that they could afford to buy, usually much simpler and less sophisticated by nature of living in the wilds with no workshops available. This helped to create the feeling for the Jawas' guns that I worked on next. I found a sawn-off Lee-Enfield rifle with a wooden stock and bolt action that seemed really suitable to go with the ragged costumes for these nomadic sand tribes. It had an ancient feel to it compared to the stormtroopers' guns, and fitted in. I found a grenade launcher that went on the end of the barrel, and this fat, squat extension gave the guns the different look required.

The Tusken Raiders had interesting clubs drawn by Ralph McQuarrie. Once more I went on a scavenge round Bapty's treasure trove of weapons. Digging around in their incredible selection of clubs and staffs I found a Fijian club called a Totokia war club. It was almost black in color; the wood was immensely dense and hard. The weapon end was carved into a round shape with notches on it that would give anyone a severe headache were they clubbed with it in a fight. The other end was pointed and just as dangerous. As these were over a hundred years old, they already had that used patina that comes naturally.

George approved these as soon as I showed them to him. We rented them as they were to use for the Tusken characters. In the movie they are called Gaffi sticks and were a fairly primitive weapon to suit these desert nomad characters, with that different look. On one of them we added a spiked metal arrow-like blade for close-up action so that it looked evil at both ends and changed the look just enough to make it stand out.

While we were in Bapty's I showed George an original black samurai costume they had on display. The shape of the black lacquered helmet and shoulder armor, and the shape of the rest of the costume, was somewhat similar to the McQuarrie painting. As it was well over a hundred to two hundred years old, the black enamel-type finish on the armor was slightly dull and it had a patina almost like a black beetle's wings. I thought it was exactly what we wanted as a reference for the overall feeling for the look of Darth Vader. The armor was articulated, an amazing suit in which the samurai could ride and be free to shoot arrows and sword-fight with a lot of movement. The articulations of the armor would protect it from arrows and sword blows. Incredibly sophisticated for its time, it was the shape of the helmet that appealed to me when I saw it. George was fascinated by it; to see an antique samurai suit and be able to feel and touch it was an experience, and the color and finish were a great reference point for us. We rented the helmet, took it to Lee Studios and set it up for a few days on the stage for Liz and ourselves to absorb its shape and detailing. Combined with the look of a German soldier's helmet, it gave Liz an excellent reference point in three dimensions to sculpt to. This really was an aide in trying to create the helmet to Ralph McQuarrie's design based on George's ideas.

Because of the huge success of *Star Wars* and the legions of fans that want replica costumes and weapons, there have been many claims about who made the first Darth Vader helmet and even claims to the design of it. The origins of everything to do with *Star Wars*, especially these iconic characters like C-3PO, R2-D2, Darth Vader and the stormtroopers, were all originally developed by George from his imagination. During the gestation period when he developed *Star Wars* he had Ralph McQuarrie illustrate many versions of these until he was satisfied. Then in the UK, beginning in Lee Studios, we began the process of making them in three dimensions, all based on George's ideas and creation. These few paintings were the reference points for all of us in the art department. Liz Moore sculpted C-3PO and ideas for the stormtroopers to George's exact specifications with John Barry, right there on that tiny stage, long before actual pre-production started. The designs were finalized and signed off by George in Elstree studios for Darth Vader, when John Mollo was employed as costume designer, and took over the responsibilities along with the art department to get them made. The biggest problem on the production was getting these complicated items made in time; the preparation period was far too short due to Twentieth Century Fox's late green light, and we only really had January and February to prepare everything for Tunisia. That is why some of the helmets and costumes were farmed out to outside companies to complete; the load was just too much in house. Never ever was anything farmed out to be designed outside, George would never have let anything be done without his full participation and approval. That was his prerogative and way of working.

George and Gary continued to traverse the Atlantic trying to get Fox to commit with a budget that worked, while we continued to develop R2-D2 and C-3PO's head. Eventually, in November, Norman Reynolds joined us and took on C-3PO. Norman sat at his drawing board for a long time engrossed in how to engineer C-3PO's arms, legs, and head. He had to move his arms backwards and forwards as if swinging and also at the same time be able to lift them sideways, manipulated by an actor inside him. Norman realized this had not been done before; it was a complex engineering problem and he had to figure out on paper how to achieve this. Also the neck had similar problems, as the head had to attach to the body and be able to swivel so C-3PO could turn his head around. We had the robot from *Metropolis* as a pictorial example but C-3PO had to have the freedom to move as much in a robotic human-like way as possible. Even simply walking became a problem to be solved. Designing the knee joints so that his legs could articulate backwards and forwards like a human walking was another complex problem for Norman.

Norman had had a lot of experience in art departments over the years and he solved most of the design elements of C-3PO on the drawing board first, and then by building mock-ups once preparation started. He had a few weeks before we moved to Elstree Studios to begin serious preparation; this time was invaluable for Norman to work out the problems. Once Anthony Daniels was cast then the main difficulty was trying to make C-3PO slim enough to look real and never seem like there was an actor underneath; also how to attach the pieces and remove them when required. Also to take into consideration was that as C-3PO was a main character in the movie, he was required to be walking in the deserts, be involved in fights and would have a lot of action around him. So he had to be durable. This equated to a lot of development time under normal circumstances, and here the clock was ticking. We had to get this right; the movie depended on little R2-D2 and C-3PO being unquestionable as characters. As Liz closed in on the final look for the head it started to look like C-3PO, and we added the dents and scratches from his previous encounters as a robot, really adding character to him. George had stressed this would give him a unique character by presenting the audience evidence of a past history These were drawn in the original paintings of Ralph McQuarrie's. The dents are like scars. Again, robots in films before this were all made perfectly and looked brand new. C-3PO was to be different, in line with the overall philosophy that everything was used and real, and nothing would stand out as if specifically designed for the film.

Gary and George continued their struggle in getting Twentieth Century Fox to understand the time restraints as there really was no precedent in cinema, and he continually stressed to them that they needed at least seven months to develop all these characters and props correctly before the shoot could begin. Both John Barry and John Stears were continually worrying about the time they would have to make everything ready for shooting and trimming down what they thought they really could not pull off in time, to help the budget.

I kept looking at the amount of work I had ahead of me and worrying. Until we could start spending money, I did what I could to prepare myself, ready for the time when I knew I would hardly have a moment to think. As Fox were used to a normal preparation time of a few weeks, George was basically still funding a lot of the work himself due to their reticence to commit. We did what we could, working on shoestring budgets right through until early January the next year when we started in Elstree Studios.

John Barry went on recces to Morocco and Tunisia to establish exactly where to shoot the locations. John had worked in the south of Tunisia a year before on *The Little Prince* directed by Stanley Donen, so knew the desert locations around Tozeur well. I had been on a recce to the south of Morocco to photograph areas John had heard about, but Tunisia seemed to be the preferred choice for several reasons. The deserts I found and valleys that were suitable for the action were then so remote that we couldn't put up a crew the size that *Star Wars* would have. I stayed in hotels that had a canvas sheet for a bed strung on poles across disused oil barrels, and tiny hovels of hotels with no bathrooms and a hole in the floor for a toilet. At least couscous was available everywhere and became my staple diet for the time I was there, along with steaming hot mint tea that was so sweetened with sugar it rotted your teeth. One had to be really careful not to get sick traveling like this, and again this was a worry for a film crew. So for us to shoot there in interesting locations the crew would have to live in a tent city. This had been done before; on *Lawrence of Arabia*, for instance. This would be more difficult on *Star Wars* as we needed a lot of technical backup with robots, sets, vehicles, etc.

Morocco was also then a little unstable politically in the deep south over disputes around the Sahara border, so all in all that was part of the decision to film *Star Wars* in Tunisia.

The variety of locations that could be used to match those described in the script were readily available and John found some amazing places to show George that were not scripted, but provided really unusual settings to build a realistic location for Tatooine.

Almost by accident John discovered the domed roofs of the village outside Djerba one day as he was driving away to get the plane home. Djerba is a tiny island off the coast of Tunisia, joined to the mainland by a bridge, and John spied these strange roofs in the distance above the more modern developments. What he found were ideal locations for the exterior of the Cantina and parts of the settlement of Tatooine. They had the perfect blend of slightly strange but very natural architecture that we could dress into and make look like another world, naturally dusty and realistic.

John also thought about using a Matmata location he had found for *The Little Prince* movie. He could create Luke's homestead in the underground caves carved off the twelve-foot-deep sandstone courtyards cut into the landscape all over the area. The locals have lived in these caves for over a thousand years to help endure the fierce heat of summer and the intense cold in winter. On the recce we stayed in the nearby coastal town of Gabès but when I was dressing we sometimes stayed in the caves, some of which had become a primitive hotel, for only a few dollars a night.

Tozeur in the deep south is about forty minutes' drive from the Sahara Desert with its very large dunes. These are reached through desert roads, easy for Land Rovers and Toyotas, so it makes them film-friendly and very hard to find elsewhere. Many dune locations are covered in scrub and don't have that classic appearance needed for the film's opening. John knew of these magnificent dunes from locations in *The Little Prince*. Also nearby are the magnificent salt lakes, or chotts as the locals call them. These are vast dried-up lake beds, where mirages are common if you stare across them in the burning light of the midday sun.

The bonus for us around Tozeur was also the amazing valleys cut into the Atlas Mountains that led to the deeper regions of the Sahara. They are right on the doorstep, perfect for the first meeting between Obi-Wan Kenobi and Luke. The number-one rule for producers and production heads is to try to get as many locations in one place as possible. Every time one has to move a crew, it costs money as they are not filming, and that's the rule: keep the cameras rolling. There was at least a kind of hotel in Tozeur, pretty primitive then, but half an hour away there were larger tourist hotels in Nefta so it was a viable place to base the first part of the shoot.

John called George and Gary over to meet him in Tunisia, and took them round the locations. He first showed George the dome-roofed houses in Djerba. They fitted his idea of a familiar-feeling location but also different and strange. As soon as George saw these he felt more secure that his search was over and the film became that little bit closer to being realized. With modifications this could easily become Tatooine, and this location also became the set for the exterior of the Cantina and Anchorhead itself.

Traveling to the south, seeing the holes and caves in Matmata he quickly realized their potential as well. George did what visionary directors do best—quickly adapted his ideas to benefit from the gift of these locations. He reset Owen, Beru and Luke's home in a hole in the ground using Matmata for the underground courtyards. The caves had primitive designs in the ceilings and were blackened from years of fires, and they felt right for the homestead. My mantra has always been 'if it feels right, then it is right'. Going on to the chotts around Tozeur, these would easily match Matmata as the exterior above the sunken courtyard and the garage roofs for the Lars homestead. The empty vast chotts would create exactly the feel of an isolated moisture farmer, miles from any township. George could see exactly where he could place Luke in that important scene when he stares out across the wastelands of his planet at the twin suns of Tatooine. Tatooine is an amazingly ancient village of small hobbit-like hovels in Tunisia that are in fact grain stores. We never filmed there on this first *Star Wars* movie but George liked the name so much he renamed Luke's home planet as Tatooine in the script.

When he saw the dunes, George knew they would work for the opening shots when R2-D2 and C-3PO get stranded in the desert having escaped in the emergency pod. They had that sweeping empty vista to them that the scene required, and most importantly were accessible by the film unit.

With the rest of the locations in mind completed, they needed the valley where Luke and Obi-Wan Kenobi first meet, and R2-D2 gets zapped by the Jawas. Right beyond Tozeur there are spectacular valleys and canyons called Sidi Bouhlel that divide the southern towns of Tunisia and the desert. These canyons are like the Grand Canyon in miniature, infused with the local red and ochre tones, and are spectacular. John took George into one of the canyons he had chosen for the scenes and that was it, the last location was approved and designated. This valley has since become very famous, and not just because of this auspicious meeting in the movie.

With locations established these helped Robert Watts, John, and Gary Kurtz to narrow the budget down to where it was acceptable to Twentieth Century Fox. My set-dressing budget was finally fixed after all the cutbacks to around two hundred thousand dollars with a small contingency. I looked again at what I had to get made for this and though I had conquered the weapons problem, I had to really think now of different ways to achieve the actual sets themselves. There are no problems, only solutions, and John Box's first advice to me ever about the plane in the desert and the director wanting it red when all one had was a small bottle of green ink, came back to me with a haunting resonance. Here I was faced with exactly the dilemma he had described.

I was driving in to Lee Studios one morning from my apartment in West Hampstead, thinking deeply about all my different options for the dressing and props. Having read the script several more times and gone through my breakdown of all the set dressings that would be required over and over again, I was pondering my different options of how to pull it off. The weapons were under control for now. It was part of our job in the art department under John Barry to try to facilitate making the movie for the budget allocated, and the more we got into it the more we really wanted to make this movie, so we had to find solutions. The time allotted was shrinking as the weeks passed. The March shoot date had been decided so that George and the crew could film the sequences in Tunisia before the fierce summer heat kicked in around the Tozeur area where we were based for most of the shoot. Tozeur is bordering Algeria and the Sahara Desert, so in summer the temperatures rise into the fifties and sixties. The locals call the week in mid-August when the temperatures reach their zenith 'suicide week'. I experienced this years later when directing the second unit on *The Phantom Menace*. One day it measured 62 degrees, and my crew had to work a twelve-hour day. 'Grin and bear it' is the British mantra, and we did. I felt sorry for the actors playing creatures in rubber suits. Despite a specially made water-cooling system for the costumes for the main characters, I had about two minutes to shoot each take or the actor would turn blue and pass out.

Gary and George kept battling away at the studio's executives and board members, whose lack of faith in this mythic story set in space remained undiminished. Alan Ladd, Jr. still stuck with it. Having seen George's success with *American Graffiti* he sensed there was a younger audience out there not being catered to, and he kept convincing the board to make it. Twentieth Century Fox had already spent several hundred thousand dollars on *Star Wars* in development costs, mostly in setting up the new special-effects department under John Dykstra, who was attempting to build a motion control camera in Van Nuys north of Los Angeles, so they didn't want to lose all that pre-investment either. Seeing George's face some days and his frustrations, and Gary's explanations of it all, made us bond together further to get this made as George wanted it made. John Barry was extremely worried as time was really running out for adequate prep time as we approached December and the Christmas holidays. Once more they returned to the US in a final attempt to solve the problem. Gary Kurtz cut the budgets down and in a sweep to get it past the board, another ten percent was lopped off the construction and set-decorating budgets. This is usually the first to be hit when budgets are randomly reduced by percentages. It's the easiest amount to focus on and reduce, as it's often the largest. Especially true in this case when it was about a quarter of the budget *Star Wars* had to create a science-fiction world.

Gary explained to me that in the beginning the Fox distribution arm had estimated the film could earn twelve million dollars in revenues; science fiction was not doing well at the box office at that time, and was not looked on as a box-office certainty. *2001* had been a commercial disaster and had taken ten years just to cover its costs. At its first ever screening in America the entire audience walked out before the end, and sealed its fate with the studios. So the studios divided the estimated earnings by three to allocate the production budget, in this case four million dollars. That was the general rule of thumb to set a budget in those days. So here we were working as the budget soared at one point to sixteen million dollars and finally, after a lot of cuts and trimming and rewriting by George, it had settled at around six.

George had employed us himself with money owed him from *American Graffiti*, which had been a considerable hit. That was the main reason that George was given the chance to make his science-fiction fantasy. For many years *American Graffiti* remained at the top of the chart of highest-grossing revenues in ratio to its cost. It was made for one million dollars and grossed well over a hundred and twenty million. I remember Gary Kurtz telling me that during the making of *Graffiti*, George had wanted to go to the local cinema, and there was nothing on that he wanted to see—it was all geared to serious adult sensibilities. He had remarked to Gary at the time that there must be families and young children all over America wanting to go to the cinema and there was very little out there for them. No more Westerns or escapist fantasies were being made. So he had decided to make one.

It was clear that to make the movie conventionally would be too costly. That meant every piece of dressing and props and weapons would be designed and drawn up and then made in the various studio workshops or by outside contractors, and this would be way above the budgets allocated to us. John Barry's set construction budget was now about six hundred thousand dollars and my dressing budget was a little under two hundred thousand dollars with the new cuts.

There had to be a solution to how to set-decorate this epic with this budget. That included making all the action props, the weapons, and robots and dressing all the interiors and exteriors of all the sets required, both in the studios and the locations in Tunisia. It was an enormous undertaking. The *Millennium Falcon* alone would eat this amount up if I did it conventionally and made all the dressings from detailed drawings through the workshops. As a child I often took model kits and adapted them by sticking other model kit parts and salvaged pieces on my cars and planes to create a used-looking reality. I used to photograph them in my back garden, making mountain roads, and tried to create a more realistic feel to my Dinky toys by dirtying them down, so this desire was somehow inherent in me already. Sometimes I'd arrange crashes and see if I could fool myself with the photographs I staged.

So how could I make the *Millennium Falcon* look real? The locations were set for shooting the scenes set on Tatooine in Tunisia, and knowing the North African landscapes, full of dusty ancient forts and desert palaces, I knew that would give the film this ancient futuristic feel. This would reduce the amount I would have to create for the dressing on location.

In the studios John and I had discussed the *Millennium Falcon* interiors as he sketched ideas for them. We both felt that space would be crammed and that this ship would be the opposite of the smooth, designed spaces in the Death Star. After all, when Luke first sets eyes on it, he describes it to Obi-Wan Kenobi as a pile of junk. Han Solo shoots back that he'd made a lot of modifications himself. I showed him reference pictures of the space pods the astronauts used to go into space at the time. Crammed with switches and pipes and functioning mechanics and electronics, they looked the part. George liked the idea of interiors packed with technology. Aircraft cockpits were like that, especially bombers and warships.

So, pondering all these things, I wondered if I could actually use airplane scrap and find junk as a base for all the dressing. This had never been done before on this scale, but I felt if I could find dressing that looked like a submarine or plane interior then it would give the sets a reality. George and I had talked about the *Millennium Falcon* and both agreed it should be like a ship that Harrison Ford had repaired himself in the garage, that constantly dripped oil and fluids, yet ran against the best of them. This suited Han Solo's character and helped to amplify his rebel nature. I thought about *Silent Running* and Trumbull's use of a ship for the craft interiors. I knew this was not practical as navy scrap from ships is mostly iron and really heavy. I thought back to my time in Emmer Green near my home when I was employed to break up the government army-surplus trucks and tanks—I knew there must be airplane graveyards in Britain filled with unused old aircraft.

I met with George and Gary Kurtz and John Barry and discussed my idea to buy airplane scrap and use it to dress the *Millennium Falcon* interiors. John was all in favor as he remarked that ILM used model-kit parts to create the ships for filming miniatures, and he didn't see why their technique wouldn't work full size. George was all for it. Secured by my success with the prototypes for the weapons and sticking airplane lights and air nozzles onto our mock-up R2-D2, he put his trust in my suggestion. It was actually music to George's ears as his entire philosophy all the time was that sets and dressings and props should be natural and in a way unseen. If you think about King Arthur, say, the swords and horses and dressings and castles are just a natural organic habitat for the characters to interact in; they never shout out to the audience 'look at me'. The great Japanese director, Akira Kurosawa, was the master at this, and I think the inspiration to all of us. My firm belief was that this should be no different if we were set in the future and this coincided exactly with George's ideas for the movie.

I remember Gary looking concerned one morning near to Christmas. He told us that he had a huge problem. Elstree was the only studio that had enough stage space available for all the sets required for the movie, alongside the massive hangar-sized H-stage in Shepperton for the main rebel base. Twentieth Century Fox had still not actually green-lit the picture and Stanley Kubrick wanted to rent the stages in Elstree for *The Shining* and was pressuring Gary and George for a decision. He was challenging the dates.

John had sketched out a lot of ideas for the sets required during this time, and realized that we could not fit the movie into one studio. The problem was not the shooting times, which are generally fairly short, but the build and removal times. These could block up the stages for a month or more sometimes. The movie needed a couple of really big stages for the *Millennium Falcon*, the Death Star hangar and the rebel base hangar. John chose Elstree as the studio main base so we could have all the stages, and Shepperton Studios, as it had the largest stage in the UK at the time,

H Stage, which was four hundred feet long. These were the two studios where I began my career.

Elstree was the studio Stanley Kubrick used. He lived very close by in Hertfordshire, always shot everything at Elstree and did all his post-production there. Stanley refused to fly in an airplane ever, so he stayed at home near Elstree and only if absolutely necessary would he sail to New York on one of the Queen-class ocean liners. So having made several films at Elstree he had considerable pull. Elstree were willing to hold the dates for *Star Wars* but needed a deposit to do so, and Stanley would be scheduled to go in on our backs. So Gary and George had a terrible decision to make. Pay it and gamble that Fox would go ahead and at least have a studio to make the movie in, or face losing it. Then the momentum would be gone, as Kubrick needed the studio for months. He was building all the sets long before shooting, then rehearsing on all of them and fully lighting each set. That way he had all the sets ready and available throughout the long shooting schedule, and as they were all lit ready, he could decide on any day where to shoot. On most movies you build and strike the sets to keep the budget down, but Stanley created his own rules as a one-man-band filmmaker and Warners gave him free rein to do it.

George and Gary took the leap of faith and paid the deposit. This was well over a hundred thousand pounds, and in the event that the movie would not go ahead they would lose it. This shows George's commitment and what it takes sometimes to get a movie made. In some ways anyone getting a movie finished and into the theaters should get an Academy Award, just for the tenaciousness required if one is outside the studio system as an independent.

Finally, on December 12, Twentieth Century Fox relented and green-lit the film. We worked right up until Christmas Eve and had everything packed up ready to move into Elstree Studios. I drove down to Sidmouth in Devon for Christmas at my parents' house, and tried to rest up for a few days to ready myself for the next months of work—I knew I would not get a day off until we wrapped.

After the Christmas break we finally moved into our new offices in Elstree Studios.

We had the first floor of one of the administration buildings in the studios. I had a room as set decorator and along the corridor, about five rooms up, were John Barry, Les Dilley, and Norman Reynolds, as we were the key heads of the art department. Peter Dunlop was hired to the production as the official buyer and worked extensively with me. It really helped to have such a wonderful man and friend to support me as Peter never questioned what I was doing; he trusted my instincts as we had done so many films together.

Spread around these central offices were the draftsmen and assistants hired to draw up the plethora of sets to be quickly built under construction manager Bill Welch. Harry Lange was also a vital member of the team; Harry had worked on *2001* and was an expert at creating the panels to be built for the *Millennium Falcon* cockpit and the Death Star. As art director he remained in charge of these right through the making of *A New Hope.*

The first thing I did was to go and re-introduce myself to the propmaster Frank Bruton and his team. Frank was like an army general in command of his troops. Having served as propmaster on many big productions Frank could organize to move an enormous film crew from country to country with a military precision that made it all seem so easy. When he was filming in Ireland on Stanley Kubrick's *Barry Lyndon* it was still the time of trouble with the IRA. The IRA decided to issue a death threat to Stanley Kubrick, and issued a warning of an imminent threat of a bombing to the movie production. In those times you took any warning like that with deadly seriousness. Stanley was freaked out by it. The line producer, an old friend, Bernie Williams, told me that he and Frank moved a crew of almost five hundred people and equipment in a weekend from Ireland to South Africa to continue filming. Frank had literally gone to war and organized everything. He was brilliant.

Peter Dunlop bought a kettle and some mugs that were set up in my room, boxes of PG Tips tea and a small fridge for the milk. It began an early morning ritual. John, Les, and I, with Norman, Frank Bruton, and Bill Welch were always in really early before the canteen opened and any other staff were there. It was catch-up time every day at 7am and an invaluable time before the start of our days that were so busy we hardly had time to think. We consumed packets and packets of chocolate-covered McVitie's biscuits, a favorite of John's.

Frank asked me a lot of questions about what we were doing, and I still don't think he realized at that stage just what surprises were to come. There were endless meetings with George and Robert Watts to decide the next moves forward, as John and construction manager Bill Welch had to plan out exactly which sets to build on which stages and Robert had to produce an accurate shooting schedule based around the actors' and sets' availabilities. It is a complex procedure on a movie where almost everything is built. To decide what to build and shoot and remove in what order takes a lot of experience, as one slip and shooting grinds to a halt and that costs money. The law is 'keep the cameras rolling', whatever the situation. John had a humongous task ahead of him. Bill had to line up an army of carpenters and painters and riggers and plasterers for the various shops to minimize the build times and at the same time work to a very tight budget. John Barry worked long hours every day at his drawing board to have sketches for all the sets ready to be drawn up by the various draftsmen they had hired. Bill Welch was on his back daily, worrying about how on earth to get it all built on time when he looked at the schedule, and smoking copious numbers of cigarettes.

John Barry had sketched out the Lars homestead interior where Luke lived with his aunt and uncle. He had photographs of the locations at Matmata all over the walls for the exterior and the *Star Wars* look. I went to see him and talk about the dressing. He liked the idea of an airliner cabin interior and had drawn it up with that shape as an inspiration. It was logical and inspired ideas in me about how to dress it.

Uncle Owen and Aunt Beru lived with Luke as moisture farmers way out in Tatooine. Discussing it with John it was logical, his idea being that they would have to have lived underground because of the intense heat in summer you get in these desert regions.

Where we eventually filmed in Matmata in the south of Tunisia this was evident. The huge circular holes cut into the ground and around each central courtyard were caves cut into the rock and dirt. These were where the population had lived for centuries. They were the perfect location, in fact, for the interiors of Luke's home, especially the courtyards. So John had taken the idea of those to convert them to a science-fiction setting. He added in vaporators and other pipe work to denote a sophisticated technology under the surface that matched the primitive and ancient look, much like an oil well in a desert setting. Then off these caves around the courtyard John had to design the actual underground living quarters that would be sealed off from the heat. The thinking was these would be built elsewhere, manufactured in component units and shipped out to these far-flung desert outposts. They really looked the part, as John's early drawings show.

My job then was to go and find all the interior dressings. Aunt Beru was cooking so I had to think about all the pots and pans and cups and saucers, all the food and equipment to put in there. We concentrated on the kitchen, as that is where the scene was set, and the rest would be on location for the dining scene with Luke and the family. I had to imagine what would be suitable for these dressings. They would be standard units, shipped out to these far-flung destinations, and things that wouldn't break easily that would be able to withstand the fierce conditions. This was not a place for antique furniture and personal nick-nacks everywhere, or beautiful family treasures like tea sets. So my thinking took on a different dimension.

In those days Tupperware was in its infancy, but growing in reputation, and it later provided a holy grail of solutions for me for the movie as they had really interesting shapes and housewares. Then another idea struck me. The metal containers used in airliners for the hot food. These were all standard sizes and easily transportable between the companies supplying the food to be heated on board. I researched airplane interiors and they could provide a wealth of interesting dressings. The food containers looked really good and, as they were left unpainted in metal, once adapted could certainly be used for dressing Luke's homestead. This reinforced my idea about using airplane scrap, so we asked Robert Watts to organize a trip for me to go round some scrapyards in England. We had found out that all the airplane junkyards were very close to airports, so they began to organize me a day's recce in a light plane, to go and search out just what was available.

Up to this point our tiny art department team had been like a small band of pioneers tucked away in the tiny Lee Studios, planning how to make the movie George's way. Now suddenly there were crews arriving daily and the film was going into full gear for preparation, and with time so short it happened way faster than is usual. Normally things build slowly, often around the production office and art department as they have the longest prep time. Here we were with crews starting and no time to really explain what we were doing, and there was a general misconception of the movie we were making, as we found out very quickly.

Things got put into perspective for me one morning early in January. Frank Bruton organized for a long table to be laid out in the prop room, and I had all the guns and props we had developed and made at Bapty's brought in and laid out for the team to see. I wanted the new team fresh to the project to look at the way that George saw the movie, and get an idea firsthand of just what we were planning for the dressing and props.

Charlie Torbett was the lead standby property master and in charge next to Frank and Joe Dipple, my charge hand dressing prop. Charlie walked around with the first AD Tony Waye and a few others in their team. Charlie looked at my guns in disbelief. He picked up my adapted Sterling sub-machine gun for the stormtroopers and laughed. "You can't show this junk to the director, he's from Hollywood—this is a big studio movie we are making. You have to make everything new from scratch. Look at it, it's old and used, it looks like an old war film. We need science-fiction guns, clean and modern ones, not this junk." He threw it back on the table in disgust. I looked him in the eyes—he was deadly serious. I told him this is what George had approved, and that I had developed them over the last three to four months with George and Gary and John Barry. The last thing we wanted was plastic. Charlie just scoffed at me and left with Tony Waye saying, "We'll see about that." He obviously thought I didn't have a clue what I was doing and went off to try to talk to the director and get everything remade as he saw it. This was a rude awakening for me. We had our work cut out for us now, convincing people just what we were intending. I knew I was in for a rough ride from that moment on as they just didn't get the script, or the vision, and my suspicions turned out to be correct that not many on the crew would ever understand it until they saw the finished film. I thought to myself that George was now going to have to justify his every move to people who just didn't get it.

We talked it over at our teatime get-together in the early morning in the art department. It would have been easy to get undermined and lose confidence under these circumstances, but George and John and Les and I stuck to our guns! We would make this film exactly the way George intended it and how we saw it.

ONCE UPON A TIME IN THE WEST

George attempts to get the crew to understand

We had to do something to make the crews understand, seeing this early reaction and the discussions going on around the studios. George screened some films he thought might influence everyone. First he screened *Once Upon a Time in the West*. From the opening it was gritty and dusty. The costumes especially were really good and George tried to explain what it was that appealed to him. For example, the dusty long black coats worn by Henry Fonda playing a really bad character for the first and only time in his career. I don't think anyone understood at all how on earth this related to a space movie.

Then George screened *2001* to show the influence of technology that he envisioned for the Death Star, but for our film it would be dark and black and evil. The shots in space were amazing for their day; Doug Trumbull had pioneered a way to shoot the craft and the space station as if we were actually there in space. I think the cerebral intelligence behind Clarke's writing and Kubrick's vision didn't appeal to mass audiences at this time, so again this was a bit confusing to a team more used to *Flash Gordon*.

The third film that really threw the non-believers for six was *Satyricon*, the Fellini masterpiece. The sets in that are amazing, aged and worn and some of a massive scale, like the strange arena that particularly impressed George. This was the kind of contrast George was seeking, and also Fellini just filmed them as if they were normal locations, especially the strange arena set. We, the core group in the art department who had worked with George for the last four months understood, maybe because we were visual artists, I don't know, but it was still hard for the crew to understand how this all related to this script they thought was a cheap children's film. The murmurings continued but undeterred we just ignored everyone and carried on.

Despite this lack of enthusiasm from the crew, I was eager to board a plane and embark on my search for suitable dressing. At 7am a few mornings later we duly met at Denham Aerodrome, a small private airfield near Uxbridge on the outskirts of London. There was me, Robert Watts, Peter Dunlop, and John Stears. A small prop Cessna was being warmed up in the cold winter air as we waited in the tiny office. As soon as it was light we climbed aboard, bumped across the grass field that served as a runway and flew into the winter skies, which were fortunately sunny. This was my first time in a light aircraft and it was exhilarating. I was put next to the pilot so was able to check out what he was doing. I was also looking at the throttles and dials and getting ideas, thinking to myself that these would be great dressing.

We arrived at our first airport in the north, I believe Nottingham, and we made our way to the local aircraft scrapyard. I entered a wonderland. There was a mountain of scrapped airplane parts, jet engines and cabins from junked airplanes, a plethora of disused jet parts lying in huge piles of scrap sometimes twenty feet high. I scrambled all over them, selecting suitable pieces, and I took loads of reference photographs for the future.

They pulled out all the interesting pieces I had marked, including quite a few jet engines as I could see their potential for dressing once stripped apart. Peter and Robert negotiated a deal with the owner. What surprised us was just how cheap it all was. No one wanted it at this stage, and scrap metal was sold by weight, not by any other value. Aircraft parts are extremely light so anything we wanted cost practically nothing. We quickly added more jet engines and cockpit pieces and Robert told him we would arrange a truck to pick it all up. I was in ecstasy. The jet engines I could see were full of the most amazing shapes and the cockpit instruments and switch panels and seats were all such a find. It just took a little imagination to see it dressed in a spaceship.

We flew to the next scrapyard, this time in Birmingham, and were greeted by the same wonderland of cheap scrap. I bought a lot of undercarriage pieces and parts of the underbelly of airliners, knowing they would be used. Again they were light and had little value in terms of metal to be re-used so we got it all for next to nothing. They were glad to get rid of it actually. I also found jet engines from commercial jet liners and bought about eight or ten of these. Seats, switches, and panels were really useful. I found a lot of the metal food containers used in the galleys of airliners to heat the food, and bought those as well as different switch panels from the galleys and cockpits. Anything I liked the shape of we bought.

Again we flew on to another airfield in Manchester and another nearer London in Gloucestershire, and I bought a great deal more interesting panels and navigation equipment. Each airfield had its own particular type of scrap so it was really useful.

It took a lot of time to exactly sort out and buy what I needed for dressing. It had taken a while for me to select the more interesting pieces; I was going by instinct, trying to imagine what I might need for the different sets. I just knew I would need a lot of it with the interiors of the *Millennium Falcon* and all the different locations for Tatooine and the Death Star. The pilot was getting a little nervous after a quick sandwich lunch in the early afternoon and said we really ought to get going. The daylight hours are very short in Britain in January and it gets dark by 4pm. As it was late he was worried about returning to Denham before dark.

Flying back it got very bumpy. Seeing the pilot wrestling the controls as we lurched around in air pockets could have set someone a bit afraid of flying into a panic. Peter didn't look too comfortable, but in the true tradition of British stoicism, we all laughed our way through it, and Peter and Robert slept through the rest of the flight. The problem was that the high winds made the return longer. I noticed the pilot looking a little concerned at the darkness fast enveloping us. I asked him what was wrong. "There are no lights at Denham," he said. "So I have to call the local farmer to drive his Land Rover to the end of the runway." Hi-tech stuff indeed. I watched as he called the farmer, and quietly prayed that he wasn't out Morris dancing or something. The farmer responded and worked out a strategy with our pilot. I looked back at Robert and Peter. Peter Dunlop was still dozing and Robert smiled and looked his calm reassuring self. Robert had worked on every type of movie and been in every type of situation one could throw at someone—this was just another day's adventure for him.

We descended down to Denham in darkness, seeing familiar lights of farmhouses and factories below us. As we lined up for an approach to the field I indeed saw the lights of a Land Rover bumping across the grass and turning to park at the end of the runway. The two lights from the headlamps made landing beacons for the pilot to aim at. Down we came and bumping onto the grass the little plane bounced around and finally slowed to a halt within a few yards of the Land Rover. We all profusely thanked the pilot and the farmer when we exited the plane and Peter Dunlop drove us back to Elstree.

The next day back at Elstree, Frank must have wondered what was going on as I explained to him that I was going to buy copious amounts of scrap from airplanes and other sources. So instead of the usual prop storage where he organized tables and chairs and room furniture, with separate shelving for all the smalls and table dressings and antiques, we would need a bullpen where the selected team could break down the aircraft scrap into dressing pieces. Here was this young, long-haired set decorator with jeans and Cuban boots telling him that the methods he had relied on for his entire career were going to be changed. Frank listened to me carefully and simply said, "Just tell me what you need and we will get it done." Frank had fortunately taken a liking to me and trusted that I knew what I was doing. I decided to wait until I had got my hands on some scrap and then show him, as it was difficult to comprehend just what we were doing.

Joe Dipple, my charge hand dresser from *Randall and Hopkirk* and *Department S* and subsequent movies we had made at Elstree, was on board and Mike Fowlie was hired as well, nephew of the legendary prop master Eddie Fowlie. I asked Frank to hire my old friend Roger Shaw as a special prop maker, as this was a new skill and Roger knew what I needed to be done. Despite Roger never having worked in the industry he was really talented at engineering and sculpting and I knew he would understand how to take airplane scrap apart and identify interesting pieces for dressing or to use as props. Frank hired Roger and got him in the union. Now I had to put my theories into practice as we waited for Frank to organize the pickup of the scrap on huge low loaders. I was praying that my idea would work; I was on the line and more than a little nervous as the production shifted into a different gear and the shoot date of March seemed to loom over us.

Meanwhile, R2-D2 was evolving. We knew that John Stears was trying to develop radio-controlled units, but John Barry was wary of his ability to pull it off in the time we had. John Barry shared the same philosophy with me on the relying on new technology, especially when budgets were so tight, and filming schedules weren't permitting any delays. George concurred; also his belief was to stick to a low-tech approach when possible. We continued encouraging John Stears, though, as we knew we would need a radio-controlled version for filming if he could make one work.

Our plywood and scrap-metal mock-up was handed to the special-effects department to make the first working model in metal. Peter Childs was given the task of doing detailed blueprint drawings of R2-D2 based on Les's drawings and our mock-up. John Stears was full of enthusiasm as to how he would make a complicated radio-controlled version that could do everything in the script. This would be the three-legged version for when R2-D2 moved quickly. For normal walking around small places he would waddle with Kenny Baker inside operating him. Kenny could swivel the head in our mock-up and they planned to make the first operating R2-D2 with the head on a roller bearing so that he could easily perform. We needed various similar robots for the Sandcrawler sequence when the Jawas sell captured robots to Luke's uncle. These were all first up on the schedule.

Also for other scenes there were R2-D2 models in varying styles and colors. We cast the first robot in plaster and had fiberglass models built and finished and painted. John Stears set to making metal-bodied versions of him. A lot of the dressings I had placed in Lee Studios stayed and became familiar parts of his body. Peter had to buy and source quite a few more of the little airplane air nozzles, but we were fortunate in having a box full when I first discovered them to use. As the first prototypes developed, Kenny was brought in to try them out and practice walking. As we developed it with him it became easier for him, though the cramped interior never got better—in fact it got worse. The amount of technical equipment and batteries that had to be hidden inside meant every inch of space was used. Kenny always complained about this piece or that piece digging into him. R2-D2 became George's *bête noir* in a way. One day in Tunisia George told me that he realized he had created the worst situation for a director, like working with a dog and a very young child all in one.

Time was ridiculously short for all the work needed to prepare all the R2-D2s required for the shoot—the little robot needed several different bodies to perform all the functions required. One had to have the third leg that could kick down and retract so that it didn't just appear like magic when R2-D2 had to use it to move quickly. Also R2-D2 took on a different stance when this happened as he leant back. They needed a remote-controlled one for both, as we couldn't get Kenny inside with the control mechanism. We made our own mock-ups as well so that we had them for dressing as we needed a lot of robots. I figured there would be several versions of the same model so I could place these around the sets.

Bill Harman was assigned to help John Stears' special-effects department, as he had built the landspeeder mock-ups and R2-D2. Bill continued to develop the landspeeder and fitted better wings on it. He carved the jet-shaped pods out of polystyrene and fixed these onto the ends of the wings so we could get a true idea of what it would look like in motion. Bruce, the special-effects assistant, took it out for a test run down the studio road watched by John, George, Les, and me. Forgetting the width of it with the extended wings and pods in place, Bruce tried to turn the already difficult-to-control three-wheeler round the stage at the end of the run. He veered straight into the stage wall and crashed, knocking one wing off. The test descended into chaos as an embarrassed Bruce limped the half-destroyed speeder back to the workshops. I think any other director would have berated the effects department and walked off in disgust. But George knew the value of these tests. In fact the speeder moving was enough to see that with the right chassis and build it could work, and that at certain angles we could make it look like it was flying. We got what we needed out of the test to proceed and George knew that he could animate or rotoscope the wheels out later in post, so work continued.

I had seen a tiny car on the road one day called an Ogle. It was from a small private car company started by David Ogle, who designed and created several sports cars. They were really tiny two-seater sports cars. I had followed up and done research in magazines and looked at them wondering whether to buy one. I was put off by their tiny size; with giant trucks roaring past I felt I would feel really vulnerable. They had amazing engineering and were pretty advanced for the era. At our morning discussion meetings John had suggested to Les and Norman that they find a manufacturer to make the landspeeder for us. He didn't see how it could be ready in time to ship out to Tunisia, and it was needed in the first week of shooting. We discussed car companies and I suggested we look at Ogle, especially as they were in Hertfordshire, near the studios. The design was approved now, but it had to be made to look old and battered and be able to drive fast over the chotts in Tunisia to try to make the illusion of floating work. It needed the expertise of a car company and Ogle might well fit the bill.

Les Dilley took over the making of the landspeeder and he and Norman Reynolds went to the Ogle factory in Hertfordshire to discuss making it.

Time constraints were one of the major issues. Ogle was really enthusiastic about the project, and agreed to do it. They took on outside commissions to design and make other work besides their car line, so were able to turn something around quickly. Fortunately for us they had developed the three-wheeled Bond Bug, a way more trendy and sophisticated three-wheeled vehicle than the Reliant Robin. Robert Watts did a deal with Ogle to build a couple of them for the main action. These would enable us to have two working and functional vehicles we could take to Tunisia that would be able to drive around the desert and locations. We had the final designs now, the mock-up Bill had made and Ralph's paintings for them to work to. The schedule was really tight so there was a lot of tension around these over the coming weeks, about whether they would be ready for the shooting in late March. They had to be transported along with everything else needed for the movie from Elstree by truck, and Frank Bruton had a schedule worked out to the last day which had to be met for shooting to start. I had to think about dressing the vehicle as well, to give it a functional appearance (and also the interior and controls), so began assembling pieces for this.

Also it was decided after watching the tests with the mock-up that Les and John Stears would build a sixty-foot counter-balanced swing arm on a mount. This would attach to the landspeeder so that it could be turned around in a full 120-foot arc, swinging it into the shot for all the close-ups as if coming in to a stop and floating. With precise editing this would also work for it taking off. A second landspeeder without wheels was built for this version. The swing arm had to be specially constructed so that it could be transported to Tunisia along with all the other sets and vehicles and dressings.

Everything was being done at lightning speed, our days were consumed with solving problems, and everyone was working from early morning to late at night—there was no other option to get this show on the road.

Peter Dunlop had purchased an expensive molding machine that made boats and kayaks for John Barry and the construction department. It was an early vacuum-molding press and it really accelerated the construction department's fabricating schedule. John was concerned as it cost ten thousand pounds at the time, but it was an absolute godsend.

Under Les and Norman's guidance, Bill Welch's team pressed out sheets of wall claddings and dressing sheets. The process was simple.

The plaster shop would create a sample panel molded from clay, and then the draftsman, having sourced suitable shapes from my store of scrap or rows of switches etc., would place them in at different places, varying the panels so that they would not all be repetitive. This would then be cast and molded. The vast amount of sets for the Death Star in particular required a lot of gray-clad detailed walls, and these panels could be stapled on quickly and removed for revamping so easily. Also, as the costumes for C-3PO, the stormtroopers and Darth Vader all used this molded plastic as a base, this machine truly saved our bacon on *Star Wars*. Brian Muir sculpted Darth Vader's helmet and the stormtroopers' costumes from Ralph McQuarrie's sketches and George and John Barry continually modified his clay sculpting until the look was correct. John Barry added the teardrop shapes to Darth Vader's helmet and then it was signed off and prepared for molding and casting. Others have laid claim to the design of Darth Vader and the stormtroopers' helmets but they were all from George's ideas, illustrated by Ralph McQuarrie and sculpted by Brian Muir under George and John Barry and John Mollo's guidance. I used to go to the plasterers' shop to watch the progress of everything going on there to keep myself informed of every aspect of the progress on the film, as everything was integral to the whole picture.

Several massive articulated lorries and trailers pulled into Elstree Studios loaded with an assortment of my airplane scrap. Piled high on these enormous low-loader trailers were my pieces of fuselage, cockpits, undercarriages, and many different sizes of jet engines. After phone calls and exchanges of information with the gatehouse, surprised at these behemoths arriving loaded with scrap metal, Frank Bruton took command and arranged for the first truck to be backed into the space he had cleared out for it. I was called down to the prop room and watched the long trailers backing in to the now empty storage room below Frank's office. The prop team started unloading the aircraft parts and placed them onto the floor in the center. I watched carefully as they pulled the parts off the truck.

Frank Bruton stood silently beside me, watching as pieces of airplane scrap piled up in his prop room. Then, without looking at me, I heard his voice. "You know you're mad, boy, don't you?" It wasn't at all malicious or condescending, just a statement of fact. I was taking a huge leap of faith in basically inventing an entirely new way of dressing the sets and getting a look that we wanted, and I guess I was crossing my fingers that all the faith everyone had put in my theory of how to achieve it would actually pay off. Seeing piles of junk on his prop room floor and having not a clue as to how I envisaged it being turned into the interior dressing of a space freighter mystified him. But Frank being the true gentleman he was just asked me what I wanted the team to do before leaving. He never ever wavered in his support. In his usual understated manner he turned to me and said, "Okay, tea's on in my office, come and tell me exactly what you need me to do." I went and carefully explained to him how I envisioned the process over a cup of extremely strong tea. Then we went down to the enormous piles of scrap airplane parts now laid out over the prop room floor and with Joe Dipple and a couple of the prop dressers I explained what to do.

Taking a jet engine I showed them the rather beautiful pipes carefully laid out along the sides. "Unbolt those and place them altogether. What I am looking for is different piles of the same pieces so we have the ability to dress in patterns, like a real plane would be," I said. I showed them the spinning fans and what great shapes they were, and especially the patina of them, which was metal but not bright and shiny, ideal for the look we were after. Each layer of pipes and metal joints exposed more underneath, and they quickly got into breaking them down. I showed them panels covered in switches, and told them to categorize them into similar pieces, so we had a store of those. The undercarriage pieces were beautifully engineered and these we would break down into sections. Everything I had bought had a purpose, and they quickly saw that by breaking the parts down we would have a supply of different pieces to create a craft interior.

Frank had understood immediately what to do, and created a log so every piece would have its own number and a place to be. He was brilliant; this was just what we needed. John Barry came down and looked through the scrap pieces. He picked up objects from the jet engines; they were a real marvel of engineering and also beautiful in their own right. He instructed the art department draftsmen to go down and take a look, as this was a new procedure for them. The way Frank categorized everything meant each piece could be identified later for the construction people to build in. Each piece had a place and a number and could be repeated. It became a military operation. Frank supported me all the way, and made it work into an efficient and workable system.

We began to assemble a huge pile of interesting pipes and shapes for my dressing crews, ready for when I would begin to dress the first set. The important thing was repetition. To stick one random piece anywhere into a set with no methodology as to how it might be conceived and viewed as a functioning piece of machinery or electronics or mechanics would not work. By selecting several pieces or the same switches and placing them in units it would give the dressing an authentic look. If one looks at airplanes or ships the panels are always in repetitive units and in airplanes in particular there is a duplicate backup of everything, so I went on this principle to create the craft interiors. By showing Joe Dipple the aircraft panels I had bought, it gave him an idea of how the dressing would be placed. Very disciplined and organized, that was the key to making it look real.

The draftsmen began to go down to the prop room and look through the stripped-down pieces of scrap as the boys stripped them to find suitable pieces to build in. Then they would measure them up and design them into the drawings, and the corresponding number identified them when the set was constructed. This was applicable to a lot of the larger pieces, but especially pertinent to the sets like the exterior of the *Millennium Falcon* and the Cantina.

Looking at the drawings John Barry had done of the *Millennium Falcon*, it was clear there were a lot of corridors, hold areas and storage rooms—then there was the cockpit! I went to the stage and looked at the skeleton construction of the sets as Bill had started the corridors and the hold area. I realized we would need miles and miles of tubing and pipe work to dress into the ceilings and walls, to simulate the conduits where the electronics and mechanics would be housed.

John had also designed the vaporators to dress everywhere in the desert, and these required pipes and tubing as well. I hit on another solution that turned out to be cheaper than making it all, and relatively easy to pull off. I was talking to Peter Dunlop about the problem and asked him about buying wholesale PVC drainpipes; this is the light plastic piping used on the exterior of houses to carry the rainwater down from the guttering.

Peter brought me in a catalogue of it from a manufacturer. They were an ideal solution. The pipes were made in sizes from about a half-inch right up to about three feet. So he did a deal to buy it wholesale and bought in a stock of pipes in all sizes that we could use for dressing. Frank Bruton set aside a large section in the prop room for it and built wooden cages to house the pipes vertically, as we would need an enormous quantity of it for the Death Star interiors and the *Millennium Falcon* corridors. There were also all sorts of fixtures and joint pieces available so he bought in all shapes and sizes. Now I had a formidable dressing kit to work with.

John Mollo had set up his office close to John Barry so he could feed off the sets and designs and get help from John in designing the color schemes for the costumes. John also inherited the stormtrooper and Darth Vader costumes as well, so he was working really closely with our department. These required the sculptors, plaster shops and molds and vacuum-formed pieces so John wisely decided to integrate with John Barry. By piecing together the look of the costumes for the main characters, John was able to establish a quick frame of reference with George and then was able to quickly create the final costumes. Brian Muir was assigned Darth Vader's helmet under John Mollo's tutelage, with input from George and John Barry using Ralph's sketch as a design model. George had cast David Prowse so they did a life cast of his body and head, and Brian sculpted Darth Vader's costume around that. I know that John Barry changed the design a little in places, like adding the teardrop shape under Darth Vader's eyes, and he continually added his input to the entire costume with John Mollo.

Once the designs for the stormtroopers' and Darth Vader's helmets were finalized in clay, they would be molded in fiberglass to make several costumes. To get the look of the samurai helmet the heads were cast with black color-injected fiberglass so they didn't require painting. This gives a way better look, and they were slightly duller so looked real. They farmed out the stormtroopers' costumes to outside suppliers to make; again they just didn't have the time or the labor to get them done.

John Mollo was incredibly experienced in military uniforms, having been the main assistant under designer Milena Canonero on movies like the *Charge of the Light Brigade*. John was creating many of the costume ideas like we were in the art department, a combination of George's discussions, Ralph's paintings and found pieces, and cobbling together elements of costumes in the vast rental stores in London like Berman & Co. Time was equally difficult for John, and he hadn't had the advantage of being with George for the previous four months that we'd had. Starting in January with a shoot in March was insanely short for the number of costumes John had to produce. Those months alone with George were an invaluable period to work out the logistics of what we had to achieve.

John was struggling a little with the broken-down dusty look needed for the desert tribe dwellers, the Jawas and the Tusken Raiders. He wandered into my office and asked what I thought. George wanted the costumes for the Death Star to have that military preciseness, but to be natural, not designed, and the rebel characters were more Western inspired. Most science-fiction films had conscientiously designed 'space costumes' just as the props had been and in my opinion they often looked fake and out of place. So John came to chat and ask my opinion about these other costumes and the use of my greeblies, as George had mentioned to John to use these. I explained that George didn't say much; he had the reference paintings from Ralph McQuarrie that we built on. He would be very precise if you were on the wrong track, but was very good at building on ideas as you showed him.

John was doing lots of drawings and his problem, he explained to me, was how to use items to create what on a normal military costume would be badges and rank details. He looked around at the guns and my array of interesting objects I was starting to assemble in my office. I explained that we would be getting together loads of greeblies as we broke down more of the scrap, and that he was absolutely free to plunder whatever he wanted. I explained the theory of attaching these to found objects and in his case he could attach them to costumes to give an interesting look. The right ones gave things a totally new appearance, as we saw by playing around with them.

He wandered down to my wonderland of dressing junk, which was growing daily. I think seeing these amazing shapes and engineered airplane designs immediately gave him an idea of where we were going with them. John spent ages selecting items he could use. My system was working—all I had to do now was dress my first set and prove the idea was valid.

John and I discussed the Tusken Raiders, in particular their eyes and breathing apparatus, as these were a prime subject for using junk pieces. It's hard to understand except by actually doing it. This had come to light when John made some initial Jawa costumes from sackcloth. They looked new and even with bits of mud he had put on them, looked like just what they were. George saw them and talked to John Barry and me to ask if we could go and show John. Les and I went down to the costume department and I asked Joe Dipple to join me. John Mollo had seen that George wasn't happy with the Tusken Raiders' look. I went and got some of our really old broken-down sackcloth we had in the prop room, and found some scrap that matched the Tusken Raiders' eyes and breathing apparatus. We wrapped one of the young costume assistants who was small in size in the cloth and then aged it down. I took some of the sackcloth and some greeblies, and had the props break the sackcloth down even more, the way we did it. Using a mix of graters and rough sandpaper they softened the cloth so it didn't sit stiffly on the actor but fell like well-worn clothes do. Then we dragged it around in the dirt so the cloth got rubbed and aged, a process that really works. George and Gary came down and approved them. John Mollo was on the right track with the dusty nomads, and his costumes for all the troops and Death Star commanders were superb. He had much to wrestle with because of numbers and his time to make everything was severely restricted and we worked really well together as a team to get the costumes ready for the shoot in Tunisia. He farmed out the stormtroopers' costumes once they were designed and mock-ups made and approved by George. As so many were required, there just wasn't the time or personnel to get them done. John also plundered my greeblies for objects to hang on Luke's belt, alongside the lightsaber and electro binoculars when required.

One day Peter came in really excited—he had found a treasure trove. One of the local London councils near St. John's Wood was pulling down an old telephone exchange to build a modern one. They were selling off the entire interior as cheap scrap. This included all the furnishings, pipes and controls. I jumped straight in the car to see it all with Peter. It was like finding another massive treasure chest. There were miles and miles of flexible metal piping and conduits in various sizes. I knew that, dressed in alongside the PVC piping, it would help make the ducting in the *Millennium Falcon* look more realistic. Peter bought everything, including all the old telephone exchange panels, as they were packed full of interesting switches and devices, and it was all bought for a song. They just wanted everything out of there and quickly.

Poor Frank Bruton got more and more inundated with mountains of scrap and piping when this all arrived by truck. He soon had the gang sorting it though, identified, and labeled into order. Some days I could see he longed for some curtains to put up, and some beautiful antiques and paintings to dress, but hey, we were ground-breaking here! I just knew as I watched the breaking down of everything we had assembled so far, and seeing how the sets ate it up as we began dressing, that we would need a lot more. I was continually thinking about the sets I had to dress, and spent time looking at John's sketches and the draftsmen's layouts as they speedily produced more and more of them. John made models for George to see the sets in three dimensions, and these were a great help to everyone. I made copious notes during this process for myself, because under pressure like this every day it is easy to forget an important detail.

We continued our ritual of meeting every morning in my office, John Barry, Les Dilley, and Norman Reynolds, with Bill Welch, Peter Dunlop, and Frank Bruton. It became the place to meet and a chance for us all to discuss the day's urgent problems and how to deal with them. My office was also filling up with junk. Every interesting piece I found that I knew I could convert to an action prop I took and kept on my shelves. As time progressed my office got so full they gave me the one next door, and this too became a wonderland of strange pieces as I collected them and converted them into action props and dressing pieces. Everybody, including George, used to come and pick through them for interesting greeblies. My drawing board was covered in superglue, as I got through bottles of it, and partly assembled ideas for action props.

Making the tea every morning brought back memories of my first job with John Box, as I was usually first in. John Barry and I drank our tea very weak or light, and often I would have Earl Gray. Bill Welch and Norman followed Frank with a pungent brew using six Tetley teabags some days. Frank used to look at my Earl Gray teabag out of the corner of his eye as it went in and out pretty quickly. One morning I think it got too much for him. I saw Frank looking with absolute disdain at my teabag as I dunked it in the water for a few moments until it was a straw color and removed it. Frank looked down at my cup with a look on his face that was an absolute picture, and pronounced another of his memorable remarks. "You just frighten the water, boy."

C-3PO was progressing. Norman had quickly worked out the entire body, how it could all function, and had made comprehensive drawings. George, who had been trying to cast an actor or dancer thin enough to fit inside the suit but also with enough character to make the robot have a personality, had found and cast Anthony Daniels. As an actor his additional skills as a mime artist made him really suitable to bring C-3PO to life. Anthony was brought to the studios as soon as we moved into Elstree in early January, and had a full body cast made in plaster. Peter Voysey, the lead sculptor, and Liz Moore worked together with Norman in the plasterer's shop making molds of each separate piece of C-3PO. Brian Muir also did some finish work. The subsequent molds were used to make a dummy of Anthony and all of the robot parts were then made to this exact shape. The head was well on the way and was starting to gain character. Norman was manufacturing pieces of legs and arms and body parts using the molding machine we had brought in specially, and trying them on Anthony part by part. The maneuverability for Anthony was a primary concern, and Norman adapted each piece of C-3PO's body as they tried them on and practiced walking.

I got given the task of developing and making C-3PO's eyes one morning at a meeting. I was suggesting we create one-way mirrors like they had for police interview rooms so that Anthony could see out and the audience couldn't see in. My enthusiasm landed me the task of creating them (as if I didn't have enough on my plate!), but everyone was stressed beyond their capabilities so I just got stuck in. I looked closely at Ralph's painting and Norman's drawings. Ralph had them illuminated with a light and it was thought that if we could pull this off somehow it would look really good. I took measurements of the exact diameter of the eye slots in the head where the eyes would fit. Behind the eyes there was really no room, as it fitted snugly to Anthony's face. All the body parts gave C-3PO the slim look he had to have to disguise the idea that someone was actually inside working him. I thought about the various problems. The eyes had to be about one-third of an inch thick to fit into the eye sockets. The problems were twofold: how could Anthony see out to be able to act and how could we disguise the fact that anyone was behind there? I hated the way you could see eyes in robots and know instantly someone was there. Also, how could I get a small glow around the eyes without heating up the metal and causing Anthony further problems of discomfort to those he was already going to have to endure?

I played around with bits of material and shapes. Peter Dunlop scoured shops and manufacturers for me for suitable materials. He found some very thin, almost glass-like Plexiglas that I thought could work, as it was very light. I asked Peter if we could have it mirrored on one side like a one-way mirror used in police interview rooms. He called around and found a company who said they could do it for us on Plexiglas. So he took a sheet of the Plexi for them to experiment with.

I checked with the electrical department and the special-effects department if they knew of any tiny bulbs that were powerful enough to light the eyes yet didn't get hot, but neither knew of anything available on the market. I then had Peter research everywhere to see what we could find. We knew the bulbs in Christmas-tree lights were tiny but they heated up. Peter dug around for information. I asked him to check into hospitals, maybe we would find something used in medical procedures. Using his amazing army of contacts he finally hit paydirt after more than a week of researching. He found that the early versions of the miniature cameras used in hospitals to investigate and look inside a patient's body had tiny bulbs in them that stayed very cool. So I sent him on a mission to buy some from the manufacturers.

The eyes themselves had to be made to fix into the head sockets and be secured. On the painting there were vein-like metal grilles which I liked, and these would help disguise the eyes behind. I had found the scrap one we placed into Liz's clay mock-up, so I searched them out. I drew up my ideas and worked out on paper how to assemble the pieces required. The main eyepieces were to be the brass round ones with vertical slots. These would fit inside the brass rings that would secure them to the sockets in the head. I had to fix three bulbs to light the eyes so that they glowed, rather than us seeing a light source. Then behind this had to be the one-way mirrored Plexiglas and then a securing ring to hold it together. It all had to be very lightweight and as thin as possible. I made the decision to have the pieces made from brass so it matched Norman's head, looked correct, and would withstand wear and tear.

Several sheets of mirrored Plexi arrived and I picked the one that was mirrored enough to act as a reflector, yet thin enough for Anthony to see through. In the center of the eye Ralph had painted a black pupil-like spot, and I decided to leave the center of the mirrored Plexi open, to give the appearance of an eye and also help Anthony to see out. The company then made up circles of the finished one-way mirrored material to the exact size to fit into the eye rings.

Peter had found me an engineering company locally to make up the brass eyepieces to the exact dimensions required. They manufactured a small clip ring that could hold the one-way mirrored piece in place. They made the fluted eye piece itself with the vertical strips from a solid piece of brass, and this fitted into the front of the head to emulate exactly Ralph's drawings and the final design from Liz Moore approved by George. In the ringed edge they drilled tiny holes that the lamp bulbs could fit into and be secured. I put the three tiny bulbs in there at an equal distance around, as that seemed to give an overall light effect and not an isolated source. They just glowed a little, even in the desert sunlight.

All the separate pieces were gathered in my office and I spent the best part of a morning assembling the eyes and setting up a battery so they would glow. It worked, so I showed John Barry first. We had to find a way to run the wires down inside C-3PO's head and down into his body. This then attached to a battery that we would have to hide on him somewhere, disguised as a piece of his costume, so Norman worked on a solution for that. I had to work out a way it could easily be disconnected and the batteries replaced, as Anthony might well have to stay cocooned in the suit all day because of the time assembling it on him.

We fixed the eyes into the head and showed George how they worked with Anthony inside. Anthony could see out. Even though his vision was severely limited, and he had virtually no peripheral vision because of the helmet's structure, he could see enough of what he was doing to interact with the action and the other actors. That's what mattered. The best thing was there was no way you could see his eyes at all. The glow certainly worked. There was another problem solved that had no precedent before it to refer to, and just another small detail to get done within the multitude of difficulties the art department was facing. At least George was encouraged as Norman began to assemble the body parts and Anthony began the process of walking in them. Already George could see C-3PO coming to life. The knee and elbow and arm joints Norman had invented the engineering for would function, and the restrictions were actually giving C-3PO a funny walking gait that has remained as part of his endearing character ever since, though Anthony didn't think so at the time when he first had C-3PO walk in Tunisia.

Les Dilley and I flew to Tunisia with Robert Watts to see all the locations so that I could prepare the dressing I needed to send out by truck and Les could get more measurements needed for some of the builds required. It had been designated by John Barry that Les and I would go out to Tunisia when the main unit commenced shooting in March. Les and I would deal with all the problems that erupted as shooting commenced and then I would move ahead to get ready and dress the rest of the sets as the unit moved on from the first location. I would also have to maintain constant visits and contact to the main unit to make sure all the props and action props were okay. So we were sent out early to note all the requirements we would need to bring down from London, and to see what we were facing. This added extra pressure on me back at Elstree. I would have to get all the dressing organized for the sets that were required as soon as we returned back from Tunisia to continue shooting, as I would be on location until we all returned.

DJERBA

We arrived in Djerba, which is actually an island connected to the mainland by a bridge, or ferry. We first looked at the main location John had chosen with George, the small town called Ajim, where we would shoot the Cantina exterior and Mos Eisley. This would be the scene where Luke and Obi-Wan, traveling in the landspeeder, are stopped by a patrol of stormtroopers and we first see Obi-Wan use the Force. It also served as the Anchorhead location. We had to build a doorway for the Cantina into an existing building and add exterior dressing. On the left where they would arrive we had to hide a tree and other unwanted buildings that spoiled the look of the location. John Barry had drawn in the massive wreck of a crashed spaceship to cover them. Seeing the size of the tree, I knew I would have to bring a ton of dressing to pull this gigantic craft off—it had to be the size of a jet liner. Looking over the dusty Cantina location, I thought it would be fun to create the dressing like the exterior of a Western bar, with a hitching post where we would tie some Banthas that John was taking down to Tozeur, and to place a few vehicles outside.

We measured out where we would put the moisture vaporators (or Christmas trees, as we called them) in the main square, to give the area a different *Star Wars* look. It was a great location, with really ancient houses and low buildings, and with our added dressing it would look like Tatooine. Les took copious photographs and measurements, as we had to add domes to houses and build cut-out sections to hide anything we didn't like. On top of the buildings around the town square we would add in additional domed roofs onto the existing structures to create a different look. John had sketched out the place for these in addition to the domed roofs that were there.

We checked out all the locations where we would shoot scenes for Mos Eisley and Anchorhead. Everything required dressing and additional pieces of architecture to hide unwanted houses or areas. I was working out how we could move around the vaporators from one location to another for my dressing to avoid building too many. Transporting them was the main problem, with the room required to get them in the trucks. John had arranged enough trucks with Robert Watts and Frank Bruton, destined to be filled with set pieces and vehicles. He had cleverly designed some of the sets so that they would fit inside each other. We would be finishing the shoot here in Djerba, so I planned on moving everything here from Tozeur when the unit went off to Matmata to film Luke's homestead in the caves. We left and drove on to Gabès and Matmata to look at Luke's homestead, as I knew I had a lot of work there. Then from there we would drive on to Tozeur.

Driving through the arid but beautiful country for a few hours, we kept noticing signs next to what appeared to be dried-up river beds, all along the long road we were driving Eventually Robert Watts asked the driver what this 'Oued' sign meant. Robert knew, of course—he was a seasoned and experienced line producer and we understood immediately that he was fishing with the look he gave us in the back.

"Nothing," replied the driver, who was our location guide.

"Doesn't it mean river or water shed?" asked Robert inquisitively.

"No water," answered the guide quickly. "No water here."

Robert smirked and gave us another look. We knew that there had to be water at some time. "When are the rains here, then?" asked Robert.

"Not in April when you shoot. No problem," was the reply. From the guide's perspective they really needed the work, and to have a movie come meant they would get paid and everyone really needed money there.

Economically it was not a great time for them. We were all trained to take notice when someone said 'no problem' and you went on a double alert—usually there was one looming. We did research the rains later and these were indeed dried-up riverbeds that flooded when the rains came, but normally we would be okay in late March and April. This came back to haunt us with a vengeance when we started filming.

We soon reached Gabès and stopped for the night there, eating in an outstanding café, The Ex Franco Arab the Third Restaurant, so named for some inexplicable reason. We headed early next morning for the thirty-minute drive into the hills to the underground caves in Matmata. These are extraordinary. All over the area are large thirty-foot-diameter holes in the earth, dug down about fifteen to twenty feet. Off these central wells are caves dug into the red-colored rock. Many are now abandoned and in bad repair but some still function, and the one we used is a low-budget hotel. You sleep in the cool of the caves that are painted with whitewash all over the ceiling, and some have ancient black designs all over them. I looked at the one chosen for Luke's homestead, which comprised of a cave where the meal sequence would be filmed, and the courtyard exterior where a lot of the other scenes were set. John Barry had drawn in a moisture vaporator in the middle and added in panels denoting the technology under the surface and in the walls. I would have to dress the meal there that the script described and add our *Star Wars* junk panels around to give that mix of an ancient world and the technology going on. I didn't want to harm the location in any way, it was an ancient and historic site, so Les and I looked at everything carefully to achieve this. Round the doorways, John had drawn in the paneled sections that became the *Star Wars* look and these could only be plastered into place. Little did we know at this time that these would serve to become a major Tunisian tourist attraction. We took measurements and photographs for reference, and then worked out how we would get the vaporator down into the courtyard.

TOZEUR

We drove a few hours down very dusty roads with insane truck drivers who rode the center of the road at seventy miles an hour and would not budge over. Another Roman road, it ran absolutely straight in some sections as far as the eye could see for much of the route.

Arriving in Tozeur we found ourselves in a small dusty desert outpost.

We were filming in Nefta, about twenty minutes from Tozeur, but there was only one tiny hotel there at this time, so Tozeur became our hotel base. In the seventies it was not much of a tourist stop and with the fierce heat and poverty, you had to be really careful what you ate and drank in those days. 'Bourguiba's revenge' was the local name given for the chronic stomach upsets from food laced with bacteria that laid many of the crew low for a few days. There were limited cold-storage systems available, especially in so remote a spot, and they were way too expensive for local merchants. Being careful what I ate and drank, as I had learned to be, I survived the challenge of working and traveling in far-flung places, and having been through so much, my system was slowly getting immune to these foreign bacteria.

We spent a couple of days in Tozeur going around all the locations, including the Chott el Jerid where Luke's homestead would be built, an awesome salt flat that went off into the distant horizon in a series of mirages. It was the same location John chose for the massive Sandcrawler set, which the construction crew had started building. Most of the locations were way out along bumpy desert tracks, not easy to get to without a 4x4, but worth it as they were exactly as George's vision required for the remote planet Tatooine. This location was about twenty minutes down a desert track, and set against a hillside and canyons next to the chott called Sidi Bouhlel. These formed the backdrop for the scenes behind the Sandcrawler.

Then we visited the canyon where Obi-Wan first meets Luke, and R2-D2 gets zapped by the Jawas. This is just like a miniature version of the Grand Canyon with spectacular colors and it was very, very hot, even at this time early in the year, but the temperature dropped suddenly as the sun went down and you found yourself wanting a warm coat.

We made comprehensive notes for our requirements and met with the Tunisian production head in Tunis on the way back, to go through our requirements. I was introduced to the art director who would be my direct assistant, Hassan Soufy. He was invaluable to me and became a great friend and subsequently worked for me on several films. Hassan Soufy was an established and very well known artist in Tunisia, and had been introduced into the film world through master theatre director Peter Brook. Highly cultured and a great painter, he became my eyes and ears in Tunisia and dealt with all the local problems for me, which became truly monumental and sometimes exasperating when we returned for the shooting. Summing up my trip I realized I would have to take everything down there I would need for dressing requirements, and also a store of spare set dressings. The only airplane I found was a white-mothballed jumbo belonging to Colonel Gaddafi that the Tunisians had confiscated, and it was standing guarded at the airport, so was no good to me.

On our return from the recce, back in England, I had meetings to discuss what was needed for dressing the sets for the locations. The recce made it obvious I couldn't find any of the type of scrap that we had in stock now at Elstree. I needed an instant supply of dressing for whatever situation or emergency arose. One just never knows when dressing a set what will make it complete and look real in this experimental way I was working. So I decided I had better take a movable stock with me that I could draw on for dressing and for the props for the shooting, just in case. It would be very difficult if we needed something quickly on location a long drive from any town we were based in. Also the locations were spread right across the country, so there was no chance if something was required when I was dressing in Djerba and the crew were in the desert in Tozeur.

I had a lot to do there after seeing all the requirements on our recce. The crashed spacecraft outside the Cantina would fill a truck alone. It was necessary as it served to hide the tree, and we certainly did not want to pull that down. John had organized for a lot of the vaporators to be built and moved around with the crew as they changed locations. These were all painted down into a desert color and aged so they would fit into the landscape. Frank Bruton and John were assembling a list of what would have to go, as it took time to prepare detailed customs papers and time to drive it all across Europe and on by ferry into Tunisia. Frank was in his element, every detail covered in his inimitable style, but I was being pressured into deciding exactly what I needed for my department for dressing. He had lists to make and wanted every box ticked for customs. I had drawings of all the sets and the experience of the recce, so I worked out what I would need and was also having pieces built and assembled. The Sandcrawler scenes when Owen buys R2-D2 and C-3PO needed a selection of different robots for sale that I had to get built. I needed spare scrap for the canyon scene when Luke meets Obi-Wan Kenobi, as the Tusken Raiders ransack Luke's landspeeder. Then there was the township of Mos Eisley and the guard posts. The exterior of the Cantina needed animals and spacecraft. Owen's homestead had various different scenes. We needed dead bodies for Uncle Owen and Aunt Beru and destroyed junk for when the homestead was ransacked. I had to dress in the smoking remains of their bodies for Luke to find. There was a good deal of wreckage required when the Imperial forces attacked and destroyed the Sandcrawler. All this had to be pre-planned.

When I announced I needed a load of scrap to have with me as back-up stock in Tunisia for set dressing, Frank Bruton never batted an eyelid. He helped me source out a full truckload of spare dressings that I could cover any eventuality with, and which we did indeed end up using. It must have been another strange request to any outsider, taking truckloads of junk and scrap all the way to Tunisia, but we were making *Star Wars*.

One other major addition to a scene I had to build was the massive skeleton in the desert behind C-3PO when he wanders away alone from the crashed pod after an argument with R2-D2. George wanted the skeleton of a dinosaur-sized animal dressed on the dunes in the background to add to the loneliness of the scene, and give it scale.

I went on a search for this as George had written it in and John had sketched them into a drawing he'd made based on the location photographs of the dunes. I could make some in the plaster shops, but there really wasn't the budget allocated for them as they were on such a huge scale, and the shops were already hard pressed to get the work done for Bill Welch. Also these would take a large amount of space on the trucks and might even add another one to Frank's army of them descending on Tunisia, so Frank needed concrete answers quickly.

I took a wander over to the Elstree prop store. Frank told me to go see what I could find, and he had an inkling there were some bones there. Upstairs in one of the prop buildings was a vast roof section filled with old film relics. There were props and models here from the earliest days of the studio. There was also a rumor going around that they were closing the store down, as they needed the space. I went behind all the racks of small props, which covered a huge amount of different periods and dressings, and into the area where all the larger pieces were stored. It was a dusty and dark roof section filled with all sorts of objects. Using torchlight I found the model of the boat used for filming the storm scenes in *Moby Dick*, and many other treasures from old movies. I dug around in the dark with a torch and indeed came across a massive pile of bones.

Apparently they were made for the Disney film, *One of Our Dinosaurs is Missing*, and given to Elstree when they finished filming a long time back. They had remained buried in the prop store for years until I resurrected them and took them to the desert. The bones were cast in a form of early fiberglass molding, and looked absolutely authentic. I had them brought down to the car park and assembled to see how they would look and to show George. Inspired, I went back and dug around some more and found a box of skeletons that looked like human beings who had been recently killed. There were still replicated remnants of burnt flesh and clothes on them. That solved Aunt Beru and Uncle Owen's bodies outside the Lars homestead when the Sand People killed them. Frank donated all these for free to me to get them out of the prop room, really helping my budget problems. They would have been junked when he cleared it out in the near future anyway, as Elstree were indeed about to close the store. John and Robert said we'd leave them in Tunisia, as we didn't need them again. It would be far more costly to bring things back afterwards, and Elstree didn't want them back.

Next I found a solution for the large crashed spaceship. John had designed the skeleton framework as large as a crashed 747 that had buried itself into the ground. Part of the fuselage and one wing and engines towered above the ground at an angle. I went to the vacuum-formed panels store used for the sets, and looked at all the Death Star pieces.

This machine had saved our bacon. John was able to build a skeleton frame for a set, and then the construction labor simply stapled these sheets that were duplicated by the hundreds onto the frames. Once painted, they looked exactly like the detailed walls of the space station. I found some panels that I could use for the skin of a spacecraft, knowing I was going to destroy them to look like years of rusting and aging from a crash way back in the past. Aged and painted, and covered in dust to match the surrounding location, they would look amazing with my airplane scrap dressed in around them. The panels were light and stackable and fitted into a crate, so took up way less room than properly made panels. Another problem quickly and cheaply solved. It all depended on getting the aging to look right, but I was well skilled at that now with all my experience.

I had to organize and assemble all the different robots for the Sandcrawler scene; this was the first scene ever to be shot on *Star Wars*.

Uncle Owen had to walk down a line of second-hand robots the Jawas were selling, and choose C-3PO and eventually R2-D2 after the first choice astromech droid unit blew up. I needed a selection of eight or nine robots for the lineup, and some spare ones to dress around. John Stears had been instructed to have some radio-controlled ones working for the action required, R2-D2 as a three-legged unit, and the red astromech droid blowing up as it moved forward. In its three-legged mode Kenny Baker couldn't fit into R2-D2 and work the legs. It moved fast on its wheels and with the body tilted back at an angle the only way to work this was by remote control. This also applied to the red R2-D2 unit when its head blew up. It was moving forward in three-legged mode, and we couldn't blow up the tiny robot with Kenny inside for obvious reasons.

John Barry was sketching out ideas and I was finding all manner of scrap elements to base the different designs on. Also required were a lot more different robots inside the Sandcrawler's hold for shooting later in Elstree Studios, so I worked on these at the same time. I got Peter Dunlop to go and buy an assortment of medical instruments and medical machinery that was being sold from a London hospital that was closing down. From this we managed to cobble together some really interesting robots. I know that one of the robots in the shadows of the hold inside the Sandcrawler is made of gynecological instruments as I thought the various pieces of equipment had interesting shapes and functions. The mantra was, 'If it feels right and looks right… use it.'

I worked with John Stears to get the look of the other robots right as John had assembled various remote-controlled bases. We had a beetle-like domed one, and a couple of square-based ones that ran on tiny rubber caterpillar tracks. I made up one with tentacle arms that were scrapped medical instruments, which gave it a kind of praying mantis appearance, a droid that could repair specialized technical problems that were mechanical. The other base we fixed a spare R2-D2 top on without the body and painted it green. Its appearance was short and stumpy and again looked different but practical. The red astromech droid unit whose head blows up as it leaves the lineup John Stears was organizing with a different-shaped head to R2-D2, but with the same body parts and mechanism.

I had found an interesting piece of airplane scrap from an engine cowling that reminded me of the wonderful science-fiction artist Chris

Foss's work. I had always been a fan of his paintings, so we built one robot that had different but somewhat similar markings to one of his early designs. That one stands in the lineup on Tatooine, and helped to make a more interesting assembly of robots.

This lineup was important to get right early on in the film, as it helped establish R2-D2 and C-3PO in a world where robots were a functioning part of normal daily life. For cost-saving and time-saving reasons we were using some of the older R2-D2 experimental carcasses repainted as robot models. By choosing interesting airplane pieces and other found elements as a base, I was able to create a lineup of robots for the Sandcrawler scene that looked real. This was going to be the first scene ever filmed, so I had to make sure this was all prepared, and that it looked like the *Star Wars* world, used and real.

John called Les and me into his office one morning and shut the door. He told us he'd been to John Stears' workshop and looked at his remote-controlled R2-D2s, and that he thought they weren't going to be ready on time for the first day's shoot in Tunisia. John did not trust John Stears' radio-controlled ambitions given the timeframe left before the shoot. Not that John Stears couldn't make them work—eventually he would—but the lack of time left worried John. Having been many times on the location and filmed in the deserts there, John Barry was deeply concerned that they would not work on a shoot miles from civilization. Without any backup, George would be left with nothing to shoot with if there were mechanical or electrical problems.

John told us to prepare our own lightweight backup R2-D2 and keep it secret. Working robots like this are difficult to categorize into departments. We had developed him, but in the ensuing construction of them they fell somewhere between being an action prop and a special-effects unit, as a lot of the working mechanism is radio-controlled or electronic. Generally they come under the art department, just as C-3PO did, but John Stears had taken over making these units, as they required so many motors to function. We had the Kenny Baker-operated ones under control.

If there is a low-tech way to do something on a movie, then that is often the best and safest way, as it generally guarantees that it will work repeatedly. So John Barry had Les and I prepare a secret R2-D2 that no one but us would know about to take out to Tunisia. We prepared a lightweight fiberglass version, fully dressed and functional. We would rely on pulling it around using the tried and tested way of nylon fishing line. This is a very fine and very strong fishing line made from a kind of transparent gut, and being so thin it never shows up on camera if the angles and lighting are right. Well used in hundreds of movies before CGI or wire removal became so easy, one could get away with a great deal. It was especially useful for flying objects on camera or pulling things along. Les and I went to work to get the robot unit ready for shipping in the trucks next departing for Tunisia. We also prepared backup pieces to take with us.

So much has been questioned and written about the lightsaber and the origin of the first one, and so many false claims have been made about creating it, I wanted to write this book and set the record straight. I have read many blogs and articles about this and there was even a lawsuit in Britain and America by false claimants trying to get the rights to sell them as they created them. John Stears, now sadly passed away, laid claim to having created the first prototype and one of his team has continued this false statement of the truth. As set dresser, or set decorator as they are now called, I was in charge of creating all the dressing weapons and props under designer John Barry, and supervised the making of all of them, exactly to George Lucas's script descriptions and ideas, most of which were detailed in the paintings he had made by Ralph McQuarrie. As described earlier, I created the prototypes of nearly all the weapons myself, armed with little more than some used guns, superglue and some found objects and scrap that I could adapt to fit George's vision. Everything I used to create these props and dressings was specifically bought in for the film by my buyer, Peter Dunlop.

I had been searching far and wide for something to use as a basis for the lightsabers, and was getting worried as time marched on. I knew how important they would be in the film. When Obi-Wan Kenobi digs it out of his old box of treasures in his cave and presents it to Luke, it's as important and mythical a moment as Arthur pulling Excalibur from the stone in the legend of King Arthur. So it had to be something a little special but also readily functional. I was considering having one made, and spent time sketching one out based on the paintings and drawings already done by McQuarrie, but I wasn't convinced.

John Stears had made up some prototypes, but they were not at all what

George was looking for. They looked a bit like an adapted torch, simply remade in metal, not a mythical lightsaber that Jedi Knights alone used with great power. When Luke examines it after Obi-Wan Kenobi gives it to him, we would see it in close-up and it had to be something special, but natural and believable in the world as we were creating it.

Everyone was pressuring me for a prototype, and I had been relying on finding something interesting to base one on as the prop teams broke down the jet engines and other pieces but nothing had caught my eye. By some lucky instinct I asked to go with Peter to the camera hire shop we used in Great Marlborough Street in London, to look for two lenses for Luke's binoculars.

Brunnings, the photographic shop, had entrances on Great Marlborough Street and Oxford Street, and sold a huge array of new and second-hand photographic equipment, which they rented to films and television companies when cameras or darkrooms were needed. Peter Dunlop knew them well, so I asked David French, who I always dealt with, if they had any old or damaged equipment I could buy for the movie. He pointed me to an area on the side where there were large old wooden drawers and boxes of equipment stacked under the shelves that had obviously lain untouched for years. He told me to have a dig through. I started rummaging through the dusty old cardboard boxes. They were full of old lenses and rangefinders, so I started pulling out anything I thought might be useful. Then I pulled one old box out from under the others. Covered in dust it had obviously not been opened for years, just lain hidden at the back underneath other boxes.

It was an auspicious moment. In a movie the music would be heralding that a major climactic incident was about to erupt, and it would be in slow motion. When I removed the lid, there before my very eyes were several silver tube-like objects with red buttons set into the handles, packed in tissue paper. I pulled one out, amazed. They actually looked like Ralph McQuarrie's paintings of the lightsaber. I smiled. Somehow here I was at the moment of finding the Holy Grail for this movie. I pulled them out. Even the red firing button seemed perfectly designed for a lightsaber handle. I discovered that these were three-cell flashgun handles made by Graflex in New York. I held one in my hand; it was the perfect weight and size. I had found the treasure that was eluding me, and I knew exactly what to do with it to disguise it. Peter bought the lot of them, and I headed straight back to Elstree Studios.

I went to my room and closed the door. I got out my supply of black rubber t-strip, the same as I had used on the stormtroopers' guns. I needed to alter the handle to look like a weapon handle. I cut the t-section rubber carefully to length and shaped the ends to look finished. I got out my constant companion (a tube of superglue) and stuck each of the seven strips on carefully so that they were evenly spaced round the handle. I had some chrome tape in different widths. I found an old strip of LED lights from a scrap Texas Instruments calculator that I liked the look of and the seven magnifying bubbles were ideal. I had broken it down to find any interesting parts inside, and had saved these in my box of found objects. They fitted exactly into the small mounting clip that I left on the original and it looked like another function round the hilt. I superglued this on to further disguise the original and to add a feature that looked like some form of adjuster, and there before my eyes was a lightsaber. I added a strip of chrome tape around the shaft to hide the Graflex name and I called George to come.

George came across to my room, took one look, held it and smiled. I knew then we had found the one prop eluding us, and that has since become the iconic image of *Star Wars*. George's only request was could I attach a ring on the end so he could hang it on Luke's belt for filming in Tunisia. This was achieved the same day. A matching chromed metal ring, bought for a few pence, was screwed on and *voila!*—we had the first lightsaber handle. Time was so short this prototype was used in the movie. I made up a second one myself as a spare, and instructed the prop boys to treat it like gold dust as we needed a non-functioning one in Tunisia. I made up a couple more for John Stears so he could work on them.

A meeting was called with John Stears to examine my lightsaber and discuss how to make the blade. This meeting was documented in the production files and has been used as evidence by a company selling replicas in an attempt to say that John Stears and his team bought the Graflex handles and designed them. This is incorrect information. Peter Dunlop and I bought all the handles for the film from Brunnings the photographer's shop where I discovered them. My buyer, Peter Dunlop, sourced them all. I bought a few myself as I loved them as objects, and made my own mock-up of the lightsaber exactly as I had created them.

I appreciated them simply as beautiful objects to keep. Gary Kurtz sold one for two hundred and fifty thousand dollars a couple of years ago—not bad for one I made for a few pounds from scrap, and an indication of the iconic status this rather beautiful object has risen to.

A lot of discussion went on as to how to achieve the look required for the lightsaber's blade. At a meeting with John, Gary, and George about it, I explained that I had experimented with front-projection material before, using it for art installations, and suggested painting a blade with it to pick up a glow. This would be at least something for the animators to key on to, as I knew it would never be bright enough to use as a source.

George agreed that we should try it out and a meeting was arranged with John Stears in the special-effects workshops. I handed over more of the Graflex lightsaber handles to be modified. I had kept my two originals to go to Tunisia for the shoot, and for Luke to use in the film. One of these prototypes is the one that Sir Alec Guinness as Obi-Wan Kenobi brings out of the box and presents to Luke as his father's weapon.

John Stears came up with a clever idea: to make a concentric motor that made the wood dowel spin off-center. The subsequent vibration would help the front-projection paint pick up any light from the set lighting. Before CGI became so advanced, the process was to animate a second image, in this case the light blade made of flickering light, and then fuse or join them together to create one image in an optical printer. Richard Edlund and John Dykstra created the first computer to create multiple moves in camera, building a motion-control unit themselves to enable multiple passes of the camera over miniatures. Without this we would never have had the amazing Death Star trench sequence. It is one of George's legacies really that he would write in his scripts sequences that at the time were impossible to pull off, and then have the faith in those around him to be able to persevere and do it. On this first *Star Wars*, though, the weight of unknowns that he had envisioned and the reality of actually pulling this off slowly weighed heavier and heavier on his shoulders as pre-production loomed towards the first day of shooting.

When John Stears had made the mock-up blade, we watched the test and it was remarkably inventive. The thin front-projection-painted wooden dowel spun around off-center really fast; it was only just noticeable to the eye. The front-projection paint glinted enough, though, to pick up light, and kind of glowed. This was yet another mock-up prescient to another novel idea of George's becoming a reality. Practically, the rods were pretty thin and about three feet long, so would need careful handling in the actual fights, but would work enough to get the film shot.

George met with Gil Taylor, the lighting cameraman, to have him test them out. Gil complained that it would never work; the light source he'd have to use to light the blade would interfere with the set lighting. However, he was persuaded, and did make some photographic tests, later claiming this was all his idea. The results were quite surprising: if a light actually hit the blade spinning it did indeed look like a light blade. Though very weak, the wooden dowel itself disappeared because of the concentric spin and the glow from the front-projection paint. It was obvious from this test, though, that George could never create a situation where we could rely on this technique to actually create the light blade. To achieve this, it meant a darkened scene and a specially focused bright light to hit the blade. However, it did work well enough even in a lit set to catch a glow now and then. This would be enough for the post-production animator doing the rotoscoping to grab onto as a key, and create the light blade later in post. So it was decided to use it whenever we could. George had faith that his special-effects team back at the newly formed Industrial Light and Magic could create a blade, and indeed they did masterfully and helped create an iconic image.

When Luke fired up the sword for the very first time in Obi-Wan Kenobi's cave, we substituted my mock-up prototype for one with a blue-screen-painted rod in it. It did pick up a bit of light from some angles and gave a small light glow occasionally. George enhanced it in post to become the true lightsaber that every fan in the world would love to own. For me, when it first fires up is one of the great moments of *Star Wars*, both for its exposure on screen as the Excalibur for the twentieth century, but also because Luke was discovering his father. Just as Arthur realizes he was the son of a king, Luke found out his father was a Jedi Knight, fighting for liberation in the Clone Wars, not an ordinary farmer as his uncle had told him. This is classical mythology, a metaphor for taking one's power growing up.

The airplane scrap was working so well, we had to go and source a lot more. The exterior of the *Millennium Falcon*, the first large-scale set constructed, took up most of one of the big stages at Elstree. John couldn't afford or have room for the entire ship, so he cleverly devised a way where a half was built, and the entire ship could be a simple matte painting when required. Models would provide the full views of it as it took off and while in flight. The draftsmen were sourcing shapes constantly to give it the look of a functioning craft. I was sourcing dressing for both the ship itself and also to place all around the stage, to create a hangar-type environment for the Tatooine segment. Taking reference and ideas from planes being refueled, I found large-scale corrugated piping from the telephone exchange to create refueling pipes. More scrap pieces created refueling junctions in the hangar floor, and equipment boxes and trolleys to move them around with all helped create the atmosphere of reality, to build up a setting familiar to an aircraft hangar. Below the craft we added many pipes and pistons to help create the landing legs that the craft stood on.

Once I started dressing this exterior and the interior of the *Millennium Falcon*, we found out that the sets just ate up the junk. I was concerned because of dressing the cockpit, and the crew holding area for the chess scenes and lightsaber training for Luke, and all the various corridors required. It was a pretty large-scale set and required encrusting from floor to ceiling with pipes and technology. I was learning as I went along really, but as the junk disappeared into the sets, I knew we needed a lot more scrap.

Peter Dunlop and I drove to Gloucestershire where Peter had found a large amount of government-surplus military equipment for sale. We drove down through the beautiful Gloucestershire countryside and turned in to a massive junkyard of old wrecked cars piled high on top of one another.

The owner took us to a field out the back, littered with abandoned cars and trucks and machinery. At the back of the field, standing like silent ghosts, were eight brand-new air force cargo carriers, huge aluminum planes that were so new they were still unpainted. Spread around the field were also pieces from some of the planes cut up into sections and engines and cockpits. There were also piles of other scrapped plane parts. "They're surplus," he told us, bought for scrap. "They were built and never ever used." I looked over one of them. It was full of interesting objects. I really liked the landing gear, which could be used for the *Millennium Falcon*'s exterior when modified and built up to a bigger scale. I asked the owner if we could have sections that I could see would be invaluable to us, and he said no problem. So we bought cockpits and landing gear and sections of the hull where there were walls of interesting switches and equipment, and all for virtually nothing. I think it cost us in all a few hundred pounds; he just wanted to get rid of them. Peter did a deal for him to deliver the pieces and, buying a few more bits from the yards, we headed back to the studios once more, ecstatic at the find.

When I look back now on all this, inventing new techniques by sourcing and using airplane scrap and other interesting junk, both on *Star Wars* and subsequently on *Alien*, I realize I started an entire industry in Britain using scrap for movie sets. This became an especially important technique and a huge industry sprang into being as so many science-fiction movies followed over the years with the success of *Star Wars*. The irony of it all is that when Rick McCallum produced *The Phantom Menace*, scrap for movies made in Britain had become too expensive to use; you could now only rent it, not buy it anymore. Rick found that it was far cheaper to fly the airplane scrap over to Tunisia and London from the airplane graveyards in Texas, and this is what they did.

Peter Dunlop found a source for a large number of scrapped office machines like calculators and typewriters and copy machines. He brought in three large metal containers used for dumper trucks for us to strip down. Like hungry vultures the draftsmen would descend on everything we brought in and pick over it for pieces to draw into the sets. John Mollo's costume assistants found these particularly useful, and plundered bits and pieces to build into the costumes.

Many years later I was invited to the huge science-fiction convention Dragon Con in Atlanta. I was on various panels and a judge on the costume competition. The producers I was with took me to the door of a lecture theater and, opening the door, said I had to give a talk to *Star Wars* fans. I had no option: a sea of eager faces awaited me as the producers left, closing the door behind them. I was supposed to do a talk and no one had prepared me or told me anything about it.

So there I was, totally unprepared, standing in front of so many faces like a deer stuck in headlights. I was introduced by a mediator sitting next to me at the desk, accompanied by a round of applause. He asked me about *Star Wars*. All I could do was launch into a series of anecdotes about working with Kenny Baker and Anthony Daniels and some of the trials and tribulations of the robots and what they went through. I talked about various aspects of the shoot for a good half an hour. It then came to question time. I answered them one by one—I take all this very seriously as there are fans out there who live for *Star Wars*.

Then I was asked by one fan in the audience if there was a certain calculator panel built into one of the army of Darth Vader's stormtroopers, and he actually named the part number, the calculator and the model type. I was amazed and thought back quickly to the three skips of junk that Peter Dunlop had brought in, and which we raided continuously for anything that might fit a costume or a set or prop. This is the amount of detail these fans go into, and as he had built himself a replica suit he had tracked down the same calculator and added it in for authenticity. I had to reply of course that it was highly possible, and if it matched the original then it was highly likely. We had used old calculators for dressing things. I obviously had no idea; we didn't work like that by sourcing specifics, but he had. He seemed well pleased that in fact he had actually identified something correctly and came and took my autograph afterwards and thanked me for my work, and for inspiring his life.

Alongside the dressings I knew I needed on location according to our recce, the script and John Barry's drawings, I looked at the panels they were making for the sets with the new vacuum-press machine. They were light as a kind of vacuum form and could easily be nailed or stapled into place. Along with the panels for the crashed spacecraft outside Mos Eisley Cantina I ordered different ones to be used anywhere I needed. I knew that I could staple them onto structures I could get Bill Welch's location standby crew to construct, and use a blowtorch to distress them and make them look authentic.

Luke's binoculars were another action prop written into the scene at Luke's homestead and thus required on the first day's shoot in Tunisia. George asked me to put something together that would look like a functioning device to scan the skies, as in the original script Luke searched to see the fight going on with the rebel alliance. We filmed the scene but it was later cut out. I sketched out some rough ideas to get my mind thinking about them, and then I dug around for days looking for something to base them on. Some days I think I drove Peter Dunlop mad, but he never ever showed it. It's easy if you want, say, an art deco tea set or an eighteenth-century four-poster bed or anything that's in daily use. You say what you want and how big you need it, a color range and the look of it, and the buyer will go off and source a few samples to choose from.

Unfortunately, with action props and dressings of objects that basically didn't exist, there was little reference to describe exactly what was wanted. Peter brought in all manner of binoculars and other objects, but they all looked like what they were. He used to bring in catalogs of equipment as well just in case something inspired me.

Digging around I found an old 8mm camera that wasn't working and had been junked. The body looked the right size when I laid it flat on my drawing table, and I liked the weight of it. There's nothing worse than actors having to pretend that an action prop that's light seems heavy—it shows on screen to me. The Eumig Servomatic camera name was on a small plate on the top of the body when laid flat, so I placed a small rectangular piece of LAD plastic strip on it and glued that in place to look like a solar charging panel. I attached a few pieces of small dials around the body to give it a more technical functioning appearance and then searched for a viewfinder for the back.

I found a large-format 35mm single-lens-reflex stills camera, identified now as a Kalimar Six Sixty by fans. I needed a viewfinder on the back and I liked the way the hood folded out on the viewfinder to protect the screen from the sun and reflections. It flicked open when touched with a very precise engineered mechanism. When open it would hide the viewer from seeing the screen that Luke was supposed to see through, as these electro-binoculars were definitely not practical. I had to get this fixed onto the already existing eyepiece and managed to do that sideways, again with quantities of superglue, so the binoculars lay widthways and Luke could hold them in both hands, which looked better to me.

I had found the two matching camera lenses for the front in Brunnings, the Great Marlborough Street camera shop, and had to make a small plate to hold the second one in place, which I managed using a lot more of my trusty superglue. Weighing it in my hands it felt just the right size and weight. Carefully painted and aged a little it was ready to present. George was happy with the look of it and liked the weight; it matched pretty well the McQuarrie sketch. We thought of a way for it to be attached to his belt so it became part of his equipment, adding on a similar ring as the one added to the lightsabers. We had the electrical department add in a light source in the viewing part, so that it looked like a lit screen on film, reflecting on Luke's face. With time now eating my days and nights getting ready to go on location and getting the sets ready, which were in various stages of construction, this prototype would have to do. I had a mock-up duplicated by Roger Shaw; this was made for rehearsals and sent with the original to Tunisia with the property master, and a strict warning to be really careful as it was a one-off. I made sure Joe Dipple and the standbys had superglue and they needed it a few times when one of the lenses came unstuck. The proof of success really is in the final film when everyone accepts everything for real. There are still blogs going on about the type of electro-binoculars Luke was using, so their authentic look did work and to me this was imperative with every detail. Even the smallest prop could destroy the believability of the world, even if everything else worked around it.

For Luke's droid caller, I searched through my shelves of junk pieces and found a flash unit, smaller than the Graflex, the right size and weight to hang on Luke's belt, which George asked for. This was from an old Kobold camera flash unit that again I had bought as part of a selection of interesting old equipment from the camera shop. I found a convex metal cap that fitted the top end and added that on, as it gave a more finished profile to it. This was one of the first props to be filmed, as Luke needed to control the robots outside the Sandcrawler on the first day. After adding the D-ring at the end, I showed George and got this one approved.

I agonized for weeks over what to dress on the table for the lunches and dinners at Luke's homestead with his Aunt Beru. Peter Dunlop brought in all manner of PVC and plastic dinnerware and containers, as we felt this would be the way to go. I managed to make up blue milk as George had written in the script using milk and a food coloring used for icing sugar. That worked and the actors could safely drink it. In the end John Barry, George, and I decided on the Tupperware sets that I had assembled. They looked innocuous and un-designed and when we tried it out on the set John was building for the kitchens it fitted in without calling attention to itself. I mixed in a few other items as well, so it was not all the same—this was a desert hovel and they would not have sets of things intact. In those remote farms you used whatever you had that was durable. They looked like they would keep liquids cool or hot as well. Correctly labeled and packed by Frank, this dressing also went on the trucks for transporting to Tunisia, along with all the weapons and action props and spares we needed. We kept duplicates for dressing back in the studio sets.

All this time I was working seven days a week. Almost every night I would head home down West End Lane and decide on the way to my flat which takeout to get as I was so tired I couldn't be bothered to cook. The choice was a baked potato from a Spud-U-Like shop, or Chinese or Indian. Who says we live a glamorous life! Fridays, like clockwork, we all went to Dingwalls club in Camden Lock and ate supper there. We listened to the band playing and relaxed for a brief few hours before Saturday morning loomed again, and I was woken by a noisy alarm clock to head back to the studios.

The *Millennium Falcon* was coming along. My prop-dressing gang ferried pipes and corrugated tubing all day from the prop stores to the craft's interior. I had to dress the corridors, the main room where Luke learns to control the Force and Chewie plays chess, and Han Solo's cockpit and the gun ports. When you look at the before and after photographs you can clearly see the density of dressing required. Every inch of space, including the ceilings, had to be covered to make it look real, like a space shuttle or a bomber. We put in so many pipes and tubes and ducting that the prop boys went back and forth across from the stores to the stages on a daily basis for weeks on end. Peter Dunlop constantly got requests from me for more pipes, more PVC drainpipes and junctions; we were getting through miles of this material.

The worst part of dressing with airplane scrap and pipes like this is that it does not look real until it is all layered in place like a thick encrustation of working detail, like a bomber cockpit or a sub. The final layer has to be carefully chosen and placed to make it all fuse together and look correct. Then when it is painted into muted tones and aged it comes to life. Before that it just appears to be junk fixed to set walls and requires a huge leap of faith that it will eventually come to life. We kept on ordering more and more pipes and tubing as it disappeared into the lengthy corridors and holds. One goes entirely on instinct dressing like this. Once the main ducting and pipe work goes in, you start to see a pattern emerging. It becomes a natural process to source the next layers, and decide where to place them. Joe Dipple understood immediately what I was up to as I showed them what to place where, a bit like layering the walls with scrap elements like barnacles. The prop boys quickly understood what worked and what didn't, and I'd see them bringing in carts laden with all manner of junk pieces they felt they had discovered in the prop stores. They really got into it, and their dedication was required to make this work. I owed Joe a lot for helping make it look so real.

Finally, almost six weeks later, it suddenly emerged as a functioning craft and looked real, as if we were standing in a spacecraft. The colors of the airplane scrap helped as well; the matte metal finish and the natural aging process helped convince the viewer they were looking at a section of a craft. Everything else was finally painted down and aged by the painters to look functional. Showing George and Gary the finished result I think helped to convince them this major part of the movie was going to be okay. I could tell from the fascinated reactions of people coming to see the set that we were finally creating a real environment. We had a spacecraft.

The cockpit itself was another major task. Many of the panels were made up in the workshops and illuminated with working lights so they functioned like a ship's controls. The overall set and look was handled mostly by Harry Lange, who gave it a modified *2001* look with a lot of panels filled with switches and Letraset-lined sections. They built in small greeblies to help the authentic look. Once these panels were all placed, we set about dressing in our own greeblies and technical pieces to enhance the idea of a working cockpit. The flight controls of airplanes are unique in themselves and visually give an immediate familiarity as to their function, so I thought it best to adapt real ones.

What I had found interesting were two controllers from fighter jets and these were fitted to the floor and made functional by my prop makers. Harrison Ford could move them, to turn the *Millennium Falcon* left or right and up or down by moving the levers forward or back, exactly as a pilot did. I kept them low so they didn't dominate the cockpit and look too much like normal airplane controls. We created a central console and this was covered in switches and small plane controls, so both Harrison and Peter Mayhew (playing Chewie) had lots of things to play with that would be always shown in camera when George was shooting through the cockpit window, as I knew that would be a well-used camera angle.

Other levers came from different scrap elements and we placed a large emergency switch right in front of Harrison that functioned as well. Once the panels were all placed into the set we went to work building up layers of small greeblies all over them to integrate the panels into a functioning cockpit look. Chewbacca could interact with lots of these and I added more control levers on his side. Lights and switches worked too so interaction looked real. Everything for the actors I worked out beforehand, and we created a surplus of controls so the actors could play around and look like they were really flying the *Falcon*. Actors love to play with these things, so before shooting the scene I gave Harrison and Peter instructions on what was operational. They played around and practiced as if flying the *Millennium Falcon*. Han Solo had to look really at home in his own ship, and would be familiar with every single nut and bolt in there. It was his baby, and in the movie, his home. Described as requiring constant repairs to keep going as part of the plot, I had to bear this in mind with regards to the look of it.

For the rear two seats, I bought two fighter-jet ejection seats, and we modified them to fit behind Han's and Chewie's pilot seats, again sourced from the scrap and junk we were still collecting. All this detailing did give the feeling for them as actors of sitting in a flight-control deck, so helped build the reality of the scenes. Harrison used the functioning levers that I placed higher up on the control panels a lot more, and used these when he had to jump into hyperspace. Indeed, George did shoot a lot of these scenes through the cockpit window so that way the audience could see Harrison controlling the ship.

Some people notice the dice hanging in the cockpit the first time we see it. I decided on these one day as we finished dressing the set and I was looking it over. I was thinking that people personalized their cars and boats, especially in America. I thought that would help establish Han's character if we did something like that, and also help to mold the set into life. I had watched George's *American Graffiti* again and seeing the dice hanging in Ron Howard's car gave me the idea. Harrison had a skull hanging in his, which I thought would be a little too rock 'n' roll for *Star Wars*, but the dice could work and kind of suited Han Solo's character. In the era in which *American Graffiti* was set, these hanging dice were everywhere adorning people's cars, especially the hot rods and street racers—in other words the rebels. Charlie Martin Smith's character, The Toad, also had a white cloth pair hanging in his Chevrolet Impala.

I had analyzed from the script that Han Solo was a wandering rebel with no particular base anywhere. He had his ship, and this was home, in a way. It was one of the only things linking us to a past for him. I thought the idea of hanging the dice would add just one personal statement about him, a symbol of reckless chance and a gambler. Also, as *American Graffiti* was so successful for George and in its own way had made *Star Wars* possible, it would be a symbolic gesture of luck to hang a pair in his cockpit. It seemed it would fit for all the right reasons and one has to approach set-decorating with this philosophy, I find. I had Peter Dunlop buy in some different hanging dice sets. George and I went down to the stage to look at the finished cockpit together. He was again relieved to see the craft looking operational and functional, and not in any way like a science-fiction-film-designed spaceship. I then suggested the idea of the dice to George. I showed him several different sets, including larger cloth ones and the small chromed pair. He liked the idea and chose the small chromium ones so in they went for the opening shots. They got removed after that by Gil Taylor for some reason while shooting the scenes, and no one seems to remember why. Gary Kurtz thought they might have created a shadow or been in the way of the mike boom and they never got replaced, but they are there in the film. A really strong indication of J.J. Abrams' determination to be true to the original, he had an assistant track down an exact replica of the dice I put in the cockpit, and has restored them to their rightful place in the *Millennium Falcon*'s cockpit in Episode VII. They are clearly shown on the *Vanity Fair*'s 'The Empire Reboots' cover of June 2015 set in the newly created *Millennium Falcon* cockpit.

John had decided that while I was with the unit in Tunisia, Alan Roderick-Jones, an art director he had hired, would help Norman keep an eye on my dressing crew so the work I had put in place carried on until I returned. We would need to come back from Tunisia to continue shooting in the studios without a break. A lot of the sets we were returning to, like the Death Star interiors, had a very different look to the *Millennium Falcon* and Tatooine. They didn't require the heavy dressing the *Millennium Falcon* required, as a lot of the interior panels in the corridors were vacuum-formed and built in. However, the Cantina was looming when we returned and this was a set and a half.

When researching or imagining a set and what the dressings and fittings will be, there has to be a certain logic to it all. So for the Cantina I thought of the familiar pubs and clubs I had frequented and also I began to dwell on the cafés and drinking bars I had seen in Morocco and other countries. Peter Dunlop bought me a book on bar and club interiors so

I could research bars in other hot dusty countries. My attention focused on some of the wonderful scenes in Western bars, and of course the infamous Rick's Café in *Casablanca*. Again, like all other aspects of *Star Wars* we had to make something different and special, yet at the same time familiar. John spent a lot of time on the design of this set, as we had to get the action right for the written scenes and one could tell from reading the script that this was a special set. John drew pictures and sketches of the behind-bar apparatus and armed with these, I sent Peter Dunlop on another mission to find unusual glass containers, plastic and PVC ones, and also to seek out all manner of ideas for drinking vessels and the complicated liquid pumps behind the bar. Of course we still had little money designated for even this set and so we had to go and buy what we could at discount rates or find suitable scrap or junk. I had to find a lot of these pieces in advance so the draftsmen could identify them and build them into the drawings.

The draftsmen had a field day with some of my scrap. The unusual shapes from aircraft fuel tanks and other storage devices, alongside pressure pumps and hydraulics, were selected for the drink holders and distribution pumps behind the bar. Some of the airplane parts were chromed to look more like drink containers. We used newer tubing and fitted these to all the pumps and vessels and created a look for the bar. I sourced some interesting plastic containers for the drinks to be served in, and some glass ones. I also found some small rubber-covered glasses that we placed on the bar as dressing. I loved the idea of a smoky haven of iniquity as it was described, full of creatures who were the dregs of the universe, pirates and buccaneers, so I had some metal and tube equivalents of the famed Turkish hookah pipes, or shishas, made up. We obviously didn't want people or creatures smoking cigarettes in there as it would have looked stupid, so I sourced reference material from the wonderful hookah bars in Turkey and Tunis and Morocco. In fact, when we were in Tunis we visited the famous Café De Nattes in Sidi Bou Said near Carthage and drank a classic café Turque. The café is dressed as an ancient Moorish café, with hookahs all over it and ceilings hung with singing canaries in cages. I felt the hookah idea would fit in with the dressings so we made a few and characters can be seen smoking them in the scene. All this was started before we departed for Tunisia so that the set could be in a well-advanced state when I returned.

FINAL DAY'S PREP FOR TUNISIA

Sir Alec Guinness signs on

Sir Alec Guinness came to Borehamwood to meet up with George Lucas and Gary Kurtz to play the part of Obi-Wan Kenobi. They took him to lunch in the local Chinese restaurant next to the studios, that made John Barry smile, as he was signed on to *Star Wars* over a seven-and-sixpence lunch special. Clearly Sir Alec felt comfortable with George's knowledge and dedication to *Star Wars* and his passion to make the film his way. It was a casting coup. That rich voice of Sir Alec's made the character a deeply resonant force in the film with a depth that made the idea of these Jedi as spiritual warriors really work. He was, after all, the grand master of theater and movies with Academy Awards to his name, and some legendary roles in *Doctor Zhivago, Lawrence of Arabia, The Bridge on the River Kwai, The Man in the White Suit*, the list is endless. However, Sir Alex was a simple man and I am sure actually appreciated the lack of fuss lunching at a simple Chinese restaurant.

Getting to know Sir Alec a little when we were shooting in Djerba, he was indeed very simple, polite and one hundred percent dedicated to his work, whether it be a leading role for David Lean or this smaller science-fiction film, which was a first for him. Les Dilley and I were the only crew members staying in the same hotel as Sir Alec and his wife at the time, so we exchanged a few words and ideas with him when we passed each other. His simple approach to his work and absolute professionalism was of enormous encouragement and help to actors like Harrison Ford and especially Mark Hamill. He was always extremely kind and helpful to them. He could also make any dialogue sound so rich and important with that voice of his. He was a brilliant choice for Obi-Wan Kenobi, and no wonder that he became so much more famous because of this role to a whole new modern and international audience. He was always most interested to learn when we showed him his props that he would use.

To be working alongside a British legend—who can forget *The Bridge on the River Kwai?*—was another honor, even for me as the set dresser, and I felt really humbled to be showing such a powerful actor how to use the lightsaber. He was, after all, in my favorite movie of all time: *Doctor Zhivago*.

Preparing for the location shoot and readying the sets, props and robots entirely consumed my life. There was nothing to distract me, nor did I have time for anything other than work. Fortunately I loved every minute of it, exhausting as it was and difficult a lot of the time to convince the crews around us that this would be a really great movie and to trust in George's vision. We sometimes lunched with George and Gary in the local Chinese restaurant next to the studios, eating the same seven-and-sixpence lunch special in keeping with the *Star Wars* low-budget philosophy. Also, there was not much else available in Borehamwood high street then. The crews relied on pubs! The Chinese was cheap and quick.

During these few weeks we also produced all the replica guns needed for the shooting. That involved creating immaculate foreground weapons that could be filmed in close-up on camera. These were made from rented weapons from Bapty's, converted exactly to match my prototype. These guns could fire blanks and would be used by the actors and the stunt men for all the battle scenes where weapons were fired. We molded less-detailed ones for middle to background use by the other stunt men and extras. For any fight scenes involving the actors or stunts they cast a mold from a real gun and molded rubber versions of it in larger numbers, as background extras could use these as well.

Should an inadvertent accident occur and someone get hit, the rubber versions, though still solid and able to bruise, could not actually damage someone. This applied to all the weapons used, and to many of the action props if a situation arose where someone could get hurt in a stunt fall or a fight. I always made mock-ups that the actors could rehearse with to get comfortable. We preserved the originals for when George was shooting the takes only. As we were low-budget and were often using the prototypes I had actually built myself, they were too valuable and delicate to be played around with during rehearsals. These were religiously guarded by the stand-by prop team and the weapons supervisor and carefully given out when the shot was being filmed, and collected the moment George said 'cut and print'. We arranged to take out the prototypes we had made of the landspeeders for dressing outside the Cantina, as we didn't have the budget to make any special vehicles for it.

George always wanted creatures tied up outside, the equivalent of the horses seen outside a Western saloon. John had had one creature made with a nodding head, which is all that we could afford and as much as the technology of the day could produce in the time allocated. This was for the desert scenes with the stormtroopers, so I arranged for it to come to Djerba the moment it was finished within the dunes. Another hairier version had also been made and I managed to get this reserved to come to Djerba as well, so I had two creatures outside. The art department had also made a *2001*-style capsule for R2-D2 and C-3PO to land in the desert and I prepared some legs to place it on so it looked like a vehicle, which I would imagine Harry Lange had drawn up, and I would be adding this to the two rejected speeder mockups. This can be seen in Ralph McQuarrie's painting. Feeling a little more comfortable I could dress the exterior to look busy and authentic, I prepared some scrap airplane parts to place around them.

I was in the production office just before we left for Tunisia sorting out the logistics of the move with Pat Carr and Robert Watts. I was liaising with Peter Kohn, who was the production runner and third assistant director. We were laughing at something he was telling me, when we heard a woman's voice asking, "Are you laughing at me?" We had not noticed a very reserved young woman who had entered the room and was standing shyly looking at us. She had a straw hat with flowers on it hiding her eyes and was determinedly keeping it low to help hide her face. It was Carrie Fisher, there to play Princess Leia. Once we had assured her that we were definitely *not* laughing at her, Peter and I shook her hand and introduced ourselves. Peter was there to look after the actors and he took her off to meet George. She looked exactly right to play the princess; she had an obvious intelligence and despite being so shy, had something of an aura about her. The family of *Star Wars* was beginning to assemble.

Leaving my dressing props team with precise instructions and a schedule to follow to continue the sets while I was gone, and John Barry to keep an eye on it all, we prepared ourselves to travel to Tunisia. The exterior of the *Millennium Falcon* and the hangar it was docked in required more dressing, as did the interiors, so Frank Bruton and I instructed the team on what to do. Peter Dunlop had his work cut out, as sets were looming fast and furious once we returned from location. I had to try to prepare everything as best as I could to be able to hit the ground running on my return.

Les and I flew out early to Tunis. It was a long drive ahead of us, so we lost no time; we met up with Soufi Hassan and headed straight out on the road to Tozeur. The drive to Tozeur is down a straight Roman road for mile after mile. Once again we played chicken run with trucks and the pressure of too little time meant that we rarely had time to stop. One bonus on the drive was the Roman Amphitheater at El Jem, which is almost as big as the Coliseum in Rome and amazingly well preserved.

Arriving late at night, exhausted from the flight and the drive, we met the construction and prop crews and caught up. Seeing the part-constructed Sandcrawler the next day was a surprise—the size of the vehicle was enormous. Despite seeing all the drawings and sketches in prep, to see something of this scale was impressive. The tracks alone were way higher than my head, almost twice as high in fact. Once construction had finished, I would dress in sand and mud around the wheels and caterpillar tracks to give it that dusty, well-traveled look. I talked with my charge hand, Joe Dipple, about building some wooden slats exactly the size of each metal track, so that we could create prints across the desert that the weight of this huge machine would have left in the sand.

Alongside it we had to prepare the various sets for Luke's homestead with Uncle Owen. Les and I mapped out where the dome roofs for the garage and Uncle Owen's house would be. I measured out with Joe and the prop crew where we would dig a large hole to replicate the entrance to the underground courtyard in Matmata. We had to dig it deep enough and build a mound around the hole so that the camera wouldn't see the bottom when filmed from the desert as Luke spoke with his uncle. It was a cheat hole, so that in any shots where Luke was standing in the desert landscape above his homestead, it would look exactly as if the lower courtyard to the living quarters was there. As the prop boys dug out the desert dirt, they piled it up around the edges of the hole, to help them match Matmata. The second hole was for the garage rooftop next to it, to give the idea of a sunken dwelling under the desert floor. The vaporators helped to sell the idea of some form of moisture farming going on, their structure reminiscent of small oil or gas wells.

Once I had organized my crew there, I parted company with Les, leaving him to get the sets built. Soufi and I drove the even longer drive to Djerba. The construction crew working there was already building what was planned for the two main Tatooine town areas and the Cantina exterior. We arrived late at night again—these were punishing drives with no cellphones and little on the way but the occasional town made up of many metal workshops for some reason, and the odd café. I always had to drive—Soufi wasn't allowed to drive the rental car—and these ten- to twelve-hour stints required concentration all the time. This was not just because of the trucks coming at us, but also camels and wooden carts pulled by donkeys that tended to veer all over the place. Then there were the young kids who would appear from nowhere and stand in the road selling sand roses or colored rocks. They were determined to make you stop and buy from them, so it was a wee bit dangerous sometimes, and that was in the daylight. At night things were far more difficult. Unless there was a full moon there was no ambient light, and the locals often dressed all in black with hooded djellabas, so you just couldn't see them.

In Djerba we organized the setting up of the moisture vaporator units around the town location. The Cantina exterior was being built and needed painting. Around the low houses they had placed all the fake domed roofs, and the profile created by all these additions to the ones already there did indeed give a natural but strange vista. They altered the appearance of the location and made it a little more in line with the *Star Wars* look. The biggest problem for me was the crashed spaceship. I discussed the structure with the construction team, who were building the skeleton in its place to hide the tree behind it. Built in scaffolding, this was a huge structure, like a Boeing 747 on its side. I showed them which of the vac-form panels would work where and we went through the airplane scrap and where to position it for best effect. Having gone through everything with the carpenters and painters and feeling they were on track, I returned to Tozeur.

At this time in Tunisia there was very limited communication available for us. There were no cellphones in those days of course, or computers or emails. There was basically one phone line available between Djerba and Tozeur to put our working situation there into perspective, and many times the line was down. If it ever rained or there was a windstorm, the lines fell and went dead. Some days I had to call the production office in London from Djerba to get a message through to Les in Tozeur and vice versa. So it was usual that we could not call each other at all. It meant me driving over ten hours each time to deal with any emergencies, which added to our daily mounting problems. I ended up making this long drive so many times that Robert Watts and his assistant producer, Bruce Sharman, booked a hotel for me permanently in both locations. I left enough clothes and a set of drawings in each room to save time carrying them back and forth.

One day we had to deal with an extraordinary situation in Tozeur that could easily have escalated to a delay in shooting. The Algerian military had gotten wind of our huge caterpillar-tracked vehicle being built on their border at Nefta. Algeria was just a few miles away across the chott. They had immediately assumed it was a war machine being built to attack them. Diplomatic relations were very low at this point between the two countries, and the Algerians were jealously guarding their oil deposits, which actually straddled the border. So they were assuming the Tunisians were building a war machine to attack, with plans to plunder their oil reserves. A military envoy was sent across the border to meet with the Tunisian army commander. This meeting took place on the chott where we were building the Sandcrawler. The name of the movie had also alerted them, *Star Wars*, most likely lost in translation and the word 'war' taken out of context. When the Algerian commander inspected the so-called 'war machine' and was convinced that it was indeed a film set for a futuristic science-fiction movie that we were building, they left satisfied. The crisis was over, thank goodness, and we were able to carry on. This has been mistakenly documented as being the Libyan army but in fact Nefta, where we built it near Tozeur, is right on the Algerian border. In places you can look across a small canyon to Algeria; it would be a five-minute hop across. Unlike Tunisia and Morocco that straddle either side of Algeria, it has remained closed and isolated from the Western world, and is far harder to visit.

Joe Dipple and the team continued dressing the homestead and placing the moisture vaporators around the landscape. As the only objects in the lonely salt flats, they looked really interesting, immediately transforming the chott into an alien desert suitable for Tatooine. One afternoon we were all helping to clear the sand of tracks made by the construction around the homestead roofs. It had suddenly rained, and the chott became a totally different place to the sandy desert we were used to. It became a mush of sticky, sandy mud that the wheels of our vehicles sunk into and made it almost impossible to drive around. It stuck onto your boots like some gooey clay that grew and grew into monstrous feet with each step, making walking almost impossible. We looked like muddy Michelin men struggling to walk as the mud quickly grew on our boots. Our days were limited, however, before the crews arrived so we had to carry on regardless. Most days the sun beats relentlessly down in the desert and after the rains it does dry fairly quickly, normally so anyway, but worse was to come.

The wind was a portent. That night came a terrible sandstorm of hurricane strength. The hotel windows almost blew in, such was the force of this tempest. There was nothing Les and I could do—it was far too dangerous to venture out and the night was as black as coal. Really worried, Les and I went out early to the set. To our dismay the winds had destroyed a lot of the work. The circular garage roof that we dressed over a dummy cavern behind Uncle Owen's homestead had gone, vanished. This was a fiberglass disc about twenty feet across. It looked like a flying saucer, as we had made windows around the sides for the director of photography to light up to help to make it look like an underground cavern for the dusk scene, and give a light source in the dark desert.

It had simply disappeared. Indeed, from the little marks in the desert where it had blown away, it had turned into a flying saucer in the hurricane-like winds. I sent one of our local drivers to follow the skid marks leading away as far as the eye could see, but even after a mile of searching, he came back with nothing. This has been documented by John Barry as happening on the first week of the shoot, and indeed a massive storm did hit us and close down the shooting, but this freak storm where the homestead garage roof flew off actually happened during prep right before the shoot. The moisturiser vaporators were blown over, but the weight had prevented them from flying. Uncle Owen's homestead had miraculously survived, but needed patching up. To put these storms that come out of nowhere into perspective, one day I went to an oasis situated close to the start of the Atlas Mountains when I was there on *The Phantom Menace*. We came across the ruins of a completely destroyed town. Just the wrecked remains of many stone and mud buildings were left in what were originally homes and businesses along the ruined streets. The local guide told me that a storm came out of nowhere in the fifties and laid waste to the entire town in a few hours of intense rain and winds. The enormous hailstones that came with the fierce winds caused most of the damage. So in a way, we had been lucky.

After the storm hit us in Nefta the British crews just got stuck in with their usual stoicism and repaired everything really quickly. Les and

I had no choice; we ordered another roof piece to be made to replace the missing one that would come out in an emergency on the charter plane. Then two days later, when we were working on the chott by the Sandcrawler, a camel train appeared in the distance, like a mirage coming out of the desert.

They were pulling an object like a sledge behind the last camels. The mirage became solid as they approached and we saw that they were pulling the roof, dragging it along behind the camels. They stopped near us and asked if it was ours. Miraculously it was still intact. They had found it over three miles away across the chott, such was the power of the winds. It needed repainting and a few dents patching up, but it was ok. Relieved, we canceled the one from London and continued working to get the sets ready, a little nervous now because of the weather. All the sets we were working on got repaired as soon as the sun dried out the ground. The chott quickly returned to normal as the fierce midday sun baked it, and the hot winds helped dry everything out very fast. But any little breeze and Les and I would look at the skies, concerned.

Once we were secure in Tozeur again, I went with my dressing team to Matmata. This involved another long drive to Gabès where we always stayed, and the next morning we drove to the underground caves in Matmata. Again, to change the feel we placed several moisture vaporators in the center of the courtyard and sprayed them the same sandy color as the surrounding floor and walls, exactly as in John Barry's sketch. We also placed prepared panels to denote the technology under the surface and painted the same sand color into the walls so they blended in. John had designed the familiar padded elements that went around all the doors on Tatooine, and these began to make the location really work and look quite different. It's a technique that requires building in as you go, and using an experienced eye to see what works and what doesn't.

The bonus of driving all this way for this location was obvious—it would add so much screen value and character to this part of the film. George was right to have added it as a location, despite it meaning more travel to the already long distance between Tozeur and Djerba. George had also liked the small grain caves in the real Tatooine that John Barry had found, but made the decision not to shoot there on this film, as it would have burdened the schedule beyond the budget. Traveling days with a crew are costly days where nothing is filmed. However, they stayed

ABOVE: One of my favorite sets I dressed—the *Millennium Falcon* hold. Encrusted with airplane scrap and an assortment of pipes and telephone exchange scrap. Luke is using my original lightsaber.

BELOW: Dressing Luke's underground home in Tunisia.

BELOW: Dinosaur bones I found and used as the giant skeleton in the desert where R2-D2 and C-3PO crashed. They are still there in the Tunisian desert.

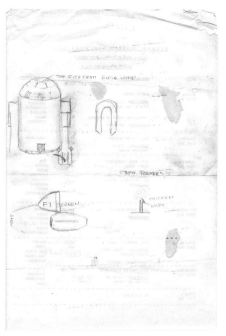

ABOVE: First ever drawing of R2-D2 we worked to; sketch of Luke's speeder.

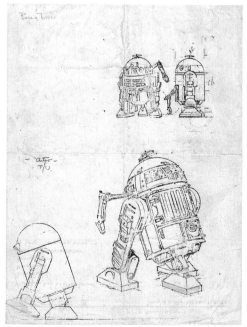

ABOVE: Sketches of R2-D2 that George brought to London.

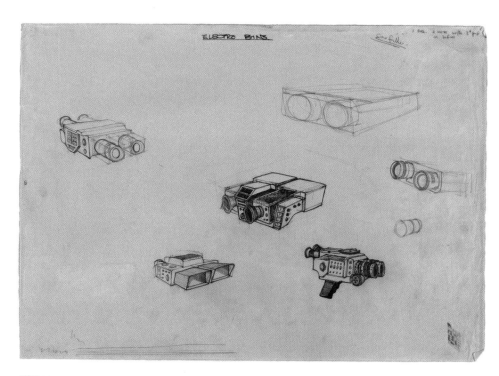

ABOVE: My sketches for inspiration to build Luke's binoculars from found elements.

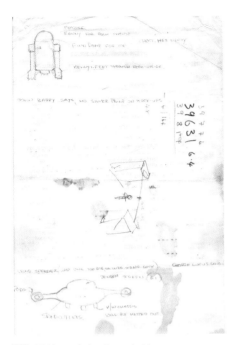

ABOVE: Bill Harman's sketches to build R2-D2; a mockup of Luke's speeder.

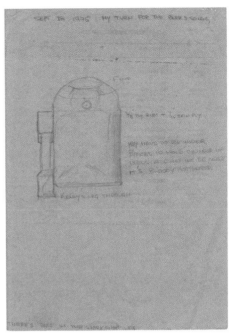

ABOVE: Rough working drawing to build our first R2-D2.

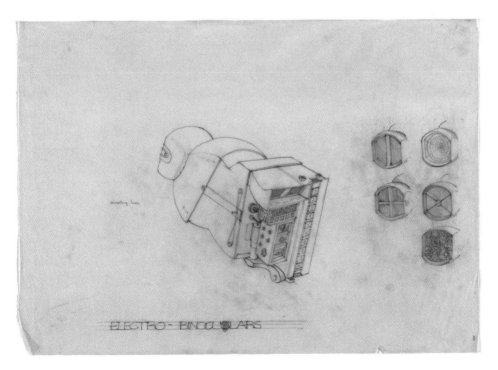

ABOVE: My first design for Luke's binoculars.

ABOVE: Me with airplane parts bought for set dressing, used in sets like the Cantina and Obi-Wan's cave.

ABOVE: Me next to a scrapped aircraft section, bought for dressing the exterior and interior of the *Millennium Falcon*.

ABOVE: Part of a mountain of scrapped airplane parts.

ABOVE: One of around twenty jet engines bought and broken up for dressing *Star Wars* sets.

ABOVE: My binoculars, made from camera parts superglued together.

ABOVE: A Tusken Raider weapon, which I adapted from a Fijian totokia war club.

ABOVE: A shot from filming when my chrome dice were still in the *Millennium Falcon* cockpit (top of picture).

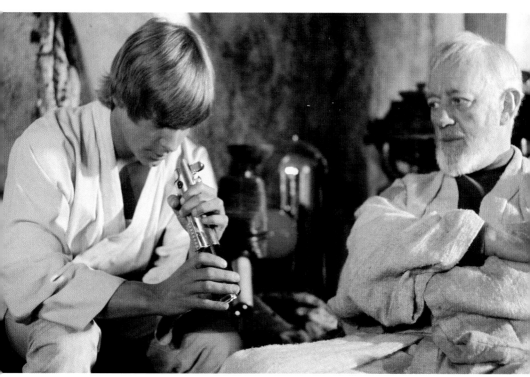

ABOVE: Luke holding the first Graflex-based lightsaber I built for filming.

ABOVE: The floor heater I sprayed black as the centrepiece for the Death Star conference room.

The first fiberglass
mockup of Luke's speeder at
Elstree Studios, without engines

BELOW: A crashed spaceship
built and dressed, using scrap
aircraft parts and Death Star
panels aged down, to hide a
tree outside the Cantina

in George's memory and he did return there on *The Phantom Menace*. What he did do was take the name for Luke's home planet from these caves, as it sounded so right for the film. Thus, Tatooine became a *Star Wars* planet.

Dressed around the courtyard, I placed groups of the metal airplane food containers we had bought as junk from commercial airliners. With a bit of dust and a few greeblies they looked natural in the setting. Again there was logic to the dressing. These looked as if they carried supplies in and out to these remote homesteads in sealed containers to preserve the contents—exactly what happens in an airplane. We also placed several gray-colored plastic bin boxes that we had converted with junk to look like storage units, which again would be used to transport goods in these hostile environments. I figured out exactly what we needed for the eating scene and arranged the dressing with the crew.

Our lunch breaks here were always the same: vegetable couscous cooked on an open fire in one of the caves converted to a hotel, with mint tea made with local mint from the mountains to wash it down. I loved these lunches, either sitting in the sun or sheltering from the cold winds inside the caves; it was a peaceful respite in our really hectic schedule. Also, eating like that in the actual location for Uncle Owen's homestead definitely helped us to understand how to dress the settings for their meal in the film. A few times we slept there in the caves in the hotel lodgings to save the drive time back to Gabès at night.

We built in panels inside the walls of the cave very carefully so as not to destroy the walls or the painted ceilings. These looked like light and heat and air-conditioning panels. I made sure we always left a location as we had found it, or better. A few in the industry do not bother about this and don't care, but we always did. Then if you ever want to go back and reuse a location you're welcomed again. (This certainly paid off here, as we came back to use the same location on my suggestion for *The Life of Brian*).

I had my dressing gang clear the rocks and small shrubs away from the edge of the circular hole where George would be filming Luke looking down at his Uncle Owen as they spoke, so they matched. George would cut the two locations together so the illusion for the audience was that the underground part of the homestead was out in the desert chott, where we built the exteriors above ground in Tozeur.

Joe Dipple suddenly yelled out and the props went into a huddle, staring down at the rocks. I walked over to see what they were staring at. Right where Joe had picked up a large rock was a red scorpion, its tail sticking angrily up in the air. "That's right where I put my hand," said Joe, alarmed. "Screw this, get the thick gloves out." So he and the rest of the props cleared the ground wearing large thick gloves.

STAR WARS FIRST DAY SHOOT LOOMS
It's finally a reality

Leaving a prop man there and a guard, as we had dressed everything but the table settings, which we would do the night before shooting, I drove back again to Djerba, another eight-hour drive. On set the next morning I supervised the building work they had completed, changing a few things, and working with the painters to get all the aging correct. We had found a technique to match the sand color; they made up water paints then we added the local sand to it. This gave a matching color and texture to the aging process, as if wind and dust had built up over the years. This looked really natural, especially after the sun dried it, and it became a technique we used in all locations.

I started the prop gang dressing the pipes and panels around the market square. Looking at the crashed spacecraft was a bit daunting. They were placing on the vacuum-formed panels, and I needed to make them look aged and distressed and burnt after the crash, then add years of aging as we presumed it had crashed a long time before. We found that by stapling on the panels they went on quickly, and as there was such a vast area to cover, that helped. Burning them with a blowtorch quickly melted them and distressed them, and then when painted down and sprayed with our dusty paint, they looked like metal panels that had rusted and disintegrated over years.

The main crew was arriving in Djerba and traveling on to Tozeur, as there were only a few days left before the first day's shoot. Once again Soufi and I took to the road in our little car on the long road back to Tozeur to do the final dressing for the first day of shooting on *Star Wars*.

Back in Tozeur, the Sandcrawler was looking awesome. I dressed more sand and mud into the tracks to give it a dirtier look and the painters put dusty layers all over the mechanics so it looked like it had traversed the desert many times. The props had made up the machine to make the imprints of its tracks across the desert behind it, and they helped create the realism. I dressed the exteriors of the homestead with junk and sprayed it all in dust, so it fit right in. The scene looked natural and really had become another world. John Barry's Christmas trees, the moisture vaporators, spread around the homestead really made this *Star Wars* look work now we could see the homestead as a real dwelling. These vaporators were the big seller to me to help create an alien planet, familiar like small oil wells but different enough to be unique to the movie. I had assembled the robots for the first scene and made sure they were all ready. Around Owen's homestead the familiar white padded detailing was all aged down and we were ready for George and the crew, who arrived ready to begin preparing for the first day.

The day George came to see the sets for the first day of filming next to the Sandcrawler, he was happy with the look. I had personally spent a huge amount of time aging everything down. From all the discussions and the way I had invented using scrap to create used and natural props and guns and interiors for the sets, our discussions and intentions with George were always the same: an aged and used look! That is why he showed the crew *Once Upon a Time in the West*—to get them all to understand the Western, dusty approach he wanted. When Gil and the crew arrived to shoot the Sandcrawler the first day it was well-aged and dusty, as can be seen in all the photographs in *The Making of Star Wars*. The caterpillar tracks were muddy and full of dust—I know, I helped dress it with my own hands. We all got stuck in with the prop boys as time and labor was limited, and aging down is a skill.

For sure they dusted all the robots down on the day, especially R2-D2, as they arrived on set fresh off the special-effects trucks—dust is a major enemy to delicate radio-controlled robots and machinery. The same happened with the costumes. Sir Alec Guinness rolled in his in the dust when he first wore it for the shoot. It makes the cloth look more aged and natural and they fit better. Actors like to make their costumes look like they have worn them for a long time in these types of location atmospheres, not hang stiff like a new costume. It's a familiar process for actors.

I made sure all the art-department robots we had arranged for the lineup for sale on the first day's schedule were ready and functioning.

John Stears and team were frantically working on the R2-D2 units, and the second astromech droid whose head had to blow up. There was very concentrated activity around the special-effects boys' trucks, with bits of robots scattered everywhere, so they couldn't have any rehearsals at all.

The prop boys and Les were still struggling with C-3PO, who looked great but was really cobbled together at the last minute, and Anthony had had little to no time to rehearse. Starting so late on such a complicated robot suit took its toll here, especially in the desert heat that had quickly returned to suffocating temperatures. Maxi was the prop man designated to deal entirely with C-3PO and look after the costume and Anthony. Maxi cleverly adapted a stand so that Anthony could remain upright throughout the day's shooting and he was working on assembling all of C-3PO's body parts and equipment, charging his batteries and helping Anthony try out walking on the desert floor. Norman Reynolds had gone to make sure he functioned on the first day as he knew C-3PO intimately, better than anyone else, and was there to supervise it working before returning to the huge builds going on at Elstree.

I showed Mark Hamill his binoculars and how I thought they would function. He couldn't actually look through them, but as any good actor can, he acted as if he could. We had fitted a metal loop on the end so that they could be attached to his tool belt for other scenes, and made sure this worked. I told Mark that they were the only ones and that I had made them by hand so to try to be really careful with them, and that we did have the second mock-up for him to rehearse with.

STAR WARS BECOMES A MOVIE

During the night before the first shooting day, Les and I stayed back late to make sure everything was ready. We worked under floodlights when it got dark. We also made sure we had our spare R2-D2 up and running, which we had assembled and still kept out of sight in secret. We prepared towing lines with the prop boys, who would work him in the event we needed it.

The first day's shooting on a film set is always exciting and nerve-wracking. Things got off to a chaotic start as the crew and George came together for the first time in a hot desert location in the middle of nowhere with a bunch of radio-controlled robots careering about. Then there were the ones operated by the other small people, including Kenny Baker's acting partner Jack Purvis. Robert Watts had organized everything as best as he could within the limitations of being in such a remote place and our time to prepare.

The first scenes filmed had the Jawas lining up the robots outside the Sandcrawler. George had children dressed as Jawas and they were being fitted out with fake guns ready and their glowing eyes tested with the batteries ready to shoot. George ran through the scene and filming began. It quickly became apparent that R2-D2 couldn't make it. During any attempt in which the radio-controlled version was required to roll forward, it suddenly veered off to one side and George quickly yelled "Cut!" before it crashed into something else. He began to film the sequence in pieces as best he could. Worried about time, Gary asked Les if he had any monofilament, and Les went rushing round the back of the set completely flummoxed, having no idea what monofilament was. Les asked everyone, but no one knew. Someone suggested it might be fishing line, so Les went back and revealed our secret R2-D2 unit, already prepared to be pulled along with the fishing line. "Yes," said Gary, "that's what I meant." I think he had an inside knowledge of our unit, and had to do something as time was being wasted while George stood around waiting for robots to be fixed. Tensions started to fray, and Gary was the one to deal with everything as the producer.

George just calmly carried on filming the lining up of the robots by the Jawas outside the Sandcrawler, cutting his way round the limitations of movement, especially R2-D2. Gary Kurtz told us to try our R2-D2 unit. We placed it in front of the camera for the shot required and, positioned correctly, the fishing line did not show up at all, especially against the sandy-colored desert floor. That ended up being how many of the R2-D2 scenes were filmed that day, and from then on in Tunisia. Whenever the radio-controlled one worked, George would grab the shot he needed. George looked on, his usual calm, unflappable self, knowing deep down that we had all had far too little prep time, and that where the result of that would erupt its ugly head was with the special effects and robots. So the only way was to find quick solutions.

Looking back, this may have contributed to John Stears being a bit upset at us, and to the comments made against John Barry. None of us in our small team had time to worry about it, nor the political inclination to do so. We knew what we had to do to help George, as this was by far the most difficult and ambitious film I had ever worked on, and the most complicated to achieve.

Looking now at the cut of the first scene outside the Sandcrawler as the Jawas assembled all the robots in a lineup, R2-D2 is absent from many of the shots. You can see that George used judicious cutting to get around the radio-control problems. He shot very quickly and as an experienced editor himself was able to make fast decisions about what would work, and even if a robot careered off course George knew where he could cut and use another shot. I truly believe that without George's low-budget filmmaking experience and editing know-how, the film would have certainly ground to a halt within days. Most American directors would have been overwhelmed with the increasing problems and apparent lack of support from some areas of the crew. Gary Kurtz took on the confrontations and problem-solving as George continued to keep his head down, work out his shots and concentrate on the actors and getting the schedule filmed.

The large black robot I had built was lowered down into the shot on a rope. John Stears pulled out the red astromech droid unit and we placed it in position with George; C-3PO was placed and stood in the line, and then R2-D2. Uncle Owen and Luke decided to buy C-3PO from the Jawas, and chose the red astromech droid unit John Stears had prepared. C-3PO went forward with Uncle Owen and Luke, chatting all the way. Kenny Baker was inside R2-D2, trying to get C-3PO's attention by wiggling his body inside the robot to make it look like he was moving around in frustration. He wanted C-3PO to get him chosen. This all worked quite well until the red astromech droid unit had to move out of the line and follow C-3PO.

To move forward, the radio-controlled three-legged version was required and was wheeled onto the set. The action, clearly described in the script, was that as the robot moved forward away from the lineup, its head exploded. This was important action so that R2-D2 could be chosen instead when C-3PO expounded on his qualities. The special-effects team looked embarrassed and announced that the radio-control mechanisms and mechanics were all in the head, so it couldn't explode. Gary did. He was furious. He demanded to know why it had not been prepared when it was in the script and spoken about in all the meetings with them in preparation. They looked embarrassed, but offered no fast solution. Les offered that he could paint our R2-D2 unit red to match quickly and we could pull it along on fishing wire. George and Gary immediately asked him to do that and Les went into fast-action mode to get it ready, painting it himself, whilst George shot another shot. Gary told the effects boys to make sure the three-legged R2-D2 unit was functioning, as that was needed next when R2-D2 gets chosen and follows C-3PO and Uncle Owen, but the next drama I think finally did it for Gary.

First up in the sequence, Kenny worked the R2-D2 unit as he tried to get C-3PO's attention to get himself chosen by Uncle Owen. Then the three-legged version was substituted for moving forward. It took ages to set up, as the operators fiddled around with the mechanisms a lot. Anthony was stuck inside C-3PO waiting in the heat. He was grumbling as it was really hot and uncomfortable, and once in the costume, which took two hours to assemble, he never got out of it on the first day. On George's "Action!" the radio-controlled R2-D2 unit moved forward... and suddenly careered wildly all over the place. I think John Stears uttered the prize quotation of the week on seeing George's frustration. John ran in front of the camera with his radio-control unit, and shouted out, "It's the bloody taxis!" At which point many on the crew just looked stunned. We guessed that working in London, blaming the radio signals from the taxis was a standard excuse when things messed up, but here we were in the desert, forty-five minutes' drive through a dusty desert road from the nearest small town. Tozeur had a few ragged taxis that for sure did not have radio contact with each other. Les went to George, who remained calm but puzzled as to what to do next, and offered to repaint our lightweight R2-D2 unit back to blue and pull it on wire again. Which he did as fast as he could.

George filmed the scenes with R2-D2 in short pieces from then on, so it looked like R2-D2 moved smoothly. On this, the first day, George demonstrated his patience and ability to think quickly and make things work in the cutting room later. He had a tough schedule to keep and no option not to get through his day's work. Dealing with several robots, all functioning differently, was a rude awakening to him of what he had written, and just what he was in for over the next twelve weeks. Due to the late start, the movie was really underprepared, the robots especially, in John Stears' defense. His problem was he would always boast what he was going to do and loudly proclaim how great it was all going to be. A mistake—better to be quiet and underplay everything and do what one can to make things work on the day. This lack of prep time really caused problems for George. Another mantra we all adhere to in the film industry is that when someone proclaims, "Don't worry," start worrying.

Gary and Robert Watts had considered moving the shoot back two weeks to give more time to prepare, but two weeks would mean the temperature in the desert climbing rapidly. It could get too hot for C-3PO certainly and then there was the problem of hotels being booked up everywhere because the tourist season was starting, and as a further blow the Italian director Zeffirelli was shooting a massive TV series in Nefta and Tozeur. In fact, it was they who had booked most of the remaining hotels in Tozeur, forcing Robert to double people up in rooms or drive a half hour to the next town, which we did. It was also deemed too costly to put the shoot back; weekly costs were high with all the construction and stages, etc., and when one adds all this up two weeks is a large cost overrun. To soldier on and make it work was the only way forward.

Most directors other than George could not have coped, I don't think. His low-budget experience and editing skills came into play big time. He knew just what he could get away with in each take, and he was prepared to get what he could out of each moment with dedicated concentration. I know how tough this is when what you really want is just out of reach, and technical problems constantly plague every scene. As a director you worry about getting everything in the can each day and on schedule, and when there is a studio behind you, not making your days is a big issue and can lead to serious problems financially. They hold the director responsible, whatever the reasons.

With the sets we always kept on top of the schedule and the great thing with aged sets is that you can more easily make them feel right for filming, especially on a location like Tunisia.

As filming progressed, C-3PO's costume had to be constantly attended to as it kept falling apart. The legs and feet were the main problem. Once on Anthony, which was a struggle to get all the pieces locked into place and then the wires and the batteries hooked up for the lights, it was better for Anthony to stay in it. It had taken two hours to get him in it the first day. Each movement caused Anthony pain; he got scratched and bruised as the parts had to fit so tightly to disguise the fact that there was a human inside C-3PO working him. We had to give the illusion he was a mechanically engineered and functioning droid. With Anthony being so thin it worked, as long as they kept the costume really tight to his body. It took a lot of maneuvering to keep him working. A special team was devoted only to C-3PO and they too were quickly learning as filming progressed what the parameters were in dealing with Anthony and the gold robot. Trouble was that in the heat and dust, Anthony was suffering. He was also trying to get to grips with walking on the salt flats for the first time, quite different from a concrete studio floor. All of this physical hardship took its toll on Anthony.

As long as R2-D2 functioned he worked, as his sounds and voice would be added later. Kenny did give him nice character traits in the way he hobbled along. Even on this first day, though, Anthony got frustrated with Kenny Baker. Anthony would act out his scenes and wait for a response from Kenny, but none came, just silence.

Whether Kenny could not hear anything inside is possible, as it was tight in there and packed with equipment all around Kenny's head. There were many batteries running to keep the lights going and mechanical parts jammed in everywhere. Kenny was sealed in for each take, and couldn't communicate until the head was removed again. So Anthony got frustrated with Kenny from the beginning. He felt that as they were the light relief for the movie and the storytellers, they should act their scenes out together.

More and more problems ensued with the robots, and one of them that became a daily headache was that the batteries ran down really quickly. Stuck out in the desert with no studio backup, with just what equipment they could take with them on the trucks, it was hard to keep on top of things. Once again I cannot enforce enough my philosophy to aspiring filmmakers to use the simplest technology possible when doing any scene like this, especially on remote locations with no studio or workshop to back you up, as you can rely too heavily on it working.

The robot hell continued. Once Les had finished painting the R2-D2 unit into a red astromech droid, the special-effects boys packed the head with explosives and set it up for the shot. The batteries kept running down inside the R2-D2 unit, and to change them took away more precious minutes of George's shooting time. Finally it was all working and ready. They packed the explosives into its head and the radio-control unit worked enough for it to run forward in a straight line and the head exploded on cue. John Stears and one of his assistants ran as close behind the robot as they could out of camera to limit the radio-control signal's range. Finally the scene worked as written and the head blew up perfectly on camera. When the radio-controlled units functioned, George shot the scenes in pieces or the props pulled the little robot in each of the shots from then with fishing wire when the radio-control units were malfunctioning. George worked out exactly where he could cut and make the limitations of having the prop boys near the camera work for him, and what angle to shoot from to avoid the fishing line.

Another problem that showed up on this first day was that the R2-D2 units could not roll along in three-legged mode on their little hidden wheels. The ground was too rough. So Les and the grips quickly devised a way of placing tracking boards down and hiding the edges with sand and dust so they weren't noticeable. Another restriction on George, as he could only shoot scenes with the running R2-D2 from lower angles to keep the boards hidden.

To top it all off for George, tension started the first day between him and Gil Taylor, the director of photography, over working methods. George was used to indie filmmaking, and the kind of camaraderie that was normal in the Coppola camp amongst the northwest-coast film fraternity. George was a filmmaker and as such was involved in the camera and lighting and every aspect of the movie. He had to be—this was a science-fiction film and it was George's original world he had created on paper and needed to recreate on film. Gil was old-school and not communicative. His way was the director worked with the actors and the lighting cameraman chose the shots and the lenses, instructing the operator exactly what to do. This was exactly the type of structured system I had rebelled against. Thank goodness I was first employed under a master designer who was not at all like that—John Box was very much like John Barry in that respect, very supportive to a director's vision.

George generally didn't say a lot except for brief comments about the work in hand. He knew exactly what he wanted and was used to getting that by working with collaborators. He had proven himself as a filmmaker with *THX 1138*, which is a really interesting and original movie, and *American Graffiti*, then the highest grossing per budget ratio movie in America, and a film that stayed in that prestigious position for many years. In my opinion he had the right to say what he wanted as he had developed the *Star Wars* world he was now struggling to get onto the big screen with a crew who maybe did not understand him very well. I was really surprised, as Gil Taylor had photographed some of my favorite movies and experimental works like Roman Polanski's early black-and-white movies, which were amazing. Unfortunately many of the crew began to side with Gil and his way of working, and Gil vocally rallied the crew around him as they were unsure about this young American director making what they thought was a children's science-fiction adventure that had no hope of ever doing anything. That was the general consensus going around, and I guess the first days of the shoot didn't help in that a lot of it concentrated on robots that were malfunctioning.

It all blew up when George was using the viewfinder to set up shots. Gil Taylor asked what he was doing, stating that George worked with the actors and showed him what was the scene and Gil would decide how to light it and frame it. George as an independent director was used to doing everything, and creating his own vision for the film. There was a standoff and from then on Gary Kurtz had to act as mediator between George and Gil. George had always maintained that the difference between any other science-fiction movie and *Star Wars* was he wanted a form of documentary style, meaning everything had to look real. Used to creating all the shots on *THX 1138* and *American Graffiti*, George could not see why this should be any different.

Reading an interview with Gil Taylor for *Red Dwarf* magazine, he states that we built all the sets looking brand-new, and he and George had to instruct that they were aged down, which is totally false. I personally aged everything down; the photographs of the Sandcrawler and Luke's homestead attest to how we finished every set and prop so it was completely aged and older-looking. All Tunisian sets and props were naturally aged and ready for shooting, George never ever had to age them down. Only the robots fresh from John Stears' trucks needed dusting down, but that's normal when dealing with radio-controlled equipment. They didn't need dirt and dust when working on them, and maybe that's where Gil got this idea from.

His comments even now, many years later, somewhat explain the difficult time George had making *Star Wars* and why it was so hard for him. The director of photography is the director's eyes and has to be in close collusion with him. Certainly George wanting to get a dusty reality to the visuals by placing a filter on the lens didn't go down well with Gil, but Gary and George pulled rank on him and made him do it. Gary Kurtz kept trying to mediate between Gil Taylor and George and sort it out, but stuck to his guns on George's side and way of working. George liked to make all the decisions, especially where the camera went and what lenses to use, in an independent low-budget shooting style as he was used to. Gill has himself expressed that George would not communicate with him in an interview in *American Cinematographer*, but Gill never attended scheduled meetings either with John Barry or the art department to go over the lighting of the sets, which is normal between DOP and designer and director.

I missed a lot of this tension erupting through being so busy getting the sets ready for filming. Les and I had our own creed developed over years of working together and it was the same for John Barry. You worked all night to have a set ready if needed; you never ever let a director arrive to an unfinished set or without the props needed for the day ahead. Les had enough on his plate dealing with the filming, especially the robots, while I was preparing ahead for the next setup when they filmed Uncle Owen's homestead exterior. I was hearing about the tension building through Les as I made constant visits to the set whenever I could to help him out. I could feel the stress and tension, though, all around the set. This was also most likely the beginning of the 'them and us' camps and John Stears would have found a sympathetic ear with Gil and his team.

Also to come to further exacerbate problems, when we began filming in Elstree, adhering to strict union hours and protocol was all a new experience for George and another very big shock, and of course the rigid tea breaks when everything stopped. The art departments that I worked in were not at all like that, and union rulings meant nothing to us because of the hours we worked. We were at the heart of the movie with the director as we were always the first hired in preparation with the production office.

Working on locations meant living in countries long before a crew arrived and we never really had structured days like a crew on a shooting unit had. We were also used to back-breaking commitments that meant we were setting up before the crew arrived in the morning, and then when they wrapped at the end of the day, often working into the night to prepare for the following day. Also I think being such a creative department helped the attitude in the art department make a difference. For my part I had also directed plays by then and music videos and so knew just how lonely the directing chair can be in reality. I felt very strongly for this script and its vision and John, Les, Norman, and I remained determined to see it get made to the best of our abilities, and took no notice of what was being said around us.

BRITISH ATTITUDE AT THE TIME *STAR WARS* WAS MADE

Looking back as I write this book, I have been questioning why George was given such a hard time. I think that there was clearly a prejudice existing at that era because it was an American science-fiction film we were making. There was also a definite prejudice in the UK at that time against American culture and movies, and there was a kind of inverted snobbery against success and being commercial that, thank goodness, has gone now. Alan Parker railed against this publicly when everyone was praising the so-called British movies like *The Draughtsman's Contract* as the pinnacle of culture. Peter Greenaway was given nearly the entire British film fund to make his opus; it was culture and 'British', praised the past, and was a costume drama.

The Merchant Ivory films were lauded as well. Though I never minded them—some were wonderful, like *Howards End*—Alan Parker had to be vocal in a revolution that was ongoing at the time to get national funding for more commercial movies. Filmmakers like him and Ridley Scott got short-changed by the critics because they came from commercials, and not an upper-class literary background. There was a definitive breakdown of the cultural hierarchy going on at the time *Star Wars* was made. Working-class was becoming popular and artists were breaking out from their shackled boundaries imposed by nationalistic thinking. Before that, one had to be educated at Oxford or Cambridge to be taken seriously. The great John Osborne really created a new voice in cinema as his works were made into films like *Look Back in Anger* and Alan Sillitoe's *Saturday Night and Sunday Morning*. Ken Loach and Tony Garnett were pioneering realism, life as it was for the poor and the disenfranchised.

David Hockney became a media star as a painter, and working-class fashion photographers like Terence Donovan and David Bailey and commercials directors launched to the top of their professions.

As I have already stated I always take exception at being judged by one's accent, not by who one is as a person or talent. It was possible that this kind of inverted snobbery against most things American at the time was directed at George and Gary, and of course they never understood that.

It was time to get the landspeeder on film. I had brought out some rectangular mirrors on the truck from England to try the experiment with the landspeeder, as we had to make it look like it was hovering just off the desert surface. From a distance, if the piece of mirror was reflecting the surface of the ground carefully placed at forty-five degrees, it could easily hide the wheels and fool the eye that the speeder was indeed floating. We tried it out. The mirror was fixed under the side of the bodywork, and to our surprise and delight when driven across the chott it worked. These chotts are famous for their mirages. If you stare out into the distance, depending on the time of day the area between the sky and the horizon becomes like a shimmering image, and gives the illusion of water. It's a strange phenomenon. I also tried tying a small broom end to the front so it kicked up a bit of desert dust and that also worked in very long shots. Later, George was able to animate out the wheels of the car underneath.

TWIN SUNS—A HERO'S JOURNEY MOMENT

The weather was really cloudy at the end of the day so they postponed shooting the scene where Luke ponders his future and stares at the twin suns of Tatooine.

After this frustrating first day George must have gone home once the crew had wrapped after the requisite union hours and wondered if he had really started something that was beyond his means.

Despite all the tension building up, George calmly carried on. The good thing with the British crews was they did work hard, despite all the grumbling, and George got through the second day of shooting. After the first day, procedures were established as to how to deal with the robots and keep them working on camera and the landspeeder. The rig on the floating arm did work really well; whenever Luke pulled up or took off the vehicle looked like it was still floating. George again made that all work with precise cutting later.

I went out to the desert dunes location to place the massive bones for the shoot the following day, and to make sure we kept the filming area free of footprints. This is always one of the hardest things to achieve, especially when a crew arrives early for the shoot. They naturally wander in to look at the sets and trample all over the sand in this case, and can easily ruin the virgin look required for a take if it is the first time anyone walks in the scene about to be filmed. We had to place the pod into the scene and then mark out R2-D2's tracks and C-3PO's footprints where they walked away from the escape pod. We had taken a pair of spare feet from C-3PO's costume with us, and used these to simulate his prints. Then with brooms Joe Dipple backtracked across the sand and wiped out the props' footprints, made when they were working.

The scene George would film started with them some distance from the pod so we set it up that way for him, and then roped off the area of sand to keep anyone from trampling across it. We found a back way up the dune where we placed the bones on the horizon, and again wiped out any footprints around it.

The skeleton looked great from the camera positions and so real in the dusty desert light. Another problem solved with little money, but this also became another truly difficult scene to shoot for George. There was no way that R2-D2 could walk in the sandy desert dunes as they shift all the time when weight is placed on them. Les got round this by laying boards into the sand so R2-D2 could run along them and filmed from the right angle you couldn't see them. Les spent a lot of his time hiding these grip-boards in every location where R2-D2 was needed to walk along. The desert and salt flats are not ever flat and are often soft or rocky ground, and R2-D2 was just not equipped to move on anything other than a flat surface.

Anthony also suffered inside C-3PO, both in the appalling heat and also with the soft sand he had to trudge along on. He was still adjusting to wearing the suit; it was really not easy for him. Pieces cut into him as he walked, especially on such a soft surface. One take when he was trying to walk across the dunes, C-3PO simply disappeared behind the dune. When George called "Cut!" he was found completely stuck, one arm buried in sand unable to move or cry out. They got him back on his feet and George and Anthony persevered until he got the shot. The desert scenes do look lonely and barren and that was the intention. In the end it worked out with George again shooting the scene in bits and using clever cuts and edits to piece it together. The illusion of film is amazing; it is a kind of alchemy I think.

All this first week of shooting, the lack of development time and preparation time really meant we were all still developing and learning while shooting. Not the best way for a director to start. George continually lost time and compromised on shots he wanted, but his persistent ability to think of ways around problems saved the day. Also postponing some shots to film later was a wise decision under the circumstances.

While the first unit was shooting in the dunes, I went back to the salt flats and dressed the remains of the Sandcrawler that Luke finds destroyed. The big caterpillar tracks we damaged as if from some massive firepower and blackened everything down from an explosion. I used a lot of my spare airplane scrap I had brought with me, spread around the chott as if a terrible attack had taken place. When he sees this devastation, Luke realizes that they must have attacked his home. He races over there and finds it destroyed and discovers the dead bodies of his aunt and uncle.

George had filmed all the scenes with the homestead intact after buying the robots, and this was next as the destroyed version. We damaged the homestead to make it look like it had been attacked and blackened it down with paint and dirt so it looked like fire damage. Our detailed planning was working. I spread more of our junk dressing around as if the place had been ransacked. For Uncle Owen and Aunt Beru's bodies I dressed the two skeleton mock-ups I had brought over from the Elstree props store and surrounded them with scavenged junk as if the homestead had also been ransacked. The skeletons looked pretty realistic after we dressed them in distressed rags and burnt these as well. When George shot it we added some smoke from the smoke machines so that they looked freshly destroyed when Luke comes across them. It had to be a shocking scene for Luke to experience; it was the turning point in his life and the launch of his *Star Wars* adventure. I was watching the skies as I was doing this, because it had suddenly gotten windy, overcast, and cold. I had no idea of the magnitude of what was about to descend on us.

The rains suddenly came down in a truly violent storm, the worst storm for years. The phone lines went down across the country, destroying communication with Djerba where the construction crew and props were readying the sets. Bruce Sharman was based there organizing everything ready for the crew to arrive. We got a call from the London office. Bruce had called there unable to get us and said that the entire set was flooded and under water. This was relayed to Les and me, so I jumped into the car and drove straight to Djerba to sort things out. This was a nightmare of a drive. I raced at night through teeming rains, a lot of the time hardly able to see through the windscreen, driving through flood after flood. I was so worried about the sets.

Halfway across the country we were racing down a long straight stretch of road and a car came racing towards us at the same speed, driving flat out. I had a feeling it was Bruce racing to Tozeur to warn us that we needed to get to Djerba, so I flashed my lights and slowed down. As it hurtled past us I saw it was Bruce, who took no notice of us whatsoever. He raced by, eyes glued to the road in some mesmerized state that happens when you drive alone for hours. I slammed to a halt and was about to turn back, but he was already way in the distance. I knew we would be on a wild goose chase trying to catch him and it would just further delay us. The way he was driving we might not catch him for hours, so we carried on to Djerba. I would have to handle things on my own now. I finally arrived at 4am and after three hours' sleep was back on set.

Early the next morning we went to the Mos Eisley set. Indeed, it was a sorry sight. There was about a foot of water in the central market square, the moisture vaporator tower was blown over, and the roofs and other constructions were discolored and damaged from the storm. I sent our local assistant off with Soufi to hire some large petrol-driven water pumps. As soon as they arrived we put them to work pumping out the water from the lake that had formed in the square. The Cantina door was also under water. We waded around in cheap gumboots we bought locally, stood the moisture vaporator back upright, and checked everything else like the dome rooftops and the crashed spacecraft.

By the next morning most of the water had gone and I put the painter and crews to work repairing the damage. I spent the day with them until satisfied that all was back in place. I knew I had to get back to Tozeur for the rest of the shooting there, and to prepare the final dressing for Luke's homestead in Matmata ready for the crew to arrive there on their way to Djerba, so I had to face yet another drive back across the country.

This was the pattern for the rest of the location's filming. Les stayed with the unit sorting out the myriad of problems that erupted almost every minute and long after the crew had wrapped to get things prepared for the next day's work. I kept one step ahead of the shooting unit, dressing the sets and getting them ready for the unit to walk onto and shoot. I would liaise with Les all the time as best we could, and if anything came up for the next day I would prepare it. That meant my driving back and forth to the set, as there was no other way to communicate. If Les needed something urgently I had to go organize it. So whenever I could I would go back to the shooting unit and ask Les and George what they needed. Things change constantly and it is necessary to keep an open line of communication all the time. Depending on a scene being shot what happens or doesn't happen can affect the next day's requirements, especially for action props and dressing. We didn't have cellphones and there was no communication to these far-flung desert locations so we relied on my visits to the set whenever I could, or assistants would drive to the production office in town and information somehow got passed along. Les and I always met in the evenings if I was working at the same location and not in Matmata or Djerba. We would go through the day and what was required for the following day. It was usual for us to be up really early and set things up before the crew arrived at 8am, so we always worked really long days. Our mantra was never let the cameras stop rolling, and prepare everything required for the next day. John was adamant about this and quite rightly. This was always how I worked and always what I expect of my art departments now as a director.

After the long trek back from Djerba I rejoined the units struggling in the sticky mud left by the rains. They had to postpone shooting as the trucks were simply bogged down in the muddy ground. It's amazing how quickly a dry desert surface can turn to mud when this amount of water falls in such a short time. The crew struggled on as quickly as they could and fortunately the sun returned and with the heat, the desert dried out quickly.

I joined the shooting crew next in the now famous *Star Wars* valley, Sidi Bouhlel Canyon. This was the location we found for the scenes where R2-D2 is captured by the Sand People, and where Obi-Wan Kenobi first appears in the movie and meets Luke and the droids. I had to help Les dress junk around the landspeeder for after the Tusken Raiders have ransacked it. Les was quickly preparing a realistic arm for C-3PO for when they find him behind the rocks where he has fallen and his system has shut down—George decided that one arm would be torn off in the fight. I had left a lot of electronic junk with Les and the props, and he made it look like the complex mechanical parts one would expect to see inside a robot, hanging out of his arm socket.

This valley we found has a special quality to it. There are really high canyons dividing the lower chott, or salt flats, and the massive deserts beyond leading to the Sahara. They create spectacular reddish-colored valleys that are similar to the Grand Canyon. This valley runs between the two areas and has spectacularly high cliffs on either side; the sun rises at one end and sets at the other, creating a gorgeous soft light that highlights the cliffs and creates deep shadows. Steven Spielberg used the same valley for *Raiders of the Lost Ark*, and the scenes where Ralph Fiennes hides Kristin Scott Thomas in the cave in *The English Patient* were also filmed here.

I talked to George when I was second-unit director on *The Phantom Menace* about filming the scenes in the same location that I was scheduled to do, where the Tusken Raiders are shooting from high on the cliffs at the pod racers, and he agreed. Just as it was on this first *Star Wars*, we had to use mules to transport all the equipment up to the top of the canyon; they were the only means of transport over the rocky and boulder-strewn ground.

It was emotionally satisfying for me to watch a few moments of the filming in between rushing around getting things ready, to see Sir Alec Guinness and hear that rich, wonderful voice of his. He can make the most simple dialogue sound like Shakespeare's most emphatic moments. It was another of those moments of realization for this boy from Reading who could only dream of being in an industry that seemed so far from reality. I believe that Sir Alec Guinness rolling in the desert sand before his first take on *Star Wars*, to make sure his costume had the dusty and lived-in look required, was a huge moment for George and the crew. This lauded stage and film actor doing this simple act broke the sense of awe that the actors were feeling. For the crew, this highly respected actor confirmed his belief and trust in George. In a way, it gave credence to George and his script that had been lacking prior to his appearance. It was a huge moment for me, and watching him do it put a smile on my face, that he understood just what we in the art department and George were striving for—a natural and real look.

Leaving Les to carry on, I said goodbye as I had to leave that day to travel to Matmata to Luke's homestead, and the next time I would see Les was in Djerba. I would leave everything dressed and ready in the cave and the courtyard in Matmata for Luke's scenes with Uncle Owen and Aunt Beru. We quickly went through what I had dressed there and again how to make the blue milk. He had plenty of props and spares, so was well covered for any eventuality.

We went back to the chott on the way to the hotel, and I quickly redressed the other sets back again ready for the next day's work. It had somewhat dried out again now after the storm, but was still very sticky in places. We just had to work round it. I then went back to gather our belongings from the hotel and checked out. For me it was the end of the Tozeur leg of my work. It was sad in a way; I had really enjoyed being here, despite the pressure of intense hours and work. There is something deeply appealing about these remote southern regions so near the Sahara Desert, where the next stop after two hundred kilometers of sand dunes in the Grand Erg is Libya—more than ten days' camel trek away. There is something mystical and healing about the Sahara Desert; its silence and remoteness, the myriad of stars at night, and the nomadic Bedouin who still populate the area. No wonder it features so much in many great writers' work.

On the way back to Djerba I stopped again in Matmata for a day and a night, to prepare the final dressing. I laid out the dinner table in the cave, as that was the first scene. Once I had played around with the props I'd had brought out, the Tupperware definitely looked the best, so I placed that as the main table dressings for the cups and containers. I matched them with various other PVC or plastic dinnerware so that it looked different to a normal meal setting, but natural, and the sort of dressing you would expect these remote farmers to use. I had organized the blue milk for the standby props so that they could put that out when the shooting started. With the technical pieces of dressing added into the cave walls, and the padded detailing around the doorframe looking out onto the courtyard beyond with the vaporator, it looked like Luke's homestead. The ancient designs in the ceiling we left intact really helped to fuse the old with the new, exactly the required look for the film.

I placed more junk in the courtyard, positioned to be seen from inside when George shot the meal scene and also for when Luke looked down on Uncle Owen from the desert above. We sprayed down all this junk dressing out in the courtyard again with sand-colored water so it blended in and nothing stood out as a prop or took one's eye. I also made sure that the dressing props left behind there brought back all the table dressings, as we had to shoot the scene in the kitchen in the studio, so everything would be used again for continuity. We had constructed one robot a bit similar to Doug Trumbull's in *Silent Running*, using the same principle of movement he had used, a small person inside a plastic bin container with corrugated plastic leggings to disguise their legs. This can be seen walking through the scene in the courtyard in the background.

Any movable dressing was placed ready for the shoot, and I left the prop on duty and guards to make sure everything stayed exactly in place for George to film the scenes. Satisfied that we had covered everything, we carried on to Djerba and the next leg of the shoot.

Back in Djerba there were no signs at all that a massive rainstorm had been there a few days before. Everything was back as we left it. I set about dressing the Cantina exterior. The construction team was replacing the vac-form panels on the crashed spaceship, as a lot had been damaged. Some were torn and broken and actually looked pretty good, so we left those. They looked like old wind damage over years. We kept going until they covered the tree behind and other unsightly buildings. We used a forklift truck and suspended the huge jet engines we had mocked up into place and then dressed in masses more pipe and airplane junk around them to make it look like the crashed craft.

The final work was with the painters, who carefully aged it with spray paint and dust to look like distressed metal. When I stood back and looked it was amazingly real, an enormous set piece towering over the small buildings around the Cantina entrance. The locals who visited the set were really amazed as they now thought it was real.

The Cantina door had been given the Tatooine *Star Wars* look by John with the paneled doorframe. Outside we set up a Western-style hitching post and brought in the dressing vehicles. These were the experimental speeders, painted down to look damaged and dusty. The owner of the building we had rented for the Cantina entrance looked on in wonder at the transformation to his home. He would periodically come out from inside and look at the change with his eyes wide in astonishment. He didn't understand it was for a movie, goodness knows what he thought, but he was getting paid a small rental fee and that seemed to make it okay.

A moment I will never forget is when we unloaded the Bantha from the truck and placed it into position as if tied to the hitching post by its owner, who was inside the Cantina, drinking. This Bantha was the only creature John could afford to make within the budget, so we took it around everywhere with us as dressing. It was placed in the desert for the stormtroopers who were supposed to be riding Banthas and then brought here. With the technology available within the limited time we had, the creature builders had managed to make its head move up and down when maneuvered. It was covered in hide and hair and when dusted down to make it fit into the location it looked okay, especially in the distance. John was never really convinced by it, but he literally could not afford more. When it arrived by truck, the owner of the Cantina location wasn't there and hadn't seen us place it. I was working nearby and watched his reaction when he came out of his house for his usual walk around to see what we were doing. He stopped dead in his tracks when he saw the creature, obviously deeply shocked. He ran back into his house and came straight back out with a huge club and started hitting the Bantha on the back. This made the head move up and down and, convinced it was real, he carried on whacking the creature and shouting at it to go away. He was jumping around its head, careful not to let the creature bite him. I was laughing, and pleased that it had fooled him. Eventually he stopped and one of our locals went and explained to him what it was. He never came out without his club after that though, and always eyed the Bantha with a wary look. I am not sure he was ever convinced it was not real.

We placed the pod from the desert into the scene, dressed on legs as another vehicle. I also had them bring the caterpillar-track maker from Tozeur. I used anything I could lay my hands on to give the impression of a buzzing space cantina. I added the second animal, giving the Cantina building's owner even more worry that there were animals outside his home. The other landspeeder mock-ups went in and with airplane parts dressed in, it started to look busy and somewhat like I imagined.

All the sets were dressed ready for the shooting days in Mos Eisley as the crew arrived and we all caught up that night in the hotel. Slowly the trucks came in from Tozeur until late in the night, as all the camera equipment, props, costumes, craft services, lighting, etc., arrived. It was a pretty big road train that Robert Watts and the production had to organize. Spirits were not terribly high with the appalling weather and conditions that everyone had faced in Tozeur, and many people were sick from bad food. Tensions were evident between the crew and George and Gary; George looked pretty depressed and tired and Gary was doing what he could to make things happen and was communicating with Gil to make things easier for George.

The first day of shooting on Djerba was on the Mos Eisley set. The old town of Djerba did indeed look like the space version of a Western when it was dressed and populated with extras and characters from the film. I had placed as many vehicles and animals and as much dressing as I could outside the Cantina and around the square.

Seeing this on film as it was shot, with the scale of the crashed spaceship as a backdrop to Obi-Wan Kenobi and Luke as they entered it, worked. The moisture vaporators towers worked wonders as well, scattered throughout the place, hiding all sorts of problems and electrical elements not right for the movie. They also added a familiar feeling to all the scenes as we had them everywhere on Tatooine. They were a brilliant idea because as the entire planet relied on these moisture collectors, they became a familiar feature for an audience, so helped to blend the reality of a different world into one that was believable.

They shot the scene where Luke's landspeeder is stopped by the stormtroopers and Luke sees the Force used for the first time as Obi-Wan Kenobi manipulates the stormtroopers to let them pass. It was a thrill for me to watch Sir Alec in the landspeeder as George filmed the scene. The power he brought to it made the dialogue work; he was so simple and unaffected in his acting. He had real presence with that voice of his. With C-3PO sat up high in the back with lack of room, and R2-D2 laying sideways, George's idea of a small sports-car version of a speeder, all that a dirt farmer like Luke could afford, worked. In the street beyond I had placed all the moisture vaporators in a forest behind them, which helped to create a street feel, a bustling port town to contrast with the lonely desert farm where Luke lived.

I only got to see occasional glimpses of the shooting, which is normal for the set decorator always working ahead of the unit. I do try to be there when the unit moves onto the next set or location so that everything is ready for them, and general props and any action props needed by the actors for the scene are there, so they can rehearse. I had to liaise with the director sometimes during the day to see what changes had come up, and it is always important to keep in touch and see how the film's look is developing through the camera.

During these last few days of filming in Tunisia, I remember an incident that shows very pertinently George's state of mind. He was pretty depressed, tired and frustrated. When they had to change over from one set to another the crew broke for lunch. There were usually a couple of hours while they shifted the trucks with the camera equipment and did wardrobe changes, etc. George came with me alone in the car to look at the next set where we would be filming. I needed him to see it and sign off on it. After he had approved the set, we had to wait for the crew and, neither of us having eaten, we stopped for a fast bite at a local café I used. As George looked and sounded so bad I ordered him and myself a Chicken Chorba. This is a soup they make from locally grown vegetables and chicken, flavored with cilantro and fresh lemon. It is always served boiling hot and thus it is always safe to eat. George looked absolutely exhausted—he had black rings under his eyes—and I spoke about this and the difficulties with the robots and the crew. I had not slept much either since being in Tunisia. I remember thinking to myself I must have looked as ragged as he did, as I was feeling exactly the way he looked and was clearly as exhausted. When one is so tired adrenaline takes over. We talked about his difficulties and I reminded him that he had written this saga so was responsible for it all, and he said, "Yes, I know." He had created robots that were like a combination of the two things directors fear most on set as they always cause delays: young children and animals. R2-D2 was like a combination of both in one, but without a trainer having the time to train him properly.

George described his feelings to me, and exactly how his days felt after two weeks of filming and all the difficulties he had encountered. It wasn't just the location difficulties that had got to him, though these were unexpectedly hard with the monsoon-like rains, or the malfunctioning robots and effects. It was the different way the crews worked to someone used to the supportive and more independently creative ways of the San Francisco-style independent filmmakers. These are the exact words he used to tell me how he felt. I never forgot them.

"I get up in the morning and as soon as I stand up they put this big rucksack on my back. Then they put a large rock in it, which means I can't move at all. Then they continue piling rocks in it until I am left on the floor immobile. I summon all my strength and eventually manage to pull the first rock out of the rucksack. Then somehow, slowly summoning enough strength throughout the day, I take each rock out one by one. Finally I take the last rock out, and I am so exhausted and so tired I go back to sleep. Then when I wake again they stand me up and put the rocks back again."

It sums it all up, really—George's exact state of mind after just two weeks of filming, and he had another ten or so to go.

Towards the end of location shooting, Koo Stark arrived to play Camie and Garrick Hagon as Biggs to film scenes at Anchorhead that were eventually cut from the movie. I had dressed the narrow alleys where Luke goes to chase down the parts for the *Millennium Falcon*. We made them sparse and unfriendly to fit the scene, and to match Tatooine's remote desert planet feeling. I covered the roof section in old lattice as it reminded me of the wonderful medina in Marrakesh; the light beaming through the smoke there makes a great atmosphere. It was easy to purchase locally sold roots and fruits that looked very unfamiliar to a Western audience, so hanging these and adding more of our aircraft junk made it seem like another planet.

The last day we dressed the remaining scenes for Anchorhead. Recycling all my props and dressing over and over on each location saved money and created a different but familiar look. They always served as a normal background to the actors; George was dead against pointing things out because they were there, and this is what makes *Star Wars* so different as a space movie, and the first really to do that.

For the Biggs and Camie scenes we used an old unused mosque-like structure. We added an air-conditioning unit onto the roof to change its appearance, painted the same sand color. For the first scene Luke and Biggs were drinking fermented beer and we gave them both black rubber-type cups from Thermos sets, so they looked the part. When they filmed the next scene they were all looking at the sky through Luke's binoculars. I had my heart in my mouth, as the actors decided to throw my one-off, hand-made electro-binoculars to each other as they acted the scene. If they missed that would be it, and I'd be stuck behind a rock trying to glue it together, but they made it work without dropping it, to my great relief. Watching the deleted scene on YouTube one can hear the clunk as each actor is catching it. Looking at the stills I see one where one of my lenses is missing on a shot of Biggs holding them to look through, fortunately from a deleted scene. I was happy George never did too many takes, and thank goodness it was the last scene they were needed for. They had held up well, far better than I had expected.

The following night, after packing and getting everything we needed ready for the return to London, we boarded a charter jet to fly us back. I was nervous and wondering if we would be ready for the next leg of the journey in Elstree Studios. The crew drank copious amounts of alcohol, as is the British tradition, and celebrated returning home. I was actually feeling the opposite, very sad to be leaving Tunisia. It is a culturally rich and beautiful country with wonderful cuisine and an amazing heritage of historical architecture, with the mystical Sahara Desert in the south.

Back in London, I went straight back to the studios as my car was parked underground there, to meet John Barry and catch up. Les and I recounted all our experiences to John that were relevant to the coming weeks. We went through all the problems that we had encountered and what we thought were to come. This was important dialogue so that the department could support George all the way through the shoot. We talked about the tensions between Gil Taylor and George. Gil didn't seem to like John and didn't like the way John was forcing him to look at alternative ways to light sets that were really what the film needed, especially inside the Death Star interiors. John was intelligent enough to ignore it and keep doing what he was doing. Gil refused to look at any drawings for some reason, and often excused himself by saying he never got them, but the production office run by Pat Carr was an amazingly efficient machine, especially at delivering information to everyone on the crew.

I went down to the stages to look at the exterior of the *Millennium Falcon*. I wanted to see if my ideas of using scrap really had worked. It was almost ready for shooting as this was one of the first sets we were filming on the following Friday. The completed set looked like a real craft sitting there in a hangar. It was huge, really impressive. The idea of building scrap into a set had worked. The painters were brilliant, especially the more senior ones; they had added dirt and oil patches to the dressing. I felt comfortable and relieved that my team was doing okay.

I went to the other stage where the Lars homestead had been built. I had duplicated a lot of the dressing we had used in Tunisia so that it matched. The jetliner cabin shape, now it was dressed, looked real and excellent. This was the first set to be filmed. Seeing out of the door to the courtyard beyond really fooled the eye. With a backing and bright sunlight artificially created it was impossible to know that the two sets, one in Tunisia and this in the studios, were not one. I added some of the airplane food containers used for the passengers' meals into the crevices at the back, which matched the courtyard dressing.

The dressing props showed me how they had arranged a heated stove element, as George had asked for Aunt Beru to be cooking in the scene. I chose some bok choy-like vegetables, because they looked foreign at the time, and the prop boys showed me the saucepan and heat rig they had made for Aunt Beru to be cooking in. I took the one they were using and added a piece of airplane junk to the top of it. It then looked like some newer form of pressure cooker, changing its appearance completely. This is the one in the final film where she is placing the bok choy into steaming water, and as it appears in close-up it was vital to get it looking correct. I would show the dressed sets to George when he returned to Elstree after the weekend, and get it all signed off.

I went home to sleep. In fact I crashed asleep, exhausted, going over in my mind what I had to get ready. I was thinking about Obi-Wan Kenobi's cave as I drifted off…

The next day I went alone to Obi-Wan Kenobi's cave to ponder what to do with it. I liked to sit in a set and let its atmosphere influence me. Once a set is built and painted, the feeling of the requirements for its dressing can change. Period sets require correct period furniture but a space fantasy set like Obi-Wan's required imagination.

I had found a wonderful piece of airplane scrap that looked like a very modern stove, traditional enough so everyone would know what it was, but different. We added pieces to it and pipes attached to the walls, and that was built into the set behind. When Joe Dipple came, we played around with different looks. I had carpets from Tunisia and fur rugs, as we thought it should be simply dressed to suit his character. He was a nomadic recluse and a Jedi Master, so unattached to worldly possessions. He had to pull Luke's father's lightsaber from an old trunk and I found one old wooden one that was suitable. It was large enough to suggest a box of treasures, and that would be his only box of possessions, we thought. I added a few more pipes and junk technology to the simple walls, enough to remove the feeling that it was simply a cave. Out of the plastic bins we created a table and seats for the scene, and covered these in furs or animal skins. That again gave the nice mix of modern and primitive. I fiddled around with this set for days to get it right.

Back on the *Millennium Falcon* stage I got the prop boys to get some corrugated tubing and attach it between the ship and the floor as if they were refueling pipes and other supply pipes. Always fiddling to the last minute, we kept adding junk pieces to layer the mechanical pieces of dressing. Then we went across to the Lars homestead garage and workshops and added lots of tools and scrap pieces to give it a used garage look. I had found and prepared a small piece of scrap to look like a tool for Luke to pry the restraining bolt off of R2-D2. This was given to the standby props to keep for the shoot. The bath was filled with oil and tested by the special-effects boys so it'd be ready for Anthony to sink into. Anthony had insisted the special-effects boys heat it for him, despite the fact that the UK was suffering a heat wave, to sit in cold oil for several takes wasn't going to be easy for him in costume. It was much easier now for John Stears' team being back in the studios as they had the backup of their fully functioning workshops. The robots went straight back in to be repaired and they worked on them to make them function. Getting the sand out of everything was the first priority.

My largest concern was the Cantina, as we were to shoot that the following week. The bar and drink-serving apparatus had been built in by the time we returned and looked very convincing. I liked the chromed look of the containers—who would have thought underneath were scrap airplane parts? I got stuck in with the props boys to make the finishing touches. I adapted some gray PVC drums into tables, which looked okay. Each table had a plastic light on it for the atmosphere, and we placed a few greeblies on the walls to help. We had made up some Cantina-style hookah pipes using scrap and other receptacles Peter had found me and made them practical so that the actor could use it in the scene. George wanted the bar smoky like a Western bar. I also added a plastic bin at the entrance, with a light inside, and hung it on the wall like a cigarette and tobacco dispenser.

On the shoot day the prop men had smoke machines to create a nice thick atmosphere. Having hookahs and other smoking devices in there gave a source for the smoke so that it looked real. Usually one man is given the lead job; it's his responsibility to watch the smoke all the time in the lights, and to get it settled to a point where it is acting like a diffusion and hangs in the air as still as they can get it. At this time we had the best smoke for film; it was based on the same incense used for centuries in cathedrals and churches. It smelt good and hung beautifully in the air.

Harrison Ford had arrived. We gave him his pistol, which he liked and felt it suited his character's persona. He went to practice with it up on the lot, where they took pictures of him in costume. They took shots of him doing fast draws, Western style. That act alone naturally endorsed the Western basis we were using for everything.

Watching the band playing as George filmed the Cantina with all the motley crew of characters, I knew this would become another iconic *Star Wars* scene. Obi-Wan Kenobi drawing his lightsaber was a huge surprise as it came out of nowhere, and suddenly before us was the world of *Star Wars* we were creating. The set looked so real in the atmosphere and the band with their instruments made from scrapped objects I had put together. Here was a classic Western bar scene, recreated as a science-fiction fantasy.

I had arranged the tables for the Greedo and Han Solo confrontation scene. Following the script as Greedo threatens Han Solo and is about to kill him, Greedo suddenly disappears in a blinding flash of light and Han pulls his smoking gun from beneath the table. George set it up that during the confrontation, Han silently takes out his gun and has it ready under the table pointing up at Greedo. John Stears had to prearrange the squib when Han Solo fired, as his blaster shot had to go through the table and surprise Greedo as he was about to fire his weapon. I had used PVC barrels for the tables and went through with John Stears how it would work for him to place the squib. I arranged a second table already melted on top as if a blaster had ripped a hole through it, ready to place back after the special-effects shot, to save George time. Everything was arranged and the famous argument took place. On cue Harrison fired! The squib exploded, creating a cloud of smoke, and Greedo fell. The controversy over who fired first was in part created because the smoke from the squib disguised the action, and in the way George cut the scene. At the time as scripted only Han fired and Greedo disappeared and no flash came from Greedo's gun. Han, like a Western fighter, was quicker on the draw and fired a second before Greedo. This suited Han's character as the renegade survivor, who always got himself out of scrapes. The one squib was set up that way. George later changed it because the *Star Wars* universe didn't uphold the idea of Han Solo being a cold-blooded killer. Also, George later had the ability to add CGI effects and could make it so that Greedo had in fact shot at the same time and missed. I thought that Greedo, being such a mean character and an obvious part of the scum in the bar, was so well set up by George, that Han killing him would be seen in the right context. Han Solo is a lovable rogue, a bandit and lone survivor with his sidekick Chewbacca, and George wrote him to be the outsider with a heart of gold and this really comes across in the trilogy, so firing first always seemed to me to be well within reason. I understand why George was sensitive as he was making *Star Wars* for a young audience as well as adults, but Han was in trouble and about to be killed, he was simply defending himself, like so many western bar-room scenes.

Once he was established at the studios, Harrison found his way to the carpenter's shop and helped out. He seemed more comfortable there amongst the fellow carpenters, working with his hands, than hanging out with the producers. Several times when I was asking Bill Harman to make something, I would see Harrison quietly sawing wood and constructing something for the film. I took him one day to see the *Millennium Falcon* cockpit. I showed him which levers he could push and pull, and what buttons had a reaction with lights. Seeing the massive exterior of his ship and the interiors gave Harrison a better perspective on what we were doing. I think the reality of created environments or sets, any sets, really affect the attitude and credibility of an actor's performance. If they feel the environment they are in is practical and they are comfortable in it, it helps them create a believable character.

Alongside this we had to dress the first scenes in the Death Star. We were dressing different sets ahead of the shooting crew all the time. Everyone had action props to be prepared, dictated by the script. On top of this work was the preparation for the week after and the one after that. I had to be thinking ahead all the time; some things took time to prepare and I preferred to show everything to the director ahead of time. It is hard enough going onto a new set and rehearsing and getting the lighting right, so it is far better to already know the set and props so that there are no surprises on the day.

The problem we were facing daily on *Star Wars* was the amount of sets we had to get ready in a short time, plus it was one of the hottest summers on record, and of course being England there was no air conditioning. Elstree Studios had eight stages and they were all full of sets. The schedule meant George was shooting for a short time on each set and moving on. We had to tear down the sets and rebuild as fast as possible. Because of the economic constraints John cleverly designed sets he could reuse constantly. The Death Star was made of units and pre-cast panels, so it could be reassembled quickly into a different set, or extended or changed fairly quickly. The *Millennium Falcon* interior was a different matter. That ate up weeks of dressing to get right, especially the hold area, which served for several scenes, and the cockpit set.

I had Peter Dunlop running all over London day after day sourcing interesting-looking dressing that we could adapt. The chairs, for instance, in the Death Star conference-room scene had to be found. We searched and searched for a design that would fit in. In the end John designed them, as we couldn't find anything that would work, and those that were interesting were horrendously expensive. I worried about every single aspect of every set, and the simple task of getting each one ready in time and never holding up the shooting was my constant battle. We never did once throughout the entire shoot, and that is a testament to Joe Dipple, Frank Bruton, and my props team, who fulfilled any task I assigned them with a smile and positive attitude.

This speed of changeover laid a really heavy burden on John as a designer and me as the set dresser. I was always on Bill Welch the construction manager's back to give me a finished set to dress, and he in turn was on the draftsmen's backs to deliver drawings so he could get the sets built. I needed a set painted and finished before I could begin to dress it, but I found we were often moving in before it was ready as there was just not enough time to dress it. As we worked seven days a week, and long hours throughout the entire period, a day off was totally inconceivable. We would often show George the sets after the shoot in the evenings to keep up the flow of information.

Friday was the filming of the exterior of the *Millennium Falcon* and the first time we saw Peter Mayhew as Chewbacca fully dressed and acting.

It was a huge set, filling the stage, and this was only half of the actual craft, as we'd see it. Declan Mulholland, the actor playing Jabba the Hutt, came to me and told me how great the set looked; he couldn't believe we hadn't found a real spacecraft. These small endorsements from people seeing the sets for the first time are important. You need fresh eyes to see the finished project to know you are on the right path, and are creating realistic worlds for an audience.

I think this set and the hold area where Chewie was playing chess were the two sets where our dream of creating a world from junk came to fruition. I watched the first setup and made sure all the dressing of the pipes and containers was right for camera, and watched Harrison perform as Han Solo for the first time. It was clear from that moment a new rebel hero had been born.

I finally finished the dressing on the *Millennium Falcon* hold set. John had constructed the chess table into the set around the banquettes, and we dressed a few tiny greeblies into that. The training droid for Luke was specially built, and had some of my special pieces in it. It was maneuvered for the most part the simple way: on fishing line hung from above and worked by a technician.

I liked this set on camera. Looking through the lens and at rushes, the idea of a submarine-inspired interior in space really took weight here. The set is encrusted with technology, and never ever betrayed the fact it was not a functioning spacecraft. It became the ideal setting in that way to establish the idea of the Force for an audience.

PROBLEMS MOUNT FOR GEORGE

I took a long walk through the Death Star interiors that were being readied with John. John was voicing concerns about Gil Taylor, who had been complaining to Gary Kurtz about these sets, saying it was hard for him to light them as they were too dark. Instead of working with John and liaising with him to get the right feel as most lighting cameramen do, he simply complained. With a space fantasy set it is necessary to build in a lot of the lighting. There isn't a central ceiling lamp or chandelier or table lamps to give sources of lighting, a normal situation in dressing a period or contemporary film. John issued drawings of each set and tried to liaise about the built-in lighting in each one, but Gil found every excuse in the book not to meet John either on set or after the shoot day and going through the placement of lights, making it work—he simply took a negative stand. This attitude takes its toll on a movie. The shooting unit are together day in day out and they all start to sing the same song, usually inspired by a leader, and it can be a negative or positive song.

George never behaved like a loud-mouthed Hollywood director, or defended his position, just concerned himself with the work and got on with it, and correctly expected everyone around him to do the same. The art department worked non-stop behind the scenes, but we didn't have a voice within the shooting unit as we didn't have a standby art director there. We didn't have one on *Star Wars* except in Tunisia where Les stayed with the crew, so we couldn't bring a balance to negative rumblings back in the studio.

Another dispute had erupted between John Barry and Gil at this point. George wanted the corridor in the Death Star prison cell section to be really long. It would give the impression of scale and also the impression of a suppressed world under an evil dictator if you saw a huge run of prison cells. Not having the budget to build such a corridor, John suggested using a well-tried film trick of setting a mirror at the correct angle across the back of the set, which would give the impression of the corridor going off into the distance. Gil refused to have it that way, told George it would never work and he could never light it. John argued his point, having done it successfully before, and George agreed it would work in theory. Getting nowhere with Gil, John stormed off to the art department and built a model of the set really quickly. He placed a small mirror across the end of the corridor and took it to show George. It did indeed work, and gave the feeling of an endless corridor. So John built it and Gil had to light it. George filmed the scene that way for the corridor master shot. This is the corridor in the 1977 film, and no one spotted that it was a trick shot done on the floor with well-tried and proven techniques. It worked well enough to fool the eye for the initial release and was replaced later by George in future versions of the film.

Frustrations were building all round. On top of this, for some reason the editor was voicing concerns to everyone about the footage, and George hadn't had time to work on the editing to make the film cut together the way he was planning as he filmed it. John, Les, Norman, and I were so overworked that we hardly had time to see each other in the day let alone listen to any of this, working fifteen-hour days.

Watching the filming during moments when we were required on stage and seeing rushes was enough to know that the core of the film was there on film as George intended it, and it was working.

On top of it all, the union restrictions were forcing George to stop every day at 5.30, even if there was only one shot left to complete a scene. These restrictions severely affected the art department and our building schedule. Robert Watts had the film planned like clockwork, and often the down time at the end of the day was when a company move was made from one set to another. This then allowed us to strike sets to build more. To move a crew the next day in the middle of a shooting day took at least two hours from George's day, so it severely impacted his filming time. He would lose the time to do what he wanted, and had to compromise scenes to try to make up the hours lost by moving. Added to this, the sound of hammering for striking the sets and building was a constant aggravation during a filming day.

This placed a lot of further stress on George. On location the shooting rules had been different: we could work longer due to the hours of daylight. Back in the studios, however, the crew stuck to their guns on regulations. The shooting crew adhered to the rulings by the minute, as if punishing George for some reason, blaming an old Associated British Pictures Union ruling. The crew on the floor all stopped the moment the clock hit 5.30 unless George had pre-empted the situation and called "the quarter," which meant he had to ask permission to film for a further quarter of an hour. The difficulty for George and any director was pre-empting whether he'd need the quarter or not. There was always a vote on the floor about the request and the union member chosen to represent the crew would say yes or no. Gil certainly endorsed the union hours. In my experience it's the DP who calls the shots on the floor with the first AD. They blamed it on the studio's rules, but rules can be negotiated and changed when warranted, and as my early career attests to in this book, rules are made to be broken. That's how you get creative and innovative work. Certainly George was breaking just about every rule in the book making *Star Wars*.

The shooting floor was therefore not a happy place for George. Thank goodness the actors had fun; though they didn't know it, they were the ones dissolving the tension. I was standing there one day when Gil said something to George that made me embarrassed to even hear it. George just carried on, ignoring it, but it must have been so tough and demeaning to him some days.

I was in John's office going through the sets that were imminent, when his phone rang. It was the shooting floor. George needed a com-link. He'd suddenly decided that a communication device was needed before the scheduled day it was required. Knowing it was urgent, John looked at me and said, "Can you do anything?" It was a rhetorical question.

I had been showing John some PVC piping and connectors for another set. I saw a small grille-like object peeking out from a pipe connector that was like a small version of the ones under a sink. This pipe was only about two inches round in diameter. I pulled the little filter out and there before my eyes was a com-link. It had a grille on the end like a mike and round the white plastic-molded case was a rubber seal comprised of rings that ran down the rest of the small filter. I showed it to John who smiled at my lucky find.

I liked it; it looked really unusual but could easily be a small communicator because of the fine mesh-like grille on one end.

I hurried down to the stage, went straight to George and showed him. As he inspected it, I asked him if he thought it too small, but he held it in his fingers and said it was the perfect size for what he had in mind, and it indeed looked like a communicator. George took it away and gave it straight to C-3PO to use in the Death Star and showed him how to use it. Phew! Another problem averted with something that looked exactly appropriate for the *Star Wars* world. There was only one of these ever made and I recently held it in my hands again.

Later on, there was a scene where the stormtroopers blow open an airlock door on the detention level and a fight erupts with Han, Chewie, and Luke. Stears set up charges around the door, ready for the shot. On George's call of "Action!" there was a countdown to one, and then a huge explosion erupted. Smoke filled the set and you couldn't see anything, we just heard George yelling, "Cut!" Everyone rushed in to make sure no one was hurt. That's always the first concern. All the actors and stuntmen were okay, just a bit dazed and their ears ringing from the loud bang. There was a lot of coughing in the smoke and laughter once everyone realized that no one was hurt at all.

Stears rushed onto the set and loudly proclaimed another of his famous quotes that Les and I will never ever forget: "It's these weak sets!" But he had clearly placed far too many explosives in there; he got overenthusiastic. The set was built exactly as they always were, with pine framing clad with fiberboard or plywood and held in place by the metal scaffolding we always used. It's a pity Stears reacted this way. He actually was a nice man and very talented.

In any event, we rebuilt the doors very quickly with the standby crew, repainted all the damage and they did take two, which worked much better. This happened a couple of times on the shoot, but in the end it looked good. Even mistakes end up in films sometimes and can end up making the scene stronger. Stears did handle a lot of the explosions and gunshot hits, and his team was pretty fast. One or two mistakes always happen, especially moving this quickly on a schedule, and the added burden of a short prep time.

I finally finished the dressing on this set. John had constructed the chess table into the set around the banquettes, and we dressed a few tiny greeblies into that. The training droid for Luke was specially built, and had some of my special pieces in it. It was maneuvered for some shots the simple way: on fishing line. The rest were created later at Industrial Light and Magic. The scene became the ideal way to establish the idea of the Force for an audience. Obviously Sir Alec Guinness created the believable drama just by being Obi-Wan Kenobi and Mark played the difficult role of learning the Force and trusting his instincts.

The Death Star conference room set heightened the tensions between John and Gil to breaking point. During the prep period, John tried out the colors he wanted first—the set needed to be very dark, so John and George wanted a steely gray look for it, almost black. The set was supposed to be ominous and represent evil and so it was natural to try to emphasize that. John tried several versions of the steely gray color. Gil claimed that John built this set without consideration of lighting and caused him a lot of problems. But this set, like all the others, was sketched and drawn up with blueprints and issued correctly to every department, Gil's included. John had built in translucent panels for lighting so they fitted the architecture of the Death Star, much like Ralph McQuarrie had drawn the illustrations.

The lighting had to be built in, but when they tested it, Gil complained about the color of the set. So John had the painters try about six different colors before they settled on a lighter gray tone. This conference room was a simple round room, with a large round table as the only dressing. It was as effective as the architecture of the infamous German architect Albert Speer, who built the striking Reich Chancellery and other Nazi buildings. They were designed to showcase power with their graphic simplicity and grandness. I didn't want to disturb this effect as it really suited Darth Vader and the evil Empire, the direct opposite of the oily, messy *Millennium Falcon* and Tatooine. This was the Death Star and it had to have that evil, clinical feel to it.

The chairs John had made in black were starkly simple and added to the feeling of the set. I didn't want to spoil the set with dressing, so I searched for a suitable communications device to sit in the center of the table. Peter brought in several ideas for me to look at, and one caught my eye: a round floor heater, very simple, with grilles circling around it. I had it sprayed black, the same as the chairs, and removed the power cable. Sitting it in the center of the table it looked the part. In front of each member of the Death Star council we placed a black pen and a pad. I found some heat-retaining cups in brushed steel and black, and these also looked great. I left it at that, graphically simple.

George's idea of the round table was interesting as it subconsciously hinted at a reference to King Arthur and the Knights of the Round Table. That power of good also turns bad as the Arthurian tale progresses, so an apt reference.

The morning of the shoot I was in my office sticking together some props for the torture robot. I liked the idea of there being a large hypodermic syringe on it, which immediately said what it was as it advanced on Princess Leia. People hate injections and I had found a very large syringe, the type that Bill Welch endured on *Lucky Lady* when he had to have rabies shots after being bitten by a wild dog. I was assembling some prop pieces when suddenly Les came in and told me that Gil had stormed off the conference room set, saying he couldn't light it. He was now in Robert Watts' office. John went straight down to the floor to see George. Everyone was standing around embarrassed. John spoke with Gary and George and said, "Fine, then. I'll light it." I do not know why to this day, but the gaffer and electricians went along with him, and John started setting the lights. He started to cut holes in the set, to backlight the scene through as he'd always envisioned it. Gil's complaint had totally backfired on him as word went back that John was lighting the set.

Gil then came back to the set. He began placing a lot of photofloods behind the slots cut in the walls and added more; these gave the set the light levels necessary. The light coming from up high gave the scene an unsettling feel. Far from being a badly lit, hokey scene, this conference room has a sinister feel. Darth Vader showing his powers by choking Admiral Motti has become another iconic moment with every new generation. It looked great in rushes.

Reports were constantly going back to Twentieth Century Fox during this time that were mostly negative about the film. I imagine the complaints (mostly from Gil Taylor, John Stears, and the editor being very vocal about how bad the footage was) and the filming now almost nine days behind schedule were creating alarming reactions with the Fox board. It was about this time that George also found out that Gil had complained about George's use of a diffusion filter on the lens, and George found out that Peter Beale, the manager of Twentieth Century Fox in the UK, supporting Gil's advice, had ordered the filters removed behind George's back. Watching rushes, the slightly more documentary reality look George wanted and had achieved by having a very slight diffusion filter on the lens had gone, and George was seeing really clean images. When George found out, he quite rightly reacted.

There was a meeting between Gil Taylor, Peter Beale, and Gary Kurtz; the subject was George. The editors had been complaining about rushes and cut scenes vocally to everyone. John Barry couldn't understand this at all, he could see the film evolving the way George was intending, so one can only imagine the talk going on behind George's back. Gary talked George out of removing Gil, saying that the production would fall apart if they lost the lighting cameraman at this stage. John suspected that Peter Beale wanted Gil there to control this young American director who he may have surmised was in over his head. Gary maintains that Gil defended George at this meeting, saying they'd gone this far and he should be allowed to carry on. One can only surmise the reason he defended George and the conversation that led to him stating this, as nothing is on record.

Alan Ladd, Jr., deeply concerned about all this negativity coming to him from reports from London, came to Britain to see for himself. He would have been relying on reports on a daily basis so who knows what was being said in those conversations, but it was enough for a concerned Alan Ladd to get on a plane. He looked at the material cut together by the editor and, according to his interview from the time, panicked. The negative comments from the editor, the DP, and Peter Beale would all have been influencing him, but fortunately he spoke to George personally about it. When George told him he hadn't cut any of the material himself, nor seen some of it, and that it was not at all what he was happy with and not at all how he was going to cut the scenes, Ladd believed him. Also that the film was not going to be three hours long as Ladd had been led to believe, but around the two hours George had timed it out to be.

The sets looked very impressive when John Barry walked Ladd around and showed him. John was very positive about George and what he was doing. George had made a huge hit film in *American Graffiti* so he had a lot of credibility to his name. The actors also confirmed their enthusiasm, and having Sir Alec Guinness there certainly added confidence. It came to light that another negative comment voiced behind George's back was that we were creating these amazing sets and George wasn't filming them to full advantage. The finished film stands better testament to what George was doing than words; George was not following the way an old-fashioned film director relied on, doing first a wide master shot, then moving in for close-ups and over the shoulders of the actors. George would sometimes start close in and reveal the location during the scene, which I actually prefer and do to this day. George's explanation to John and me one day at the time sums it up. When a character walks into a building, you don't first show the building, as if saying, "Wow, look at this," which is the temptation for science fiction as it involves new worlds never seen before. You just show naturally what the action requires, and that was George's approach to *Star Wars*. For executives used to watching the film dailies and not seeing what they expected—first a big wide shot of the set—it had most likely caused concern with the budget being so high in their eyes for the time. Also, the disaster of *Lucky Lady* was ringing in their ears.

Alan Ladd returned to Los Angeles to convince the Fox board that everything would be okay and somehow George just carried on trying to ignore all the stress surrounding him from every side. His belief in his own vision and ability kept him going. Other directors might have given up or just started exploding at everyone. George looked ill and tired and stressed beyond belief, but he kept his calm demeanor and still managed to laugh and play with the actors and get what he wanted. It was an important lesson to keep all this tension and attitude off the shooting floor and away from the actors, so they can play. They at least trusted George and were unaware of the dramas going on.

The presence of Sir Alec Guinness was an ongoing factor. His complete mastery as an actor and his simple and kind way of working certainly impressed everyone and he gave tremendous credibility to George and the script just by being there. He never spoke badly about anyone and worked kindly and professionally with George. Alec did his scenes with honesty and a full respect for George and his mastery of every detail of the film, without any signs of ego.

George's casting of Mark Hamill and Carrie Fisher was also very astute (in this he was aided by the great casting director Fred Roos, who also cast *American Graffiti* and *The Godfather*). But I used to cringe with embarrassment some days on the set for George and the way the crew treated him. Chewbacca became known as the big walking carpet, in a derogatory way, not a kind or fun way. It's true that the stormtroopers sounded weak when they walked as the fiberglass and plastic costume pieces clanked and fell off every so often. Darth Vader performing on the shooting floor with a thick Somerset accent as Dave Prowse was playing him did not have that epic feel that would come later. R2-D2 and the robots never got that much better, either.

Things went wrong all the time but there was something there, that something special that is the alchemy of cinema. I was thrilled and excited every time I watched filming or saw rushes. Here was a world being created and coming alive before our eyes. I had little time to dwell on that, however, as I raced from hour to hour trying to keep ahead of the shooting unit. Thankfully only rarely did George ever complain about any of the dressing or props. I cannot remember one time ever, in fact, except the market street on location where it got overdressed and we had to simplify it right down. The dressing crew followed the real market or souks in Tunisia that were laden with goods and fruits and vegetables, but George needed the planet sparse and dry, so we echoed that in the re-dress and made it really empty and devoid of much produce. George removed John Jympson, the editor, feeling bad about it, but George did not have the time or the energy to explain what he wanted—you either got it or you didn't. So George would rely on his own skills as an editor— the part of filmmaking he most prefers—and Marcia Lucas, his wife, an experienced editor herself. He eventually hired editor Richard Chew to work with them as a team.

Looming towards me on the schedule was the interior of the Sandcrawler and the Death Star garbage disposal room scenes. I was gathering props and dressing together for both these sets. The main unit moved across to Shepperton Studios to film the hangar sequence, so Les covered that while I stayed in Elstree and tried to catch up. For the Sandcrawler interior I had the robots we used in Tunisia but needed to fill it with a lot more. The scene called for a huge amount of junk they had picked up, and robots everywhere. We ended up building so many different robots by taking any interesting piece of scrap that I thought suitable and fixing other pieces onto it to assemble different characters. Medical instruments, bits of vacuum cleaners, aircraft parts, any robots the special-effects boys had made, anything was used disguised with greeblies and scrap to make up the numbers. Old C-3PO suits were adapted for more robots, and I finally managed to assemble enough to make the scene work. They had to look real but I had an advantage in knowing that the hold would be quite dark, a lot easier to disguise the more background robots than when seen in the glaring desert light.

The garbage room was a huge endeavor. The middle of the set was built into the tank in the stage and flooded so I had to prepare some junk to float and create a large amount to pile up around the sides of the incinerator walls like garbage. My biggest problem was that Harrison had to grab a long pole and try to wedge it between the closing garbage incinerator doors. The gap at the beginning of the shots was really wide, about fourteen feet, and I couldn't find anything that long that was not too heavy for Harrison to lift. I tried so many things to find a solution, including some specially made-up very light polystyrene ones, but the length meant they broke too easily with just the weight and length.

I tried to join two lengths of plastic tubing together but they always looked bent as it was too long to support itself. I needed it longer to reach between the garbage incinerator doors as they slowly closed in shot. I finally found a solution. We put two lengths of light PVC drain piping together, which made it long enough. I had found some interesting sleeve pieces and that created a way to join them together so it looked like natural junk. It would even bend a little as the doors closed in. I made up several different lengths so that they could work with each segment of the scene as the doors closed in on the actors. I had to go to the set and show Harrison how it might operate. I needed his help as it was not too strong and could easily fall apart. Harrison was great. Being a carpenter and manually skilled he understood very quickly the underlying problems of making things up that could work—not always the case with actors and props.

Thinking the action through for this scene I was worried about the actors getting hurt. The set was flooded and the actors would be standing throughout the entire scene waist-high in water filled with garbage. It was planned in the script that the monster would rise from the filthy water and grab Luke and drag him under the water. I needed a lot of specialized junk, that was obvious. Rocks for filming are usually carved from polystyrene, which is light and can't hurt an actor. Shaped and painted they are indistinguishable from real rocks. So I had the prop team make up large numbers of polystyrene junk, painted black and gray, and they made enough to fill the garbage room. The trick was to inject the paint into the sections, so that when a piece broke off the surface it was the same color inside and didn't betray what it was actually made of. This was important as when the walls closed in the junk became squashed and moved around so was easily damaged. I found all sorts of great shapes to place in there around the edges. I used masses of rubber pieces and pipes and larger aircraft parts that were light. We even cast some junk in lighter-weight materials so that it was softer.

This was another set that took a long time to get right. Everything in it had to move as the doors closed in on the actors until it looked like they would be crushed, and also so that the monster could rise out of the debris to grab Luke. George only ended up with a tentacle as the monster never looked right—once again the budget and time was just not there to make it work as George originally envisioned it. However, in the end the scene worked.

After running for weeks, if not months on adrenaline, I realized that the end was in sight, though about fourteen days over schedule. The strangest thing with movies is that there is no winding down, especially for the designer, set decorator and directors. One day you are worried sick, thinking you can't get through and the next day it stops, like a train hitting a concrete wall.

Les Dilley and I had met Brian Eatwell, a designer friend who came to Elstree Studios and asked us to work on *The Last Remake of Beau Geste*. It was to be directed by Marty Feldman and filmed in Ireland and Spain. He needed me immediately and as the dressing on *Star Wars* was really finished, I was the one to leave first. They were fracturing the main unit into different units on Twentieth Century Fox's orders, to finish within fourteen days. The sets that were left were all covered and under control. George wanted a larger white corridor for the main opening scene where the rebels battle the stormtroopers and we first see Darth Vader. This corridor was made up from cast elements and there was very little dressing required, a few pipes running along the ceiling, otherwise it was not like the *Falcon*. A few of my large drainpipes were set upright in the airlock areas and painted white but really I didn't have to worry. Also the gun ports where Han and Luke were fighting were already covered. Norman had drawn these up to work as the gunners swung around firing, all based on WW2 gun ports and adapted into the *Star Wars* look. So I agreed to be the first one to go from the main team and help the budget cuts, which Gary and Robert needed to make.

John came to me on one of these last days and thanked me profusely. He was about one hundred thousand over in his construction budget. But he told me that by inventing the way of using so much scrap and junk and found material, I had brought my set-dressing budget in almost a hundred thousand under budget, so his entire total worked at about where it was meant to be. Certainly my ideas about creating the weapons from older guns had really saved a lot of money.

Quite frankly these last weeks were pretty much a blur, and reading the interviews of the time and the account in Jon Rinzler's wonderful and comprehensive book *The Making of Star Wars*, it seems everyone went through the same experience. Gil Taylor was sick, we were running ahead of the unit as sets had to be ready, and right on the back of the rushes being approved, the sets filmed on were torn down or revamped into something else.

I do remember the San Rafael effects team came over to see George and Gary and go through what they had done, and what they had to do. I was with them on the *Falcon*'s exterior stage, where they were blown away seeing it full size. They laughed, as it came to light then that John had scaled up their model to design it from. They had used aircraft model kit parts and one part was a mistake, but it had become a part of the *Falcon*'s exterior forever. This was some polystyrene that was not meant to be part of the structure. Speaking with Joe Johnston he surmised that he had pulled off a piece of model kit he didn't think looked right, and we had recreated the shape of the glue left behind; in small-scale model form it looked like part of the ship. Aged down and painted no one ever noticed. I just loved how impressed these experts were by our spaceship.

Harrison and the other actors were disappearing fast. I went around saying goodbye to everyone; it was one of the more difficult films to leave because I was really attached to this world and to George, Gary, and John Barry. I sadly said goodbye to George and Gary. Poor George hardly had time to think, he looked absolutely drained, but as a director you just have to keep going on and on. (Not long after the strain of the last few months caught up with him. George was so exhausted that he was admitted to hospital for a weekend with severe chest pains. He was fine physically, just beyond exhaustion.)

It was hard to say goodbye to John Barry—we had really been through a lot. He too was exhausted, both by the weight of hours he had worked but also the mental strain of the politics that were constantly aimed at him. It's tiring defending oneself all the time and also constantly repairing the false politics and accusations that keep coming from elements on the shooting stage. But John was a survivor. He was excellent at politics and was able to keep his head and ours above water and clean, despite all the shenanigans that had occurred. George to this day still values John's support on this film and his unwavering dedication to him.

Peter Dunlop, my stalwart friend and buyer throughout, was also getting on a plane to Madrid to join me on *The Last Remake of Beau Geste*. Les would stay to the end of the *Star Wars* shoot and then come out. So I parked my car in the underground parking and disconnected the battery—it would stay there until I returned from Spain in a few months' time—and a production car took me home. I didn't have time for mourning or feeling the usual withdrawal symptoms after an intense movie—I was on a plane the next day and into the madness to follow…

STAR WARS SUMMATION

After George added the special effects and color-timed the film, the result looks as George intended, a space Western, and despite the difficulties he created, Gil Taylor's inherent professionalism came through. The film looks well photographed. Gil Taylor recently stated in an interview before he passed away that his one regret was not getting to know George better on *Star Wars*, a frank admission that he had very little communication with George. In fact in the same article he states that at the first interview with George and Gary he wondered why on earth they had hired him, he couldn't see the connection from *The Omen* to a space fantasy. The connection was clear: George did not want *Star Wars* to be made the way science-fiction films were made before, showing off the sets and props and costumes, all designed to be what designers imagined future worlds would be like, all clean and plastic. George wanted and achieved a natural look for *Star Wars* as if the world existed for real, and we had simply gone and made a film in it as if on location.

Many people tell me they prefer this first *Star Wars* film to the others. I think the Western style, the positive emotional content and deep connection to mythology of the hero's journey, and being the first film ever to introduce such spectacular effects to tell a story helped a global audience to connect in huge numbers. The style of the film, with sets and props that were real and not looking sci-fi designed, definitely helped an audience connect. The underpinning of classic mythology set in an epic space fantasy world with heroes and heroines and evil lords, set the box office alight for families hungry for a film to go to as a family. These underlying themes connected at a deeply spiritual level to the audience who, though they didn't know it, were very hungry for this. It is clear when looking at cinema in general—the movies that have connected like the great legends of old did are *Star Wars*, *Lord of the Rings*, *Harry Potter* and *Avatar*. All are deeply concerned with myth, retelling the ancient fables.

Joseph Campbell was right, in creating *Star Wars* George showed he is the one true mythologist working today and has created a new and lasting legend in cinema as popular as King Arthur. The huge success of *The Force Awakens*, so reverently made, respecting George's vision in *A New Hope*, is proof of how enduring the world of *Star Wars* is.

MARTY FELDMAN'S *THE LAST REMAKE OF BEAU GESTE* AND THE SEX PISTOLS

Before leaving, I had gone to meet Marty Feldman in the drafting office, where John Beard was drawing up designs for some of the sets. Marty explained some of his ideas, which were pretty funny and fitting to his crazy sense of humor. He had cast Peter Ustinov, whose character had a wooden leg, so on a legionnaires' march Marty wanted his horse to have a wooden leg also. The movie starts with a spinning globe of the world, and in the tradition of movies from the thirties and forties a finger points to a map of Africa on the globe. We cut to the desert and the finger sticking into a dune and then legionnaires marching. When the finger is pulled out the legionnaires fall in the hole.

The script was full of gags like this and I knew right away it was going to be a huge ordeal for the art department. Also, Marty was coming up with ideas all the time so we would have to be adaptable and ready for anything. With our experience to date Les and I were used to this, especially working with designer Philip Harrison who was a long-time friend of Brian Eatwell's. They had both come from the BBC, and worked in a more unstructured way than the traditional designer's route of working their way up.

So I signed on, despite being exhausted; the chance to keep earning money and work on another interesting movie with many problems to solve suited me. It was also a chance to work in Spain, a country I loved. Ireland fascinated me as well, a very mystical and beautiful land full of myth and magic. We had to film on the west coast in Limerick; the coastline there is recognized as one of the world's most beautiful spots.

So I found myself on a plane heading for Madrid to meet the team. Bernie Williams was the line producer in charge of the entire production. He had set up the production base in a house in a suburb of Madrid and we all stayed in hotels nearby. We hired a wonderful young Spanish assistant called Benjamin Fernandez, who would make it very easy for the transition to working in Madrid. He knew all the best people and suppliers and solved any problem we threw at him. I sat in the office in Madrid and made my usual breakdowns of what we needed and discussed budgets with Bernie. Once I had done this and set up the early stages of prep in Madrid and got everything in motion, I flew out to Dublin to sort that out there and have a look at the locations.

I spent the next few weeks on planes, virtually commuting between the two countries as we had so much to get made and dressings to be sourced. It was easier than *Star Wars* because the film was a period piece and the dressings required could all be found and rented, but there were still a lot of special props needed. One scene Marty had created was the drawing room of the mansion where the adopted Beau Geste grew up. We had rented Adare Manor, a stunning Gothic mansion in Adare in western Ireland. It needed modernizing and repairing but the building, a stately home standing for four hundred years, was full of Gothic towers and wonderful paneled rooms. I could use everything already there, but in the hunting room for the movie, Marty had written his own visual joke. Alongside the usual moose heads and hunting trophies like stuffed lions' and tigers' heads mounted on plaques, Marty had written in an entire range of animals as a visual gag. These went all the way from large elephants' heads down through dogs, cats, mice, rabbits, guinea pigs, all manner of domestic pets, and little birds too, like sparrows and blackbirds and starlings.

So I had to deliver all these; that was my job. As shooting was looming and Marty wanted what he had written, we had no choice but to deliver. Marty Feldman found it extremely difficult some days and enormous fun on others. Designer Brian Eatwell and our small art-department team were there solely to support him and make his movie happen, but he took a strangely defensive path with everyone as shooting progressed. He smoked from morning to night, lighting each new cigarette from the embers of the last one. I think he got insecure about his own movie. It was his first directing gig and he was also starring in the movie. Directing a movie of this size is not easy to start with—the load on the body and mind is just massive—then add in playing the leading role where everything hangs on your performance and the fact that comedy is the most difficult of the cinema arts to get right.

Marty was following Mel Brooks' example, but Mel had had time to build his reputation and experience. We carried on as normal, making sure every set was as amazing as the last. Brian Eatwell was a very involved and supportive designer and worked as hard as anyone. Also, Marty had good producers on board in William S. Gilmore and Howard West who were all extremely supportive to him, and Bernie Williams was a great line producer, highly experienced. Later Marty said in an interview that he thought he should have stayed in Hollywood like Mel Brooks and made the film there, but that was never an option on his budget. To film ancient British mansions, foreign prisons and African locations and deserts with forts and outposts, Spain is the natural country to film in, and at that time very, very cheap and with great crews available.

Spain is a wonderful country and I am still happy every time I go there, having explored much of it over the years. It is no wonder *Doctor Zhivago* was able to film so many different countries there and *Lawrence of Arabia*—it has such diverse locations. So in the end it was the right choice for *The Last Remake of Beau Geste*. Marty's slapstick-style comedy was unfortunately left behind by the success of the Monty Pythons and their domination of comedy, and in America by Mel Brooks who caught the public's attention with his movies.

At the end of the film I spent three days in the Canary Islands, sleeping in my room and sunbathing in the warm winter sunshine, before returning to England. I was so exhausted that I needed to do absolutely nothing, so I retreated from the world and ordered room service for three days and slept and read. That was it, my rest and recovery period before returning to London for Christmas.

It wasn't long before the phone rang for me. It was the *Life of Brian* producer John Goldstone. He offered me a very difficult project and I listened carefully as he delicately tried to lure me in. He was producing a project for Malcolm McLaren, the Sex Pistols' manager, called *Anarchy in the UK*. He introduced into the conversation that the legendary American director Russ Meyer was directing it, was in London and wanted to meet me. He really wanted me to design the film for him.

I was not sure about this. Russ was famous for his movies like *Beyond the Valley of the Dolls*, and *Faster, Pussycat! Kill! Kill!* among other movies he had produced and directed. His forte was to cast women with enormous breasts, like Edy Williams who he married, and that became his signature. I actually really liked his movies, they are cult classics, but wasn't sure that this was the right move after *Star Wars* and the serious movies I had been so involved with like *Akenfield* and *Mahler*. Then there were the stars of the movie, the Sex Pistols. They were at their most obnoxious zenith at this time, upsetting the entire music industry after having a hit with 'God Save the Queen' and they were out to cause havoc everywhere they went. It was actually a brilliant marketing strategy by Malcolm McLaren, who engineered the entire success of the band. He cleverly caught a revolutionary wave that he spearheaded with the Pistols, as music turned from the sixties behemoths into anarchic chaos.

Robert Lee, my oldest friend and also my lawyer whose law firm Lee & Thompson handles a good deal of the music scene, had refused to deal with the Sex Pistols in his own office when he was a lawyer at entertainment law firm Harbottle & Lewis. He had been asked to do some contract work for them at the time. The Sex Pistols had a reputation for eating cans and cans of tinned tomatoes at business meetings until they threw up, a rebellion against what they considered were boring establishment meetings they were forced to attend. So Robert, being well aware of this, made the meeting somewhere else. He warned me about them and their behavior, but at the same time I was thinking the film could become a cult classic... Robert Lee became well known when he got the record deal for his friend Brian Ferry and Roxy Music signed. Brian Ferry thanked Robert on their first single, 'Virginia Plain', by writing the lyrics, "Make me a deal and make it straight all signed and sealed, I'll take it. To Robert E Lee I'll show it. I hope and pray he don't blow it." Brian added the E because British lawyers are not allowed to advertise in any way.

John Goldstone was very persuasive and after several phone calls convinced me to go and at least meet Russ at his apartment in Mayfair. I thought it would be interesting to go and meet this legend, not sure what to expect as I drove there.

I parked near Sloane Square, and was met at the door by Russ, who reminded me a little of the wonderful Karl Malden. He turned out to be a highly intelligent and fascinating man, deeply devoted and passionate about film. To make his movies he had even built a house that could be turned into a studio. This house was situated in Los Angeles right under the Hollywood sign, an ironic statement as Russ is credited with inventing mass-market soft porn. His living room was really a disguised studio room to shoot in. He could pull back the dividing walls and the room converted into a studio. He had his own lights and cameras and did absolutely everything himself, from script to shoot and lighting to editing and sound. He was a true one-man band, and then he distributed himself, so he was able to make his movies his way without any interference. (His films have since become even bigger cult classics. Quentin Tarantino is reputed to have based the idea for the *Kill Bill* movies on *Faster, Pussycat! Kill! Kill!* and cites Russ Meyer as a driving influence behind his directorial work.)

John Goldstone's ploy worked in getting me to meet him "just to say hello" as Russ really loved *Star Wars*. We spent hours that afternoon discussing movies. Then we went into *Anarchy in the UK*. His ideas were intriguing and he also liked the suggestions I came up with. Before I knew it, John had a contract under my nose and was paying me to design the movie. The script was actually very good; it was written by the acclaimed critic Roger Ebert, and was hilariously funny. I thought the combination of the Pistols with Russ was another flash of genius on Malcolm McLaren's part.

Russ and I drove around London looking for locations and planning out designs for the sets. One day we were driving down Kensington Church Street; it was early evening and Russ spotted an Italian restaurant. He begged me to stop so we could eat, as he loved Italian food. I pulled in and as we got out I said I should hide my camera case that I had bought on *Star Wars*, as it would get stolen. He was crossing the road and said, "It'll be fine, don't worry—we'll be quick, I promise. I'm starving."

We finished plates of pasta and going outside we went to continue on with our recce. To my horror I saw glass all over the pavement by my car. Russ was also horrified as he stared at the back window of my car, which was smashed in—my camera was gone. Russ never forgave himself. I tried to tell him not to worry, I would get another, but he insisted he would buy me a replacement; he had special deals in Los Angeles. I explained about London as we continued to look for locations; that you just could not leave anything, it was not safe—even in the higher-class areas like Kensington. It was my fault, I should have taken it in with me. Lesson learned.

Malcolm McLaren decided that he needed a studio where they could keep the Sex Pistols under control. Bray Studios, the legendary home of the Hammer House of Horror movies, was deemed ideal and it was free to rent the entire space. Malcolm McLaren planned to move in there with them when we were filming and live in caravans, so they couldn't ever escape. He had planned it all out. There would be guards with them and they'd lock the gates at night and keep them imprisoned. Many of the great Hammer films were filmed inside this wonderful old mansion house with a famous staircase, which has been featured in so many Hammer classics like *Dracula* and *Curse of Frankenstein*.

We set up an art department and went to work. I hired John Beard as my assistant. I designed all the sets, which John then drew up, and hired Peter Dunlop to source all the dressing and props. As it was a long drive from London I found a cottage for rent nearby when looking for locations to film in. The cottage was in the grounds of the manor house on the banks of the River Thames that was the inspiration for Toad Hall in *Wind in the Willows*. It was a beautiful estate, and I was lucky to be chatting with the gamekeeper when he said they wanted to rent out the cottage. I was negotiating to buy a flat in Earls Court at the time, and this served as an interim place to live, was close to the studios and avoided the rush-hour drive out of London every morning.

I had some fascinating interiors to design. I created a Dickensian-style orphanage and changed it into a nightclub. We managed to source some classic Victorian iron beds that I placed around the walls for seating. I created arms coming out of the walls with the hands holding lanterns. The walls were based on John Box's Victorian canals from *Oliver*, with the same damp appearance and patinas. My experience from *Oliver* really came into play and we aged the wooden floors and walls to look like a Victorian orphanage. I created interesting graphics for the club that looked like Victorian workhouse signs.

We completed all the sets, including council-house interiors and canteens, all sorts of real environments. A set I loved that I came up with was a record industry CEO's office. Russ had a scene where the Pistols threw the CEO through a huge stained-glass window, so I had Mick Jagger's face created in colored glass around fifteen feet high. It was written as an anarchic act against the establishment and what the Pistols considered old-school rockers.

We were all ready to go for the first week of filming and the movie was then retitled *Who Killed Bambi?* by Roger Ebert. Russ went on location and shot a day and a half's footage of the killing of a deer for the opening of the movie, which can actually be seen on YouTube on Jonathan Ross's 'Incredibly Strange Film Show' episode on Russ Meyer. I had supplied the crossbow and they managed to find a dead deer on location to use for the scene. Russ came back to London and as we were getting ready to roll in the studios—Malcolm McLaren fired him. According to Russ in the interview with Jonathan Ross it was because Malcolm didn't want to give up any part of the rights for an investment, he wanted to keep it all for himself. Whatever the truth, Russ was fired and disappeared overnight. It was a great pity, I thought; it was obvious this would become a genius cult movie with him at the helm, and it was a perfect combination. Russ seems to be confused himself as to why he was suddenly on a plane home and writes about it in his autobiography, still upset as you read his explanation of what he thought had happened.

Russ turned out to be an honorable man. A few days after he returned to Los Angeles a courier package arrived at my home. Inside was a brand-new Nikon F camera and accessories. Added was a thank-you note from Russ and a goodbye message. That camera stayed with me for twenty years, and was an absolute warhorse. Sadly, a thief broke into the house and stole the Nikon and its lenses, the loss far more that it was a gift from Russ than the value of it.

Another American director, Jonathan Kaplan, arrived who had made a film called *White Line Fever*, and I was introduced to him. I walked him round the sets, and the ones he liked stayed. It is always a very delicate situation as one defends the last director's position often as a lot of preparation work and discussions go on based on his vision and the script. Here was a totally different director, about to rewrite everything. I sensed trouble brewing. Jonathan and I got on well enough, but he was different, not so cinematically educated as Russ and not so auteur-like. He had a kind of Texas truckers vision, which is where *White Line Fever* came from, a cool movie for its day, fast, full of action and crazy.

Jonathan's film has also become a cult movie but, being a totally different kind of director to Russ, I had to go along with what he wanted, whilst trying to stay on budget in discussions with Malcolm. He wanted to change everything else and we were wrestling with this new vision when suddenly the movie was canceled.

Many rumors exist surrounding this. I recall an incident that I believe was the truth behind Twentieth Century Fox pulling out. I was reading the newspaper at home and saw an article on Princess Grace Kelly, who was married to the King of Monaco. She had been appointed to the board of Twentieth Century Fox. She stated in the interview that everyone presumed she was merely a token member of the board, but it was quite the contrary, she was going to take her position very seriously. She said that she was going through every project Fox had on its books to give her opinion. I drove into Bray Studios the next morning and went straight to Malcolm's office. We were still then only a few days away from the main shooting in the studio, despite the upheaval over a new director. I put the article down in front of Malcolm, and said to him, "Have you seen this? We're dead."

He read it and got on the phone. Within a few days the film was canceled. Princess Grace was linked by marriage to European royalty, and I think the album cover with the Queen on it with cut-up letters across her face and the lyrics relating the Queen to fascism was just too much, so it's possible Grace wielded her influence and canceled the movie. At Bray Studios we pulled down the sets and went home; sadly, as I thought with Russ Meyer directing it would have become a cult movie, and it is always difficult to see creative work go to waste.

MONTY PYTHON

John Goldstone was soon on the phone again; Monty Python's *Life of Brian* was starting up, financed by Elstree and its chairman, Lord Delfont. I was asked to go and meet Terry Gilliam and Terry Jones, who were co-directing the film at the time. I had met the Pythons before in West Hampstead when they had wanted me to design their previous movie, but by the time the finance had come through I was contracted on another.

I guess you could call them the true pioneers of the modern-day comedy series and I loved their work. I don't think anyone can underestimate the impact they had at the time. In London on a Thursday evening, which was the night each new Python episode aired, the streets were visibly emptier as everyone was inside watching. I remember one night racing up Tottenham Court Road—I was working on another movie at the time—and the street was absolutely devoid of cars. It was eerie, as if the apocalypse had finally descended. Seeing the time was Python time, I just pulled over at the nearest pub and raced inside. Most pubs had the TV on and Python airing on it, so I watched the episode there.

We had a very Python-esque first meeting in a flat in West Hampstead on West End Lane. This was actually a continuation of Abbey Road that the Beatles made famous with their walk across the pedestrian crossing outside the studios. Getting to the meeting I found Terry Jones wandering around in the street looking for samosas. He asked me if I had seen Michael Palin, but I hadn't. He looked up and down the road, confused, as if I had the answers to Michael Palin's disappearance. "We must have samosas," he said. He was on a hunt for them and was not about to give up. I pointed him to an Indian up the road that I knew as I lived locally there for quite a few years, and asked where I was going for the meeting. He showed me the door to the flat and disappeared up West End Lane on his samosas hunt.

He returned with a large, brown, grease-stained bag filled with them. We all ate the greasy goodies as we chatted about their new film and my experiences so far. A lot of banter and laughter went on, and they were very apologetic over what they thought were the miserable efforts they had made so far with impossibly small budgets. I told them that they were funny, the budgets didn't matter as long as it worked, and in a way made them funnier. They literally couldn't afford horses, which is where the coconut shell idea came from; these were used in the radio sound-effects department to create the sound of horses' hooves clattering on pavements. That's become part of Python folklore now and shows how once again budget constraints can make one push the envelope and be creative.

I read the script of *Life of Brian*. It was a first for the Pythons as it was a complete story, and I thought it was really good. Funny and epic, a real challenge for a designer. I met up with the two Terrys and John Goldstone at John's office in D'Arblay Street. John had produced all the Monty Python movies, and Tim Hampton, who was the associate producer and line producer, was with him. We went through the film with them and the requirements. It was described as epic but the budget wasn't, of course, and I made some suggestions as Tunisia had been the location chosen to film it. They asked me a lot of questions about working there and what we could do. I was hired on the spot. With Tim Hampton the line producer we discussed the possibilities of shooting all the Roman sets in the ruins in Carthage and in Monastir, an ancient fortress town next to Sousse. Italian director Franco Zeffirelli had just wrapped *Jesus of Nazareth* there, and all the big sets were left standing. I also suggested Matmata as I thought the area around the caves would serve for the crucifixion scene. Terry Gilliam had noted the strange location on *Star*

Wars, so it seemed fitting we would go to Tunisia and do a recce.

Charles Knode, who designed all the costumes on their previous films, was also hired. We found out that all the costumes and props from *Jesus of Nazareth* were in rental houses in Rome, and could be rented very cheaply, saving us thousands of pounds. It was not a high-budget movie so once again we had to do what we could to make a shoestring epic. There was also a scene in the movie in a Roman coliseum and we decided to go to Arles in France on the way to Tunis to see the one there. It is perfectly preserved and has full three-hundred-and-sixty-degree seating. One could film without any major construction.

Terry Gilliam and I began sketching out ideas for the sets. We spent time in his studio at home in Hampstead, a treasure trove of reference material. Terry collected anything that caught his eye that he could use for his animation sequences, especially anything unusual or bizarre. We began looking at artists like Piranesi, who had a unique view of ancient Rome in his drawings. He was obviously intrigued by the massive scale of the buildings they constructed, contrasted with the narrow streets and alleys of Rome. His was a contemporary vision and, being relatively undeveloped at his time, was a view of exactly what Rome must have been like. Following Piranesi's genius, Terry loved the idea of creating massive-scale sculptures and buildings alongside the normal-scaled living dwellings.

Over the next weeks we did an enormous amount of preparation work on *Life of Brian*. Terry Gilliam, Terry Jones, and I decided to go to Tunisia to look at the locations and see if the huge set of the interior of the Roman Forum that Zeffirelli had left behind intact in Monastir would work for us.

When we landed in Tunis there was a strange atmosphere in the air and many soldiers with guns at the airport. Terry Jones got really nervous, and had a fight with the security officer as he was going through the checkout, his voice rising in tone as he confronted the ridiculous demands of the officer. He was sent to the back of the queue like a naughty schoolboy; the look on his face was exactly that as Gilliam fell about laughing as if a Python sketch was being enacted in real life with us all involved.

We checked into the hotel amidst a lot of security and discussions about what had transpired a few hours earlier. There had been a major shooting in the Kasbah, the large old market area of Tunis. These are a labyrinth of market stalls that run for miles and where everyone goes to buy everything or anything you could ever want. A lot of people had been killed and the army had imposed a curfew; after 9pm no one was allowed on the streets until the morning.

For some reason the two Terrys had got it into their heads to go to a restaurant out of the city and despite the curfew decided that's where we had to eat. We all left the hotel and piled into two chauffeured cars, which drove us out over a bridge to the restaurant, a good half hour away. It was really great food, I think our local producer had strongly suggested to them that we go there, and the lure of great food to both Terrys was something not to be ignored. We were talking and telling stories and having fun as one does with these masters of comedy, when the drivers kept saying we must go. None of us had ever been in a curfew before, so we ignored them and continued as we were, eating and having fun. We wanted dessert, and we were going to have it. Eventually, the drivers' anxiety got to us—they kept looking at their watches and interrupting us with more and more angst: "Please to go, please to hotel." Then came the order, we go... now! Tim Hampton, who speaks fluent French, then understood.

So we paid and bundled into the cars. The driver looked quickly over at us as he spun the wheels and accelerated fast away from the restaurant. "Please hold on tight, we have twenty minutes to get to hotel."

Terry Jones was in a relaxed mood. "Oh, we'll be okay," he said. "What can happen?"

The driver looked at him in the mirror. He spoke slowly and clearly in broken English with a French accent, "Anyone in the streets after 9pm will be shot."

That made us sit up. "What do you mean? We are tourists!" Terry laughed. "We'll never be shot."

The driver looked back as we left the ground flying over a small bridge. The car lurched and its tires bounced as they hit the road and screeched as they found their grip again; we must have been doing eighty miles an hour now. The driver didn't smile, he looked really nervous. "Doesn't matter who it is, after nine o'clock they are shooting anyone on the streets, army has taken over. We have to get there so hang on." Our knuckles were turning white now as those on the outside gripped the handles to steady themselves as we flew over potholes and dusty roads at between eighty to ninety miles an hour. We realized we had to make the journey that took us half an hour going in less than twenty minutes back.

We raced through streets that were fast becoming eerily empty as people got themselves indoors. As we hit the outskirts of Tunis it was getting tense. Tanks were rolling into the streets and soldiers were appearing everywhere with guns. Now we were worried. The tires were screeching as we raced round corners and we were thrown together. We were all nervously checking our watches as the minutes ticked down. As we raced through the main streets to the hotel, no one was left but us. Soldiers were looking at us as the car raced into the street where the hotel was situated. It was one minute to nine as the car screamed into the front parking of the hotel, and we jumped out and raced for the door. It was exactly nine as we got through the doors; the second car was right behind us. Inside we all went upstairs to the bar and looked out the windows. The street was empty, deserted. Just tanks rumbling through and stopping, the gun barrels sweeping the area. Soldiers with guns were also searching the area, patrolling. We heard shots—someone obviously had chanced it and paid for it. It was pretty scary.

The curfew lasted a few days, so we got out early the next morning and drove to Carthage to visit the Roman baths and ruins. These were extraordinary and amazingly well preserved. The Romans built them so that the various heights of the baths flooded with seawater and because the water was different heights the sun heating them created different temperatures. One could see the plumbing and water pipes they had made. They were so cleverly designed; these stunning locations must have been amazing in their day. We could easily adapt them for the film, and the Tunisian producer said we could film there no problem.

We went for coffee and pine tea in the famous Café de Nattes in Sidi Bou Said to see that famed area of Carthage. Every building in this beautiful little city on top of the hill is painted white with blue shutters and doors; that's the rule there and it's religiously obeyed. The deep azure-blue Gulf of Tunis, part of the Mediterranean Sea, surrounds the hillside on both sides, and with its exotic palm trees and Moorish roofs, it's a paradise. The café sits right at the top of a steep cobbled street. Inside it's a typical Moorish café; large square stone plinths covered in carpets are all there is to sit on. When we went, there were canaries singing in cages all over the ceiling, and locals in djellabas sitting around smoking hookah pipes.

We wandered around looking at the narrow streets, photographing ideas before heading back to the souk to bargain for gifts and take photographs of the market streets and stalls for reference.

But as the evening hour of nine approached we made sure we got back inside the hotel to safety. We watched the tanks rolling into the empty streets around us and soldiers armed with guns sweeping the area for strays again.

The following morning we left early for Sousse. It was another crazy drive, just like I had endured many times on *Star Wars*, but now it seemed worse. Terry Jones remained wide-eyed as trucks bore down the center of the road at seventy miles an hour, straight at us. It was a new experience for the two Terrys as these monsters billowing black smoke drove nearer and nearer. Most of them looked pretty old, but were dressed up like Indian trucks with chrome bits and religious paraphernalia. Our driver always waited to the last minute before diving off the road onto the dirt shoulder, once again raising plumes of lung-coating dust before swerving back onto the road when the monster had passed. Terry Jones took no comfort from the carcasses of smashed cars and trucks littering the side of the road.

Barreling down the long, straight Roman road, the driver was going as fast as he could; there was nothing but road for a good hundred miles. Finally a shape became apparent in the distance. I smiled, as I knew what it was: the Roman Amphitheater at El Jem that we were going to stop at and recce. It is the third largest amphitheater outside of the Coliseum and as one approached it slowly got larger and larger. It dominated the tiny town, a few small houses and a café spread around it. Terry Gilliam was excited. We had driven straight into a Piranesi drawing; the contrast of scales was exactly what he loved. We looked at the amphitheater and though Terry loved the size of it, it needed far too much work to make it look new, as it would have been in Brian's time. We bought lots of coins so we could duplicate them later for props.

In Sousse, the massive set left by Zeffirelli proved to be a godsend to us. It was a huge complex and extremely well finished and detailed. The Italian painters are fantastic, especially at duplicating marble and stone, and the sculptors were able to make realistic-looking statues and moldings. There was a wonderful mosaic floor too. We decided it would fulfill all our needs for the Roman forum interiors, and looking under the set I saw that the floor was raised about four feet off the ground on scaffolding. We just had room to get the Revolutionary People's Army under there, and by cutting a hole in the mosaic floor we could have them appear. All of this made the scenes possible on a scale we had only dreamt of, as construction costs would have been far too high to build the requirements from scratch. The Forum set had been constructed right next to the ancient ribat, a vast Muslim fort, which had the potential of being used for a lot of the scenes in and around Brian's home.

We walked across and into the impressive ribat. It was on a huge scale and well preserved in places. Looking around we found most of what we needed for all the scenes in Jerusalem. The high wall on one side could be used for the writing on the wall scene when Brian is punished. I explained that it could then be revamped, and by building a Roman portico we could build the platform for Michael Palin to play the stammering Pilate, and have a huge crowd below reacting. We found cells for the prison scenes.

There was an older part that was not so well preserved and by creating a window we could shoot the exterior of Brian's house and Terry Jones' famous speech to the crowds below, wanting the messiah. There were also plenty of rooms and balconies to create scenes for the revolutionaries, and other courtyards we could use for other scenes required. I found a place where we could build the market scene and have streets any time we needed them.

It was an incredibly positive day as the scale and variety of locations in one place was fantastic. We looked at the city walls and gates behind the ribat and they also worked for us; with a bit of dressing they could easily be returned to biblical times. We had the gates into the city to make, and the stoning scene ("Jehovah, Jehovah!"). All were easily doable around the ribat; it was so vast and had different vistas. We photographed everything and took measurements to draw up ideas for the sets.

These two locations meant that at least eighty-five to ninety per cent of the film could be made here, so we drove the two kilometers to Sousse to take a look at the hotels as nothing was available in Monastir to accommodate a film crew. Sousse is a very big tourist holiday destination, right on the sea, and that meant there were many hotels there.

These were built right along the golden beaches, so the production could easily be based nearby—and what a great place to be located for a crew. We then recced a hillside just out of the town. This was a deserted, scrub-like desert, and this would do really well for the crowds heading for the town of Bethlehem. Nearby was a greener area with trees where we could place the 'three shepherds at night' scene, for the opening. So we had everything covered if Matmata would work for the crucifixion scene.

Next day we drove on to Gabès and stopped for lunch. I took the two Terrys to the Ex Franco Arab the Third restaurant we'd enjoyed regularly on *Star Wars*. They all loved this simple roadside restaurant with paper tablecloths and the best calamari and chips ever. Refreshed and happy, Terry Gilliam drew doodles on the paper tablecloths. (If the owner knew what was coming he would have kept them and framed them and sold them on eBay.) We drove the twenty-five minutes up into the hills and Matmata. I was reminded as we drove into the area just what an amazing location this was. These vast holes in the ground covered a huge area. Some were crumbling and broken and a few, like our *Star Wars* location and the ones functioning as primitive hotels and a restaurant, were intact. I showed Terry the one we had used for *Star Wars*. The dressings were still there, and the moldings we had added around the doors as they fitted in. It was less damaging than removing them and the owner had requested he keep them, as he liked what we had done. (A fortuitous decision as it happens; he is now a major Tunisian visitors' location and trades off it very well with the legions of fans who go around seeing all the *Star Wars* locations.)

Each film has its different requirements and for *Life of Brian* we looked at the broken-down and more ruined holes. Some of these holes had been really neglected and had caved in, and these are the ones that caught Terry Gilliam's eye. They were like Gothic ruins with collapsed stone entrances and very much like some of his drawings. We settled on one for the crucifixion scene after I had inspected the ground around it to ensure we would be able to dig in the crosses and make them safe.

Returning to the UK via Rome we met up with costume designer Charles Knode. I went to look at the prop houses where all the props and dressings from *Jesus of Nazareth* were stored, and Charles searched through the costume houses where they had kept hundreds of costumes from the series. Almost everything we needed could be rented, and being Zeffirelli everything was made to historically accurate detail—what a bonus, as it was far cheaper than making it. Charles found enough costumes to do almost everything for the film; this was a massive find for him. Tim Hampton found out that it was a simple overnight ferry ride from Genoa to Tunis and was used all the time by the Italians for film materials, so this trip turned out to be highly cost-effective for us. We were low-budget but after this trip we were satisfied we could make an epic out of the script, way bigger than anyone had envisioned we could.

Terry Gilliam and I wandered around Rome at night looking down narrow alleyways at the vast out-of-scale Roman buildings that are all over the city. I had spent months there earlier in my career working on a film with David Niven called *The Statue* and had stayed on after the movie wrapped to explore the city in full. It's a remarkable city at night. Unlike London's neon glow of over-bright street lamps everywhere, Rome's ancient cobbled streets are often lit by a single yellow glow from a lantern high on a wall. It makes the city romantic. I remember the first time I ever visited the Trevi Fountain was at 1am. This was before the ugly glass curtain walls were erected around it. As we came on the fountain, a couple in evening dress and dinner suit were dancing in the water. Obviously inspired by *La Dolce Vita* they had decided to follow in Anita Ekberg's famous footsteps.

Back in the UK, all was going really well. Terry and I assembled all the photographs and began drawing up all the plans for sets to create exactly what we needed. Using Piranesi as our main reference and other Roman architecture books we were creating ancient Roman buildings and the city of Bethlehem exactly as we wanted them to be. Working with Tim Hampton on the budgets, we allocated what we thought we would need, and having found so many riches in Tunisia we had an easier time making the vision required for the small budget of four million dollars (again). Peter Dunlop came on board as the production buyer and we began sourcing what we would need to take with us. John Beard was also hired as the draftsman and assistant, and was busy drawing up plans of the sets.

Terry Gilliam had a studio in Neal's Yard in Covent Garden and we decided to build the spaceship interior there as we could fit it into the first-floor studio. It had a loading dock leading onto the small cobbled yard below, so we could winch anything we needed up to the area using the old lift contraption that was still hanging outside.

We went through exactly how to create the flying sequence when Brian gets rescued in the spacecraft. We had to create him flying through the meteor shower, and we decided to do it all ourselves as it would be more fun. Below ground level Terry had the animation camera and stand where Kent Houston created Terry's animated sequences and tabletop animation, so we had him to go through technical explorations with.

At the same time as we were preparing *Life of Brian*, Ridley Scott had been given *Alien* to direct through Sandy Lieberson for Twentieth Century Fox. They had set up production at Shepperton Studios. Michael Seymour, who had designed commercials for Ridley, was chosen to production-design the movie and Les Dilley went on board as art director to supervise the actual set building and construction, based on his experience on *Star Wars*. I knew Ridley and Les wanted me there, but I was locked in by contract to the Pythons. The time came for us to go to Tunisia and begin prep, as we had quite a lot of set building to do. Terry and I had done as much as we could to prepare and everything was packed up into boxes for transport to Tunisia. I was preparing all this on the Thursday, ready to leave the following week, when I had an auspicious phone call. I was asked to go to see John Goldstone and Tim Hampton at the office in D'Arblay Street in Soho.

As I entered the office I could see that something was amiss from the subdued and somewhat glum looks on everyone's faces. John and Tim were both looking serious and depressed, so I expected the worst. We had been working together for several months, and John was always bright and funny. I knew there was trouble brewing as Lord Delfont, whose company, EMI, was financing the movie, had finally read the script. John and Tim explained to me that he had pulled out overnight, deeming the script blasphemous, and could no longer be associated with it, leaving the movie with no funding. He felt like many other people did, that parodying Jesus was derogatory to the Christian faith. We always argued back that our film was about *Brian* of Nazareth. John and Tim explained that they were going to try to replace the money as quickly as possible but were not sure how long it would be. We were all shocked, of course, as everything was arranged and ready to go that weekend.

They had been aware for a few weeks that Ridley Scott really needed me on *Alien*, which had started preparation at Shepperton Studios. My experiences on *Star Wars* and the used look achieved with the dressing in parts of the *Millennium Falcon* was similar to the look Ridley aspired to for the *Nostromo,* but no one knew how to do it there. Indeed, calls had been traded that morning as news was getting out about *Life of Brian*'s demise. But I had agreed to design *Life of Brian* with Terry Gilliam, and having worked really closely with him, the visual genius within the Pythons, he wanted to keep me on board as I had done so much work on the film, and we shared the same vision.

Tim and John proposed a solution. They put me on a small retainer as they were convinced they could find the funding for *Life of Brian*, and they had some funds from the EMI deal left over to carry them through. They explained that they really did not want to lose me as we had done so much preparation work, and both Terrys were comfortable with me. The aspirations Terry Gilliam and I had on the creative side were enormous, and it would take considerable skill and experience to pull it off. Having worked so recently on *Star Wars* in Tunisia was another boon. They didn't know the timescale involved in raising the rest of the budget, and they knew I would go straight onto *Alien* if Ridley still needed me, so giving me a retainer secured my continuity with them. Then when and if they could retrigger the movie I would return to the *Life of Brian* fold. I accepted, of course, as I was really enjoying the work on the film, and I could see the enormous potential of the movie.

ALIEN

The moment I left Tim and John's office I got a phone call. It was Ridley Scott, telling me to get my backside down to Shepperton, right there and then, so I drove straight there.

I first met with Garth Thomas, the production manager, who I knew from *The Last Remake of Beau Geste*, and Ivor Powell, Ridley's associate producer, who I knew from the commercials I had made with Ridley and Tony Scott. They introduced me to Gordon Carroll and David Giler, who were really keen to have me aboard. I had a quick discussion with them about how I made my set-decorating department work on *Star Wars*. They asked me if I was free and could I start immediately as art director and be in charge of the dressing side of the movie. I was happy to do this and went to say hello to Ridley, who was locked away storyboarding, carefully illustrating each shot in the movie using his very precise storyboard frames we called 'Ridleygrams'. Looking at H.R. Giger's original paintings placed around the walls in Ridley's office, much larger than I thought they'd be, was amazing. I liked his work and to see originals close up is always a more tactile experience. With the vision of Giger's paintings in my head, they gave me a script and put me in a room alone to read it. I read it through in about forty minutes straight—it read like a bullet train. The script was stripped down and bare, the drama was all there, clean as a razor, and I could see what it could be under Ridley's powerful eye. The story, like a claustrophobic horror nightmare, really piqued my interest as I like the horror genre when it's done well. Here it was unique, having been combined into a science-fiction tale, a simple and powerful story like the ten little Indians all being contained in a space adventure inside one ship, a really clever idea. It's interesting to me how many of the crew hired to work on *Alien* didn't get the potential of the script and doubted the film would be any good. (Even the model makers, used to science fiction, explain in their documentary interviews on the *Alien* makers' site how they all thought the script was weak and pretty bad. None of them knew Ridley except for his commercials, and could not see the potential about to erupt.)

With the massive success of *Star Wars* taking them all by surprise they needed another science-fiction movie to follow on. This package, with Walter Hill originally at the helm and Gordon Carroll and David Giler producing, was intriguing enough for them to make the movie. It was never a B movie as so many people say it was. I guess the stripped-down script could resemble one of the Italian spaghetti horror films being made at the time. In the hands of a less visionary director who would simply film the script as it read, it might have turned out to be a B movie, especially filmed in sets that were more to do with the way science-fiction craft were made before *Star Wars*.

Even so, with Ridley at the helm as an unknown director to Fox with just his film *The Duellists* to go on, and despite Sandy Lieberson's strong endorsement knowing he could put powerful images on screen, Twentieth Century Fox were still unsure of the film being more in the horror genre and R rated. I think they were wondering if *Star Wars* was a one-off phenomenon. Being an unknown genre and an R-rated movie, the sales estimates were not high; they told me at the time the budget was set at around four and a half to five million dollars when Fox said they would first make the film, and for this ambitious project that was about half what was needed, exactly as it was for *Star Wars*.

I went back in to see Ridley and looked at the paintings of the alien. There was the movie right there—the colors and sensual shapes mixing body parts and sexual organs with pipes and sinews; they were deeply disturbing and would bring a new and powerful creature into the horror arena. Glancing through Ridley's storyboards, I could see immediately the detail of the corridors and airlocks, and the color of Giger's paintings became the inspiration to me for the overall color to aim for with the dressing. Ridley's sketches are very precise if you know how to read them. The designer Ridley had hired, Michael Seymour, had worked on many commercials with Ridley over the previous years. Ridley had hired Peter Hampton, another of his television commercial designers for his first film *The Duellists*. *The Duellists* was a stunningly beautiful period epic, and despite being made on a shoestring budget looked amazing. But for *Alien* Ridley needed a totally different approach.

The disappointment of not leaving for Tunisia that weekend had vanished due to the prospect of helping to make this amazing project. I knew I was in for a tough few months, though—this was almost more daunting a prospect in the time and budget allocated than *Star Wars*, and on *Star Wars* I had had no reference point to gauge what could be done or not in the time allotted, just a fierce determination and blind faith to succeed.

Ridley explained that he wanted to get the used look of an industrial cargo freighter for the *Nostromo*. He'd had Michael build the layout of the craft over two large Shepperton stages that linked together. This was designed that way to enable Ridley to open the movie by tracking around an empty ship, through corridors and crew quarters, past the infirmary and onto the bridge. This gave the exact impression of the famous galleon, the *Mary Celeste*. She was found drifting in the ocean with all of the crew missing. A ghost ship sailing along on her own that had struck a chord with people everywhere and which has since become an urban legend.

Ridley was determined to begin the movie tracking around this silent ship, so wanted the set built as a complex, allowing him to track through it in one go. Then as the ship suddenly woke up it would bring a tension to an audience not sure what to expect next. The advantage of having the craft built for real as a complex meant you entered into the corridors and felt trapped inside, like in a submarine. This would naturally create a sense of claustrophobia, an element that would help Ridley create the tension required to really scare the audience later in the film. Once inside the craft, there was no way out.

The basic frames of the *Nostromo* sets were already built and the octagonal corridors and airlocks were like wooden skeletons snaking around the stages when I came on board. The corridors needed dressing now to turn them into a real spacecraft. The use of scrap had worked on *Star Wars*. Having invented the technique with an inherent knowledge of how it would eventually look when finished had given me a unique talent. Ridley was dependent on getting this look right, of an industrial, used spacecraft, looking like a 'truck in space' as he described it. Also on board was art director Les Dilley, and he knew what was needed as he had gone through the *Star Wars* journey with me. *Alien* was a different look to *Star Wars* but needed the same techniques to achieve the reality Ridley aspired to.

Star Wars was pure fantasy but set in a real world and filmed that way by George. *Alien* had to be a hardcore industrial reality. The crew were bickering workers basically, trapped together inside a space submarine. If this world could be created the film would work. The reference Ridley and I talked about when I met him that day were the *Millennium Falcon*'s interiors. The crew quarters in particular were like an ancient barnacled ship, and I would have to cover every inch of it with pipes and machinery and greeblies. This is what Ridley wanted. The *Nostromo* was more military in its look than the *Millennium Falcon*, but the same feeling of reality was required. What was different was that the entire world of *Alien* took place inside this ship, except for the brief section where Kane, Dallas and Lambert leave the craft to explore the alien craft on the planetoid, and discover the eggs. So it was enormously important to create this claustrophobic world with a crew trapped on board a working spacecraft, and for the first time on film make it totally realistic and acceptable to an audience.

This was more than exciting to me; it was like another dream come true. To be paid to create my dreams and aspirations of how I saw ships in space, guided by Ridley's master hand, was a gift from the stars.

Michael Seymour had hired Ian Whittaker as the set decorator. I knew Ian very well as we had made *Akenfield* for Sir Peter Hall and Ken Russell's *Mahler* together. Ian was truly brilliant at period films and conventional dressing (his talent was widely acknowledged when he went on to win an Academy Award for *Howards End*). But I knew Ian would be hard-pressed to work with airplane scrap and know what to do with it. I read science fiction, collected graphic novels and was familiar with the work of most of the science-fiction artists—it was a world I understood. Ian was up for anything, though, and similar to me in the way that he just got stuck in and did the work to the best of his ability, and never complained about long hours or missed suppers. Ian had art-directed many films for Ken Russell and had to cope with extraordinary demands made by Russell, who pushed his fantasies onto the big screen, and Ian always came through. I knew I would have a reliable ally on the floor with me.

Michael Seymour was already doing a stellar job interpreting what Ridley wanted with Ron Cobb and Giger's design influence. Having built the *Nostromo*'s corridors and interiors into a massive complex spreading over two stages, now it all needed to be dressed. It was getting that look that Ridley had seen in parts of *Star Wars* and adapting it to the *Nostromo* interiors that was causing Ridley to be a little concerned. Michael had hired a very inexperienced assistant into the art department, who had somehow convinced him he could do what I did and was in charge of buying all the scrap for the dressing. The assistant had never actually worked on a movie before. Michael had sent him out to buy as much junk as he could find over a few days. This was assembled in the props areas, but it seemed to me that no one knew exactly what to do with it when I got there. None of the dressing had actually been started or tried anywhere, so making it all look like a working ship was the next major phase and that's where I came in.

I walked round the sets with Ridley; the wooden skeletons of the corridors and airlocks in their basic construction stage were built like a spider's web. They gave a strong impression of how the *Nostromo* could end up. I described in detail how I created the reality look for the *Millennium Falcon* on the *Star Wars* sets, and how I had come up with ideas for all the action props. But *Star Wars* was an escapist fantasy aimed primarily at a young audience; *Alien* was to be a horror film, a mix of *2001* and *The Texas Chainsaw Massacre*, with a dash of *Star Wars* thrown in. Ridley instinctively knew *Alien* would work if he could get the same used and totally reality-based atmosphere that *Star Wars* had. This was necessary for him so the actors would become an organic whole with their environment, and one would never question the story's authenticity. We had to take the audience on a journey inside a working spacecraft.

Claustrophobia is a proven method to get the tension required to get an audience on edge where there is no way out and they are being chased by a monster. Combining that horror genre into a sci-fi environment was a really historic leap of creativity in the film world. I assured him that I could give him that look he wanted. Fortunately for me I could understand without a lot of explaining.

I walked straight over to the art department to meet designer Michael Seymour and Les Dilley. Les had a unique skill because of his experience in being able to translate complex two-dimensional drawings into three-dimensional sets. This was especially pertinent where sets like the Space Jockey were concerned, and the exterior of the alien craft. Based on Giger's paintings they were formed of bone-like structures and soft contoured walls and floors. Not a straight line in sight. Les knew exactly how to prepare the drawings from which the modelers sculpted clay formers.

Les Dilley and I had our tasks on *Alien* clearly defined as the two main art directors on the movie with our *Star Wars* experience. Les looked after the construction side, as he had done on *Star Wars*, especially the soft Giger areas, and I was overall responsible for all the interior dressing and look, the weapons, and action props. Peter Voysey, who was the best modeler working in the film industry, alongside Liz Moore and Brian Muir, was on board working very closely with Les. He sculpted the pilot and the alien and other landscapes, and also worked closely with H.R. Giger when he came on board in Shepperton. Sadly, Liz Moore, the brilliant young sculptress we had on *Star Wars*, died tragically in Amsterdam when the car she was in crashed. It was a very sad loss; she was a really bright and talented woman.

When Peter had sculpted the set piece full-size, molds were made for casting the finished pieces to assemble together to create the huge sets. The casts were made in plaster and fiberglass, a truly difficult procedure when they are as complicated as these were required to be and on such a large scale as the Space Jockey and alien spacecraft. It was, however, the easiest and cheapest method of fabricating sets to the scale required, relying on centuries-old techniques. This way the panels could easily be cast off in batches and duplicated, then assembled in repeat patterns over the large-scale sets. Les was in charge of all this aspect of *Alien*, the 'Giger world' part as we called it.

Michael was already hard-pressed under the work strain to keep up. It was the same situation as *Star Wars*, and the pressure was on Bill Welch the construction manager, who had come across with Les Dilley. Bill was doing his usual, smoking heavily and worrying. The prep time was an impossibly short eleven weeks due to the budget restraints that Twentieth Century Fox had imposed on the film, but everyone was supporting Ridley in getting his vision to the screen intact. Just as *Star Wars* was totally undervalued in the original estimates of revenues due to the lack of box-office history of science fiction, *Alien* suffered the same lack of confidence. Despite the overwhelming success of *Star Wars* for Twentieth Century Fox, *Alien* was a completely new and risky genre for them.

Though there were in fact only three main set complexes—the *Nostromo*, the alien planet, and the exterior and interior of the alien craft—they were massive, intricate, and highly complicated sets. The *Nostromo* complex and other sets took up most of Shepperton Studios' stages. The alien planet and interior, the landing leg and the famous pilot set were so massive they had to be built on H Stage, one of the largest stages in Europe at the time. Giger's designs for the alien craft's interior and exterior were unlike any spacecraft ever seen. Organic in nature and developed from his paintings of auto erotica, they were unique as Giger used an airbrush technique to fuse women's and men's sexual body parts into soft machinery-like shapes. It's well known that the three vent openings in the exterior of the alien craft are vulvas, and the alien head itself needs no words to describe its origins. The alien creature was developed from his painting *Necronomicon IV*, and adapted by Giger under Ridley's vision to become the unique monster required for the film to work.

The art department had their work cut out for them and Peter Beale, the managing director of Twentieth Century Fox UK, was keeping a tight rein on art-department spending and the overall budget. Already way too small for the work required, Ridley was adamant in keeping his vision intact and adding more sets he really felt essential to the plot, whilst Peter Beale was ordered to cut costs and was trying to cut the script down. So Michael and Les were working round the clock with a small art department at the core.

Michael Seymour talked at length with me about all his requirements and problems he perceived. Les and I looked at all the drawings they had prepared and the skeletons of the sets already built. I explained again to Michael exactly how I went about the dressing process, and what we needed. They had tried to emulate what I had done, and Michael explained that the assistant he hired had bought in two jet engines amongst other junk. I told him that for a way smaller area on the *Millennium Falcon* I had bought in at least ten jet engines and ordered more and more as we broke them down. The sets eat up the dressing to get that encrusted industrial look. I told him we would need miles of different-sized PVC drain piping and fixtures to create ducting along the corridors. I could see the bridge alone was a monster.

My working mantra has always been 'don't complain, just get your head down and do it', so hitting the ground running was not a problem for me; as I told all the students I mentored, dive in the deep end and you'll survive. It was as exciting to me as those first days on *Star Wars* and I experienced the thrill of entering into the unknown creatively, yet at the same time feeling as if I had entered a world I belonged in. Having seen Ridley's storyboards and looked at Giger's designs for the alien, it was obvious this would be an amazing film. Ridley has a unique and rare visual talent, and through his camera this would be a new and visionary movie in a genre I loved. So to be able to be part of a first again, another pioneering experience in filmmaking, got my creative juices flowing overboard.

I tried to make everyone aware that during the dressing process, as the aircraft parts and piping and wiring are layered in, it looks like nothing until the absolute final days, so an amount of trust is required. Then when it is painted to unify it all, dressed with Letraset symbols and identification codes and detailed with specially made props for the actions required for the sequence, only then does it suddenly emerge almost magically into a believable interior of a spacecraft. Aging this all down is the icing on the cake that will make it live.

I explained to them the problems of the time that it had taken to dress the sets for the *Millennium Falcon*. The bridge of the *Nostromo* was at least ten to twelve times larger than the cockpit of Han Solo's craft and way more complicated. It would have seating for a crew of six, each with their own console and flight-control equipment to pilot and navigate the ship. There was to be a large navigation area at the back, where a lot of meetings would take place in the script. Around this were grid-like walkways to move around the cockpit. Beyond this in the front section was a walking area and more wall space that had open cupboard-like areas. Then behind the control section was a large area with the navigation table, again surrounded by grid walkways. Beyond this the walls were compartments and storage cupboards designed to hold all the computing equipment.

I walked back through the skeleton-like framework of the set complex being built and looked at the computer room, called Mother's Room. I was relieved to see there was little dressing required here, even the central control console to access Mother and the control chair were designed and built in. What a relief—one set that didn't need my attention. The entire room was a mass of Christmas tree-like lights set into in cream-colored panels in the walls and ceiling, denoting a pure and sterile environment. It was the special-effects boys and the electricians who had the nightmare of wiring all these up to be practical, as Ridley wanted those to be the light source.

As I was walking back to see Ridley in his office and the producers, it became even clearer to me why Ridley had called me down that very day. Ian Whittaker, the set decorator, came across to see me the moment he heard I was there. He rushed up, said hello, and then said, "Thank goodness you are here." Ian was totally honest and knew me well enough to speak his mind. He told me he had no idea why they had hired him. "I am fine with dipping curtains in tea to age them," he smiled, "but I have no idea what to do here, especially with all this scrap." He was a brilliant dresser, totally committed to the movie he was on, no matter what it took, the hours it took, and though this hardware-oriented movie was a little baffling to him, he was plunging in headfirst. He had had to come up with some innovative ideas for Ken Russell but it was never for science fiction, and certainly not on this scale. He asked me to educate him in what to do and was happy to get on with it with me, and support me and learn. Movies are a team effort, we all have to play the same violin, and Ian was highly experienced and dedicated and knew what was needed.

I met with the inexperienced assistant, and looked at the scrap he had bought, and where he had tried to emulate the same dressings I had created on *Star Wars*. I could see that he was very uncomfortable with me being there; I guess that I threatened his position in his eyes. It wasn't the case, I was not there to threaten his position, just use my experience. I was hired in the position of art director with Les so I was in effect his direct boss, and I was hired with the mandate to oversee the entire look of the interiors and the dressing side of the art department, and get it done. It was very quickly clear to me that he simply lacked experience and over the next few weeks it became increasingly clear that he was also very unwilling to learn anything, until things came to a head.

STANDBY ART DIRECTOR

No one wanted to go on standby as the on-floor art director who controlled the shooting on a day-to-day basis. The work entailed sorting out anything that was required or needed doing immediately for filming. Michael had told me it was open if I wanted it. I don't think many people like the pressure of being on a demanding set all day. You were there from early morning until shooting wrapped, and then working to prepare for the next day with the team. I understood from the quite nasty directors of photography I had sometimes encountered, and similar directors, that it could be a thankless task, but not here with Ridley and Derek Vanlint. I also knew Ibbo, Paul Ibbetson, the first AD.

Planning to direct myself, I knew the experience of being the standby art director on set beside Ridley every day would be an invaluable experience. It all depended on the dressing being finished and under control. So I offered to do it, as for me this is where the heart of filmmaking lies, and it was a way to learn and experience it firsthand. I loved that kind of pressure on the floor and solving problems fast, as the one rule was never to hold up shooting. I knew the load I would be under was going to be a tough one. This would be seven days a week, and really long hours. I relished the pressure to come; it was a rare chance to make two movies in a row that I felt creatively in my blood.

I was told years later when I was given a reading by the very great Vedic astrologist Chakrapani that I should do two films at once. He smiled and told me I surpassed under pressure, and the more the better. He looked at me, laughing. "Even make three at once—you are one of those rare people, the more pressure the better they do." But I laughed at him; one movie at a time's hard enough.

I shook hands with Gordon Carroll and David Giler, the *Alien* producers, spoke to Ridley and joined the production on the spot. Gordon and David Giler welcomed me with open arms and seemed hugely relieved that I was there. *Star Wars* had become a massive success and the look of the film was talked about a great deal. As a huge bonus, especially for me, Ron Cobb, the illustrator, was working with the team in Shepperton. I soon became friends with Ron, and going through his concepts for the movie I could see that they were outstanding and a huge help in visualizing the sets. The drawings he had done for Ridley for the bridge were really detailed and expressed Ridley's desires to make it like a bomber interior. Some of the earlier concepts had first made it look open and ballroom-like, more like the feel of the early *Star Trek* movies, but that was the opposite of Ridley's conception.

DAN O'BANNON

Dan O'Bannon was there in Shepperton when I joined the team, and was involved in a few of the meetings I was at. He was designated by Walter Hill to be in charge of design after they had rewritten his and Ronald Shusett's script over a few drafts. We had all appreciated Dan's movie *Dark Star*; it was innovative and funny and having been made on a real shoestring was pretty impressive. Dan seemed to survive on cola and cigarettes and lived in the dark, even covering the windows at home with newspapers, and maybe that fueled the claustrophobic atmosphere of *Alien* that was such a large part of its success.

Much has been written about Walter Hill's involvement and rewriting it when he was originally directing it. He most certainly brought a hardware-fueled attitude to the script, and made Ripley a woman, a cinema-changing act that has empowered women action heroes since to take center stage. For sure to have a film this strong requires a very good original screenplay. Dan O'Bannon created the *Alien* idea and slaved mercilessly at the story with Ron, and it's their original script that made *Alien* so unique an idea. Ron Shusett takes a huge credit for inventing the facehugger and inspiring the chestburster scene. The chestburster scene made *Alien* a hit in a way, and has since become recognized as one of the most seminal scenes in modern cinema history.

Dan was working on various aspects of the production when I was there with Ron Cobb, and it was Dan who introduced Giger to Ridley in what in hindsight was a masterstroke of design genius. Dan was helping with computer material for the playback on the monitors as he had done on *Star Wars* at ILM. He was suddenly sent home, though, by David

Giler, for something to do with copying computer printouts. There was a blanket of security around the movie as there had been on *Star Wars*; everyone was paranoid about any detail getting out to the press. I was too busy to really take much notice at the time; sadly Dan had simply disappeared one day. He and Ron Shusett were great friends and an interesting duo to talk to when they were together.

In *The Book of Alien* by Paul Scanlon and Michael Gross the very first heading in the 'making of' section are my words, "It's just a monster of co-ordination." Researching this chapter and looking back, these words are pertinent indeed. This was how I described the work on *Alien* to Charlie Lippincott when asked at the time in interviews with him. Charlie was employed to create a book on *Alien*, and I knew him from *Star Wars* as he was doing the same then, documenting the making of.

The second day working on *Alien* I arrived early at the studios and Ridley had organized a screening of *Dr. Strangelove* to try to get the design crew to understand the look he wanted. Michael Seymour came to me, baffled after the screening. He asked me, "What does Ridley mean when he said he wants the bridge to be like hair? I don't understand his reference to hair." I explained: the bridge was to be like the B-52 cockpit, jammed with switches on every surface, like they are in the film, every inch of space around the pilot and co-pilot covered in switches and controls and instruments. We had to create the same look, but for a spacecraft. Every surface was covered, a little like the crew area I created for the *Millennium Falcon*. It was a way of trying to create a visual reference, as it is difficult to explain when there are no references or precedents.

I explained to Ridley and Ivor how I had trained the prop men under my longtime associate, charge-hand dressing prop Joe Dipple. I had shown them how to break down jet engines and scrapped airplane parts and recognize shapes and pieces, and then how to place them. Ridley and Michael asked me what I needed and I told them that as time was so short rather than try to train new people we should hire Joe Dipple and a couple of his prop men. It wasn't just the breaking down of the airplane scrap, but the placing of it in the set that really mattered.

Ivor and Ridley hired them immediately, and they came down to Shepperton and started work with me. I went to the prop and dressing team and discussed what we would need in supplies, and that it was to be obtained quickly. We needed a lot more engines to break down, and a lot of airplane switch panels, navigation instruments, control units, and pipe work. Also we needed to source the right scrap for this, and we would need a great deal. Fortunately it was still very cheap. I put the art-department buyer Jill Quertier in touch with our *Star Wars* buyer Peter Dunlop and he gave her all his contacts to help her source more.

The assistant was in charge of buying the scrap, and wanted to maintain control of it, but I was worried. He clearly did not want to listen to what I was saying, and still defended his choices. When I explained to him again what we needed scrap-wise, he argued with me and defended everything he had bought, saying he knew best how to do it. Knowing that time was really short to get the sets ready and there was not a minute to lose, I pulled rank on him and ordered him to do what I said or face the consequences. Not a great way to start, but the film is the ego and I was not about to let Ridley down, which I could never do, whatever the cost. Making a movie like this under budget and time restraints requires a massive team effort. It was an auspicious meeting. I told him exactly what was needed, and that was it; he was to go get on with it because there was no time to argue.

NICK ALLDER AND BRIAN JOHNSON: SFX

Brian Johnson, an innovative and skilled special-effects master, was hired by Lucasfilm to replace John Stears for the sequel to *Star Wars*, *The Empire Strikes Back*. Brian was incredibly experienced with model shooting as he had worked a lot on Gerry Anderson's television series like *Thunderbirds* and *Space 1999*, as well as being one of the best special-effects heads in the UK. Ridley really wanted him for *Alien* so Twentieth Century Fox did a two-picture deal with him and Lucasfilm to start *Alien* and then jump across to *The Empire Strikes Back* when pre-production began. Brian hired Nick Allder to work alongside him and to take over *Alien* when he finally had to leave for *Star Wars*.

Nick was an invaluable part of the team. As an effects designer and supervisor he is without exception one of the best. Nick had the same attitude as me—do it, or find an alternative. The more complicated an idea he was thrown, the happier he was. He could solve immense problems with his team. Soon after *Alien* started pre-production, Ridley, knowing Brian's amazing contribution to model building and shooting on the *Thunderbirds* and *Space 1999* series, sent him to Bray Studios. All the exterior models of the *Nostromo* and the mothership were to be built and filmed right after the main unit had wrapped shooting. So Brian went over to Bray and Nick took charge of the main unit.

One cannot underestimate the influence Gerry Anderson's puppet series had on science-fiction movies. The models and the filming of the ships and exteriors were groundbreaking. Series that developed from *Thunderbirds*—*Stingray*, *Fireball XL5*, and *Space 1999*—were revolutionary, and the latter has become a cult classic. Often derided at the time because of the use of puppets and characters like Lady Penelope all dressed in pink, in their way they influenced the making of *Star Wars* and *Alien* in terms of the detailed model-making and shooting of the craft exteriors. My first ever try for a job in the film industry was with Bob Bell, the designer of all these series. I managed to get myself an interview and he showed me around the sets, which were amazing and real. I desperately wanted to be a part of the production, but the series was winding down, sadly for me. Brian Johnson and Bill Pearson were both working there then, garnering valuable experience to bring to *Alien*.

I set up a meeting with special-effects head Nick Allder, the special-effects department, and the electricians. We would need to make up a large number of electrical panels that could fit into the console sections in the corridors and the panels in the bridge set. As we wanted them to be practical and to look right to match the dressing we were going to do, it would be a very large task. Nick Allder suggested we put Guy Hudson, Roger Nichols, and Dennis Lowe onto making them; they had been working on different areas in his department, and understood what would be needed. We agreed that they would make up two samples to show us, using different designs to see which worked the best. They went away to search the airplane junk for suitably interesting pieces that George christened greeblies on *Star Wars*, and Nick's workshops had mountains of gadgets and suitable switches. We were going to have to buy in hundreds of small lights to fit into panels in sequences, and I wanted them wired to switch panels so the actors could work at their consoles in a real way. Fortunately we had done a lot of research on *Star Wars* for lights that were small enough and didn't generate too much heat, as that was always the main problem on film sets.

I spoke to Michael and Ridley and the producers about Roger Shaw. I had needed someone on *Star Wars* with an artistic and engineering capability to head a prop-making department, sorting out the scrap and identifying which pieces could be used where and making up specialty pieces. Having convinced Frank Bruton to start Roger on *Star Wars* with me as a special prop maker, he had excelled at this and developed the technique, so I had no problem in convincing the producers on *Alien* to hire him. Roger had really developed a new key position on *Star Wars* as a prop maker who understood how to create action props and dressing requirements from found objects plundered from the scrap.

So here I was, art director with a larger team under me, with less time and a far bigger load than *Star Wars* in a way. We were contained in one massive spaceship. While working out a plan for the bridge set, I was also planning in my head what to get and how to make work the military-style infirmary and the canteen area, which would come up for shooting very fast behind the bridge set. There were also a lot of action props to be prepared and approved by Ridley, so I was also listing these out and thinking about them. My days were really long. I left the apartment at 7am every day and rarely got home before ten, seven days a week… again.

While we continued building the sets and developing the set dressing at breakneck speed, Ridley was casting the roles in the film. Mary Selway and Lucy Boulting were the UK casting directors. By coincidence my old friend Mary Goldberg, who I stayed with in New York when I first visited America with my actor friend Chris Plume, was casting *Alien* in America for Ridley. Mary was the casting director for the highly prestigious Joseph Papp director of the Lincoln Centre theater when I first met her, and she really knew her actors.

She had found Sigourney Weaver, who had only done one movie before but had been doing stage work in New York. Mary highly recommended her for the part of Ripley. Ridley thought she was exactly right for Ripley: she was both beautiful and athletic and would make a strong leader amongst a group of pretty macho men. He really felt he had found his Ripley in Sigourney and wanted her in the role above everyone else. Fox wanted a bigger star in what was really the leading role as she was the one who survived. Ridley remained insistent on her as she was so right for the part and had agreed with Fox that they fly her over to Shepperton Studios and he film a screen test with her.

Ridley didn't want to shoot the normal actor's test. This is usually filmed against a wall with a potted plant in a studio. They get the actor to turn this way and that, and talk, but really it gives little indication of what the actor can turn into when in character. Ridley decided to have a special section of corridor built for the test, and also for us to create a hold area, so he could film her in action as if hunting the alien.

Talking it through with Ridley and Michael, Ridley felt the best way for everyone to understand how the look of the *Nostromo* interiors could evolve was for me to prepare the test corridor for real. That way I could create the look of the *Nostromo* that Ridley had talked about and sketched out in his storyboards. They could all see exactly what was involved and the time it took to complete the dressing. Also it would give a very good idea of exactly the right scrap we would need, and what exactly to buy from the airplane junkyards.

Ridley and Michael Seymour agreed I should take charge and start work on the section of corridor for the test immediately. Bill Welch, the construction manager, had already constructed the skeleton frames of these corridors and other areas of the *Nostromo*. The *Nostromo* corridor was more military-looking and by making the corridors from a standard element that could easily be duplicated, it saved a huge amount of cost and also looked authentic. This is how it would be done in the real world. Safety and the cost of construction would be the major considerations for any type of craft, and the octagonal-type structure could withstand the atmospheric pressures of long-haul space flights. In between each section were handholds built in, so that any crewmember passing through could grab on in case of turbulence.

Ron Cobb created illustrations for designs for the corridors. He had an inherent engineering understanding of the requirements for space travel and its hardware. They were designed in sections with angled panels that we would cover in switches and lights and all manner of small technical gizmos and pipes to encrust them. I could visualize that once they were painted in a dark shade of military green and aged down they would look amazing.

I took Joe Dipple and the crew to look at the scrap that the assistant had bought and the problems started to surface immediately. Some of it was salvageable, but it was obvious it had been bought without experience and consideration of how it would break down to be used for dressing. I

ALIEN

tried to explain that it is not as simple as buying any scrap and sticking it into a set and expecting it to work, but that there are serious disciplines involved and procedures to follow. You start with the basics, like pipes and larger pieces, and add in to it in layers. Every piece has to be placed with logic behind it, as if it's a real working craft. We are asking an audience to believe they are in a craft and never to question it.

I had Jill buy us quite a lot of the various diameters of the plastic drainpipe we had used so copiously on *Star Wars*. There were small holes in the design of the corridor sections, both along the ceilings and the walls, where I could run piping. This would look exactly like ducting to carry liquids around the ship, and also for all the electrical wiring that one could imagine would be there by the mile to run a complicated craft like this on space journeys. Also I had her go buy more suitable scrap for us. She was in contact with Peter Dunlop and sourcing all she could find for us. As Ridley needed the test corridor built as fast as I could, I also ordered the assistant to do the same.

I went to see Nick Allder in the special-effects workshops and went through exactly what we required. He was also under huge pressure because of the time constraints. His team was really hard at it and his workshops were crammed with all manner of hydraulics and pieces of equipment that would be needed to build parts of the *Nostromo*. He had a large team assembled, and they were working like dogs to try to get ahead of a seemingly impossible task with a shooting date looming. I needed a really great-looking big gun for Sigourney for the screen test, so we discussed ways to create one from found objects.

Ridley wanted Sigourney to look really tough, in a way playing a masculine role but as an attractive woman. The team making the corridor panels showed us two versions. One like *2001* with a few switches and lights linked by Letraset lines and graphics. The second was covered in switches linked to lights and with pipes and pipe connectors built in and small, interesting airplane pieces tucked into it. That was the *Alien* look, so we chose the latter. I could see their reaction as it required way more work to make them up, and we were going to have to make a huge number for the corridors and the bridge set. They agreed, though—the latter did look really good, encrusted as Ridley had envisioned, like 'hair'.

With a structure built to create a length of corridor, Ridley had the idea to build a hold-like space alongside it to create a kind of lower pen in the craft. Jill had bought in a lot of PVC-molded crate palettes exactly as we used on *Star Wars* to use for the corridor floors and other sets. They were painted red when they were manufactured and we repainted them green, black and gray depending on where they used them. Shaped like grids, they were perfect to use for all the floors in the *Nostromo*.

Painted in the ship's army-green color, they were indistinguishable from a metal grid floor and also gave Ridley the opportunity to underlight them when needed.

For this hold section of the test corridor we left them painted red. Bill quickly assembled wooden formers to support them; they were placed upright into the walls to look like metal grid sections. They were also laid on the floor to make it look like a grid passageway and on the ceiling as well. It was a cheap way to make a hold area, and stood end-on-end looked fantastic. The corridor and the hold area created two *Nostromo*-like environments for Ridley to shoot an action scene with Sigourney for the test.

The floor grids were laid down first in the corridor set and then we began the process of dressing the walls and switch panels. From carefully selecting the junk they had already bought and continued to buy, Joe Dipple and I sorted out switch panels and interesting-looking aircraft panels like navigation and cockpit units to add to the ones Dennis Lowe and crew were making. Also I found scrapped calculators, office machinery, any other really useful components, which we had discovered worked so well for us on *Star Wars*. Jill bought a lot of the same small switches and lights. I placed these in repetitive patterns on panels that we set into the corridor walls themselves and around the consoles. We got the electricians to wire them up so that we could light them in any sequence we wanted; small glowing lights like this really give a craft the appearance of being alive and functioning.

Finally, it began to look like the real thing. The next process was to make it assimilate together as if it was designed and engineered for trucking interplanetary mineral runs and had been worn and aged on its many interstellar journeys. All the dressing was carefully sprayed in the *Alien* metallic-green color, which immediately unified everything.

Any form of functioning machinery, like pipes carrying liquids after long periods of constant use, creates aging and leaks and stains. I had the painters duplicate this in certain places along the corridor. We also sprayed an aging kind of mist over the red crates in the hold area so they looked more like metal gridding. It's amazing how quickly well-painted aging suddenly turns a corridor full of junk and scrap into a spacecraft corridor that has seen many trips across a universe. The technique I had learned from John Box of adding paint powder into wax polish came in really handy.

Michael Seymour had assembled a huge store of sheets of Letraset, both lettering and numbers, and had made up a lot of special sheets of Letraset with various sizes of the *Alien* winged symbols on it in the greenish color. These we rubbed on in various places where it looked correct. Then, taking sheets and sheets of Letraset, we created numbers under many of the switches and pipe outlets. Most working machinery has these so that one can identify the pipe in case of an emergency or when one needs replacing. It adds authenticity. Some of the Letraset had computer-type graphics and these were carefully placed as well. It took ages to do, but really helped integrate the working machinery into a cohesive look.

Finally we used wax polish with fine particles of metal mixed in to give an authentic patina in places. I used to make fiberglass casts of objects like apples and pears when I was an art student. I mixed into the fiberglass bronze or copper metal particles that made them look strangely real but metal. I showed the painter what I wanted by grabbing a rag and the wax polish we used and adding in dark brown and black paint powders. All of this was time-consuming. The test corridor took a couple of weeks to get right at least. Even then I was always adding and fiddling until Sigourney arrived. I took Ridley down to the finished corridor and felt his relief as he walked through it. The corridor looked authentic, the dark-green hues and aged metal pipe work making it look like a complicated piece of machinery that had seen better days in many long-haul flights collecting ore and transporting it back to Earth.

With the little lights working and oil drips placed in, I knew we had found the look of the *Nostromo*, and Ridley felt that too. He was finally beginning to see that his vision was coming to fruition.

Ridley filmed Sigourney, dressed in an army jumpsuit, hunting the alien under different lighting scenarios. Nick Allder had cobbled together a mock gun and we dressed it to look the part. Adding backlight, or simply lighting her through the shafts of light through the crates, was a chance to see how it might work for the below-decks cargo areas.

Ridley filled the hold area with his signature incense smoke to diffuse the atmosphere, a look he'd used on *The Duellists* and many commercials. Though illogical in a spaceship, it worked. If something works, if it looks right, then the rule is: use it. The props burnt the incense in their bee puffers, softening the look on the set as it works in three dimensions, unlike a simple filter on the camera lens, which softens everything in the foreground and the background with the same diffusion. Smoke is far more natural as it is dimensional.

The corridor scene was a chance to watch Sigourney as a crewmember at work in the *Nostromo* corridor. With the low ceilings and the pipes and dressings running the length of the set, it did look like a spacecraft, except for the windows, which I felt lost the idea of the claustrophobia. Giving Sigourney switches she could operate and functioning bits of machinery, it looked like she was at home, not an actress trying to make something feel real.

Sigourney was very good in the tests, and the powerful strength of an independently minded woman and leader was all there. Sigourney showed the strength, intelligence and vulnerability that Ripley needed, so no one would question her authority as she took over the reins of control on the ship. She was obviously attractive but being tall and athletic made her convincing. Here, for the first time, we had the privilege of getting a brief glimpse of a new breed of action hero, a woman in peril who could fight her way out of a situation and win, and the audience would believe it.

There was originally an idea that Ripley and Dallas had sex, an element that often seemed to be added into Hollywood scripts, I guess to satisfy the execs at the studios that every base was being covered. Ridley had hired an actor for the test, and this scene was one of the pages from the script tried out. It was there to show the boredom of long-haul flights across space, and also that with seven people isolated together for months, a sexual relationship could easily happen. The scene and any intonations of it were dropped from the final film, for the better in my opinion, as it would have placed a small dent in the tension that was building from the first frame. More pertinently I think it would have somehow weakened Ripley's credibility as the emerging leader and ultimate heroine of the piece.

Watching the test later in rushes I was studying the colors and density of the dressing and how it had worked. I could see where to go with it, especially seeing how Ridley had brought his amazing stamp to the visuals. I remember someone who knew him well at the time telling me that Ridley had a camera for a head; he somehow instinctively knew exactly where to get the best shot from every time, and how a color scheme worked best. This is true.

After seeing the rushes I knew we were onto something. It was a huge relief seeing these tests and knowing what we could now aim for, not just to me but also to Ridley and the producers and Michael Seymour.

Ridley made the decision to remove all the windows to make the corridors more claustrophobic. We could now go ahead and dress all the corridors in the *Nostromo* after experiencing what it took to create the test corridor, with the knowledge that it would take time and that we would burn through a lot of airplane junk and PVC pipes. I showed Dennis and the crew that we needed more switches and encrustations of lights and pipes to make it look real, and they went away to set up a kind of factory to duplicate them and the large number required.

This screen test can be seen on YouTube, the *Alien* Quadrilogy anniversary edition and the Blu-ray release. It gave me the chance to show everyone what we could do with scrap to create the dressing, and how to go about it. It was a great training exercise and served its purpose really well. Sigourney looked so strong in the test that Alan Ladd, the president of Twentieth Century Fox, signed off on her (after asking all the women in the screening what they thought).

Soon after I started, H.R. Giger came to visit, arriving at Shepperton with his girlfriend Mia, who acted as his assistant. He came to look at all the designs and to sculpt original models for the facehugger, the alien eggs and to look at the baby alien ideas. He was just going to visit at this stage and go back after a couple of weeks. I think he felt that being away from home and his studio for months would not suit him. Like most major artists he prefers seclusion to being in large teams of people.

But once he got involved in the movie with us, saw the scale of the work, the commitment to the look and feel of *Alien*, and the passion of the team making it, he decided to stay with us and help firsthand. It was to be a huge bonus for us, as he could then help with the alien landscape that Michael and Les had to create on H Stage, as well as the alien itself and all its many components.

We set Giger up with his own private and secluded workshop on one of the stages by building him a sectioned-off area using the wall panels used to build film sets. Here he was uninterrupted and he could work alone as he liked. Ridley felt the best way forward was to have Giger create three-dimensional models of the sets for the alien planet, the alien itself and the facehugger. I spoke with Giger to find out exactly what he needed to make this happen. He told me he needed real bones to sculpt these scaled miniatures of the sets with, and lots of them. He also needed all the usual sculpting tools and materials to create the miniatures, like modeling clay.

Getting bones didn't faze me. From past experience I knew that we couldn't just go out and buy bones, they were considered dangerous. Human bones, unless treated, can cause anthrax in humans, so there were suppliers who sold medically prepared and safe-to-use bones for hospitals and research facilities.

Jill went out and bought him a truckload of these specially treated bones. They turned up soon after and were delivered in a huge pile to his studio area, much to the consternation of some of the crewmembers. On top of this, Giger was always dressed from head to toe in black. This was his character and personality as a great artist. His persona was further enhanced by his art, which was all around him here in Shepperton, and I noticed a few people were very wary about ever going near his studio.

For us he was just another member of our small unique team. We used to have lunch with Giger and Mia in the King's Head pub in Shepperton every day for weeks on end. It was always highly interesting to me, as I was a great fan of his talent as an artist, and lunchtimes were a rare time when we all lived a pretty normal existence. Giger and Mia used to deliberate long and hard over the menu, carefully choosing the daily fare as we translated what bubble and squeak and Yorkshire puddings were. Spotted dick and custard was a difficult one to explain to a German-speaking Swiss and an Italian woman.

We had many interesting conversations, as you can imagine, but chiefly we centered on the movie and the problems involved with getting everything up and running in time for shooting. Les Dilley worked the closest with Giger, as he was in charge of that portion of the film's sets.

Giger would disappear into his cabin in the morning and only surface at lunchtime and the end of the day. He was very focused as he began building a model of the alien planet landscape. Carefully selecting the right shape and size bones from his stockpile, he created the model landscape with modeling clay. In a few days he had built an entire scale model of the planet exterior that we see when the crew of the *Nostromo* go in search of the beacon they have found on the way home, and where the alien eggs lie.

Les was drawing up the Space Jockey set, and wrestling with the cost of building it full size. Peter Beale, representing Twentieth Century Fox, was adamant it was too expensive for the budget and the scene needed to be cut out of the film. So Les, Ridley, and Michael worked out that by building the Space Jockey in the center of a revolving platform and building only a small section of the wall surface behind it, Ridley could use that same section again and again as a background to the huge pilot in the center by turning it round for reverses and other angles. The cost would be way lower than building a circular set of walls right around the pilot. This was creative thinking, but it meant building a huge turntable large enough to build the Space Jockey set on, which Nick Allder helped design.

Ridley fought the studios long and hard over these scenes, those he felt were essential for the film to work. The gigantic Space Jockey set kept Les busy for weeks on end; having to make full-size sets from Giger's bone-like constructions with never a straight line anywhere, they had to be drawn up by the drafting team. Way more difficult than simple walled sets. Alongside these day after day, he was in charge of constructing the full-size sets for the interiors and exteriors of both the *Nostromo* and the alien craft and trying to get the alien itself to work.

Carlo Rambaldi was employed to make the complicated and brilliant extending jaws of the alien and the facehugger, and was causing concerns over the time he was taking. Ridley had fortunately cast Bolaji Badejo to play the alien so Les had something to cast around to make all the alien pieces. He was developing the eggs, which had to open. Just as on *Star Wars* we hardly saw each other, we were so consumed with getting completed what we had to do, and time was running out.

Les and I had to take a few days off and fly to Los Angeles for the Academy Awards, as we were nominated for *Star Wars*. It was a thrill and an honor and it was a huge surprise when we were first informed that we had actually been nominated.

We landed in Los Angeles and went straight to the Westwood Marquee where we were staying. John Barry and Norman Reynolds were there and we all had dinner and caught up.

Next day we had a long brunch and drank a toast with champagne and orange juice. George Lucas had invited us all to the Entourage restaurant at 8450 West 3rd Street to meet before the awards ceremony. It was exciting to see George and Gary again, entirely vindicated in their success. George looked a lot less tired than when I last saw him in Elstree Studios.

They gave us each some Plexiglas stars, with engraved wording on them saying *Star Wars* and *The Empire Strikes Back*, as that was in early pre-production. Each star was wrapped in strips of 35mm movie film. George told us that the strips of film were from his cutting copy of the original print of *Star Wars*. I kept mine as an amazing souvenir, and still have them to this day, a precious and extremely rare memento from George's actual original working print. You can see a chess game going on in the *Millennium Falcon* hold.

We then all traveled by limousine to the Academy Awards theatre. In those days it was nowhere near as massive a worldwide phenomenon as it has become today, and it certainly wasn't beamed out to the world reaching sixty million people as it is now. We did walk the red carpet with a huge crowd of fans watching for the stars. Richard Dreyfuss was there as the star of *Close Encounters of the Third Kind*, and the other stars of *Annie Hall*.

A very young John Travolta was also there for *Saturday Night Fever*. John was a special guest. At one very memorable moment during the ceremony, the music played the main theme song from the movie, composed by the Bee Gees, and John walked, or rather strutted, on stage in black bell-bottomed tight tango trousers and a flowing white shirt, a grin on his face and his hair flowing. He walked forward on stage and said, "Hi," and it brought the house down. He was the biggest star there and adored by everyone.

When the special-effects team won for *Star Wars* we were ecstatic, but a little embarrassed by the English ones and their behavior. Eight of them went on stage dancing and yelling, and each one in turn took ages thanking copious people. There were no instructions and cues in those days to limit the speeches to a few seconds. John, Norman, Les, and I looked at each other and unanimously agreed that if by some remote chance we did win, John was to speak for us all, to avoid such embarrassment. John was an erudite speaker and storyteller and we knew he would say the correct words.

After what seemed like an age, it finally came to the moment we were waiting for, the art-directing nominations. Henry Winkler, 'The Fonz' from the series *Happy Days*, one of the biggest television stars at the time in America, and screen legend Greer Garson walked on stage to announce the nominations. These were *Airport '77, Close Encounters of the Third Kind* (which we thought would win hands down), *The Spy Who Loved Me, Star Wars* and *The Turning Point*. I cannot say I actually remember them being read, my heart rate had increased and my concentration had wandered for sure.

The drum roll sounded as I heard the winners' names called out by Henry Winkler and Greer Garson. I don't think I can actually remember those words when they pronounced the winners.

"For art direction, John Barry, Les Dilley and Norman Reynolds, and for set decoration Roger Christian."

Everything froze into a kind of slow motion. We were numbed into silence. Then came the daunting realization that I had to walk onto the stage. I followed the others up; somehow I managed not to trip up or fall over the steps onto the stage. Thank goodness we had had enough alcohol at breakfast and the pre-party to loosen us up a bit. Les was quite overcome with emotion. For a plasterer's apprentice from Radlett, who had really struggled and fought his way up through the ranks, this was a moment to relish.

Suddenly I found myself on stage in front of a crowd including Jane Fonda, Vanessa Redgrave, Jack Nicholson, Warren Beatty, and many other famous faces. I stood transfixed as Greer gave each of the others a hug as she gave them the awards. Henry Winkler gave me my statue last as the set decorator, as it was a separate category, and as I was last I didn't have time for a hug on stage. As he presented my award to me and shook my hand, I accepted graciously and thought to myself, well, if my father could see me now he might finally think that I did have a proper job.

John stood at the microphone. He thanked the Academy, and then looking down at George Lucas who was sat right below us, he held the statue towards him and spoke these words:

"We are very pleased to accept this beautiful award on behalf of all our friends and compatriots, who worked so hard to make the sets of *Star Wars* a success. And there's one man whose name should be engraved on this above everybody else and whose name should be on every frame of *Star Wars*, and that's George Lucas. Thank you, George."

Holding the Oscar up he saluted George. They were the most apt words that could have been spoken. George had nurtured this epic through from beginning to end and in his own quiet way shaped and controlled every frame of the film and how it looked and sounded. Against a mountain of negativity on set and difficulties with the studios George had pulled it off. Tenacity is one of the main traits we have to have as filmmakers, and George has it in buckets.

We left the stage to loud applause, and I just remember George's smiling face below me, sitting next to Marcia, his wife, and Steven Spielberg. George's smile said this was all worth it.

We were ushered into a freight elevator behind the stage. Greer Garson looked at me and suddenly I was enveloped in an enormous warm hug. "I'm sorry," she said. "I didn't give you your hug on stage, I missed you out." Many thoughts went through this young man from Reading's mind at that moment: how I got to this point, struggling to get a job, often broke and being lambasted by parents and bank managers to get a proper job. All those put-downs on the way up and also the fantastic support. It all melted into this one moment –being hugged by a legendary film star in a freight elevator, clutching an Oscar.

The first thing you notice is how heavy the Oscar is.

The most disappointing part of the entire day was *Star Wars* not winning for best picture or George winning for best director, which the film and he really deserved. I think in terms of epic filmmaking, groundbreaking filmmaking, and massive audience appeal, which is where cinema actually came from, *Star Wars* and *Close Encounters of the Third Kind* are deserving movies.

We went straight back to the *Alien* set when we flew into Heathrow. Not an hour could be lost. I had now got the set decorating under control, and the departments working. Under Joe Dipple an army of prop men began dressing the many corridors. Airplane scrap was coming in daily to build supplies and any other useful material Jill and Ian Whittaker could find was being sourced. Ian started to concentrate on the infirmary dressing, as we needed to fill that exactly like an army field hospital and it needed white and stainless-steel props to make it different from the rest of the craft.

As our workload increased daily, everyone quickly forgot *Star Wars*. Our concentration on getting the sets built and dressed became almost the entire focus of our lives. It's interesting to look back on it now. *Star Wars* won six out of the ten categories it was nominated for, and a special achievement for sound effects. I think it puts it all in perspective, the value shown to the awards in Britain at the time, in that there was hardly a single mention or piece written in any newspaper congratulating us, or even recording the fact that the movie was filmed in the UK. The British view was that you kept the Oscar in the toilet to hold the door open, which was the acceptable way to handle winning one. To brag or merit its importance, like winning anything at that time, was just not 'British'.

In a way, winning one was the worst thing you could do career-wise. Times have changed now, thank goodness. The Oscar is the most celebrated award in the world in terms of recognition and prestige in the film industry, and is far more exploited in the media than, say, the Nobel Prize.

To illustrate the general attitude to the importance of winning at the time, a few days after we returned Peter Beale thoughtfully threw a party for the British Oscar winners. We assembled at about 6pm at his offices at Twentieth Century Fox House in Soho Square. Les and I left Shepperton early to attend. We met John Barry and Norman Reynolds and the rest of the team; John Mollo and John Stears and the sound crew were there as well. There were a few Twentieth Century Fox secretaries who we had got to know during the making of the movie and Peter Beale's assistants, alongside Peter Beale himself and guest Kenny Baker. We had a glass of wine and a few hors d'oeuvres. Peter was kind to do it and at least celebrate the moment. There is a picture of us at that party that made it to *Screen*, the British film paper, and then it was all over, life went back to normal, and indeed I had to hide my Oscar away for fear I'd be called arrogant. But I rather liked mine, it's a beautiful design, so it went into my office and remained there on the shelf.

NOSTROMO BRIDGE SET
A turning point

I left one dressing gang to continue the corridors, and went to start the bridge set.

The bridge scenes were chosen to be first up on the schedule when filming began. It made sense as the story begins there after the crew wake from hypersleep. It would give the actors a chance to bond together as a crew. This really was a huge set, built up above the floor on a four-foot rostrum. I first went alone and spent time looking at the set still under construction, and tried to imagine it dressed, and what we would need.

Ridley had asked Michael Seymour to lower the entire ceiling of the bridge several times during the construction of the set; he wanted that claustrophobic feeling to the scenes. Though this process drove Michael Seymour and construction head Bill Welch mad because of the work involved, it was really the only way to see how it looked. By lowering the ceiling down he could get it in the CinemaScope frame all the time, so it really looked like a giant airplane cockpit: crammed and suffocating. Filming the widescreen format with a ratio of two to one meant that you saw a wider view of the scene but less height. Most filmmakers who do epic-scale movies prefer this format as it fills the cinema screens with a much larger image, a huge landscape. Gordon Carroll, who was about 6ft 5in tall, complained about the height as he had to stoop, as did Michael, who is also tall. Both had to bend to walk in it and Michael's problem was he had to absorb the cost of changing the set so many times and the time it took from an already too-tight schedule, but the only way to really see how it worked was trial and error. It got lowered a few times until Ridley signed off. Working in the set it reminded me of sitting in an aircraft cockpit, with all the overhead switches and controls just above in reach, and once we began dressing it that way it began to look so real. It was claustrophobic and that was the intention.

Having analyzed in detail what I thought would be required for the bridge, I called a very important meeting on the unfinished set with my dressing team—Nick Allder and his crew, Guy Hudson, Roger Nichols, Dennis Lowe, Roger Shaw, Ian Whittaker, and the electricians—to go through what I saw we needed to plan for. I told Nick we would need to have pilot and crew seats and he would have to make them functional on sliders and adapt them for each crew member. We needed harnesses, and they had to look like real flight-deck restraints. I suggested we find discarded seats and harnesses from fighter jets, as these would already look the part. Even if we got one or two in it would be great reference to begin with. I also suggested they buy in scrap from large jetliner cockpits, and from any military aircraft if they could find them. These could then be adapted by Nick's team and made practical. As they fought the turbulence descending to the alien planet we would see the crewmembers fighting to control the ship as it bucked and jerked around. Each crewmember had a flight position and particular requirements as the *Nostromo* descended down to the alien planet and landed, so we needed six sets of flight controls.

We needed television monitors in each cockpit face, and playback of computer-style elements to read on them when we turned over the cameras. That was another department, but I had to organize it. We reckoned that with the small monitors available they could run playback for all the monitors synced together. Nick knew of small Trinitron monitors and we could build the consoles around them so they sunk into the control panels. Each control station had to have a sea of switches and levers and controls, emergency lights, helmets, and equipment.

At the back of the bridge behind the flight-control sections, was a large underlit navigation table. Stanfords, the huge map store in Covent Garden, had transparent sheets of maps of the star systems so we ordered some of those to lay on the table. We needed navigation instruments as well, and I figured that even if they had a computer-controlled ship, they always had backups and old-fashioned maps in case the systems failed. Again I related to ship movies with the captain working out sea routes and adapted the ideas to space to keep a familiarity.

Everyone was happy with the plans we cemented at the meeting, except the assistant, who seemed to still be threatened by me. As we began assembling everything we would need for the bridge dressing, and the corridors and medical room for the *Nostromo*, things with him came to a head. His attitude was affecting my schedule to get the sets ready, and this I could not accept any more. Driving home late one night, tired and frustrated, I made a decision that he would have to go.

That evening I tried something that my girlfriend Patricia suggested, as she was a Nichiren Shoshu Buddhist. I often practiced the mantras early in the morning before leaving as I found they focused my energy and mind for the day. Before eating that night she had me focus on a solution and do an hour of the Nam Myoho Renge Kyo mantra before her Gohonzon. I did this, concentrating on shifting this block, trying to change the negative energy to positive.

I drove in the next morning to Shepperton prepared to have the assistant replaced. I had the blessings of Garth Thomas and Ivor, who were aware of the problem and had given me permission to do whatever was needed. The assistant came to see me in the morning. He walked into my office and sat down.

"Look," he said, "I have come to apologize. I realize I have been totally out of order these last weeks, and I have come to apologize to you. I realize you know what you are doing, you are far more experienced than me, so I would like to knuckle under and learn."

I was... 'gobsmacked' I think is the right word. Inside I was thinking this mantra had really worked. I kept a calm demeanor and said that he had been very obstructive these weeks and I was not a threat to him, I was there appointed primarily by Ridley to get the interiors of *Alien* working and ready for shooting. So I needed my team behind me all the way, not challenging what I was doing at every turn, and this was not arrogance or ego, just experience and an ability to understand exactly what the director wanted. So I accepted his apology and discussed what exactly I needed him to go do, and left it at that. I would see how he did and if he was true to his word then he would stay and help, and goodness knows we needed all the help we could get.

Les and I suggested we get Benjamin Fernandez on board from Madrid, the brilliant young Spanish art director who had worked with us on *The Last Remake of Beau Geste*. We persuaded them to hire him when it was suggested we needed another hand in the art department. We needed someone to draw up sets like the hypersleep chamber (the 'flower-opening' scene). This set had been in and out of the script several times due to budget cutting, and this was one set that got put under the hammer each time as being too costly. We figured if we revamped another set and used found objects, we could get it built for Ridley, who felt it essential for the drama to work. The problem was Michael and Les and I were up to our necks in work. We needed someone who could think like us and take this set by the scruff of the neck and get it made.

ALIEN

So Benjamin was hired and came to work immediately and did indeed prove to be a hugely valuable asset to us. (Benjamin subsequently designed all of the sets for Ridley's brother Tony after *Alien*.)

As we were working I watched other sets being built and going up, and kept my eyes on the dressings that we would need to add for mechanical reality. The landing leg was a massive structure, almost into the roof of H Stage, which was 35ft high. Michael built the leg from Ridley's desire to give scale to the *Nostromo*, when we see the crew descending down to the alien planet's surface. This was the scene when they go in search of the warning beacon. The back wall was hung with black velvet and Michael relied on Ridley backlighting the leg and putting atmospheric smoke all around it like hydraulics and steam vents to make it look real. It was built one-sided to save cost, and was really well painted to make the wooden construction look like metal. Again, being carefully dressed and aged by the painters, who placed oil and grease stains around the giant pistons, it is absolutely foolproof in authenticity. We sourced some tubing and odd bits of scrap dressing to add on to the surfaces as well.

For the illusion of it being a real craft, there needed to be a second landing leg behind this one, but costs prohibited the construction of two. Michael relied on the atmosphere of the planet being thick and polluted, and built a second leg as a two-dimensional cutout, again almost 35ft high to the ceiling. This was made on a frame of hardwood with a plywood skin. When it was scenic-painted and aged down, standing behind the other leg with smoke pumped in for atmosphere, the leg would look one hundred percent real. Scenic-painted cutouts like this were art-department tradition to fool the eye of the viewer, and absolutely foolproof on camera.

The legs were duplicated in a smaller scale when the model of the *Nostromo* was filmed at Bray Studios, and then the feet made practical to film the underside of the landing shuttle as it descended onto the alien planet surface.

For the elevator to descend or ascend the crew from the airlock to the ground, to save money we dressed a scissor lift. These were used to raise or lower workers on the sets, and this model could elevate the platform to the height of the airlock door. Once we placed steam vents coming out of the pistons, and simulated it with the dry-ice machines and added in smoke and lights, I knew this would pass the reality test. I talked with the scenic painters during the days I inspected the work going on and assembled scrap tubes and pistons that I could dress on to help its authenticity.

I went every other day to H Stage, at that time the largest stage in the United Kingdom, to watch Les's progress with the Space Jockey set. It was growing daily and despite being skinned with panels of plaster and fiberglass you could see how awesome the set would be. The scale was huge; an army of plasterers and modelers were working on the central Space Jockey, and Giger himself with Peter Voysey spent a lot of time carefully sculpting the details of the strange pilot figure lying in its seat where it had perished.

The floor was made in sections modeled on the sinuous organic shapes in Giger's paintings. The set would be what it was, so no dressing was required for this one from me; everything was there, built into the walls and around the central Jockey's skeleton sitting in the chair that he was fused into. What I had to assemble were the torches the crew would carry when they descended and discuss the wire harness Kane would wear to drop down into the egg chamber.

In the central part of the stage they were constructing the alien landscape that the three crewmembers had to walk across to get to the alien ship. This was comprised of a lot of strange-shaped rocks and pipes made in plaster molded over chicken-wire frames, on a vast scale.

At the far end of H Stage a section of the wall of the alien craft was being built, with three entrance passages based on women's vulvas as portals into the alien craft. Ridley planned to see the full craft only in model form, again constructed at Bray Studios. Both these sets in their unpainted stage of construction looked pretty unconvincing as they were being built, and the planet surface especially was going to need a lot of atmosphere to fuse it into reality. Giger and Peter Voysey spent time whenever they could sculpting finishing touches to both sets, especially the alien ship. They sculpted bone-like shapes in plaster, adding in pipes and larger-scale modeled bones to bring the look closer to his paintings for both scenes. He airbrushed colors into the alien ship when it was being finished, exactly as he did on the massive pilot set. We wondered if this would ever work; the scale of the sets and the amount of work they took ate up the weeks, but we had faith that Ridley would find a way to shoot these scenes to make them look authentic.

ALIEN

Somehow, miraculously, the Space Jockey set had survived and was being finished in situ by Giger and Peter Voysey. Giger was airbrushing the final details and colors himself. Almost finished, the scale of this set was absolutely dramatic and Ridley's insistence that this set would bring a huge scale to the film was apparent now to everyone visiting the stage. What it represented to me, looking at it, was a history, a past where something terrible had occurred and showed the audience a race of very large aliens. The organic sculpted walls, like Giger's art, filled with bones and erotic curves, created a world that no one had ever seen. As the three crewmembers ventured into the craft we were truly entering an alien world, yet it was real.

We now needed to think of a way of creating a membrane across the alien eggs as described in the script. The English band The Who was huge at the time and had a permanent stage booked at Shepperton for rehearsing. Anton Furst was developing the lasers for them that they were experimenting with, and trying out ideas for using them for a coming live tour. These lasers were newly invented at this time, so were really novel. Prior to this I had visited Anton in his workshop to see some holograms he was working on using laser technology. He wanted to show them to me with an idea for using them in films. This was the first time I had ever seen a hologram live, and it was fascinating—right in front of me was a three-dimensional image. Les and I went across to see him about the egg membrane in the alien egg chamber. The Who were rehearsing. Anton showed us the various laser beams and effects they were pioneering, and being new to us, they looked spectacular. Anton showed us how they fired like bullets into the air in different patterns, or shot out like veined light beams. We are used to them now, but this was the first time we had ever seen anything like it. We liked the green and blue laser beams when Anton showed us how they could spread like a membrane across the stage, and we knew we had found an answer to another problem, as long as they looked as good on film. Ridley took one look at them and approved them. When he added his customary smoke and tested them out they worked better than expected. The bonus is that when someone broke the light beam by standing in it, it created shapes in the membrane like reverse shadows. With the smoke added for atmosphere the tests looked great, another simple and somewhat lucky solution to a problem that we were pioneering.

One of the action props required was the alien tracker device. I had been searching the scrap materials for some time to see if anything was useful to base one on, in my tradition of prop making for *Star Wars*. One day I was looking through lists of TV and radio equipment for sale and came across a small portable Sony television that had been designed to look like an army field receiver for some reason. It was made in an army-green color, rectangular in shape with molded speaker and controls, and looked really interesting. It could also be programmed to work as an oscilloscope; I got the buyer to get one. I spoke to the video boys to ask if they could play back our pre-recorded alien-tracking graphics on it as per the action required, and they could, so I went to work. I essentially redressed the exterior with interesting parts using superglue again. I found a suitable tube-like piece for the front to give the idea of it being a tracking probe that could register changes in air pressure and track movement. Then I just stuck on different switches and electrical parts from our junk store to change its appearance from an army receiver to a tracker. I placed buttons and plastic shaped pieces to look like control mechanisms, and left some practical so Ash could turn it on when demonstrating it.

Aging it a little and adding a few of my own graphics with Letraset, I took it up to show Ridley in his office. Very few people were allowed in his room at that time as the producers wanted his storyboards as fast as possible and had basically locked him in for the three weeks it took him to draw them.

I showed him the finished tracker and how it worked, and the tiny TV screen in its mode as an oscilloscope looked like a working tracker device with all my additions to it, and not at all like the television it was based on. In its aged-down military-green color, it took on the *Nostromo* color scheme we were aiming for. Nick Allder had positioned a few functioning switches for me, and the television itself was functioning on its own batteries, so worked.

This was the very first action prop I took to Ridley, and as such was important to get his confidence. He approved it on the spot. It was an exact repeat of showing George Lucas the first gun I hand-made on *Star Wars* and his relief that I was on the same page. Ridley now knew for sure that I was thinking as he was.

Art-directing the look of the *Nostromo*'s interior on *Alien* and coming up with the action props was an enormous undertaking. I ended up, just as I had on *Star Wars*, working for at least three to four months without a single day off. I was living in Earls Court at the time and by the time I got home from Shepperton it was always around ten or eleven o'clock. It was a rare day that I didn't fall asleep whilst eating a late meal. I remember asking Ridley one day what the red mark was on his forehead that had appeared over the last few days. He was so exhausted driving home, usually between twelve and one in the morning, he had fallen asleep at the wheel of his Rolls-Royce each night. He banged his head on the large steering wheel and relied on that to keep him awake. That was Ridley's dedication to this movie and what it took to make it what it was.

In one of the main holds we decided that there would be various vehicles stored in there suitable to use when the *Nostromo* was at the mining location. I went to Ron Cobb and asked him for a few ideas for vehicles we could construct from the larger airplane scrap pieces we had brought in. One of these sketches is in *The Book of Alien* by Paul Scanlon and Michael Gross called the 'two-place helijet'. The functional detail and ability of Ron's to quickly fire off a sketch is remarkable. Even the type of engines the vehicle would have Ron knew in precise detail, depending on my description of what a vehicle might be required to do. Ron did several sketches like this for us, as we talked about their different functions. The helijet would be the main vehicle so I put an assistant in charge of sourcing the scrap and making it with a small team of prop makers. They built a rough mock-up and they sourced larger pieces of airplane junk to use. We knew they would be seen simply as shapes in the dark lower hold areas when they were grabbing supplies or hunting the alien, but the detail would add authenticity and confirm the reality required to make an audience believe they were on a real ship.

The talented French designer Moebius had been commissioned to come up with various ideas on the Jodorowsky production of the film of the classic science-fiction book *Dune*. Jodorowsky had put together an incredible team of visionary artists including Moebius, H.R. Giger, Dan O'Bannon and Salvador Dali. When that film collapsed Dan O'Bannon went back and wrote *Alien* and when Twentieth Century Fox picked it up and Ridley Scott was hired as the director, Dan introduced Giger and Moebius to Ridley Scott. Moebius came onboard for a few days and designed various spacecraft and alien planets, before H.R. Giger took over the entire alien side of the film. Ridley decided to use Moebius's designs for the spacesuits and the costume designer, John Mollo, built these locally. John had also been employed after the recognition of his work on *Star Wars*. The leg pieces and other padding were actually adapted from ice-hockey padding, American-football uniforms, and cricket pads, all altered and colored to change the look of the originals. Various fiberglass panels were added on, all using small pieces of aircraft and office machine junk to add detail, and inspired by samurai costumes, which Moebius loved. The helmets were sculpted in clay and then molded in fiberglass, and were particularly interesting.

Once again when they were sculpted in clay John added in lots of our sourced small scrap objects that created a technical functionality to match Moebius's design. He also cobbled together various pieces of old junk for the backpacks and belts. When Nick added in small lights inside the helmets as if it was a functioning control panel seen through the glass visor, they added a light source for the faces and therefore a reality.

Ridley wanted an air exhaust as if expelling the astronaut's used breath so liquid-nitrogen jets of steam were added, functioning on small timer batteries to simulate the timing of each breath. I thought they looked spectacular—they were the first spacesuits I had seen on film that I really believed were real. The actors could be clearly seen through the large glass visors with the self-contained light source glowing on their faces. Moebius had designed a light built into the top of each helmet and this became an invaluable addition. It focused the eye on them when Ridley created a thick storm-like atmosphere on the planet's surface. Later when Ridley filmed the model set of the alien planet in Bray Studios, Nick Allder made a simple miniature track with little stick figures that moved slightly as he pushed the three figures along. Adding the tiny medical pea bulbs, they got away with a really wide angle on the planet surface, to create an immense landscape and scale. No one ever guessed. Nick was experimenting all the way with anything that worked, and unusually he was blessed with a director who had the courage to say, "Go for it."

There has been a lot written about how the early version of the baby alien made up by Giger for the chestburster looked more like a dead turkey. Ridley kept showing Giger ideas, in particular Francis Bacon's triptych called *Three Studies for Figures at the Base of a Crucifixion*, and this influence led to the turkey-like creature. Bacon's painting is pure horror, relying on the imagination to fill in what the eye can't see. Giger had his hands full at this time creating the actual alien itself, which of course the film relied on being great. Working at the same time on the planet's surface and the alien ship, plus the Space Jockey, Giger's days were already filled up, so it was suggested they hire Roger Dicken to take on the chestburster sequence. When the baby alien broke out of Kane's chest it had to be articulated, to open its mouth and look around, so had to have an experienced puppeteer to operate it, and Roger was able to do all this.

The development process continued under Ridley's eye when they hired Roger. His design for the baby alien, based entirely on Giger's, had all the right elements to scare the audience when it burst out of the chest. Roger went to the art department, I remember, with Dan O'Bannon and they worked on a final rendition of the design using Giger's paintings and ideas as the main inspiration. Roger also inherited the facehugger. Carlo Rambaldi was supposed to make this alongside the alien head with a full working jaw in his studio in Rome, but it was taking a lot longer than planned. This also went through a development stage with Giger and Dan O'Bannon, and finally with Roger to get the look right. Ridley and Roger liked the long fingers Giger had painted in a cross-section of the egg, and liked the idea of them wrapped around Kane's head, gripping onto him when it was attached to his face. This certainly made it creepy along with the long snake-like tail wound around his neck. So these elements were designed into the finished creature.

The facehugger seen in the infirmary on Kane's face, made and operated by Roger Dicken, had little air sacks on either side of the body that looked like lungs and gave it the appearance of being alive. We needed another facehugger for when it had appeared to die, and seeing as Roger Dicken's time was being consumed with making the chestburster baby aliens and the practical facehugger, Bob Keen, the horror legend who created many prosthetic creatures, was commissioned to create a second working facehugger we could use in the infirmary. Bob Keen worked for Clive Barker for five years and had created such epic characters as Pinhead. He later worked on *Return of the Jedi* as part of the team working Jabba the Hutt. Bob also created some of the alien eggs for the alien nest scene as so many were required. Several of these were still in Bob's workshop in Pinewood last time I worked with him.

I was dressing the bridge set one day when I was called to the other stage, and went across to the corridor section. Walking through the corridors transforming into the now so-familiar *Nostromo* was always inspiring to me; I felt I had come home. There were several different sections of corridors created to distinguish them as different crew areas. I walked through them to one section outside the infirmary. Some were made up of just the padding, as this area was. As I walked in Ridley was standing opposite Michael Seymour in silence, and there was a tension in the air. Les and Bill Welch were also there to one side. I looked at the padding, and they had painted a few pieces in gold. Ridley explained he had suggested a gold color for the padding in this area, and thought it would work. Michael was worried it would look like a hair salon.

They had come to a standstill over the decision, so Ridley had called me there to see what I thought. Talk about being put on the spot. Les wasn't sure, as he didn't delve much into color schemes. I was immediately placed in an awkward position—Ridley asked me what I thought he should do. He really wanted the gold color-coding, to separate the area from the other corridor areas. Michael was correct in that just sprayed gold the panels would look somewhat gaudy on screen, and might not work.

I decided the only way was to be honest, and give my opinion for the movie. I liked the gold idea, as space vehicles from NASA use a lot of gold, and it's familiar because of that. I said that it would work in my opinion, but Michael was right in that it could look very like a cheap gold fabric as it was, and that one has to be careful with gold on film, like silver paint. I explained to them about the technique John Box taught me of blending metal dust into wax and applying it, to soften the color. Ridley said, "Let's see what it looks like."

Bill got the painter over, and I suggested a copper-colored pigment to blend over the top of the gold. They added copper and black pigments to the wax and applied it gently with a cloth over the gold padding, and it did look way better. I was taught by John Box and John Barry to always listen to a director's idea, and try to make things work for them. Ridley liked it so they did the entire area like that, and that became the way the padding was finished throughout. It was cheap and easy to apply, and meant that we could safely color the different sections.

Budget restraints are obviously a problem and one simply cannot always do what is required, but where there's a will there's a way. Michael was facing a lot of pressure from Peter Beale to cut sets, and getting in trouble for supporting Ridley, determined to build what Ridley and *Alien* needed. Peter Beale was under orders to cut scenes from the film and reduce the budget, and the hypersleep chamber was still under threat as the Space Jockey set had been.

A few weeks from shooting, Twentieth Century Fox made the firm decision to cut down the budget. Before preparation started they had agreed a budget of around four and a half to five million dollars. No one seems exactly sure anymore what it was exactly. They had set it low and it seems to have been in line with *Star Wars* from two years earlier according to what we were told at the time. Then when they had seen Ridley's storyboards and the really promising screen test for Sigourney Weaver, which Ridley filmed like a piece of the movie in action, they increased it. Some say to eight million dollars and others eleven. I clearly remember Peter Beale slashing the budget by six hundred thousand dollars. Both Ridley and Ivor Powell state they are not sure of the exact final budget when asked recently, but I clearly remember discussions in the art department with Ivor that it was around seven and a half million.

What was fact is that several hundred thousand dollars were cut from the art department budgets overnight, like an ax falling, just as they were on *Star Wars*. The art department and construction budgets are the largest chunk of money in a science-fiction film that comprises of sets to create the environments. So it's the easiest one to attack by the accountants, little knowing the serious impact it has on a science-fiction movie like this. I remember the day these cuts happened. There were a lot of depressed discussions about what sets to lose. Some sets were amalgamated with each other to save costs, and some were destined to be revamped, which did save a lot of money. Ridley didn't want to lose any at all, and in fact kept adding sets and scenes he thought were essential. The hold area under decks, where we see the water dropping from above, was basically reduced from a set to building walls from revamped set pieces and floor sections and using the stage roof above. It was so high and with smoke and water no one would know that the roof of the hold area was looking up into the stage gantries above. The set has huge scale this way, and worked, so rather than destroy a sequence or set it into a small space, this was a way more creative solution. In one section of it, Michael built a structure and placed the same crates we used on the floors in the corridor and other areas as a ceiling, leaving it open for Ridley to light through. Suitably dressed with the vehicles we were building and plenty of added pieces like old oxygen cylinders to represent cargo, it became a natural part of the underdecks of the *Nostromo* as one would imagine it to be.

We were determined to give Ridley what he wanted. Benjamin was put to work to redo those sets that were to be eliminated, and find ways to keep them in, by reusing other set materials already made and props and dressings. The biggest loser in this, I remember, was the hypersleep set as we see it with the opening 'flower petals'. This was deemed too expensive and one that Peter Beale kept targeting as unnecessary. It had been through several designs to make it work, and was down to a simple inexpensive set. If Peter Beale had his way and unless it was simplified it was in danger of elimination. Benjamin and I went to see Nick Allder as Michael and Les decided with me that if we could find a way to adapt what we had already purchased on the film, we could make something work for Ridley. None of us wanted to give this up; the set is synonymous with sunrise and awakening, and helped accent the idea of the crew waking up from a long hypersleep. The idea of the sleep chambers opening like flowers at dawn light was one of the only light moments really in the film, and was important, we thought, to be able to deliver to Ridley. Plus it was another memorable set adding huge production value to the film, again all helping the film to be seen as a major movie. We decided to try to make the set the way I had been dressing the rest, using airplane parts and found objects.

Nick showed us seven or eight hydraulic rams he had bought but was not using in any sets. These could be used to open the flower-like pods. They also had the PVC canopies so these together were enough to create the basis of a set. This would have to be built in secret so Peter Beale wouldn't realize what the art department was doing, and use an existing set and revamp it when it was finished with. Benjamin went to work and drew it up, using anything existing he could find to keep the cost to a minimum.

As the days diminished and shooting arrived, way faster than any of us realized, the workdays got longer and longer. The bridge looked amazing; everyone was attracted to it and kept looking at it, trying the seats, wondering how on earth we had built a real cockpit environment. It was good to hear this for our team, as it boosted confidence. We kept on adding and adding more layers. Once it was all painted into the green color and aged a little, the prop boys and our apprentices spent several days just placing Letraset numerals and letters and the Weyland-Yutani symbol, like an Egyptian winged bird.

Nick Allder adapted the flight controls from the airplane scrap we had bought and made them so they could tilt back and forth and side to side like a plane's. We also had throttle-type sliders placed in beside the seats, like engine thrust controls. When you sat in the seats and slid them forward into position it really felt like a sophisticated yet highly practical flight-control deck of a flying craft. The military-green color cemented this idea that it was some kind of long-haul working craft that had seen a lot of service. There was tangible relief all round from the producers and in particular Ridley—this bridge was something special for sure and was going to set this film far apart from anything that had come before it.

On the bridge, Ridley needed emergency lights that could come on when the turbulence knocked out the power system for the cockpit lights. I thought about this for a while, as I didn't want to make lights especially for it; the cost would be prohibitive and also time-consuming for the already stressed and overloaded art department. I remembered Lee Electrics had some adapted handheld lamps called Red Heads, with handles that actors could walk around with. I asked the electricians to get me one of these out. I took it to Roger Shaw's workshop and we added a few interesting pieces to it and tried it in the set. We left them in the red color they were painted as it matched the red we were already using. Ron Cobb had drawn in red symbols in the airlocks anywhere that emergency services were located, so it fitted the design element. Sited behind one of the crew seats I thought they fitted into the dressing without looking out of place. It looked really good, especially the red contrasting the green of the set, and added to the idea of the red for emergency. We showed Ridley this one in the set, and he agreed it looked exactly right. I placed another in the ceiling above the crew stations.

I made a very thorough breakdown of every playback required in the bridge scenes for each monitor. It was a detailed list that became another roadmap for everyone of exactly what was needed. At a meeting I called with the special-effects boys and the video playback team, we went through it. Garth Thomas from the production team arranged for the graphics required to be created by an outside team he knew.

Computers were rather simple in those days and we got a lot of binary-based numerals and numbers, which poured across the screens. It looked real as it was real, but they generated a lot of meaningless graphics for us. Also for exact sequences we needed star maps and detailed maps of the outer systems, which are seen in the film. They created these and then put them on videotape and the playback team synced them up to playback monitors that are wired into all the monitors on set, both in sync and individually, so Ridley had freedom to play back whatever was required of a scene quickly. We had sourced tiny eight-inch Sony Trinitron monitors through Nick Allder that had amazingly detailed images on the screen, so these really helped. We bought quite a few of them to place in each console and anywhere that playback was required faked as a computer screen.

I made the breakdown, individually numbered for each scene, and then gave each playback section a code and thus the tapes were easily identified. Experience taught me that the time wasted on set whilst waiting to roll the cameras, trying to find the correct playback piece, could be long. So this way there was a precise log. Also in those days, because of the film frame rates, the playback had to roll with the camera until they fell into sync, to avoid seeing bars scrolling across the monitors, so each playback section had a long intro to allow the cameras to roll and sync up. When we tried the playback out the tiny Sony Trinitron monitors worked amazingly well; the image was higher-resolution than anything else for the time. The alternative way was to rear-project the images as we had done before. Nick Allder ended up doing this on the models for the sequence where the crew sees Ash in his blister from the planet's surface. It immediately gave scale and life to the model of the *Nostromo* landing craft and you can even see Ripley moving around behind Ash at one point. Ridley determined he was going handheld, especially in the bridge set, so matching the image into the monitors later was not really an option. In those days the only tracking devices were expensive and cumbersome motion-control units, impossible for this set; Ridley would be down to filming about three setups a day, they were so slow. You could hand-rotoscope them in later in post, but it was a painstaking procedure and Nick Allder opted for video playback direct into these tiny monitors on set as he knew how well it worked.

In Paul Scanlon's book about *Alien* the pistol is credited as being a

Roger Christian special. This is based on my creating and making all the prototypes on *Star Wars*, adapting them from real weapons, and being the first to do this. For *Alien*, the crew all needed weapons, though Sigourney was the only one really seen holding one at the end. The crewmembers going to the alien planet were supposed to have weapons, but again these were hardly seen. As they were written in the script and planned out as action props we had to make them and have them available at all times for filming.

I did my usual pitch on creating weapons based on interesting-looking existing guns so they looked real. Everyone agreed and I had no resistance to the idea as they had worked so well on *Star Wars* and had looked so realistic. I based the crewmembers' weapons on an M4 assault rifle, and this time had the luxury of a prop-making department assemble one for me, adding on interesting pieces of scrap to change its appearance, and my customary scope addition this time added onto the bottom of the weapon to distinguish its look from *Star Wars*. We changed the magazine as well, and did my customary altering of the barrel shape.

For Sigourney's end action sequence Nick and I mocked up a flame gun to look like a really powerful weapon. Dallas also used this in the ventilation ducts when hunting the alien. Nick really went to town on the flamethrower. He, like me, was disappointed with feeble-looking weapons, so he developed one that could shoot flame a good twenty feet. It did look spectacular and Ridley, who was always operating the camera, nearly got fried a few times, especially in the ventilation ducts. However, the shot looks spectacular when the flames travel up the shaft right at the camera, a very effective shot for the audience watching. The weapon looked like it could deliver once we had dressed it up and added on scrap components. It really helped Sigourney's overall look in the final scenes where she is escaping from the alien and rescuing the cat; her physique and the gun made her look like a very cool warrior woman. It is seen clearly in action in the deleted scene when she fries Dallas, cocooned by the alien as food. She has no choice but to kill him, and fires the flamethrower at the alien's large wasp-nest-like cocoon covering the entire wall.

On any big film, because of the amount of work that occurs daily on the shooting floor concerning the sets and props, it is often required to have an art department head as part of the floor shooting crew. *Alien* was certainly no exception as the entire film is in sets. As Ridley had a really tough schedule to adhere to every day, any hold-up caused by the set or dressing and props could seriously affect his day's work. I had my team working in unison now, and nearly all the corridors and the bridge were dressed. Ian Whittaker and I went round the crew's quarters, corridors, infirmary, holds, and lower corridors and all the sets on H Stage. We went to the bridge and placed the final crew's personal dressings.

These are the little things that personalized the environment, like the dice in the *Millennium Falcon* cockpit. I left used coffee cups with the Weyland-Yutani emblem placed on them around their consoles as these are symbolic as familiar objects, and other small details that may or may not be seen but personalize the dressing.

In the crew quarters we decided to leave the commissary table as if they had left a meal in progress, and Ridley came up with the idea of the pecking birds that work by perpetual motion. The beaks dip into the water and as the balance changes with the weight of the water, it swings upright. As the water evaporates from the beak, the weight distribution changes, and they dip back into the water again in perpetual motion. These were very popular in the seventies; people placed them in the back window of their cars for some reason in the UK.

Just as Americans loved their hanging dice in their cars, we thought this would be something that would not be a normal dressing, but would add a light personal touch. Also when Ridley tracks around the empty *Nostromo*, to get the *Mary Celeste* deserted-ship feel for the opening, the birds would be moving on the eating table, an eerie reminder that something was missing—a crew! The buyer managed to track some down, and we placed these on the commissary table for the opening shots.

For the next scenes when the crew have woken up from hypersleep, we thought a lot about what the crews would eat from, where their food would be stored and what kind of food. As the first meal we see them eat is breakfast, crews like the *Nostromo* truckers would eat basic stuff like cornflakes, as this could be easily stored. We added this in PVC containers, much the same principal applied to the containers in Uncle Lars and Aunt Beru's homestead. We sourced suitable designs of plastic tableware and containers that felt right. The other surefire breakfast necessity amongst a group of truckers waking up and having a first meal is coffee. So we found some interesting-looking plastic cups and placed these and coffee-making equipment and a jug on the table. We placed personal items around; this added the last bit of reality to the dressing.

The prop dressing crews were all well in sync now as well, just adding more and more to the corridors and the airlocks, always trying to encrust more and more pieces onto the walls and ceiling to give that industrial reality. We never stop until shooting starts as one can go on and on layering material in.

The assistant who'd worked against me was working in sync with his team now creating the vehicles for the hold. He was constructing a mock helijet from Ron Cobb's sketch that was beginning to look real, and a couple more vehicles on caterpillar tracks that Nick Allder had in the workshops. The helijet would be the main object in the hold area and would give scale to it, so was important to get right. Seeing that the bulk of the *Nostromo* was done, Ian and I concentrated on the infirmary for the last few days before shooting. I was able to go as standby art director on the floor. No one else wanted to do this, as it is pressured and leaves little time for anything else. I was planning on moving to directing as soon as I could, and being at the heart of a movie alongside the director and actors was the best way to learn. Also I knew Ridley and wanted to be there—as I was the one who most understood the workings of the dressing and props, it seemed better that I did it.

Les still had his hands full getting the alien planet and Space Jockey set finished, and dealing with getting the alien itself working around the actor Bolaji Badejo, I could easily still look after the rest of the dressings as we were contained in the studios on the main two stages. It was easy for me to be on set most of the time and supervise everything else going on in preparation for the next day's filming and the next week's. I could shuffle between the set and the workshops. Joe Dipple would be on the floor with us as well on standby; he was a trusted prop on the floor, brilliant at dealing with actors and their requirements, especially their action props. Joe is especially good at smoke—using a bee puffer and a piece of cardboard, he was skilled at getting it to hold still quickly and not look like smoke. It was agreed by Ridley and Michael that I should start with the shooting crew on the following Monday. I could solve any problems that arose immediately as I knew all the teams well, and this freed up Michael and Les to get on with the rest of the sets without worrying about the shooting-floor problems.

One of the standby jobs I had to constantly do was touch up the sets. We had a standby painter with us all the time, who had a full stock of all the paint colors used on the set and different aging paints and waxes, so we could repair any damage done really quickly. As the sets were basically wood underneath the finishes, it was easy to knock them with a dolly. A patch of wood exposed would ruin the illusion of us being in a real environment. Often the heat from a lamp will mark the set or burn the paint, so these had to be watched all the time. The general work procedure for me once Ridley had set a shot and the lighting was being tweaked was to look through the camera and check for any details that needed fixing. This happens hundreds of times a day, sometimes when shooting fast and using a lot of different setups. There is nothing worse than sitting in rushes and spotting something we missed that spoils the illusion.

Along a narrower corridor on the set lay the door to Mother. In the movie, a complex series of entry procedures allowed only the crewmember that knew the codes in, in this case the captain, Dallas. In the movie that was enough to show that he was the captain of the ship without actually saying it in dialogue, and therefore an important procedure. We had Nick Allder engineer keys and locks to make the secure-entry procedure look correct. Roger Shaw made up the entry key for me from scrap computer parts encased in Perspex. It gave the impression of a different type of electronic key, all designed to support this idea that no one could enter Mother unless permitted. This original key was recently sold at auction at Bonhams. Certainly it was never expected when we built all these props from scrap and found objects that they'd become iconic items sought after by collectors. Ivor Powell tells the story of visiting Shepperton after the production had wrapped and finding a large waste container filled with discarded Alien props, smaller scale-models of the sets, and even the alien itself. Ivor could only grab a model of the pilot, not the surrounding set. One can only imagine what these container contents would have been worth today and the collectors salivating over them.

We placed locking mechanisms amongst the specially chosen aircraft pieces to help create the idea of a wall of security locks. Mother's room itself, covered in tiny lights, seemed like a womb. The central console that controlled Mother and its built-in chair moved backwards and forwards and turned using power motors, again installed by Nick's crew. This room was all painted in a warm cream-like color and had a view screen. We only had the older computer keyboards in those days, and I used these extensively throughout the *Nostromo* as we had bought in a large lot of scrapped ones.

Placed into their respective consoles, and painted in the matching colors, they looked as if they belonged. I firmly believe that in the real world, cost would determine the use of uniform parts in building a craft like this, as the company would put out bids to tender, much as building ships for the ocean. So it felt right like this, and my own philosophy on filmmaking is if it looks right it is right, even if it might not be historically correct.

When lit with the ambient bulbs, which is how Ridley wanted the set lit, Mother was a warm environment, a secluded hidden room, and the heart of the ship's control system. There were alcove-like shapes in the roof section, and these were the only way to add light through diffused glass panels. There were monitor screens around the walls in each part of the octagon shape, and the console and control chair moved around and close to the one opposite the door that functioned as the main access control to Mother. It was very well designed to give a sense of power and control, the true brain of the *Nostromo*, and helped give the feeling that Mother guided the craft much as a plane flies on autopilot; the crew merely did perfunctory duties and were expendable. Mother could do it all. Arthur C. Clarke and Stanley Kubrick had set the idea in motion with a force by inventing HAL as a character on *2001* who believed humans were flawed, and this idea enabled the audience to understand Mother's role, by setting the idea in everyone's mind that a computer could control everything. Also at this time in the late seventies, the world still regarded computers with a suspicion that they would somehow take over the world and there was always a nagging doubt about them in people's minds—not like today where they function almost as a body part in our lives.

All the actors drifted in during the last few days before the shoot. Sigourney had already been in Shepperton for the test, and she came and looked at the cockpit and the corridors. I think the look on her face and on those of the other actors as they first walked around the sets, or anyone's faces for that matter when they entered the *Nostromo* for the first time, said it all.

There was a small wall panel left out in one of the airlocks to enter the labyrinth. You entered into a section of the ship that was like a hold area. Beyond stretched the corridors, dark and brooding like a submarine asleep. The floor looked like metal grating and was left a dark red color. Some crates were placed in the wall and ceiling sections and also left in their dark red color, with the pipework shining with oil drips and aging from much usage. As you walked down you were encased in a working spacecraft, and turning the corner at the airlock, painted with red emergency symbols and dressed with fire-fighting equipment and spacesuits, you entered a labyrinth. You passed the infirmary, which had a large glass wall in the corridor so you could see the white sterile hospital and diagnosis room beyond.

Derek Vanlint had placed small fluorescent tubes all along the ceilings, gelled to color-balance them to give that off-white color to the sets. They added an atmosphere of dim claustrophobia and shadows and then the airlock sections at the end of each corridor were brighter. Michael added corner sections so that the corridor became more labyrinth-like in places. In one area Les Dilley suggested to Ridley using the same mirror trick that John Barry had used on the *Star Wars* Death Star corridor to make it look way longer. This was implemented and has never been spotted by anyone as a trick. Angled correctly the mirrored reflection can make a corridor look like it's going to infinity, a massive cost-saver when needed.

After several corridors you came to the commissary. Like a kitchen in a large house, it became the central place of the ship. The wall units contained food in jars, and storage containers. We had tea- and coffee-making equipment built in, and we designed various units that looked as if you could get milk, water, juice, etc., much like a future kitchen might be. I liked some PVC white cups we had found that looked utilitarian and were in the same color as the units; I think they were designed as picnic cups. We placed these in a row over the main delivery unit and I added the Weyland-Yutani logo. Using different sizes of PVC downpipe and a coffee jug, I built an automatic coffee dispenser. Units from airplane galleys were also built in and painted in the same off-white to blend in. There was a delivery hatch and the crew could press the suitable button to order what they wanted, exactly the principle of a modern food-vending machine. It was all designed to give the impression the crew was looked after and all their needs catered to. They just had to fulfill their respective roles and endure the boredom of long-haul space flights.

This set was left sparsely dressed at this time in readiness for the first shots as Ridley was drifting through the empty ship. Just the odd coffee cup, a crewmember's jacket, and those pecking birds, slowly, rhythmically, bending their beaks into the cup of water. This gave the impression of life being there on the ship, but human life was nowhere to be found.

Then you came into the bridge. Entering from the rear door into the claustrophobic yet quite vast cockpit area for the first time was overwhelming. No other set had ever been made like this, so organic and utilitarian and to all appearances a real cockpit we had borrowed for the shoot. I think somehow it exactly matched people's subconscious idea of what a spacecraft would be like.

Sigourney came to visit and I showed her the cockpit. She was amazed at the controls she was able to use, like flight control levers and throttles we had adapted from airplane cockpits. Her seat moved on sliders back and forward and then there were all the switches and levers that were all interactive. For her first major film this was something else. As this looked like a long-haul vehicle it was much easier for her to imagine her part in it and get into the role. She sat in the seat and played around. Certainly the environment is as much a part of creating a character as the internal work and the clothes, hair, and makeup. Being in a world you didn't question the authenticity of certainly helped on *Alien*.

I felt fully justified seeing the reactions of the actors, visitors, and crewmembers as they walked around the sets. Looking at the *Alien* sets was like looking at a dream I had had in my head since a child. Film is magical, and here was the alchemy—from wood and scrap we had created a spacecraft in all its glory, and knowing how Ridley lit and photographed his films I knew this would be a major leap in cinema revolution for sure. The script was simple and read like a straightforward drama, and that to me was a huge advantage. It wasn't bogged down with details and descriptions and erroneous drama, it was a straight-as-an-arrow thrill ride and scary as hell. It had a new vision to it and included some sequences that were destined to be cinema landmarks if we could pull them off, and I never doubted that not only would Ridley succeed, but also that his visionary eye would far exceed expectations.

I was on the finished bridge set a few days before main shooting began one day with Ridley and Nick Allder talking about the opening sequence when the *Nostromo* wakes up. We were going through all the playback required and where it would be located and in which monitor. Ridley had drawn in his storyboards the computer readouts suddenly firing up, projected as a reflection across the glass of the emergency helmet I'd had built behind the crew stations. No one could come up with a solution for how to do it. There was a discussion of trying to animate it in afterwards— not so easy then as no CGI existed; everything had to be rotoscoped in and combined together in an optical printer. I had been working with an artist friend who created projections as art. We had made little 8mm films to project in art galleries, and some were created from graphics and lettering. We could project the films onto objects and see them in three-dimensional space. I told Ridley about this and said that I thought it might work and give him what he wanted. All we would need is a small 16mm projector, as that would provide the light level that would give an exposure on film. If we could get the computer readout transferred onto 16mm film, it was worth a try. We'd project it back onto the helmet.

Ridley was always game to try something if it sounded logical, so he said to give it a go, much the same as George sanctioned experimenting to get results not achieved before. Garth Thomas and I picked a suitable piece of computer readout to play back on the helmet, and he arranged to have it put onto 16mm film.

As soon as we had the projector and the film back, we tried out the idea. They lit the corner of the set where the helmet stood on a console, placed in front of the wall of the bridge set. This was layered with switches and computer elements that were in cupboard-like alcoves, fronted by glass, so it looked like the mechanisms were kept free of dust and atmosphere. When everything was lit, I handheld the projector up at the right height so it was level with the helmet, and we ran the film. I did this by hand so that I could position the projected image to get it to be at its most solid in the visor. It worked immediately: the numerals and lettering showed up in the glass, better than anyone thought. I moved around with the projector to get the reflections sharply in focus, as it depends on the distance from the screen, in this case the helmet's visor, on how bright the image is and also how sharp it is.

Ridley watched closely, as he was really an experienced director of photography himself, having operated everything he had done before this, including thousands of commercials. He gave me the thumbs up when everything was correct and we fixed the projector on a stand.

Killing all the lights except for the set lighting, they filmed a test on it as the lettering fired up. Then, changing the helmet position and the camera angle, several takes were filmed to make up the opening chatter from the computer. This test became one of the opening shots on *Alien*—it looked so good when we watched rushes.

As shooting progressed the first day, Ridley worked his way around the *Nostromo* for the opening of the film. I love this opening shot. It sets up an uneasy tension for the viewer, as the camera drifts around the empty *Nostromo*, lulling one into a false sense of security as it is smooth and unthreatening. Drifting through the corridors and airlocks with just a fan blowing the air conditioning and a bird pecking into a beaker, its all disquieting as there is no sign of a crew. I had to make sure everything was in order and that the audience was seeing a real ship. We see all the details as we pass through airlocks and corridors and the commissary. This is why so much attention to detail went into these sets from the dressing crew; everything, every detail had to stand up to scrutiny.

We placed the pecking, perpetual-motion birds on the commissary table; their movement as they bend into the glass of liquid is silent, and strangely lonely. Over a banquette there is just one crew jacket to remind us that a crew must have been on board. The camera drifts into the bridge along the walls of computer technology behind glass panels and over the consoles. We added three little bouncing toys on top of the console, not focused on, just there to create an illusion of life.

Then the camera moves over the flapping paper on a bridge console blowing eerily in the draft from the air conditioning. Ridley asked what we could do to make this happen quickly, so I thought for a moment and then came up with an instant solution.

There was no time to get it prepared in the usual way with an air blower and a hose. Also there was not much room under the console filled with wooden struts from the construction of the set to be able to set up a blower. Ridley needed to shoot quickly and was adjusting the shot through the lens.

Thinking quickly I suggested the fastest way was to get a hairdryer. I'd hide under the console and blow the papers by hand. That way I could adjust the airflow to make it look right. Ridley immediately said, "Let's try it," so the props went off to find me a hairdryer with several speeds on it. I looked at the shot Ridley had set up to see where I'd be safely out of the frame and maneuvered myself under the console. Blowing the papers by moving the hairdryer around gave the exact effect as if the air from an air-conditioning system was blowing them. We shot the scene quickly with no hold-ups. Once again, the lowest-tech way worked, and we got the shot. That's all that matters.

After this shot the camera comes over a console, coming to rest slowly for a moment on a monitor. I carefully placed the used cup on the console into the frame—this is what people do, leave dirty cups around. It gave the impression that someone was on board the craft, and begged the question—where were they? We cut to a helmet. We now know we are inside a spacecraft and a real one because of the interiors; everything is functional, but silent.

Then suddenly this computer chatter erupts on the monitor, reflected in the visor. It's the first real noise on the soundtrack, and loud enough to make us uneasy. It's a great image: a space helmet with the ship's cockpit reflected around it suddenly waking to life as the computer chatter starts scrolling across the dark glass of the visor.

So begins an uneasy tension, a hint of what's to come after the almost lyrical feeling drifting around the empty craft.

During these first days of shooting, a lot of tension surrounded the set as all the producers arrived and sat around nervously. On most days there were about three or four of them, and on one day with all the American executives and producers from Twentieth Century Fox there were about six people watching Ridley and watching the clock. It was tough on Ridley as he had not had any lighting test time allowed except for the test corridor earlier for Sigourney and the time pre-lighting the built-in lights all around the *Nostromo*. This would normally be budgeted for on a movie of this size, but they had imposed a really tight schedule, and the producers were there in force to ensure that he stuck to it. Derek Vanlint was the director of photography, and Ridley was very quick to explain exactly the lighting he wanted.

This film used built-in lighting to create the atmosphere, rather than normal film lighting, where a bright exposure level was all that mattered. Having most of the lighting built in meant that Ridley could shoot anywhere and quickly, and it also helped ground the sets in reality. Some of the corridors had the crates built in as wall sections and these were backlit to give a depth to them. They under-lit the floor grating running all over the corridors and bridge, but after an hour or so the lights started to melt the PVC grating. From then on after every take the lights were killed, whilst the team of electricians replaced the rest of the lights in the set with less hot fluorescents. We were all getting the soles of our shoes melted as we had nowhere else to stand when filming commenced around the cockpit control areas, but it looked awesome on rushes, and that in the end is what mattered.

The first scenes filmed on the bridge with the crew began after they had woken from the hypersleep and eaten. It picked up as they all got into their positions in the cockpit and started firing up the *Nostromo*'s guidance systems. The crew arriving and sliding their cockpit chairs into position looked incredibly natural to me, as they began firing up computers and flicking switches to get their guidance systems under their control. I think the color of the costumes and the pale faces of the crew just blended into the set and looked natural. The crew quickly realized as the system's locations started to appear on the monitors that they were not where they were supposed to be. Mother had woken them up, but they weren't home—they were in a totally different galaxy.

Ridley always operated the camera himself in those days, this way he composed the frame himself and watched the actors and the action through the lens so that he observed the scene exactly as a film frame. Stanley Kubrick did the same. Where atmosphere and framing is as important as the performance it is the best way by far, and Ridley is one of the best camera operators around. His framing on everything he does is always just about perfect, meaning the camera is always in the right place to observe the scene.

For the overall look of *Alien*, Ridley had decided to pioneer a more documentary style so that it again reinforced the idea that this was a real journey the audience was watching. He had Panavision cameras for the main unit, using anamorphic lenses with a 2.35:1 CinemaScope ratio. He also had a smaller Platinum camera with a shoulder harness, so that he could operate the camera handheld, and a good eighty percent of *Alien* was shot on Ridley's shoulder. The anamorphic lenses were huge and heavy, so it was a considerable weight Ridley carried daily for many hours.

When Ridley shot the corridor sequences early on in the shoot, he walked around the low corridors with the camera on this shoulder rig. Behind came the various technicians holding batteries and cables attached to the camera. The focus puller, the wonderful Adrian Biddle, walked alongside Ridley with the focus control on a long extended wire. I walked right behind camera with Paul Ibbetson, checking that the set was always correct. I used to see Paul Ibbetson, or 'Ibbo' as we all called him, cringe as Ridley walked forward. The magazine that held the film was mounted on top of the camera and sometimes Ridley missed the ceiling pieces at the airlocks and junctions by less than an inch. The grip followed as well, so either Ibbo or the grip would hold their hands ready to push the camera down if Ridley banged into a crosspiece above. As Ridley's eye was glued to the eyepiece on the camera it would have been dangerous if he did run into a set piece; it could damage his eye.

But Ridley has an amazing sense of framing, and never once did he ever hit anything. His instinct and concentration level meant he seemed to know within a half inch where everything was around him. The end result of shooting like this is that immediacy is added to the frame, a slight movement as the camera breathes with the actor's movements, and it feels alive. It worked remarkably well for all the opening tracking shots around the *Nostromo*. It gives a sense of fluidity but also of a little tension, as if from the point of view of someone, in this case the audience.

THE CREW FIRE UP THE *NOSTROMO*

Watching the actors fire up the *Nostromo* on the first day, working their stations, they looked remarkably like a well-seasoned crew who had been flying missions together for years: Kane sitting in his seat and seeing it slide forward into position as he switched controls above his head on the overhead units we had built in, like a bomber cockpit; Ripley moving her seat forward and studying the monitor; and Lambert starting up her console and realizing that they weren't home. It's extraordinary how a strong set can make the actors feel so at home. Having given them logical things to do that made sense, when none of them had ever piloted a plane before, they made it seem so real, without any real practice or rehearsal time on set. They just got it instinctively.

As standby art director, I was able to show the cast how things worked and give them suitable instructions before the shot started on how things matched the actions. Joe Dipple also helped me and was constantly making sure the actors had their cigarettes and props they needed for each shot. Ridley was shooting pretty fast, and having the camera handheld most of the time is a much quicker way to work than the camera fixed to a dolly or a tripod. He could quickly adjust the framing by subtly moving the camera to get the shot right, whereas on a dolly it takes a combination of people, with the grip and electrician and focus puller all walking alongside. Looking at the pictures of *Alien* now, especially this bridge set, one can see a very small concentrated crew around the camera with Ridley, and this made the filming much more intimate. I could see it giving the actors another layer of comfort.

The floors were getting really hot every time they were switched on for a shot and the set, being confined, was also really hot. They continued working fast, working through the opening scenes as the crew discovered they were in a very different system, and that Mother had picked up an emergency signal. The smoky atmosphere and heat was clearly affecting Jon Finch, who seemed very pale and tired. In the middle of a take, he turned yellow and seemed to collapse. Ridley stopped the shooting and they took Jon away to be treated. It turned out he had diabetes and had suffered an insulin failure; also I think the incense smoke was affecting him as well, as he was diagnosed with pneumonia. He was deemed to be too ill to carry on. It's ironic really that his character would have an alien growing inside his lungs a few scenes into the film. Ridley kept going, shooting around the now absent Kane. It was possible for him to do this as Ridley wasn't filming a lot of wide master shots in the bridge scene, more relying on tension-building closer shots of the characters and filming across the side-by-side consoles, with one character in the foreground and the other in the background.

Derek Vanlint was sweating to keep up, I remember, and smoking copiously. Ridley was shooting fast, and it added to the energy of the scenes. Derek was always worried about the lighting, but Ridley knew exactly what he wanted. The first day was really testing for Ridley as well in terms of getting the look right, and it was only in rushes that he could judge how the look was resonating. Most of the lighting was from the practical fittings built into the set but Ridley, operating through the camera, added in small highlights where needed, mostly adding backlight behind the actors and set. Using smoke as a natural diffuser creates an atmosphere in three dimensions, which softens the look of the scene naturally, and is way better than adding a diffusion filter on the lens.

Watching these rushes the next day was a mixture of excitement and a learning curve. Michael, Les, and I were carefully watching the sets and details to see how the look held up and if there were any moments that let the reality down, but the way it was shot and the intensity of the moments worked. We were used to the rushes process, as these are the full takes and shots and one looks at them knowing they will be selected for the best moments and cut together to make the sequence work. So only small parts of the rushes are used. I thought the look was amazing and justified those long days and weeks getting it right. The color schemes made the craft look very utilitarian, and the best thing for me was that the crew was working the controls. Ridley was analyzing everything, especially the lighting, to see how he could improve it and what to adjust. The actors had very little makeup in keeping with the 'space trucker' feel and that also helped embed them into the organic look and feel. So far so good.

It is well documented how John Hurt was persuaded by Ridley that first night after we wrapped to take on the role of Kane, and ironic in a way as Ridley had always wanted John for the role and he wasn't free. The film he was supposed to be on collapsed, and by a stroke of fate and destiny he was suddenly free. John is such a consummate professional and such a great actor that he slipped into the role the next day with no fuss or demands. As the shooting started back up again, he sat in Kane's chair and Ridley reshot the scenes with him that had been filmed the day before. John immediately seemed at home in the console area destined for Kane and, after a brief explanation of the controls, got on with his job.

Ridley didn't allow the actors to watch rushes. In my experience most actors don't want to watch them as they feel it makes them conscious of the character they are creating, and then they start imitating what they did on the previous day. Most prefer to create a character and then let it be, trusting the director to guide them. Also the exterior image may not exactly match what they imagine in their heads as they become the character, and many of the great actors in fact never watch the films they have made until many years later. Sigourney wasn't fully used to the process yet as this was only her second film, and first really major role. I spent a lot of my time near her as she was always asking me questions

ALIEN

about the bridge and how to make her actions look functional. She then began to ask me how she was doing every day when I returned from rushes. I always told her not to worry, it was all one hundred percent believable and she was Ripley.

At the early stage of the movie she was one of the crew, and only later as the story progressed did she take command. She built into this really well, slowly gaining power as she took over. As the rest of the crew was killed off one by one she grew into the role of the female warrior, determined that the alien would be destroyed. Ridley didn't say much to his actors; he wanted them to remain insecure and a little tense about what was happening, just as their characters would be. I told Sigourney when she asked me about this not to worry, if Ridley sees something is not working, he'll tell you immediately. We could see in rushes that the actors were really blending into the atmosphere of the *Nostromo*, and like truckers they were in a way ordinary characters thrust into extreme danger, into the unknown. Sigourney was the new girl on the block as the other actors were all seasoned film veterans, so she was a little more insecure than the others, but her character demanded that. So it worked.

In the case of *Alien* the script was utilitarian, stripped down to the bare essentials and seemed like natural dialogue between grumbling below-deck workers who always felt hard done by. It emphasized a kind of 'upstairs and downstairs' scenario, the 'them and us' syndrome so familiar in ordinary life. Below-decks continually moaned and pressed for more pay and less hours and did what they could to make it seem their working hours and difficulties were far more than they actually were. Above decks there was the subtle posturing for command of the ship between the other crewmembers, who all had ambitions to be captain and who had ended up on long-haul ore-collecting missions, maybe dreaming of much more creative jobs or better conditions. So the script was not dwelling on complex character explorations, or difficult scenes of emotional complexities, it was merely a group of truckers at work coming under an unknown threat causing tension and duress, as shocked as the audience watching them at the horrific events unfolding. The actors did improvise and make the dialogue better when needed, feeding off the atmosphere on set and each other.

Sigourney has a graceful and natural beauty. She needed little to no makeup to help her portray her character; the more natural the better.

Ridley only added water, spritzed on by the makeup standby to denote sweat in the hot, humid atmosphere of the *Nostromo*. Combined with her athletic body and loose wild hair, it gave her a tremendous appeal as Ripley. She could play her as a determined, intelligent, and tough woman, whilst still keeping her really feminine. By fearlessly playing her so well, she created an icon and revolutionized the way women were portrayed in films.

I will note that having read the script and knowing it so well, it was really interesting for me to watch Ian Holm work. The subtle way he made Ash develop; there were tiny clues in his acting that were inherent in being an android, a robot created in human form. The audience never guessed but there was always something a little odd about Ash, and only on rediscovering the film after the first viewing do these intricacies of performance get noticed. As an intended director these were the best master classes, to watch actors at work on a set constantly day after day, building their roles.

Once the first scenes had been established and shooting repeated with John Hurt, Ridley moved onto the scene in the cockpit where they have to unlock the shuttle and fly down to the planet's surface. This required a lot of vibrations as the shuttle bucked and shook when entering the planet's turbulent atmosphere. Dan O'Bannon's idea, based on numerous flying experiences when turbulence rocked the plane, wrote it in this way to garner more authenticity. Also, the delay caused by the rough ride and landing as Brett and Parker repaired the ship was a plot point. The set was far too large and heavy to build on rockers, so it depended on the actors looking like they were being buffeted and shaken around whilst strapped into their seats. Ridley gave cues to the actors as they filmed each segment and he shook the camera in sync. He jerked it around on his shoulder and asked Ibbo and the grip to bang the camera and make it shudder. When Ibbo had to cue the actors to lean left or right, I had to join the grip and bang the camera around to make it shake violently. It worked so well, and in rushes you could see those moments of magic when all was in sync and it did look like the *Nostromo*'s landing craft was flying through terrible turbulence. His idea was to create chaos, and not the all-too-familiar soft landing of spaceships in movies before that. The papers flying, the electrical faults causing fires, and the crew trying to control the bucking bronco made a scene as real as anything and kicked the film off onto the path of authenticity for the audience watching.

The special-effects boys had rigged up sparks and fire for the final landing sequence, so that the *Nostromo*'s shuttle looked like it was getting damaged in the turbulence. At the same time the film lights were rigged to a central control board and Derek Vanlint worked this so that the lights kept dimming and flashing, eventually going out completely as they landed. All of these elements, combined together with the actors' reactions like spraying a practical fire extinguisher I had dressed in as an electrical fault sparked, gave the scene a tremendous force. It looked incredibly tense as the craft looked like it was nearly losing it. The shoulder-mounted camera really came into its own here, and Ridley was able to recreate a storm and the ship reacting violently in it so easily. All done with no CGI or tricks, just simple on-set co-ordinated instructions from Ridley to the crew to move in sync with each designated movement of the craft, and a lot of camera shake and grips moving what they could on set. I still prefer this reality-style filmmaking, and despite the illusions created now so easily with CGI, I don't think this landing scene has ever been matched on film.

I watched rushes carefully. It was exciting stuff. The fire extinguishers we had dressed in with Nick's boys helped make the scene look real as smoke and sparks created chaos as the crew struggled to put out the fires. Then the lights came back on as the emergency generator kicked in. It all worked. I cannot remember ever having seen anything like this before. Submarine movies for sure had captured the fear and claustrophobia of the crew as a fire broke out or a problem erupted, but never before had a spacecraft been created and filmed this way. Heady stuff indeed, and a portent of what was to come.

For one section, Ridley was shooting down the cockpit across the consoles and needed a light in the background. He got the gaffer to set up a small lamp on the steel-colored stands and place it in the shot. Derek Vanlint watched in horror and argued with Ridley, saying, "You can't do that," but Ridley was absolutely firm that no one would notice it was a film light, and that the shot looked great backlit with it in. Derek didn't want to give in. He kept arguing. Ridley looked at me: "Can you dress it up?" I nodded yes and told him not to worry. I went round the back to our stage supply of scrap and found some suitable pieces. With the prop standby we attached them to the lamp stand and disguised it as best we could, carrying on until Ridley was ready to shoot, and Ibbo called standby. I understood Derek's point: if the lamp showed up on screen, as director of photography his reputation would be challenged. However, Ridley knew exactly what he wanted, especially where the lighting was concerned, so he pulled rank and said, "It's fine, let's shoot." I looked through the camera and it was true—with the light burning into the lens one could never tell the source, it looked very strong visually. Next day in rushes it looked great, but Derek just couldn't get over the fact that it was a lamp on a stand. It is the power of the mind; what one knows stays in the mind but you have to leap over the fact and look at the result with fresh eyes. To me it's the end result that counts, not how you got there.

Whilst filming was going on I was preparing for a major prop to come in the next few scenes. We had made the alien tracking device and the video playback team had that ready with the material that played back on cue to show the position of the alien in the air ventilation shafts, and Dallas. The other prop we were going to need when shooting moved to the navigation area behind the bridge consoles was the cattle-prod-like device that Brett had made up and demonstrated. Nick Allder had made this up from an electric welding iron. This sparked when the tip touched metal, so we rigged up a hidden steel plate on the overhead console that Brett could touch, and the short made a large display of sparks. We dressed up the finished prod to look less like a welding iron and more like something Brett had cobbled together in the *Nostromo*'s workshop down below.

After Brett shows them how his alien prod works, Ash demonstrates the tracking device to the others. I showed Ian Holm the tracking device we had made up, and how it functioned. The video playback technician showed him how the tracker worked. Ash describes to the crew how the tracking device works on air-density changes when questioned about it by Ripley. Both these action props are right there in close-up on the screen and are both used to hunt the alien so they had to look right. He shows them how the tracker zones in on movement. This is important as the script calls for a moment when they think they have found the baby alien, and it's Jones the cat. This is a false shock to lure the audience into a state of tension, not knowing what might jump out on them next.

During that first week of filming, while Ridley was setting up the next shot, he asked me if I could quickly come up with a notebook of some kind for one of the crew to write notes in. I went off set to think about what I could quickly assemble that might look right and fit in with the *Nostromo* look. It was a bit challenging—nothing came to my mind that instant and I knew it had to be a quick solution. It was obvious we couldn't have a conventional notebook of any kind—I had my small black Daler one in my pocket with me always to make notes in, but that really wouldn't fit the *Alien* world. I was thinking fast, standing just off the side of the set of the bridge next to Kay Fenton, the continuity lady's worktable. I knew I would have to go off set to the prop store where we had the selected airplane junk when at that instant Kay opened her Polaroid camera, took out the empty cartridge and threw it in the waste bin. It was another of those slow-motion moments for me. As it hit the bin I watched in amazement, reached in and grabbed it.

Continuity people use Polaroids as they are instant pictures and easily recorded. In those days a lot of them used the simple Polaroid SX70, which had a small cartridge-loaded film pack holding about eight pictures. These Polaroids can be seen in the 'making of' on the boxed *Alien* DVD sets. I reached in and took the small cartridge out of the waste bin and blessed my luck. It was about four inches square, and the eight pieces of instant film were held in place by a small spring-loaded clip so that they were dispensed one by one. The Polaroid snaps were fired out the front of the camera. It was finished in matte black, and looked like a small engineered device. I could easily convert it to a notebook that looked futuristic but fitted the style of the *Nostromo*. I rushed out to the art department and found some graph paper, which had green squares printed on it. I cut them in a guillotine to the exact size and fitted them into the pack where the film was placed. Then, taking the Letraset symbols of the company logo with the green Egyptian wings, I stuck this on the top bar. I added a few more numbers on the lower bar and it looked exactly how a future notebook might look.

We had some pens we had dressed already as they were steel design and looked suitable and, grabbing one of these, I quickly returned to the set. I showed Ridley, who immediately added it into the shot. Then I went back to Kay and took the other disused cartridges from the bin, as she went through quite a few of these in a day. She looked at me amused as I took an extra full one, telling her I'd replace it. I had the prop makers make up three more for dressing for the other crewmembers. Another problem solved quickly. The notebook shows up in the scene in the infirmary when Ripley is questioning Ash about the facehugger and the baby alien. Ash is making notes in it.

These were my days over the coming weeks, as these things erupt on set all the time. It's a natural part of the filming process as directors or actors tend to add little details to help a scene, and it often falls on the art department to invent something on the spot. One has to be used to thinking fast and being inventive.

TENSION ON THE SET

Watching rushes for the first four days of filming it was clear how good *Alien* was going to be. The storm sequence looked so real, this was truly a cinema first. Also, the amount of footage Ridley was shooting was impressive. He was moving very fast, doing a lot of setups a day.

When I came onto the stage I noticed a lineup of chairs along the stage wall. There were several producers and executive producers on set all the time in those first days. Amongst them were the film's actual producers, Gordon Carroll, David Giler, Sandy Lieberson and Ron Shusett, and Ivor Powell who was Ridley's producer from commercials. Added to these producers were several American execs from Twentieth Century Fox, over for the start of filming, and the UK's manager, Peter Beale, working directly under Sandy Lieberson. Some of them were looking at their watches rather noticeably.

As I walked back to the set, one of them walked up to me and asked me why I thought Ridley was so slow. I told him I didn't understand as Ridley was doing easily a minimum of thirty to thirty-five setups and most days way beyond that, and shooting really fast in comparison to other directors I had worked with. Filming nearly all of the film handheld is a very fast way to shoot. Not laying down dolly tracks saves an enormous amount of time and, being handheld, Ridley could easily change his setup quickly. I told the producer that I thought the rushes were awesome, there was so much rich material there, and that you could see how fast he was going. Technically it was running smoothly and we didn't have huge, long lighting setups at all, the lighting was mostly inherent in the set, built in. They just gave it small tweaks as they went. So I told the producer I didn't

ABOVE: Me, Les Dilley, Norman Reynolds and John Barry at the 1978 Academy Awards.

ABOVE: Me, just back from filming in Tunisia, with Les Dilley, John Barry, Bill Welch and Norman Reynolds in the *Star Wars* art department.

BELOW: Harrison Ford tries out my adapted Mauser for Han Solo's gun of choice.

CHEWBACCA'S RIFLE

SW 5804

SW 5804

BELOW: The first weapon I ever made on *Star
Wars*—the Stormtroopers' gun. Adapted
from a Stirling sub-machine gun with rubber
T-strip and army rangefinders glued on.

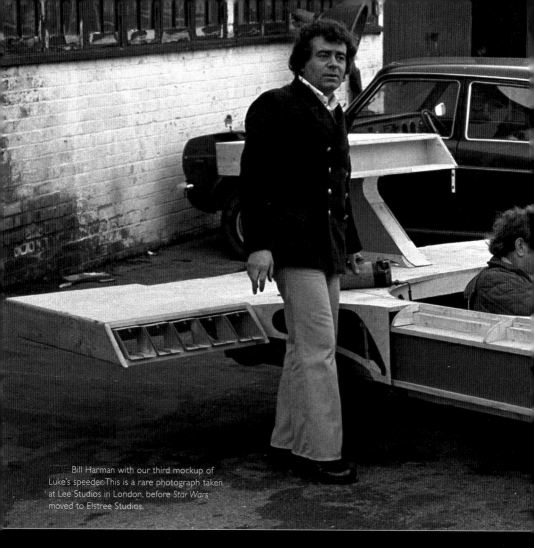

ABOVE: Bill Harman with our third mockup of Luke's speeder. This is a rare photograph taken at Lee Studios in London, before *Star Wars* moved to Elstree Studios.

ABOVE: Airplane scrap and robots I created for the interior of the Sandcrawler's hold.

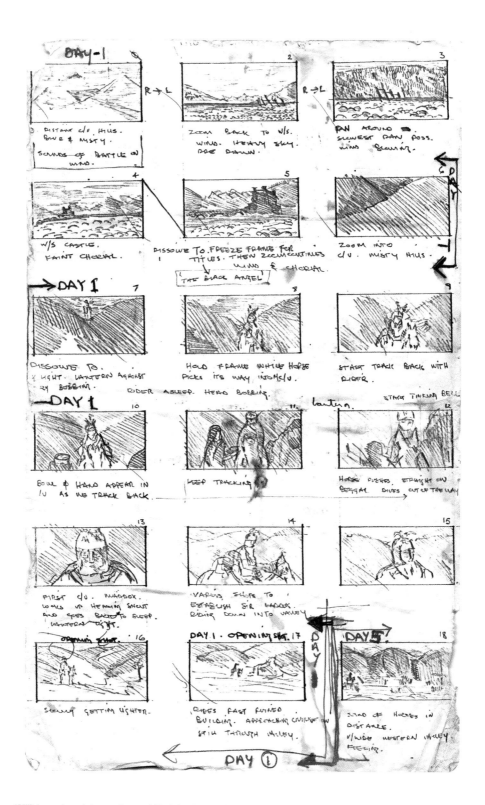

ABOVE: I storyboarded every frame of *Black Angel* to get through filming in seven days, using film stock limited to the ends of film left over from *The Empire Strikes Back*.

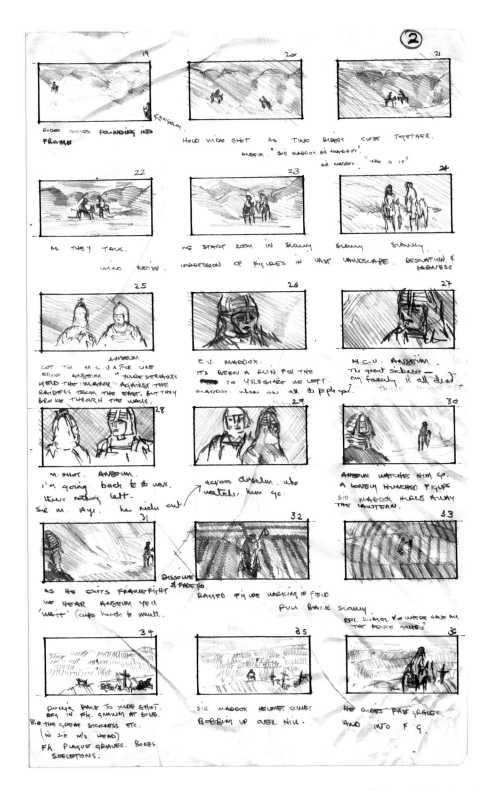

19

RIDER COMES POUNDING INTO FRAME

20

HOLD WIDE SHOT AS TWO RIDERS CLOSE TOGETHER.
ANSELM. "SIR MADDOX SIR MADDOX."
SIR MADDOX. "WHO IS IT"

21

22

AS THEY TALK.
WIND NOISE.

23

WE START ZOOM IN SLOWLY SLOWLY SLOWLY.
IMPRESSION OF FIGURES IN VAST LANDSCAPE. DESOLATION & DARKNESS

24

25

CUT TO M.C.U A FOR LINE FROM ANSELM. "YOURE SERVANTS HELD THE MANOR AGAINST THE RAIDERS FROM THE EAST, BUT THEY BROKE THROUGH THE WALLS.

ANSELM.

26

C.U. MADDOX.
ITS BEEN A RUN FOR THE PAST 20 YRS SINCE WE LEFT.
MADDOX. WHERE ARE ALL THE PEOPLE GONE?

27

M.C.U. ANSELM.
THE GREAT SICKNESS —
MY FAMILY IS ALL DEAD.

28

M. SHOT. ANSELM.
I'M GOING BACK TO THE WARS.
THERE'S NOTHING LEFT.
SIR M. AYE. HE RIDES OUT

29

ACROSS ANSELM. WHO WATCHES HIM GO.

30

ANSELM WATCHES HIM GO.
A LONELY HUNCHED FIGURE.
SIR MADDOX HOLDS AWAY
THE LANTERN.

31

AS HE EXITS FRAME RIGHT
WE HEAR ANSELM YELL
'WAIT' (CUPS HANDS TO MOUTH.

DISSOLVE & FADE TO.

32

RAGGED FIGURE WALKING IN FIELD
PULL BACK SLOWLY.
RPT. DIALOG. V.O WHERE HAVE ALL
THE PEOPLE GONE?

33

34

PULLING BACK TO WIDE SHOT.
BRING IN FK. GMMM AT EDGE.
V.O. THE GREAT SICKNESS ETC.
(IN SIR M's HEAD)
FK. PLAGUE GRAVES. BONES
SKELETONS.

35

SIR MADDOX HELMET SLUMS
BOBBIN UP OVER HILL.

36

HE RIDES PAST GRAVES
AND INTO F.G.

ABOVE: *Black Angel* storyboards.

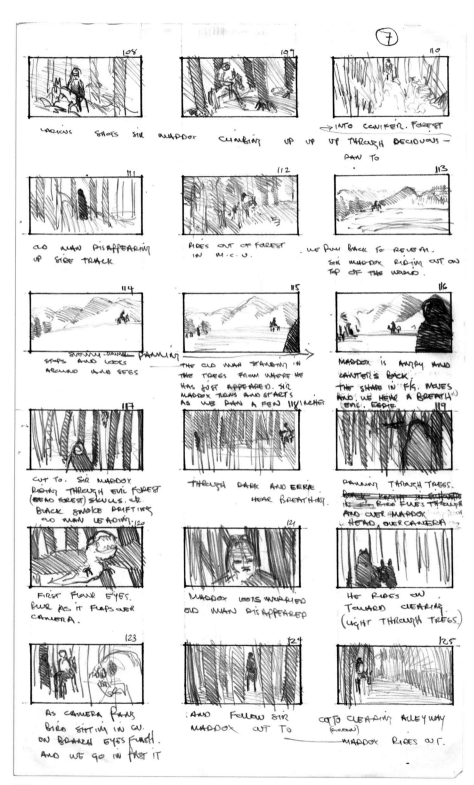

ABOVE: *Black Angel* storyboards.

126

HIS GIRTH SLIPS AND
HE STEPS TO FIX IT

127

HORSE TURNS TOWARD
US AND WE SEE THE
BLACK ANGEL...
SILHOUTTE. SITTING WATCHING.

128

M.C.U. SILHOUTTE.
EVIL. BLACK
LEATHER MAN.
FRANZETTA SHOT.

127.A

SIR MADDOX AWARE.
TURNS AND LOOKS

REGISTERS HIS OPPONENT.

130

REGISTER HIS LOOK.
HE FEELS AND TAKES
HIS AXE FROM THE SADDLE.

131

AND SUDDENLY
CHARGES TOWARDS US

132

CUT TO.
MADDOX CHARGING
AND BLACK ANGEL CHARGING
TOWARDS CAMERA.

133

THE PASS THE
ANGEL EASILY AVOIDING
THE BLOW.

134

ANGEL IN F.G.
SIR MADDOX DISTANCE
THEY HAVE TURNED FOR
ANOTHER CHARGE

135

AGAIN BLACK ANGEL
SEEMS TO EASILY
AVOID BLOW.

136

SIR MADDOX RIDES INTO
F/G. OFF BALANCE AND
STOPS.

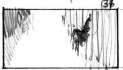

137

BLACK ANGEL SUDDENLY
CHARGES AROUND CORNER
INTO TREES.

138

CUT TO. CU BLACK
ANGEL.
SEE EYES FOR FIRST TIME
CAMERA WEDS EYES FLASH

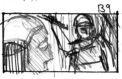

139

HEAD TURNS.
MADDOX CHARGES AROUND
CORNER.
AXED RAISED.

140

STRAIGHT INTO
ANGEL. AND
OUT OF SHOT.
CUT. TO.

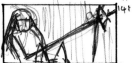

141

AXE   HANGING ON
ANGELS   STAVE.

142

HE FLICKS IT AND IT
LANDS IN THE GRASS.
HALFWAY BETWEEN
HIM & SIR MADDOX.

143

SIR MADDOX RIDES TOWARDS
THE AXE AND
DISMOUNTS TO PICK
IT UP.

BELOW AND INSET: Directing Tony Vogel on the last day's shooting sequence for *Black Angel* at the Riverside swimming pool, Dunoon.

BLACK ANGEL

A FILM BY
ROGER CHRISTIAN

PAINTED LADY PRODUCTIONS LIMITED PRESENTS

A ROGER CHRISTIAN FILM

STARRING TONY VOGEL AS SIR MAROK

AND INTRODUCING PATRICIA CHRISTIAN

JAMES GIBB   JOHN YOUNG   DIRECTED AND ROGER CHRISTIAN
PRODUCED BY

ASSOCIATE LESLIE DILLEY MUSIC BY TREVOR JONES SCREENPLAY BY ROGER CHRISTIAN PHOTOGRAPHED BY ROGER PRATT ART JOHN BEARD EDITED BY ALAN STRACHAN SOUND MICHAEL BATEMAN DIGITAL RESTORATION BRICE PARKER AND DAVID H TANAKA
PRODUCER   DIRECTOR   EDITOR   PRODUCED BY

FILMED ON LOCATION IN SCOTLAND   AVAILABLE ON iTUNES   FILMED IN PANAVISION ® WITH HELP FROM SOUNDESIGNE POST PRODUCTION AT PRODUCTION VILLAGE   082 1001   CANADA LIMITED

© Copyright: ROGER CHRISTIAN 2004

understand what they wanted, it was obvious from the first days of rushes how powerful this film would be. Ridley had elevated what was on the page to visionary cinema, and I didn't see how he could go any quicker. True, Jon Finch had fallen ill and Ridley had to reshoot all his scenes with John Hurt, but I am sure insurance covered those costs. I walked away thinking, *What the hell do they want from him?*

RIDLEY PUNCHES THROUGH THE BRIDGE CEILING

A short while later I was standing on the bridge set right next to Ridley. We had opened the side panel to the bridge to allow for easier filming from the side across the consoles. Garth Thomas, who had obviously been sent down as an envoy by producers afraid to do it themselves, came and talked to Ridley in a low voice. As Garth turned and left, Ridley exploded like a rocket—he launched himself up in the air and punched the ceiling of the *Nostromo*, his fist going straight through a small section of the roof. He let out a yell of pent-up frustration as he rose, and a "Fuck!" came roaring out of his mouth He landed and looked around, swore at the producers and then got on with the next shot. Garth was actually a friend of Ridley's and had been chosen by the American producers to deliver their dirty work, telling Ridley he was being too slow and to hurry up. Ridley looked around as we carried on and said, "What the fuck do they want from me?" I replied, "I don't understand them, they just asked me why you were so slow and I told them you were shooting faster than any director I had worked with."

It was baffling but Ridley, knowing what he had to get on camera every minute as they'd for sure never give him any extra time, just knuckled down and carried on, getting the best of each shot. You can't let this stuff affect you or you lose focus and concentration. It always seems to be the same complaint from producers to directors. You are shooting too slowly or you are using too much stock—they are the continual complaints a director receives shooting a movie, whatever the budget.

The shooting carried on regardless and the rushes got better and better. As long as the director makes his days, that is gets the work completed each day that is laid out in the schedule, that is the thing most accountants worry about, and those reports go back daily to the studio heads and the bond company who insure the movie's completion if anything goes seriously wrong. It is a huge pressure on directors, as the budgets get tighter and tighter as finance gets harder to find. It becomes a daily battle to get through and sometimes the creative moments have to be sacrificed. It's the director's job to structure his days and find a way to get what he wants in the can, and that's why it's hard if there are disputes on set, or actors aren't on the ball or on the same page, which happens sometimes. It's somewhat easier on a huge studio movie, as there is room to maneuver when the schedules run over several months and the daily shot number is far less.

Ridley worked his way through the bridge scenes to the back where the navigation sector was. Here the alien tracker prop was introduced and functioned perfectly (thank goodness) and then came the scene with the cattle-prod tracker. We showed Harry Dean Stanton the metal plate in the overhead console and that worked perfectly; sparks erupted each time he touched it. It is always a worry as major props are filmed, but having someone like Nick Allder and his team there took that away, as he never let us down. Nick was on top of everything and made sure it worked perfectly. The actors ramped up their performances as the alien was on the loose for these scenes. Films are very rarely shot in continuity order of the drama; it is too expensive and time-consuming to go back and forth between sets, especially lighting them. It would mean leaving sets lit to go somewhere else and returning again. The cost of having a huge amount of lighting equipment to have each set lit ready to shoot at any time would be prohibitive and also the time wasted changing from one set to another is huge. We all try to avoid moving, as hours go by taking down the cameras and re-setting, and changing actors' costumes and makeup all takes its toll. But the Nostromo complex was built and ready to shoot, so Ridley could go anywhere at any time.

JONES THE CAT IN THE LOCKER

Thank goodness animals and children don't normally fall under the art department. Ridley was about to tackle Jones the cat. The animal handler had trained several cats but in the 'working with animals' manual by directors, cats come number one in 'avoid at all costs.' Dogs can be trained to do amazing tricks and perform, and of course now computers can generate them to undertake impossible feats. Cats are far more difficult, willful creatures that just don't like to be told what to do by humans. In those days it was get the animal to do it or cut it from the script. I once spent over four hours in the famed Cinecittà Studios in Rome trying to get frogs to jump for one shot for a commercial for Vespa, finally getting one to do it at four in the morning. After trying every trick in the book we got one shot—that was it.

Knowing cats are on the schedule puts the fear of god into any director; they are really hard to train. Trainers also have an unwavering optimism about cats, and Jones's trainer was no exception. Jones had to be found in a locker, and when the door was opened by the crew, prepared to catch whatever was in there with a rope net, Jones was meant to jump out snarling at them. We as the audience were to think it was the alien trapped in there, ready to leap out and kill. Easier said than done, but the trainer said the cat was trained to do it, and she had a stand-in trained as well. Michael had designed the locker in the front area of the bridge, so we had rear access to it. The shot was carefully set up with Jones inside, with Ripley, Brett and Parker approaching the locker holding up a cargo net to catch the alien. When they opened the door on the first take—nothing, no cat. It refused to budge. They tried the second cat after several failed attempts, and the same, it wouldn't move. No shot. The special-effects boys were called in. They blew CO_2 at the cat from behind, and nothing! They needed to get a huge reaction from the cat as the scene depended on it, so lunch was called and decisions had to be made.

After lunch they set it up again. Nick Allder recounts the story in the *Alien Makers* documentary of how they got the cat to finally do it. Of course the animal lovers might look on this badly these days but they had to get the shot, and without hurting the cat. Phil Knowles, who was a major part of Nick's team, made it work, and Nick 'lets the cat out of the bag' in the documentary made by Dennis Lowe regarding how Phil did it and how Ridley finally got the shot. Phil went behind the locker when the scene was set up and the camera was ready. He wrapped the cat's tail around his fingers and waited. Upon 'action', the crew opened the locker door once more and the cat screamed and fired out of the locker like a rocket, shocking everyone on the crew, not just the actors. This is the shot we see now in the film. Nick Allder says that Phil kinked the cat's tail in his fingers and that made it flee with a scream. Whatever happened, it worked, and you only need one take that works with animals.

Ridley moved onto shots with Ripley looking for Jones in the corridors. To film Ripley running through the corridors later in the script, when she is trying to find Jones to get him into the shuttle, required Ridley to run after her in the corridors, or be her point of view with the camera on his shoulder. First AD Paul Ibbetson who we called Ibbo, Adrian the focus puller, the grip, Derek Vanlint, and I ran after Ridley for each take. I was trying to make sure the set and the dressing was all okay. This time watching Ridley run through these corridors with their low ceilings was scary. The camera magazine would barely pass the airlock architecture, and either Ibbo or the grip would always have a hand ready to push it under as Ridley was moving so fast. The shots looked great, though; the movement on wide lenses rushing through the *Nostromo*'s army-like corridors really looked impressive, adding to the tension of the moment.

It was here when Sigourney carried the cat that she broke out in an allergy. Thinking it was due to the cat, it was a massive worry for her, as she had several scenes to come with Jones. After a lot of researching they realized that it was the glycerin they were putting on her skin to make her look damp, to create the slightly sweaty look to help sell the idea of the enclosed hot atmosphere of the *Nostromo*, and add to the feeling of fear. Somehow the two things together created a reaction on her skin. So they sprayed her down with water in a spritzer for the rest of the film. Without the glycerin she was fine with Jones and could carry on acting with the cat, immensely relieved.

The bridge shooting schedule went on over the next three weeks or so. There were a lot of scenes to be covered where the action took place there. I went off set when the setup didn't require me to be there and worked with Ian Whittaker on the dressing of the crew quarters.

CREW QUARTERS

The next scene up after the bridge was the breakfast scene when they wake up from hypersleep. First up was Kane, who woke first from hypersleep, and he wandered in from the corridors and made himself a coffee from the automatic dispenser. The only dressing we placed on the table for this was the two perpetual-motion birds and a cup of water we had for the empty *Nostromo* shots in the opening sequence. I am sure that the space-science purists would argue that after a long period in hypersleep the crew would be drip-fed minerals and vitamins to get the body functioning correctly again, but this was a movie. And what would space truckers do? Go get a coffee. A scene played out in the majority of American households as a daily ritual. So whether true or not, it offered familiarity for an audience watching a space film for the first time. The script called for it and we dressed it that way to set the scene for the crew together later.

As soon as this sequence was filmed, Ridley would have to move straight onto the breakfast scene, so we prepared all the props to create a normal breakfast morning for the crew of seven. Once all the dressing was prepared, I went back to the bridge and the shoot.

NOSTROMO COMMISSARY

The crew shifted location to the main galley set. Ridley set up for Kane entering from the hypersleep chamber. He walked through into the food and dining-area set, smoking a Russian Sobranie cigarette. I had used these cigarettes in the *Jason King* TV series, as I liked the color of them, a beige kind of faded-yellow color that looked much better on screen. Instead of the usual white paper, they had cardboard filters to smooth out the smoke. It gave them a more interesting look, I felt.

As the camera tracks and pans around with Kane, we see a lot of the set for the first time; the alcoves where the crew rest and the details of the padded environment are all seen. It adds depth and reality—it's not just a four-walled set as many previous films had made do with. Kane turns into the main area and pushes a button at the food-delivery hatch. The hatch door slides silently up and pushing another button, grinds coffee and serves him from the built-in coffee maker. What more natural way to start the day from waking? The scene was cut out of the final movie as it was deemed to slow the pace of the movie.

Shooting progressed on through the crew breakfast scene as they all arrived. This took ages to shoot and somewhat frustrated Ridley. Ridley allowed the actors to improvise on the script dialogue to try to get the scene as natural as possible as they shared breakfast.

John Hurt was ad-libbing at a really slow pace, smoking his cigarettes and drinking his coffee, and the actors were enjoying this moment. Ridley hadn't rehearsed, just let them gather and chat to try to get a scene as normal as possible. We could all sense Ridley's frustration as the takes dragged on and on and never got to the dialogue scripted as Ridley had instructed. They were trying to create a bored crew awaking from years in hypersleep. It was obvious this would all be cut from the script; just the pertinent dialogue to the story was needed. Eventually, John delivered the lines in the script and the scene does look natural and that's all that matters.

This was the only really relaxed crew moment in the movie and in a way the discomfort of the actors working together without rehearsal makes the scene a bit edgy and real. Life is like this in the real world, after all, workers and bosses are pushed together in a confined space, like being at sea in a submarine for months on end. Cutting can pace a scene up very easily in the editing room if there are enough different takes. We also met Jones the cat, who was on the table drinking milk.

As they were filming this part of the scene I took the opportunity to go through my breakdown of everything required for the infirmary set with everyone on the set. Kane would be brought back here from the alien planet with the facehugger attached under his helmet.

In the script it called for a scanner-type machine used in hospitals that could X-ray Kane. The crew could see the facehugger had a tube down inside him, keeping him breathing. Michael had designed the scanner like a built-in alcove in the infirmary wall, again based on Ron Cobb's sketch. I spoke with Nick Allder and the electricians to work out how to have a light slide across Kane's body in shot, and slide back just as an MRI scan would. The controls were mostly dressed in switch panels from an abandoned electrical control room, painted in to match the set, and specific panels were made up by Guy and Dennis.

Kane was placed on the hospital-type bed Michael had designed within the set, and for the action we needed Kane's helmet, made in various stages of being removed. When he was brought into the infirmary after the facehugger attacked him in the egg chamber, Dallas and Ash cut the helmet off his head by slicing through it with a small high-speed saw. So we needed to make that up and prepare several helmets to save time.

MOTHER

During these early weeks we also filmed inside the Mother set. Dallas has to take out the security key in the corridor leading into Mother, and go through a security procedure.

Dallas places the electronic key into the device and goes through the various procedures to open the door to Mother; this again gave visual reference to the secrecy surrounding Mother and that Dallas was the only one with license to enter. We had prepared another key-in code panel at the door; by entering the correct code the door slid open. These were worked by the grips, on a slider mechanism, working almost perfectly every time; it was merely a question of getting the cues correct. Bill Welch had built all the airlock doors in the craft on slider mechanisms in combination with Nick Allder; they operated like giant sash windows. On cue the grips could pull the doors up or down, and the addition later of a hydraulic 'swish' sound made the illusion work that these were powered airlock doors.

Inside Mother, Dallas sits in the chair with the keyboard console and on operating the controls, the chair swivels round and moves into place (Nick Allder's work again).

The set around Mother looked absolutely original and authentic with all the lights on; we had built in scrap computer keyboards for Dallas to operate under the monitor, all painted in to the same cream color of the set. These still look functional today and fit the scene, slightly retro but truck-like—that's what the *Nostromo* was. During the filming of this, we went back to the commissary to set up the chestburster scenes to film next on the schedule.

Alien still sets the benchmark for horror today, and the chestburster scene is regarded as one of the scariest moments in movie history. To create this sequence required four stages of preparation and filming. First the eruption in Kane's chest with a blood squirt, then the hydraulic ram to break through his chest. Third was the baby alien puppet and then fourth the escape.

First up we had the commissary table modified with a hole cut in it to allow enough room for John Hurt's head and shoulders, the mechanism for the hydraulic ram and Roger Dicken's puppet-controlled baby alien to punch through the false chest. We made the panel so it could be placed back to look like a solid table to film with first. I knew that the dressing for the eating scene would hide any evidence of the joints; this was the scene in the schedule filmed later after Kane had been attacked by the facehugger and it had died later in the infirmary sequence. Kane had recovered and all seemed to be fine again, and we see all the crew eating together.

I had the crew prepare several duplicates of all the table dressings in preparation for the chestburster scene to come. As Kane went into spasms, he had to lie on his back across the table to be positioned correctly for the ensuing scene to be filmed later. I knew there would be a few takes around the first part of the scene where Kane is struggling in pain and that a lot of the table dressing would go flying, so I had prepared replacements for each time the scene was reset for another take. I imagined there'd be a lot of blood flying as well, so we'd have to duplicate everything for second takes. This is always an important part of our planning with set dressing. If shooting grinds to a halt because items have got broken and there are no replacements on hand, it would be a severe problem for a director. Continuity in the scenes would jump if suddenly things were missing, so we always made sure we had several duplicates of everything.

Benjamin Fernandez was put in charge of drawing up the sequence. Again, Benjamin was very clever at understating these mechanical processes and drawing it up to make it work. He worked closely with Nick Allder, who did very rough drawings of how the creature would burst through Kane's chest based on Ridley's storyboards of the sequence. They had worked closely with us to make the special dining table with a hole in it for John Hurt to fit his head and shoulders through. Nick planned to make a false chest from fiberglass, which matched John Hurt's head and shoulders. By positioning him lying at an angle under the table on a chair or a sloped support, carefully aligned it would look like his chest thrashing around. In the end John was in fact sitting in shorts on a cushion on a chair. Benjamin took measurements of Nick's hydraulic rams that he would use to punch the alien through for the first hit. Benjamin had to carefully align John's body so that the rams would go through past him, but look like they came through the middle of Kane's chest. He also had to make sure there was room for the operators to handle the pumps and pipes for the blood to be pumped through.

The main consideration was the angle of John Hurt's head and shoulders so that the fake chest looked real and unquestionably his. They had to make sure as well that John was comfortable, being able to act in the scene whilst all this was going on around him. The setup would take a great deal of time while John had to sit there—there was no way to set it up any differently. On the day, they fed John his Gauloises cigarettes and glasses of wine to keep him happy throughout the entire process. Then once the first push through was filmed, Roger Dicken, who had made the glove-puppet version of the baby alien to shoot with after the first breakthrough, had to get under the table to operate it, alongside the special-effects blood-squirting operators. He had to be hidden under the table and have room to be able to work the puppet in shot. It was all precisely prepared using the old trick that had been well used in cinema before.

On the day of shooting, Ridley had to build the shots as he went along to see what worked and what didn't. He needed to trust his instincts in the edit room, trust that he could cut together those magic moments of horror and reality to make this the seminal scene that it has become. It's not easy relying on puppets—they can look pretty hokey if not filmed correctly. You must get the right angle and lighting, and allow enough different cuts to reduce the possibility of failing to convince an audience. I think the savior here was the blood pumping, as this itself hides a myriad of possible failures.

I believe Nick Allder learned this technique of how to achieve the shot from the legendary special-effects supervisor Les Bowie, who they all call the father of in-floor effects in Britain, and all pay homage to as the instigator and inventor of many of the techniques still used today when CGI costs prohibit its use. CGI certainly did not exist at this time so everyone relied on in-camera techniques. Personally I think the organic nature and resulting realism that you get using these techniques, all be it in a different way, are still often far superior. I like the little random accidents that occur—these make the magic happen. The way the blood sprays out, and little tricks of light that occur naturally as the action happens, all create a reality that an audience accepts. This is especially true of filming models for scenes; when made by expert model-makers and filmed the right way, they give spectacular results.

Everything was prepared in detail, and worked out with Benjamin in conjunction with Nick Allder and Roger Dicken. Roger had prepared a solid baby alien head and body for the first shot that would sit on top of Nick's hydraulic ram and burst through Kane's T-shirt. It had to be strong, and capable of punching through the cloth. Attached to this baby alien were four rubber tubes attached to small rubber pumps. These worked the tiny veins either side of the alien head to look like pulsing veins, and the others were for blood to pump out at the same time. Several T-shirts were prepared. Tiny Nicholls, the wardrobe master, distressed the cloth so it would tear easily in shot; they usually did this with some form of acid. Benjamin drew the entire thing up, and that way made sure the exact angle that John Hurt was positioned in made it look like he was attached to the false body. It was all carefully sketched out and drawn up in detail to ensure it worked and fooled the eye. We redressed the table to match the shot exactly before we cut to this.

Filming commenced on the sequence in the morning, as the actors sit around the table eating, full of loose banter and chatter, Kane happy to have survived. Then Kane suddenly chokes and goes into spasms of pain. While Kane is fighting the pain the other characters turn him round and lay him on the table so that he is correctly positioned for the chestburster sequence.

Once Ridley had got that scene, Nick Allder hid a blood pipe under Kane's T-shirt and a squib with a blood pack. On cue this let out a stream of blood to stain the T-shirt red as if something terrible was going on in Kane's chest. The actors picked up their positions where they left off, surrounding the choking Kane. I think being nervous and inquisitive they crowded in on Kane. On the first take the blood pump didn't pump much and the squib caused a popping sound and lifted the T-shirt as a stain of blood spread. It looked pretty scary, as if something had broken through the skin. The rest was imagination as it hadn't broken through the material, but it shocked the actors. In a way this false start helped, as you could see it increased the actors' anxieties about what was coming, letting their imaginations run wild. On the second take the blood pumped into the T-shirt and stained it heavily. The actors were sufficiently shocked at this, enough for Ridley to move on, feeling he had captured credible reactions. Paul Ibbetson then sent all the actors except John Hurt to their dressing rooms, and told them it would be a few hours to set up the next shot. Ridley did not want the actors to see the setup, just to experience the horror of the moment the baby alien actually breaks through. To practice how this would all work, we had set up a separate secluded area off stage for them to try it all out, so the actors were truly unaware of what was going to happen next.

Nick Allder set up the next stage. Roger Dicken had prepared the solid baby alien and Nick had fixed it on top of the hydraulic ram. Nick went to work with his team to set it into position under the table, and set up the separate blood lines and pumps. It was a bit of a squeeze to get everyone in under the table, around John Hurt's body and legs. John still parodies this moment.

We removed the dressing on the table, careful to Polaroid exactly as it was left after the previous setup. We had to replace everything around John to match the last take, or objects would jump in the cut. The panel in the top of the table was removed and they set the false chest into place. John kind of lounged on the chair under it on a cushion so that he was correctly positioned. He lay there throughout the long process of the setup. He had to be in position the entire time as everything was geared to him being able to move his arms and head, while the effects boys moved the false chest piece in sync with him. The assistants plied him with glasses of wine and kept lighting up his favorite Gauloises cigarettes. He kept smoking and drinking, unable to see what they were doing below the table, smiling and joking as the assistant filled his tumbler to keep him happy.

Ridley kept the other actors at bay throughout all of this setting up on purpose, so the surprise would be real, and their reactions would not be acted but genuinely horrified. They knew the scene, of course. They knew what was called for but had no idea what everyone around this table where Kane was lying, were planning. Ridley knew full well this was the moment in the film when he got the audience or lost them.

In conversation with Ridley, Nick Allder, and me about making this scene more shocking, Ridley had decided to add bits of intestines, liver, stomachs, and any offal we could source around the baby alien. Nick had done this before, and I had too when trying to make an operation look authentic using a false prosthetic. Ridley immediately wanted it to look like the baby alien had launched its way out of Kane's chest through his lungs and heart if he could, and knew that adding bits of fat and gristle around the puppet would further disguise the possibility it could be seen as just that—a puppet. I sent one of the team to the local abattoir to fetch a bag full of bloody animal innards. The buyer returned clutching a plastic bag full of liver, intestines, kidneys, and lungs—whatever organs they could find. This was washed so that it was sanitary, but it still smelt. It was sanitized in formaldehyde, which in itself smelt bad, making the set smell like an operating theater.

We redressed the table as it was. Then, when that was approved by the continuity lady, we made sure everything matched the dinner table contents to the Polaroids she had taken. Ridley was ready to film. The chestburster rig was primed and set. Paul Ibbetson called the actors down, ready in makeup and costume to shoot right away. I think they suspected something, as the cameras were all covered in plastic, and most of the crew were wearing plastic rain macs. They gathered around the table in the positions they were in for the last take, and prepared themselves to carry on with John writhing and screaming and them trying to help him. You could see they were all nervous; no one knew quite what to expect. I think that seeing John half-buried in the table with cameras set up all round him, and the blood-stained T-shirt from the last setup, made them a little jumpy. The special-effects crew was bent under the table, and the set was pretty hot already from the lights setup. Dan O'Bannon and Ron Shusett were there in the back, watching and talking, as were other people, adding to the sense that something was about to happen.

The rigs were all charged and ready, Nick Allder working the ram and the effects team working the blood pipes. The actors couldn't see these properly hidden under the table, so were really not sure what to expect. Tiny Nicholls had the T-shirt prepped and on the dummy, all ready to shoot.

Ridley didn't really explain to the actors at all what would happen, just gave them positions for the cameras. When everything was ready the cameras were rolled and action was called. As Kane squirmed and rocked on the table, the props men also rocked the false chest to make it look like it was Kane writhing. As the second action was called for, Nick released the hydraulic ram to fire the baby alien through the T-shirt and the effects team worked the blood pumps. Kane's T-shirt bulged up as if something was about to burst through, but the head didn't actually break through. It still looked pretty horrible. Another splatter of blood suddenly appeared on Kane's shirt, staining it further, but did not spray out as Ridley had hoped. It still shocked the actors, who were all leaning in closely over Kane, trying to help him cope with the agonizing pain. What the eye doesn't see the mind makes real, and maybe this false start increased their anticipation and in the end it was another cut that helped Ridley create the tension for the audience.

They quickly reset the rigs while Tiny scored the fabric even more on the T-shirt with a razorblade, so it would definitely break through this time. Once Tiny had finished, we redressed the table and the actors moved back to their positions. Looking down on Kane struggling like crazy with this huge patch of blood on his chest, they moved in even closer to try to see what was going on. The cameras were all duly set running and Ridley called action.

This time the blood-covered baby alien broke through the T-shirt, but the blood lines clogged up and no blood came. Ridley called out to Nick to try again while he was still rolling the cameras. Nick withdrew the head and rammed it up again; a small amount of blood came with it, so Ridley cued Nick to ram the head through a few more times, and then he called cut. This small baby alien didn't really look as shocking as it was planned without blood flying everywhere. Ridley quickly assimilated the reactions of the cast and spoke to Nick Allder, who said that during the next take the blood would flow.

Ibbo called for a reset. Ridley knew he had the breakthrough moment okay; the baby alien was nicely soaked in blood so looked correct for the first moment as the T-shirt rose and the head appeared and could work if cut quickly. They closed up the T-shirt so only a tiny hole was left, but it meant that the baby alien head would burst through now. He quietly asked Nick to add another blood line pointing at the actors at the back, and Nick told him this time he'd make sure the pressure was fully ramped up.

What happened next is better watched on the film than described. Suffice it to say that Ridley's idea to add a second blood line and focus it on the actors and Veronica Cartwright paid off better than he could ever have expected. The actors were feeling a little more comfortable, as they had now seen the baby alien. The cameras rolled when Nick had the setup ready and the dressing was placed to match. On 'action', as the bloody baby alien head burst through Kane's T-shirt, a massive spurt of blood shot into the air with it. Then another came out like a stream, and horrible as this bloody snarling head was, that one spurt of blood that caught Veronica in the face was far more horrible for her. She screamed in shock, recoiled back against the set, and dropped to the floor out of the shot. The others also got splattered in the fountain of blood, and they all recoiled. Ridley kept on instructing Nick to keep ramming the head through the T-shirt, searching for that perfect moment of creature and blood squirting. Veronica appeared again as she stood up, but looked white and shaken and she was crying as more blood kept flying around. Poor John Hurt was soaked in it, but kept on acting until Ridley called cut. This was a real reaction from Veronica, a true moment of method acting, as she was beyond playing the character—she was in distress. After Ridley cut the cameras they all stood around in shock, covered in splattered blood. And they all went back to their dressing rooms as Nick set up the next scene in the sequence.

For the next shot Roger Dicken took over with the puppet version. The animated baby alien was worked from underneath via a series of pumps and mechanics. Roger was squeezed out of sight under the table as they prepared for the glove-puppet baby to pop up and look around. He had tubes running into the baby alien that made its veins pump and its lungs work, and metal wire controls to make the baby alien turn, and open its mouth like a birth cry, all adding to the terrible reality of this monster. All around the chest cavity where the baby alien came through, Ridley dressed in the offal and intestines, which by now were smelling quite bad in the heat of the lights. Under the table the special-effects boys were working the blood lines.

Ridley spent ages himself carefully dressing in pieces of fat and gristle and lumps of meat around the baby alien. Now that the shock of the breakthrough had occurred, we would see the actual puppet Roger Dicken had built pop its head out, look around, scream, and flee. Ridley wanted it to have pieces of Kane's organs hanging off it as if it had eaten its way out of Kane's chest. John Hurt was plied with more wine and cigarettes as he had now been several hours in position, and it was deemed too time-consuming to take him out of the rig and set it all up again. Soaked in blood for continuity, he seemed okay, and I think the wine softened his discomfort.

Nick added yet another tube to fire blood into the air around the baby alien, timing it so that as the alien burst out it would look like it had burst from the heart and would spray everywhere. The rest of the actors were in their rooms wondering what was going to happen next. Veronica was extremely shaken up, and really didn't want to go on anymore. It was very intense activity around this simple table, preparing everything to work. Roger Dicken was incredibly uncomfortable tucked under the table, almost leaning over John Hurt's legs to get a hand on the puppet's operating system. Roger held it up while Ridley finished dressing in pieces of meat around its mouth and gills. Dressed in this way it would add to the authenticity as the baby alien had to break through from inside, and would tear its way through organs and body parts.

Ridley assembled the actors again for the next shock. On 'action' the baby alien reared its head from Kane's chest, blood pumping out around it. Roger Dicken manipulated the puppet creature to turn its head, look around and then scream as it opened its jaws. Ridley called out each movement and action to Roger under the table. The actors were again shocked as the little monster looked pretty frightening with its fearful-looking jaws covered in blood. Ridley had Roger work the puppet a few times to get the full impact of it emerging. This shot is eerily beautiful, and terrifying for the crewmembers as they look on in horror at the twitching, dying Kane covered in blood, and this birth from inside his upper body.

This is another example of a terrifying sequence in a horror film where the writer and director exploit these deeply buried subconscious fears, connecting big-time to an audience because of that. It never seems to fail. Something deeply primal connected with the actors and was transmitted through to the audience. To see an actual creature burst from a friend's chest inspires a deeply rooted fear in all humans. Whether you think of a cancer growing or an insect or animal growing inside, these are ancient phobias. More pertinent is the devil that has been feared throughout history and legend, living inside humans who have become possessed. The most graphic of these is the Incubus, a tiny devil that emerges from inside the possessed victim's stomach, and in its way is the most awful. So all these fears arise in the subconscious and this beast emerging out of someone's chest brings up those fears. It's no wonder this sequence has become recognized as one of the most seminal moments in modern cinema.

Of interest to note here, and something that no one seems to have spotted except me and a few dedicated fans, and which truthfully shows just how impressionable and shocking this moment was and still is for this never to be noticed, is that if you look closely you can see the screwdriver of one of the special-effects crew poking around the innards to help the baby alien through the layers of offal. The blood and action disguise it, but it is there clearly if you pause the moment. These things happen, but when the shot works and is the best moment one has in the editing room, it barely registers with an audience. It certainly never ever did when this sequence shocked the hell out of the American audiences when the film first premiered.

Once this scene was in the can, the last element of the sequence was filmed. The little alien had to move fast into hiding. They set up the next prepared baby alien for the moment it runs across the table and disappears. Again, this was all carefully pre-planned when Nick Allder came up with another really low-tech way to do this. Benjamin Fernandez had drawn the table up, under Nick's careful instructions, to have a central slot running right through it. The specially prepared baby alien was fixed to a dolly track under the table where Roger was able to control it when the grips pulled him through really fast. Shot from a low angle all the dressing on the table we had placed for the meal would hide the track and the gap running right across the table. The narrow cut across the table would just allow Roger Dicken's puppet controls to pass unhindered through the objects on the table.

We reset all the dressing on the table and matched the blood. When they filmed the first take the baby alien shot successfully across the table, but didn't look real. Ridley wanted the tail to lash around just like on an animal. Brian Johnson suggested to Ridley and Nick Allder that hooking up a compressed-air line to it would make it snake around. The air pressure is really strong when worked from a compressor and if you tie a tube to it, the tube snakes and twirls dramatically. Nick prepared it this way and it worked really well on the next take. Combining the way Roger Dicken could make the baby alien move and the expressions on its face, he used tiny air tubes running up the puppet mechanism to look like veins pumping and lungs breathing. It really helped to create the illusion of a live animal that had just been born. Covered in blood and coming after the burst through Kane's chest, it left the crew of the *Nostromo* gasping in shock at the moment they had just witnessed and this translated exactly to audiences worldwide. This was the first sighting ever of the alien to come. So Ridley got the shots, building the sequence bit by bit as he went, making sure he had got the required pieces of film to remove any suspicion of trickery creating this now famous sequence.

Using a sequence of cuts, Terry Rawlings, the editor, and Ridley composed this sequence into a huge shocker, and by inter-cutting the different shots of the alien and the reactions of the crew, the sequence is truly one of the best moments in horror cinema ever. The sound also adds enormously and the shriek the baby alien gives as it emerges sends shivers down the spine. This is the moment the movie kicks into pure horror.

We shifted into the white infirmary set. There were two sides to these scenes as most of the crew wait outside the glass viewing screen in the corridor and look on, as Ash and Dallas work on Kane inside.

We had made up a tiny saw as an action prop for cutting Kane's helmet in two, again in combination with Nick's team. Nick had adapted a cutting tool that had a tiny circular blade that could cut through fiberglass and could cut into the helmet. We had prepared the various helmets cut in two already for this sequence so that Ash and Dallas could easily pull it apart and reveal the facehugger. The helmet had the Perspex visor melted down to show where the facehugger had melted through it. It was also made milky as if acid had burnt it. The cut helmet was made in various stages, and Ridley shot it carefully from different angles so it didn't betray that it was already cut, or that the saw was just an action prop and not able to actually function. The helmet was placed on John Hurt over the facehugger, so that as they cut through the helmet and visor, the creature's spine was showing.

Once it was cut off, the two sides of the helmet were broken away from Kane's head by Ash and Dallas and the truth was revealed of the horror of what had happened. The facehugger covering Kane's face, the tail wrapped around his neck, and the strange, long, thin articulated fingers gripping his head, was pretty horrible. Roger had made little lung-like sacks on either side of its body; these really fooled the eye, helping to make anyone in the audience feel the suffocating effect that Kane was under. When Ash tries to move one of the facehugger's fingers it tightens, and the tail tightens itself round Kane's throat. To make this work we went back to basics on the floor techniques. We had the prop boys tie a fine wire around the end of the tail and hide out of shot under the table.

Then when Ash touched the finger, they pulled the tail on cue. It certainly looks real, and betrays to the audience this monster means business.

The X-ray scan worked practically and Ridley dimmed the lights in the room to make this stand out more visually. The video team played back previously created footage for the X-ray to show what was going on inside Kane; a combination of X-rays and animated footage made up the image of the facehugger's tube going down Kane's throat into his lungs. When Ash goes to cut the facehugger's finger, the laser knife was specially designed and made up to look as if it could work—it had to look different, as it was going to be seen in intense close-up. The acid dropped and burnt its way through the hull. This was filmed separately as an insert, and Nick used a combination of a polystyrene set and acids that ate it away and smoked, creating the illusion of the metal hull melting down through several layers of the ship.

The next scene filmed in the set was when the crew come back to see Kane and the facehugger has gone; it's nowhere to be seen. We used a probe light from a reading lamp that had a long flexible shaft, to make up a scientific-looking device that Ash could use when he first examines the facehugger. He uses this here to search in the dark crevices around the ducts in the set, writing notes in one of the notepads I had made.

Dallas and Ripley search for the facehugger in corners and behind pipes we had set up, Ridley creating a good deal of tension following them around, building the expectation that it would jump out at them at any moment.

To use during the scene as they are looking for the facehugger, we had found some interesting-looking clear Perspex office trays, and I thought these looked better than metal ones as scripted. Ash had one of these to catch the facehugger in if they found it. To create the shock as it drops down onto Ripley's neck, we simply placed the facehugger on a pipe above where Ripley was positioned. Paul Ibbetson then poked it with a stick on cue, so that it fell right onto Ripley and scared the hell out of her and made the audience jump. This is the facehugger Bob Keen made, as Roger Dicken was so overloaded with work creating the baby alien puppet and the baby alien head with Nick Allder. It wasn't animated as it is dead when they find it, he just had to create a reflex movement when Ash pokes it.

In the next setup in the infirmary, Ash is looking at the liquid from the facehugger, trying to analyze its DNA and source, when Ripley comes in for a quiet talk with him to find out information. We had set up the console like a laboratory and everything was sprayed the creamy-white color. Using suitable and interesting scrap pieces the prop-making crews had found, we had created a microscope analyzer, and spraying this the same white color immediately made it look the part. Adding in some adjustable knobs, Ash was able to look like he was using an analyzer. The video team also played back pre-recorded material on the monitor so it synced in with Ash's scene. Ripley's dialogue here confirms that he is the science officer, so as this is Ash's station and work place, he had to look comfortable with all the action props.

Once Ridley had got this in the can we placed the specially dressed facehugger in position. For this version we used oysters, clams and mussels—anything that looked right. It had to be filmed quickly as the smell became pretty bad under the hot studio lights, but it looked fantastic, and that is what mattered. It had to look like a dying organism with suckers that had attached to Kane's face, and a mouthpiece where the tube that went into Kane would have been. With oily liquid poured on it before the take, the face part of the hugger looked like a moist, soft underbelly.

Ash places the carcass in the glass tray and puts it on his analysis table to look at it closely. Here we see a huge close-up. The props brought in a freshly prepared one with more oysters, clams, and other fish innards, entrails, lungs, anything that made it look the part. With moisture on it, Ian Holm was able to lift up a piece of the oyster that looked like the alien facehugger's flesh. We had made up another probe-like instrument for him to do this with, this time from scrap material. The prop makers ran a green transparent tube down to the instrument's point to give an added functioning type of mechanism. Ash used a surgical instrument to hold back the fleshy bit from the large selection of surgical instruments we had dressed in for his workstation.

Shooting moved outside the infirmary into the corridor section with the huge glass view screen. This echoed the hospital areas where people are placed in isolation or babies in incubation cots so people can see them. The corridor padding really held up, with the aging process in wax applied all over it. Being off-white with cream and gold it looked like another section of corridor in the *Nostromo*. The occasional pipework and electrical panels all color co-ordinated kept the space vehicle reality look.

Michael Seymour designed Ash's blister (a kind of cockpit) from a Ron Cobb sketch and ideas as the only area in the *Nostromo* we see in the film which connects it to the outside world, alongside the airlock where the crew exit and re-enter after inspecting the alien planet. These scenes are closely connected as Ash watches their progress. Ridley was able to show the alien planet surface as Kane, Lambert, and Dallas go out to seek the source of the distress signal by cleverly filming the image on Ash's monitor through a crewmember's video camera and distressing the image. Worried about how the miniature set would hold up, Ridley was able to have Ash watch their progress on the stormy planet's surface and show the alien craft through a distressed video signal. Matched in with the live footage filmed on H Stage, filled with smoke to give an alien atmosphere, this made a low-budget solution to a highly important moment in the movie work amazingly well. It helped to perpetuate the mystery of the planet and create a more tense visual of it. For close-ups of the actors it was fine as Ridley was able to make it a really dense atmosphere using a lot of smoke.

A lot from my store of scrap dressings were added to encrust the panels and window frames to make it look more hardware-driven. Ash's console chair was designed on a long track mechanism like the rails we use for tracking the camera on a dolly, and made functional by Nick's mechanical crew. Ash got into the console chair and it slid all the way into the blister, which created the viewing platform with green-screen panels beyond to matte in the alien landscape. Psychologically this isolates Ash, alone in the blister, another little layer in the audience's subconscious of what's coming. Monitors were placed all down the walls built into housings. Below were more panels with lights and switches made up by Dennis Lowe and Guy Hudson and the team. We gave Ash a swiveling monitor in front of him, like a suspended television set, so he could watch their progress as they walked towards the alien ship.

The blister was not only an interesting way to show Ash isolated and alone, carefully watching everything, it also avoided having to have windows anywhere else in the *Nostromo*. This saved both green-screen time and costly replacements of it with specially filmed exterior views. Also it kept the claustrophobic atmosphere for the audience. It's here after a second viewing that one starts to see the little things Ian Holm did to build the character of Ash, like his running-on-the-spot moment as if warming up his system. We find out slowly that he is an android and his intention is to find the alien and to bring it home. To him the crew was dispensable. His role was pre-destined on Earth, as we find out. Alone in this blister it's the only contact with the outside world in the entire movie when visiting the alien planet. A fog-laden polluted planet with a warning beacon and a strange craft—ideal horror film territory.

It is also here we first see Ripley take command of the ship. We come to know that she is the second-in-command and has to try to rule over a disrespectful bunch of testosterone-heavy men—Lambert is clearly not intended to command. The first sign of antagonism between Ripley and Ash is engineered to begin at this point in the movie, and erupts when he lets the crew back into the ship after Ripley, following command orders, refuses them entry, so it was important plot-wise to have Ash be able to see exactly what was going on outside the ship.

Filming moved on to the airlock door sequence next; we get a glimpse of the planet's atmosphere when they open the airlock door to descend to the planet and return. Wind machines and smoke machines created the atmosphere, barely seen beyond the door, which slid on cue and with an added sound design that made it look heavy and airtight. We had dressed in the fighter-pilots' suits I had bought with my airplane scrap near the airlocks and dressed in some white coats. These played an important piece of dressing, not just to add personal items amongst the hardware and make the ship live, but Ridley had the effects boys place big fans outside the airlock doors, so that when they opened it a blast of wind from the changing atmosphere blew the coats. This was the only soft thing capable of moving like that so helped again to visually tell the story. The suits, designed by Moebius, really fitted in with the hardware-oriented look. They were truly beautiful designs, art objects on their own.

The alien planet on H Stage was filmed in the central part of the stage, with the side of the alien craft at the far end. The work on the planet and the side of the ship went on right up to shooting, taking up a lot of Les Dilley's time, with Peter Voysey and Giger working on sculpting onto the basic plaster set pieces. To the eye it looked like a series of sculpted mounds of set, placed indiscriminately across the huge stage on the concrete floor. Once the gravel and sand were laid down it began to fuse into something more like a planet surface when sprayed down and aged into the alien blue-gray look.

For filming these scenes Ridley wisely saw the problem with them being a set on a stage filmed against black velvet walls, and had Nick Allder's team fill the stage with smoke. That immediately changed their appearance to a dense atmosphere on the planet's dark surface. Then, by adding large wind blowers, they emptied bags of the carpenter's shop's discarded wood shavings, and suddenly the planet became real, truly inhospitable and alien. When Ridley filmed the wide shots using his children, Jake and Luke, and Derek Vanlint's son in the miniature spacesuits, their smaller size effectively doubled the scale of the planet.

The characters Kane, Dallas, and Lambert were filmed in several sections of the planet set. In the smoke-filled half-light, the lights on their helmets and the CO_2 gas escaping from their backpacks as they exhaled breath created an image that was undeniably real. The difficulties the actors had with breathing while encased in the suits have been well documented, with Ridley's children, John Hurt, and Tom Skerritt almost passing out during the long shoot days as there was no way to get air to them, except to cut the shot and remove the helmet. Just as on *Star Wars*, all the departments involved were struggling with technologies that were being invented as we filmed and a lack of budget and time to create elements that were fully developed. The results speak for themselves so were worth the discomfort during filming. There is an absolute authenticity to the look of these scenes, which could so easily have been missed in the hands of another director without the right vision.

To increase the scale of Giger's alien craft, Ridley once more filmed his children in the miniature suits, again more than doubling the size of it by illusion for an audience. This trick worked remarkably well, and by slightly slowing down the shot when filmed, the different way the children walked disappeared and they gained more weight by illusion.

Ridley used the same trick for the wider shots of the three astronauts descending on the landing leg when first encountering the planet's surface. The already huge landing leg took on the apparent height of about fifty feet and dwarfed the astronauts.

The alien egg chamber was created and filmed in the revamped Space Jockey set. Despite Peter Beale's instructions from Twentieth Century Fox, about one hundred and thirty eggs were made, not the six that

Ridley was told he could have. These were cast and duplicated to create the egg chamber as painted by Giger.

The egg for the main action with John Hurt was made once again with a combination of sculpting based on Giger's design (after several attempts) and Roger Dicken working with Nick Allder on the hydraulics. Bob Keen again assisted Roger Dicken in making the hydraulics for this foreground main egg. Giger's designs were clearly based on vulvas and Ridley vetoed these as just too graphically sexual. There was also a cross-like version Giger tried but in the end Ridley evolved the flower-like opening as the best way. Several versions were prepared: a complete egg for all the wide and master shots and a cut-away version for close-ups and for the operators to make the various actions work. Inside, before the facehugger jumps, a sheep's stomach was laid in carefully. With the pink membrane-like skin and white veins of fat all over, it made an unsettlingly real egg interior and being almost transparent clearly showed some movement below. It is well documented that due to lack of time and resources, when the close-ups were shot, Ridley himself put on a rubber glove and shot his hand out at the camera to create the shocking moment required to make the audience jump.

What I had to assemble were the torches they would carry when they descended and discuss the harness and wire rig Kane wore to drop down into the egg chamber. This would be a stuntman in the suit as it was quite a long drop from the stage ceiling and no one could tell it wasn't John Hurt in any of the wide shots. Then for Kane's close-ups they used the same harness and wire rig used for stunt work for John Hurt to drop the last few feet.

For Ash's demise, Michael constructed the console top with a hole for Ian Holm to place his head through for the live-action pieces when Ash spoke. A live-action cast was made of Ian Holm's head for the sequence when they push the head upright to re-activate Ash. This is a claustrophobic procedure that most actors dislike intensely, but suffer for their art.

Two drinking straws are stuffed up their nose and then wet plaster of Paris is wiped on by the modeling team. This is left to dry on the actor and—this is the part they really sneer at—the plaster shrinks as it dries. This is when they can feel really uncomfortable, and if they are in any way suffering from claustrophobia, it makes it very hard to bear. Then it is cut off and there is a perfect mold of the actor's face—with their eyes closed, of course. These are opened by the fine work of the sculptors and a silicone mask is then made from the mold.

The silicone rubber in those days that was available was way inferior to the amazing products now, which is much finer-textured and almost transparent like real skin. Once it was cast and molded in latex it shrank so the head was smaller. Ridley had no choice but to use it; there was no time or budget left to sculpt a second larger version of Ian's head. I remember when shooting this scene the problems the props had trying to hold the fake head upright; the latex collar just kept preventing it from staying in place and the head kept slipping over. The tubes connecting it to the body prevented them from holding the neck pieces down as the base was so uneven. It was a matter in the end of rolling the camera and when it was right and the smoke was transparent to camera, Ridley rolled and got the shot before it fell back over.

Ash's fake, headless body was dressed with small rubber tubes to look like liquid veins and marbles were placed in between them, an idea that Ridley suggested. Covered in condensed milk and real milk, it looked for the first time like a working humanoid robot.

The scene really relies on Ian Holm himself, with his head through the table and the matching neck skirt in latex, covered in milk and cream and sweat. Ridley kept feeding Ian with milk so that as he spoke, fluid from the damaged body was flowing from his mouth. Ian made this entirely convincing despite his intense dislike of milk.

The set where the alien kills Brett is another testament to what one can do with limited resources. The set was constructed into the sound stage using the grid ceiling above as the high roof of the *Nostromo*. The stages in Shepperton have chains hanging down to floor level, to move around the grids and lower them, and hang scenery from. Ridley used these in shot to create atmosphere. The walls of the sets are filled with scrap pieces to look like an industrial hold full of equipment. Michael Seymour hung large pieces of revamped sets from the chains as well, like an unused landing leg segment to disguise the view looking up. This is where the alien is hanging when it attacks Brett.

The assistant working with the prop-making team had assembled several mock-up vehicles, inspired from Ron Cobb's sketches. They made up the bulk of the floor dressing. One was a mock-up of a helijet Ron had designed and the other was built on caterpillar tracks to resemble a moon buggy. A large amount of the palettes were used around the floor section and walls, and painted down to an oily dark metal color. Then loads of repetitive junk pieces were applied to look like working machinery. Anything we could find got dressed in here.

I think the *coup de grace* here was Ridley suggesting to the effects boys to put water pipes above in the roof girders and let them drip down below. With the smoke placed in for the shoot to create a softer atmosphere, that gave the feeling of it being really hot down there like in the bowels of a ship, near the engines. The water dripping constantly from above really gave an eerie yet realistic feel to it. There was a lot of discussion from the purists who said there would never be water dripping in space, but in the end what looks right is right, and if it works use it. When the water drips onto Brett's cap during his death scene and makes that loud plopping sound as he lifts his face to cool himself down under the water and drinks, it adds an eerie sense of calm, but at the same time is somehow threatening. We sense something bad is coming and the music is building tension, telling us so.

This set complex gave a huge sense of scale as if a massive hangar-type area was below decks and was used several times from different angles. Using pieces of walls and junk and hanging the ceiling pieces and letting it fall off to the darkened stage around it meant Michael could create a very large-scaled set, again for a limited budget. In one section, Michael placed small beams across the top and laid the palettes on them like ceiling pieces. Ridley placed lamps above the ceiling pointing down and with the smoke in the set they created shafts of light, like a cathedral effect in a forest. This look was inspired from his test shoot on Sigourney, where Ridley tried out different looks lighting through the palettes. It gave the effect of a hot industrial hold or cargo area below decks, and the atmosphere was perfect for the scary scenes filmed down there.

This set was used again when Lambert and Dallas go down to search for the fuel cells to take to the escape shuttle. Using an adapted metal-wheeled trolley we stuck additional elements on as a type of carrying dolly, and scrap aluminum oxygen cylinders from the airplane junk as fuel cells, we created the action for the scene as scripted. Whilst Dallas and Lambert frantically collect the fuel cells from below decks, Ridley aided the reality of the scene by adding the sound of heavy steel cylinders to the soundtrack each time they carried one onto the trolley, which made them unquestionably, realistically heavy.

During the *Alien* filming I learned that I had been accepted for a place at the National Film School in Beaconsfield. I had applied for the directors' course as I thought it would help bridge my path into directing, which I was passionate to fulfill now. I had gained a pretty impressive credit card in Hollywood, especially for *Star Wars* and now *Alien*.

When *Alien* was near to wrapping the shoot, the Beatle George Harrison, a huge Monty Python fan and friend of Eric Idle's, put up the entire budget to finance *Life of Brian*.

Rather than give it to the taxman under the tax-exemption scheme operating at the time, he chose to invest in the movie. George also mortgaged his mansion in Henley; I went there to see him and can stand testament to how beautiful it was, so it was a risk for him because it was his sanctuary. George Harrison formed HandMade Films with Denis O'Brien, his business partner, specifically to finance *Life of Brian* in 1978. John Goldstone restarted the production up again and a new shoot date was set. Tim Hampton and John Goldstone contacted me and I worked out with them when I had to leave for Tunis, as I was driving down and would take the ferry across from Genoa to Tunis. I had to give notice to Ridley and Ivor Powell as I would have to leave shortly before the end of the *Alien* shoot, but as all the sets were now up it was just a matter of completing around one week of shooting, so I was able to go. All the action props were built and completed, and I spent the next weeks making sure Ridley had everything he needed.

Les was still there and Benjamin, so Ridley was well covered if I departed. It was part of my deal as they had me on a small retainer for *Life of Brian*; I was lucky that the film had started up again so late as I was able to see *Alien* to the end.

Once again I sadly said goodbye to the team. It is always with regret, these goodbyes, because with the pressure and the intensity of a movie there are no pretenses with crews and you get to know people really well. In addition, when it is such a heartfelt and unique project like *Star Wars* and *Alien*, quite simply you don't want it to end. These were the creatively inspiring films that really got me excited; doing groundbreaking work, in a tight team as the budgets were too small for the intended vision, really bonds people at the top end together. I got a hug from Ridley and massive thanks from Ivor and Gordon and Garth Thomas, who were genuinely aware of my loyal support to Ridley.

BACK TO *LIFE OF BRIAN*

Immediately the next day after I left *Alien*, *Life of Brian* started up preparation from where we left off. I set off in the Matra Rancho through France for Genoa and the ferry to Tunis. It was an absolute pleasure to be back in Tunisia, a country I love being in as much as Morocco.

There are of course many crazy stories from this shoot about what really happened behind the scenes. That will be told one day.

One of the most memorable, however, was filming the spaceship sequence. Terry Gilliam called me, as we had to film the sequence with Brian inside the spacecraft. I went and met him at Terry's Neal's Yard base, and we decided to make it in his studio upstairs because filming there would keep the costs to a minimum.

We employed John Beard again and Peter Dunlop, my buyer, and sent them out to scavenge scrap. Terry got the puppets built with his people who made prosthetics for the Pythons, designed in Terry Gilliam's style, with the hand holding their one eye.

We also decided to do the special-effects sequence ourselves. The spacecraft had to fly through space and a meteor field avoiding rocks and meteors, and was chased by an enemy spaceship firing lasers at it. We just had enough room in the studio if we built the spacecraft on a gimbal at the back so it rocked to simulate turbulence, which left just enough room at the front of the studio to build a black velvet backdrop and the meteor field. We decided on the old technique of tracking through the meteors suspended on fishing line with the camera on speed rails—these are perfectly aligned camera tracks, so no bumps.

Roger Pratt came in to light the spaceship and the space sequence. He worked with us on building the interior of the spaceship as we decided to have the light sources built in. It was a bit of a struggle in the small studio space, and lighting is the secret to making a space scene with meteors look real. It works best with a single bright light source to simulate the sun, so that the meteors are half in darkness and half in light. This shows their shape, like seeing the moon half-lit. That requires getting a single light source at a distance away, so we had to compromise that to make it work.

Terry Gilliam, John Beard and I built the spacecraft with our grip Tony Andrews, who also doubled as carpenter and mechanic. It's always more fun to do it this way, it keeps you grounded and aware of what goes on at grass-roots level. I always prefer to try to get epic production values and never betray the true budget and if you get your hands dirty and make things yourself, it really helps in planning out how to make effects sequences work for other challenges. We always storyboard what we want to achieve as precisely as possible and work to them.

Terry did sketches of the design of the spaceship. A typical Gilliam retro design, it somewhat resembled a Messerschmitt bubble car that Gilliam was fascinated by, and was later used as Jonathan Pryce's transport vehicle in *Brazil*. John drew up working drawings of this design for the craft for us so that the gimbal to rock it back and forth could be worked out; a low-budget grip device worked the gimbal with old rubber tires for suspension. We started assembling scrap to build the shell and the interior, and found seats and junk to make it look real. John found us some scrapped side panels from an aircraft with windows intact so they became the base of the set. We added a round cupola ceiling piece behind Brian, like a conning tower.

The feeling of the dressing was much more *Brazil*-like with wires and tubes everywhere. We hung the plastic tubes and bags used for drip feeds from the ceiling, and placed any scrap we found that looked retro. Applying the same technique of panels with lights and having them wired up gives life to a set like this. We found some round valve-type wheels and used these for the steering wheels for the two aliens, another Gilliam touch. We had to design the area under the spaceship so that the two operators could work the aliens with eyeballs held in their puppeted hands, and Graham Chapman as Brian could enter from below. These two alien pilots were Gilliam-inspired aliens who could talk and move; it was a bit different to *Alien* and *Star Wars* in scale and intentions as anything a little over the top was okay here. It was not your conventional craft by any means. The puppeteers simply held the eye in their prosthetic-covered hands and acted out the scenes as the spacecraft veered left and right to avoid the meteors and laser fire from an attacking ship. Their eyes were actually huge eyeballs that I had made with the company who create fake eyes for the movies and glass eyes for medical purposes. The puppeteer's other hands worked the aliens' mouths, red-lipsticked toad-like orifices. Their fat bodies were created from the simple prosthetic latex available at the time and painted a gray color.

Brian falls into the ship behind them so we had to create a hole in the ceiling large enough for him to fall into and disguise it with pipes and tubes hanging everywhere. In the end there just wasn't room to do this, and it looked a bit unsafe for Graham to drop down into the set, so Gilliam simply cut around his actual entry in the sequence. We got all the junk assembled around a wooden frame we had built so we could move the craft around. I liked some of the switch panels and lights and we wired them up so the lights helped create a working-craft look. We found two retro-looking warning lights, one white rounded glass and the other red, so we wired them up and had them flash when the warning hooter went off when they came under attack from the pursuing ship.

For the attacking spaceship we built another version, painted black. Kent Houston, Terry's animation chief, added in laser fire later, matching them to the flashes we created on the spaceship set with a lightning striker rented from Lee Electrics. This made it look as if the spaceship was being hit, and adding lots of smoke from a simple smoke machine helped create the idea of it being under fire.

It was an absolute homage to *Star Wars* by Terry Gilliam; the entire sequence is like a scene from a space attack in the first movie. Even the attacking ship being black alluded to Darth Vader and the evil dark side. If you listen to the music it's a definite homage to John Williams' famous

Star Wars theme, re-recorded by Terry and his musician friends. The way I made and dressed the ships was done using the same techniques I had developed on *Star Wars* and *Alien* but done in Gilliam's Python style. It was a fascinating full-circle memory for me, from the very first days on *Star Wars* in Lee Studios when George Lucas, fascinated by the way the Pythons made their films on shoestrings, had Bill Harman my carpenter bring in some of Terry's sketches made on old call sheets to look at.

When shooting the scene we had two puppeteers work the puppets; one was the grip who helped us and I remember Terry operated the other puppet as I looked on and directed with Roger Pratt operating the Arriflex camera. Graham Chapman got back into costume helped by Charles Knode the costume designer, who always worked with the Pythons and who is coincidently the man who watches bemused as Brian falls into the spaceship and as he returns and walks past after it crashes, calling him a 'jammy bastard'.

We filmed the entire puppet sequence in a day, and it was lots of fun. The puppets behaved themselves and were great actors. Terry and Graham rewrote the dialogue as they went along and it stands out as a crazy scene in the middle of a film about Brian of Nazareth. People still wonder what it's doing there. It's traditional Python; Terry Gilliam always had weird and wonderful animated sequences in every Python series broadcast and the movies.

We then set up to film the meteor sequences and the exterior of the ship. We got a model builder to make the ship. Terry had Kent Houston working in the basement with his animation table that he used for all his graphic animated series on Monty Python, so we could add in the moon and other planets using still shots manipulated on film. Kent added in the animated laser shots when the alien craft chasing Brian's ship comes under attack. That was the way they were done in those days, one animated them frame by frame.

We hung black velvet drapes around the studio, and having had the prop makers make us various different-sized meteors we painted them and aged them. These were hung on nylon fishing lines from the ceiling. Roger set the camera up on a long track and we carefully placed each meteor on a path as if the craft were flying through them. Roger had to create space lighting, which should be a one-source light and shadows, so he blasted the meteors with a large light and we adjusted it until it looked real. He had many small black flags everywhere blocking light flares as they always get in the lens as you track through, and he was creating shadows where needed. Some of the flags we had to pull out as the camera tracked through; everyone was on board to do whatever was required to get the shot. Getting the speed right in the camera is the trick to model-shooting to make the scale work, and balancing it with the focal lengths (or F-stop).

To film the exterior of the model spaceship we placed the ship on a long metal rod, painted black and set against the black velvet, so we could turn it when required. Then tracking towards it with the camera on a dolly, we could travel past it in various positions, and on film it looked like the craft was flying over us and under us and to the side of us. Each shot required careful lighting and exposure so that it looked real and defied the scale. It took time to do this, and endless fiddling with tiny paintbrushes and spray cans to age it correctly.

When it crashed into the meteor after being hit, we simply did it for real. We placed the model spaceship on a vertical rod and smacked the model sideways into the rock; it works, as it fools the eye. Kent Houston removed any sign of the rods afterwards.

When John Goldstone saw our footage of the aliens and the spacecraft he laughed. I went across to D'Arblay Street to his office and John asked me to direct a cinema teaser trailer for them, as we still had the aliens and the set. Terry had written a dialogue sequence for them as a trailer.

We assembled the team again and filmed them on another day. It was pretty funny, with the aliens talking about *Life of Brian* coming to a cinema nearby. Somewhere in the archives John Goldstone kept this must exist, as we finished it as a 35mm print.

The film has a massive fanbase and following, so it will be interesting for them to read some inside stories, but that is another book.

However, one typically Python-esque story that I must recount happened when I succumbed to Bourguiba's revenge. Bourguiba was the old ruler of Tunisia and we changed the famous Montezuma's revenge quote to suit our Tunisian experiences. Everyone on the movie got sick at some point. Working for months in ancient locations, and often relying on local food, even in the first-class tourist hotels it is inevitable. Tunisia was still a poor country at the time and, as in any hot country like this, the refrigeration and preservation facilities were extremely limited.

I was in bed when our lead actor Graham Chapman knocked at my door and entered. He was dressed in a long white doctor's coat and had a doctor's stethoscope around his neck and was carrying a black doctor's bag. He walked over and asked about my symptoms. Now this is a Monty Python troupe member and our leading man! He was playing Brian, so I was unsure if this was a sketch or a wind-up. I went along with it and answered the questions diligently. He proceeded to feel the glands in my neck and my back and he checked my blood pressure. I thought if this was an act he was very good, as he diligently checked me over. At the end he said, "Well, it is a bacterial infection in the intestines so just take twelve aspirins a day, and rest, and you'll be fine." He wrote out a prescription for the aspirins and politely left.

I checked back immediately with Tim Hampton, who told me that Graham had indeed qualified as a doctor and had decided to be the unit doctor and was treating everyone. He must have had some yearning as after qualifying he had decided to join the comedy fringe group and became a Python. I didn't actually take the twelve aspirins a day, I had the local Tunisians give me some medicine, and it has always been my way to use the local experience and expertise, especially after Mexico and my experiences there.

BACK TO FILM SCHOOL

Returning from *Life of Brian* I spent the next six months at the National Film School in Beaconsfield, for the rest of the winter and spring terms. For me it was a threefold decision. I wanted to study the various other aspects of filmmaking and actually get my hands on editing equipment and lighting sets, plus I got to do workshops with actors and writing workshops which I found really helpful. I also needed to cement my decision to direct and cease production design for a while. It was hard—earning a living always becomes a prevalent necessity when paying the mortgage and car payments, etc. I figured if I was sitting around at home, and the phone was constantly ringing offering me highly paid work, it would be hard to say no. Fellow film-industry comrades who had also decided to be directors had faced this and none of them stuck it out. I decided to stick it out at all costs. Going to film school every day helped me ease the transition, as I was learning different crafts and working and talking with fellow aspirants, and that encouragement meant a great deal to me.

Then the third point was that I needed to make a movie to prove myself. Talk is cheap and the cafés of the world are full of wannabe directors talking about their wonderful unique projects, but you have to actually go and make one to be taken seriously. I was highly respected now with my art-directing credits and over the last few years had directed several theater plays and commercials and videos. I now needed to convert all of this into a movie-making career.

I was really determined to make my short film, and I was writing and researching ideas. I kept on returning to the same theme: the knight's quest and the last act of chivalry as a knight facing death. This was somehow deeply embedded in my thinking. I realized that I was relating it to the stories from my childhood, and fueled by the Pre-Raphaelites and their vision of the romantic world of Arthurian tales and gallant adventures, I began jotting down ideas.

BLACK ANGEL

had taken the decision to start making my own films very seriously and after long and hard thought, I realized that if I didn't pursue my dream then, it would get harder and harder to turn back. It was difficult, as I loved designing films and art-directing. I loved the visual aspects of the process and being at the heart of movies that required creating new worlds and being pushed to the limits. I knew the best way to learn was to direct one or two short films and learn the ropes that way. Shorts are hard to make as the disciplines of telling a story in twenty-five to thirty minutes are quite hard, and also the budgets are just not there to make epic movies. So I decided to write *Black Angel* as a short film for myself.

THE SCRIPT

I settled down at home and concentrated on a story centered on a knight and his last quest. The historical structure of the great tales of knights and warriors, samurai and other epic legends are all centered on the hero's journey. These tales relate to our subconscious and to our role as humans, and I was interested in exploring a theme associated with this. I wanted to tell the tale as a fantasy, not realistically as the portrayal of a medieval knight, but based on that archetype. I loved Kurosawa's movies and the way the samurai warriors were portrayed, and was keen to film in his style of movie-making. Kurosawa was a master at using the widescreen frame in a different way to Western filmmakers; his films were like epic moving paintings. Movies are a combination of visuals and drama, and I was keen to explore a way of putting on screen images I had in my mind, like images I had seen in paintings and romantic illustrations, if I could capture these, I knew an audience would relate in a more poetic way. I had all my books at home for reference and spent time in my favorite book store, Foyles near Shaftsbury Avenue, reading the classic myths and looking at painters I loved. I also went to one of my other favorite places to hang out, the science-fiction and fantasy bookstore Forbidden Planet. I spent many hours in there over the years buying graphic novels and art books. I wanted to look again at Frank Frazetta's work. He was an inspiration to so many creative people, and one of his paintings, *Death Dealer*, was in my mind as I was assembling my story.

I had the idea of Death as a dark knight who my hero had to fight at the end, and it really helped to have a visual image to fire my imagination into deeper realms. The idea of dealing with death appealed to me. It's a great taboo in Western civilization, but Buddhist teachings make us look at death as just a part of the journey and thus remove all fear of it. Their teachings near the final stage in practice are to make one stand in one's own death, to experience it, to go through the process. Not pretend or act it, to actually go into deep meditation and experience it. Once you have achieved this, you remove all fear of it and this attachment to the fear. Removal of attachments is the work. Not easy to do but necessary to achieve any form of realization. I was figuring all this out for myself, and it was only after I had made the film and was introduced to the *Mad Max* director George Miller that I truly began to understand what my subconscious had led me to. I allowed this to be my guide and let the story evolve from the alpha stage of consciousness, where one's psychic powers are elevated and we plug into the collective unconscious, which enabled me to come up with a basic story. Admiring the way Andrei Tarkovsky made his films to connect directly with the subconscious I decided to attempt the same. *Black Angel* would be a visual story to connect with spiritually.

WHERE DO STORIES ORIGINATE?

Writing original stories raises a really interesting subject, not only related to film but to any creative artist. Where do stories come from? Where and how are they given birth to? What is the absolute root of a story? Joseph Campbell explains in *The Hero with a Thousand Faces* that all great myths are basically the same story told in a million different ways.

Obviously emotional incidents and personal journeys deeply affect us and shape our lives and the way we live them. Profound emotional scars and wounds are often the fuel for these stories, as is the healing of those wounds. Love of course is always the big one, the big story. It is truly the only thing we can have and keep and take with us on our journey, so it is the fuel for most of the world's greatest stories, and whether about falling in love, losing a loved one, or the yearning of ever finding it, this is the universal concern of all human beings.

Robert Bly has written a comprehensive study of the spiritual meaning behind a story in his book *Iron John: A Book About Men*. Bly has taken this classic fairy story and explains how every stage in the drama relates to the stages of boys becoming adolescents and men. Here is a story written with deep inner meanings and keys, and in reading the story the keys trigger emotions in our subconscious that enable us to mature into healthy adult males. A wonderful tale in itself and a drama unfolding that keeps the reader engrossed, but all the time it is a metaphor for something far deeper. What intrigues me is a question that I asked many times and never ever had a response to. What came first, and what is the absolute root of the story? Did the ancients who wrote these wonderful myths and legends think of the deeper subconscious messages they wanted to impart to people and make them understand and learn things about themselves, and then build myths and legends around them as dramatic stories? Or did they write stories as myths and legends and somehow subconsciously touch on these deeper keys that resonate with us as humans and our path through life?

All of the great Greek myths and stories have tremendously complex ideas contained within the dramas, underpinnings to the words that have deeper meanings. It's an interesting discussion and relates to *Black Angel* now that time has passed and I have had to examine the story for this book. How the story I wrote came about and what its influences were

were unbeknown to me at the time and never analyzed until now. My influences for sure were the great British myths and legends I connected to as a child. King Arthur and the Knights of the Round Table, and the stories and legends surrounding the Crusades. As a young boy these were captivating tales to me and I imagined myself in them. It's interesting how every child, I think, at some point wonders where they came from and if they came from a far richer heritage than their parents, just as Arthur finds out and then has to make a choice to follow the path of destiny. Luke Skywalker finds the same thing about his father when he meets Obi-Wan Kenobi. It's all part of the understanding towards taking charge of our own destiny, which is separating from our parents and becoming adults.

I had a tough time comprehending the world of the fifties in Britain and the closed emotional world I grew up in. No one spoke about feelings and emotions, in fact my father believed the common saying that children should be seen and not heard. So how we were able to grow up mentally healthy intrigued me. I constantly challenged the society I was born in. That is why I loved the Pre-Raphaelite painters and the great romantic stories of the Knights of the Round Table and Robin Hood and William Tell. These were romantic heroes who fell in love with beautiful maidens and fought battles for honor. It was a magical world that I could retreat into and it seemed full of passion and color, a marked contrast to the gray world I was surrounded by. I loved the fairy stories of Enid Blyton; I must have read *The Faraway Tree* a hundred times. I also had some strange imaginative children's books, like *The Wonderful Isle of Ulla-Gapoo* and another with beautiful illustrations about a strange electric duck that went around villages terrifying people. These were written and illustrated by some serious fantasy writers and more than likely were responsible for fueling my imagination and also a love of movies that are tense and frightening.

THE TRUE ORIGIN OF MY STORY

Writing this today I have been deeply analyzing where the story of *Black Angel* really came from. All the above are potent ideas, but deep in my subconscious lay the true origins of this story. Relating back to my time in Guaymas in Mexico, described at the beginning of this book, is the moment I stared death in the face on that hospital bed. On the wall was a poster of the lochs in Scotland. I was facing that moment when the life-force energy in the body has almost gone, yet some deepest survival instinct from primitive times kicks in, and I fought to live. I had now written a story of the dying moments in a knight's life and the fulfillment in those last seconds of his deepest desire; the classic knight's quest, a disguised hero's journey, told in a different way.

Something deeply connected here, somewhere at the bottom of the well of my subconscious. This connection to some inner truth that is hiding inside everyone is open to all, and going on a spiritual path is the only way to open that door. The threshold of fear must be overcome, much as the hero has to find his strength when he faces his deepest adversity: his own mortality. When death stares you straight in the face—that is when the true self is revealed. All the great religions and philosophies make one stand in one's own death to release fear, as this is the last boundary to awakening. When that moment of spiritual catharsis arrives, that is when there are only two ways to go: up or down. Just like the hero in every story. King Arthur went down in the end, a tale that was resonating in my head as I was lying there. I think subconsciously the idea for my first short film, *Black Angel*, was born there in that simple room in Mexico, with nothing but a life-or-death decision that had any value to me.

THE SCRIPT EVOLVES

The story finally came to me as they always do for me—in the early hours of the morning. This is when the brain is naturally in the alpha state and at its most receptive and creative. With meditating, the alpha state is the best way into the center, as it were. It is a way to access this level through training, closing off the brain chatter that is so destructive to the creative process, and to the body's self-healing process as well.

I had read some interesting stories about the Crusades and how knights returned to a land devastated by the plague. The knights were given a code when they were sent by the church to fight in the Holy Lands: the more heathens you kill, the closer to God you will be. You were supposed to die in the Holy Lands, never surrender. It was not permitted to leave and return home unless you won in battle. The belief in God at this time was above all else, so it was a perfect way to get armies to go and kill, and not surrender under any circumstances.

I had read some stories about how some of the Crusaders were defeated at Acre and fled the Holy Lands in ships when the Turks and the armies of Saladin pushed out the armies. So I imagined the interior conflict going on in a Crusader's mind and psyche as he had broken a code, which in those times was sacrosanct. I was also trying to find a way to construct a story around the knight's quest. The Crusades were deeply linked into the knights' stories; I had read those like the tales of Sir Galahad and others like *Ivanhoe* and *Perceval, the Story of the Grail.* I loved the idea of the English knights' code of honor when they were to go out and help people in distress. Their greatest success would be to find a maiden in trouble and rescue her; classic King Arthur and Lancelot territory. But I wanted more. The idea of fighting death came to me. Inspired by spiritual practice and the painting by Frazetta of the Death Dealer, I tried to think of a way to combine all of these elements into a short story.

The structure occurred to me when I thought about a book by William Golding, one of my favorite authors and one of the great mystical writers of Britain. His novels use deep allegory and symbolism often relating to mythology. Most people know him for *Lord of the Flies* and the wonderful film directed by Peter Brook. I was extremely fascinated by his novel *Pincher Martin*'s structure and I found an inspiration for mine. The novel begins with a seaman drowning in a shipwreck and struggling to get his heavy sea boots off so that he can swim to the surface by ridding himself of their weight and so save himself. He struggles and finally pulls them off as he is about to take his last breath. Swimming to the surface he is washed ashore unconscious. When he wakes he goes on an amazing journey, part analysis of the loneliness of man and part an examination of his life in flashbacks. The book ends with his body being discovered on the seashore by some seaman, and one of them pronounces, "The poor bugger never had time to get his sea boots off." So it's a full circle, an imagined drama in the few moments of dying. The book uses an anti-hero as a hero, a man fighting a lonely and seemingly hopeless battle, a theme that recurs in many of my movies. In the end it's his refusal to accept death, even at the hands of God, that makes this extraordinary novel so powerful.

BLACK ANGEL

One morning I awoke with a story in my head. I created a character called Sir Maddox to tell the narrative through, a knight who returns defeated from the Holy Lands with his servant Anselm, to find his lands and house in ruins and all his family dead from the plague. He has nothing left to live for and, tired and defeated spiritually, he decides to go back to the Holy Lands to fight to the end, if that should be his destiny. As he crosses a fast-flowing river he slips and falls into the deep water. He is sinking fast, weighed down by the heavy iron helmet and as he struggles to remove it off his head, he hears a woman's voice saying, "Stay your hand, Lord Death, take me instead." Spurred on by hearing the voice of a damsel in distress, he launches into renewed action and finally yanks the helmet off his head and swims to the surface.

He emerges in a strange land with odd-shaped trees growing into the water, and a mystical atmosphere pervades. He sees a maiden, an eerie ghost-like figure on the shore, and asks her why she wants to die. She tells him she is bound to the Black Angel. She turns and walks away. Maddox has finally found his true quest and speaking aloud to his horse says, "This maiden has saved my life and needs to be rescued." He sets off to follow her.

She leads him to an old man, a strange figure who mocks him and says that he will lead him to the Black Angel but it's a dangerous path to take. The journey takes him to the Black Angel through strange landscapes and a confrontation and battle to decide his fate. In fact the Black Angel is death.

I wanted the script read by other people and took it to the film school for a few peers to give me notes. Everyone liked the story a lot, but all asked how I was going to make this with the budgets we had. I realized that it was going to be a struggle, as I did not want to film it in any other format than widescreen CinemaScope, and needed spectacular landscapes to pull it off. I already had my eye on Scotland. My influence was Kurosawa and the lone samurai movies, and I wanted to set my film in similar epic landscapes.

During this time, Ridley Scott had edited *Alien* and was by now doing the final sound mix at EMI Studios, so I called him and asked if I could sit in to watch and learn the sound-mixing process on a big movie. Bill Rowe was one of the best mixers in the world at this time. He did the final sound mixes for all of Stanley Kubrick's movies, including *A*

Clockwork Orange and *The Shining*. He also mixed the award-winning *Chariots of Fire*. I knew it would be like observing the best, and that's the way to learn.

I went to the studios and sat in every day watching Bill work, his fingers moving across the soundboard like a magician, maneuvering the sound to exactly what Ridley wanted. Sound and music are the last elements to be added to a film, and they can be what makes or breaks a movie, adding the final elements to create a cinematic experience. The wrong sound, the wrong music, can throw a scene totally off balance. You could clearly see here that this movie was going to be a huge hit; the sound was awesome when combined with the music and created a really tense atmosphere. Sound plays a massive role in the way a movie is received by an audience, and shapes the way an audience watches a film. A skilled sound mixer can really raise the bar on a movie, given the right sound effects and music, and create a flowing sound that amplifies every moment.

One day I was watching the sequence where the *Nostromo* is going to explode. The alarms are going and the voice of Helen Horton is announcing the ship will explode in T minus the minutes on the countdown as Ripley races around the corridors in a panic to get Jones and get into the pod. The sound was loud and awesome. The sound of the ship's engines going into overdrive was filling the EMI sound theater; it was giving me goosebumps to hear just what sound was turning these scenes into and Bill was making it all balance with such ease.

Sandy Lieberson came to visit and take a look at what Ridley was up to. He sat enthralled next to me on the carpeted steps of the theater, so we were center screen, watching the massive sound sequence being built up layer by layer by Bill. When there was a break Sandy asked me what I was doing. I told him I had written a short film script but felt it was outside the realm of the budgets allocated at the film school. He asked what it was about and I told him it was a medieval fantasy story about a knight returning from the Holy Lands and rescuing a maiden and a fight with Death. I wanted to film it in CinemaScope ratio, same as *Alien* was, in Scotland, and it was about twenty-five minutes long. Sandy then told me that George Lucas was really disappointed with the short film they had put with *Star Wars: A New Hope*, and wanted a film especially made to go out with *The Empire Strikes Back*. As the British government had the Eady fund in place to help filmmakers make short films there would be about twenty-five thousand pounds allocated to make one. He asked me if I could make *Black Angel* for that—I said, "Of course." I did know how to make things really low-budget having filmed music videos and documentaries and I knew being in Scotland I could use a very small crew to get what I wanted. Sandy asked me if he could read it to see if it might be suitable, knowing my relationship with George and Gary Kurtz would help.

I went home and faxed him the few pages of the script that evening. Sandy called me back almost immediately and said he really liked it, and it would be a perfect fit with *The Empire Strikes Back* as the story was about dark and light, and a myth. He told me he would fax it over to George and Gary, with a recommendation to make it. I would produce it with my company, Painted Lady Productions, with the twenty-five thousand pounds from the Eady fund.

I waited anxiously for an answer and continued to go to EMI Studios to watch the mix. Bill Rowe asked me at lunch what I was doing, and I told him how I was trying to make my first short film. He asked what it was about, what sort of genre, so I told him the story and how I wanted to make it. Bill said that I had to let him mix it there at EMI. I told him I could never afford it; we would be on a shoestring if I got permission for the funding. Bill said, "Don't worry about that, I really want to help you; I will do anything for you. You just give me whatever you can afford out of the budget. You are doing the sound here, agreed! And you have to do this in stereo sound." I was blown away; if the film was to happen the best mixer in the world wanted to create my sound mix! This was another Holy Grail moment.

In case the news was positive from George and Sandy I went to Neal's Yard to meet up with Roger Pratt. Roger looked after the cameras for Terry Gilliam and in return was able to use their equipment. Terry had told me that Roger was really talented and I had seen it for myself. I went to talk to him about *Black Angel*, as I needed his thoughts on the project. I knew I would have very little money to make it with and so it was not a choice of mine to go with an established director of photography. To come to Scotland with me for the time it would take to recce and prep the film and shoot it under pretty difficult conditions would take someone very hungry and ready to go out on a limb with me. Also artistically and creatively I wanted someone who loved cinema and Kurosawa, and had that kind of sensibility. Roger loved painters and spent his time looking at how they arranged light, the true inspiration for all the great DPs. He also loved Ingmar Bergman's films and hero-worshipped his DP, Sven Nykvist.

I was also looking through all my reference books, particularly several I had of castles. I settled on Eilean Donan Castle near Dornie at the head of the Kyle of Lochalsh. I had never seen this castle on film, yet it was located dramatically at the head of three lochs. It stood on a small rock island connected to the mainland so in silhouette it was stunning. It was also completely intact and restored, not in ruins. I needed a vista like this to start the movie and set the tone and style of the remote lands of a medieval countryside like Britain was at the time. The film was to be a fantasy but familiar to eleventh-century Britain.

Les Dilley wanted to be a producer and asked if he could produce it with me. I knew the sacrifices I had to make and with Les and his children to support it would be more difficult, but we met and talked about it as I needed help producing and directing. I explained what I wanted to do and how it would have to be a very small, dedicated crew eager to do anything and work long hours if necessary under pretty different conditions to what most crews were used to as I only had twenty-five thousand pounds and that would be eaten away very quickly.

I had to have the heavy horses with long untrimmed hair for the knights—they would look wrong if we used the modern riding horses. That meant going to the horse trainer and owner Reg Dent, who we both knew well from movie work we had done together. Whenever a carriage and horses were required, Reg was the man. He had many trained film horses and had massive experience at handling carriage and fours for period films. Reg would have to transport the horses to Scotland and look after them, so it would most likely be the largest expense I had.

Sandy called me into the Twentieth Century Fox office in Soho Square. I got on the Tube and went there, not sure what to expect. To my absolute delight he told me that George really liked the script and had sanctioned *Black Angel* as the film to accompany *The Empire Strikes Back*. George had also told Robert Watts, the producer, to give me the short ends of film left over from filming *The Empire Strikes Back* and to let me go make my movie. His orders were that no one was to see *Black Angel* until I had finished it. George would be the first to see it. This was a supreme act of faith by George and a thank you to me for standing by him on *Star Wars* and never faltering by his side with John and Les.

The script had to have been strong enough for him to agree, this is a tough business after all, and the second *Star Wars* going out would be a big deal for Fox. George had been supported by Francis Ford Coppola when starting out, and retains the independent spirit of a filmmaker to this day. The small group of filmmakers based in San Francisco stood by each other with unwavering loyalty, especially when beginning a career; it is vital to have peers who encourage. I am forever grateful to him for this act of generosity.

So here I was, finally on the brink. I went home and created a budget to make the film. I had to go and make a recce to put absolute costs on paper, so I booked a train for Inverness.

I drove from the train in Inverness to Dornie. Scotland, especially then, has a wild and unaltered beauty. Ancient castles dot the landscape and it was easy to imagine oneself in the medieval times. Seeing the light, even in mid-summer, I knew my instinct had guided me to the right place to make the film. I had found the castle I was heading for in my old book of Scottish castles in my reference library. It was ideal as an image of the romantic Pre-Raphaelite world the painters had imagined. I needed images like this to set the scene for the film at the opening, and then slowly to reveal the world destroyed by the plague.

Dornie is a tiny hamlet on the shores of the Kyle of Lochalsh. Eilean Donan Castle was even more beautiful than any picture I had seen. With storm clouds in the sky and the water of the three lochs, Loch Duich, Loch Alsh, and Loch Long, framing the castle and reflecting its image in the still water, at the right time of day, reflected in the water with the hillsides surrounding it, it was indeed a truly spectacular setting. Spotting a small guesthouse that was looking right onto the castle from the mainland shore, I booked a room for a couple of nights. The little private hotel was owned by a Mr and Mrs Snowie. They were closing for the winter season at the end of September, but I offered to do a deal for my small crew and actors for eight days. The shots of the castle would work early in the morning at sunrise in one direction and at sunset in the other, so I needed to schedule the shoot accordingly.

I explored the area for the other locations to match the script. I needed an abandoned castle for Sir Maddox for his ruined mansion but could not find one anywhere. Then, by accident, I found a landscape for their ride through the country. The valley had stone walls, which must have been placed hundreds of years before, that covered the hills as far as the eye could see. It looked like an abandoned country left to ruin, and would more than visually amplify the story I was trying to tell. In this same valley I found a magnificent vista high up in the hills with a view across the Scottish Highlands. This again was far better than I imagined and worth searching for. I worked out with a compass a time of day to shoot this as well, so it would be backlit.

I also needed a waterfall. It's a symbolic image included in many myths and paintings, and always used in ancient stories. Water actually represents the subconscious, and moving and falling water can be interpreted as the storyteller wishes, but often is used as an image of cleansing and transformation. It is also a deeply romantic visual, often used by the Pre-Raphaelite painters. Mr Snowie told me about a waterfall that was up a long dirt road. Every location I had found was way off the beaten track up really rough roads used by farmers and shepherds. Having planned a tiny crew I knew we could get to more interesting locations—when one is dealing with a major film and a crew of hundreds it's impossible, so I could consider using locations like this, amazing locations normally unseen by tourists and certainly never seen on film before.

Walking through the lower marshy ground with small springs everywhere, I came on an area of ancient gnarled trees that looked dead, covered in lichen and moss, and really strange. It was a kind of otherworldly landscape and I took pictures, absolutely ecstatic that destiny was giving me such amazing gifts. I had written in the screenplay Sir Maddox in this kind of different landscape, like a more surreal world.

Walking on up the valley we could hear the waterfall and had to cross a fairly rickety bridge over a dried-up stream bed to get to it, the sound of falling water guiding us to it. When we found it, though small, it fell about forty or more feet down a rocky escarpment, and it looked very like one in the Pre-Raphaelite paintings that I had referenced. Though tiny compared to something like the Victoria Falls it was still impressive. Water falling in a great swirling, tumbling mass has fascinated man since ancient times. Crossing back over the bridge I spotted an area of the dried-up riverbed, perfect for another location I had imagined and written in the script. I found a few more locations that I required: a forested area to walk Maddox through, and another area with broken-down shepherds' stone huts.

Now I had most of the locations to make up the background for the story, although I still needed a stretch of lake with a small inlet and strange trees. This location proved to be impossible to find here, but I had seen pictures of a lake near Dunoon, and decided to go there to search for a location for this part of the shoot, and split the shoot in half, as we had to film the underwater sequence in the swimming pool in Dunoon. I also needed a strange forest for the meeting and the fight to the death between Sir Maddox and the Black Angel.

I had made very precise notes of the locations so far, how they fitted together and what time of day I needed to be at each one to film for the correct light. I would have just enough film at most for a few takes at each one and that was it, so I had to go home and storyboard exactly how and when and where to film each section. This meant doing my own shooting schedule, working out exactly how far between locations it was for timing and how long I would estimate to shoot each section.

My intention was to make this twenty-five-minute film as epic as possible and try to put the poetic and romantic images I had in my head up on screen, as I had not seen this done outside of Werner Herzog's early movies, and the most stunningly beautiful images in Ridley Scott's *The Duellists*. I realized that the budget was stretched beyond limits and I had to limit what I could shoot for each segment. I barely had enough film, so I had to work out how much I could use for each shot and location. I took a hard decision to limit the dialogue to a minimum to allow me to film each segment, as recording sound would be restricted and I could only do one or two takes. If I could connect the locations in Dunoon, the added cost of travel and hotels could be absorbed if I cut the script to the minimum and could still attain my goal of filming a poetic and visually inspiring film. I had to go to Dunoon, as there was no swimming pool available in Dornie.

So my first stop when we reached Dunoon was the local swimming pool. Because of my timing I lucked out; Scotland gets pretty fierce winters and they closed the swimming pools. This school was going to drain the pool so didn't mind us filming in the water. I did a deal with them for a day's filming, and explained that I would need to hang black velvet into the pool to give the right background and we would bring an underwater camera. They were fine with it, as they had to drain the pool anyway and would wait until the day after we filmed, so I now had another element in place, another location ticked off the list.

Searching around the area I found a location beyond my imagination for Sir Maddox's emergence from the lake into a strange land. When I walked into this bay on a lake, to my absolute amazement there was actually what looked like banyan trees growing into the lake with huge entwined roots. They certainly did not look British at all, but very strange and mystical. I shot photos of this from the water, not believing my luck, and I could see that backlit this would be the perfect location.

The small river I found was exactly like a Pre-Raphaelite painting of a brook, and beyond it was a natural amphitheater formed by the trees, where I could frame the Black Angel like a painting. I wanted to recreate the Frazetta vision of the knight on his massive black charger as an inspiration, but against an amphitheater of trees.

Now I had everything, so we returned to Dunoon to fix up accommodation for the crew and anything else we needed.

I found my last location required, an abandoned castle in ruins nearby. An eerie and sad place with a chapel attached, it had no roof and open windows, but structurally had a lot to offer with its gray stone edifices and arched doorways still intact, and a stone staircase leading up to the ruined first floor. This was perfect as an abandoned and derelict castle for Sir Maddox and it could be shot anytime during the day, so this would be tacked on at the end of the schedule as it was just outside the Scottish border.

We drove back to London and I created my schedule myself, taking into account the different locations and the times of day I needed to film to get the light right, as this really created the correct image I needed for each scene. It was more difficult than normal, as the daylight in Scotland at the end of September is short. I think I only had usable light from about 8am to 3.30pm, a very short day. However, right before October starts and the snows come is when Scotland is at its most beautiful. The skies are just stunning, with sequences of clouds racing across them and the sun bursting through in veins of cathedral light. I needed to connect the different locations together to make the journey of Maddox work as a story. I had limited time at each location, and I fitted them together like a train, using my Polaroids to place them in a sequence. *Black Angel* was told visually as a story. I only had Sir Maddox alone in many scenes, like the opening as he rides home, and then after he leaves his servant behind. I had no one to construct simple dialogue with to tell the story.

I made very rough storyboards for myself to help put the pieces together for the story to work and to aid my crew in understanding what I was planning in my mind for the film. Communication of ideas is paramount when time and money are so tight. I spent a lot of time with Roger Pratt going through this, and exactly how the light worked for each shot. We wanted to benefit from backlight wherever we could.

As a massive bonus to us my favorite cinema, the Electric Cinema in Portobello Road, was having a retrospective of Kurosawa and were showing three of his movies a day. So we spent hours in the darkened cinema watching them all. In between each film the Electric had a small booth and a kitchen at the back of the auditorium, and served tea and hard-boiled eggs with bread and butter. So we ate between the screenings, absorbing exactly how this master of CinemaScope used the frame to tell the story. The two owners used to come down the aisles in between films dressed in fifties usherettes' gear, with pillbox hats on an angle on their heads, and sell ice creams. To cram in my film education when I moved to London I lived as close to the Electric as I could off Ladbroke Grove, so I could go any time, day or night, to see obscure movies and art movies— anything I could to educate myself.

I missed this wonderful cinema when it finally sank into mediocrity and was bought out as a mainstream Odeon. Now it is transformed again into a Soho House venue and restaurant, and the old projector is preserved in a glass case. It's just not the same, though. Portobello Road and Ladbroke Grove were the places in the sixties and seventies, alive with a vibrant atmosphere. They were heady days in the sixties, seventies and early eighties and movies became the means of escape and also my means of earning my living, so it was like living a dream.

The wonderful and highly experienced casting director, Irene Lamb, very kindly agreed to help me cast *Black Angel* for a very small fee compared to her usual, but she was always glad to help and knew I was serious. Having cast *Star Wars*, I knew her, and at that time she was one of the best, so I was in good hands. Casting is really one of the most important elements in making a movie, equal to the strength of the script. She had narrowed down a list of actors who could play the lead knight for me to look at. Taking into account I was making a short film, and the payment for actors would be small as the budget was very tight, the list was easily compiled. I needed that masculine look that could carry the physique of a medieval knight, and a face that could pass for the era. Irene heavily recommended Tony Vogel, who came to my attention. He was the lead in a television series, *Dick Barton*, he played a role in *Jesus of Nazareth* and he looked absolutely right for the knight. When we met he had a beard and his hair was grown so he really looked the part, and he could ride horses. We talked about my vision and Kurosawa, and he liked these types of movies so had an inherent understanding of what I was after. He read the script, and was passionate about making it. We talked about the language and whether it was possible to speak in the way that medieval men might talk; it was worth an experiment with that type of dialogue and we decided to try it.

I had met John Young on *Life of Brian* and became friends with him whilst shooting in Tunisia. John was a regular in the Python films, always cast in a central role. I remember John telling me that they always cast him in roles that required some terrible physical activity. He said they dropped him in a vat of custard on one film, and did several takes of it. I needed an elder wizard-type character who would lead Sir Maddox to the Black Angel. John was perfect for the role, and knowing him well was a great help. He agreed immediately to come to Scotland for the few days required, especially when I guaranteed we would not drop him in vats of custard or boiling oil.

Having so little money for the casting from the budget, Patricia wanted to act and was determined to play the maiden. The character I needed was an ethereal and sad young woman who was bound by the Black Angel, an almost ghostly figure who would be extremely pale. I needed someone with a mystical air about her and I knew that Patricia looked the part and was convinced that she could pull it off. The maiden had very little dialogue, the main line being, "I am bound to the Black Angel." With her French accent it gave the maiden a more ethereal presence so she was cast.

I needed one other knight, Anselm, who rode in with Sir Maddox and had important dialogue. I went on a search in Scotland for a casting director. It made more sense to cast a local actor from Glasgow. Having settled on the only casting director there, Ruth Parks, I sent her a long description and examples of the type of character for Anselm and arranged to meet her there on the way to the next tech recce.

I traveled to Glasgow to her home office and I went through all her choices one by one. With each headshot and resume I looked at, my face dropped. They all looked like handsome, contemporary television actors; not one had the face of a medieval knight, or the structure that I could easily build on. I wanted a natural look, without any makeup or false hair or beards, so I needed faces that looked right. Ruth just could not understand why I rejected them all, and kept trying to point out their relative qualities, and why I should hire them. I think she was more concerned with getting a job for local actors who were her friends than fulfilling the brief I had carefully gone through with her for the part of Anselm.

I suddenly had an inspiration. "Can I see who you rejected?" I asked. She looked at me most astonished, as if I had asked for the unthinkable. I think that by now she had seen and recognized my determined and stubborn side, which was about to display itself, so she went away and fetched three photographs with resumes. They were all interesting and all possible, and all had good experience. One actor really caught my eye: James Gibb. He had deep, strong eyes and a face I could see with hair extensions would jump back in time and look really authentic. There was something about this actor, a presence and a force, and I just knew he would be strong. I had had some experience, having directed some stage plays and music videos, and I had a basic understanding of the actor's skills. Being around actors all my working life, watching them perform, watching endless movies, and being close to some directors and learning from them, I had developed an instinct about casting. At Beaconsfield film school one of the bonuses of being there were the regular actors' workshops that I participated in and you could work directly with them on scenes and record them. I had discovered for myself through all this that there are no rules to casting, just intuition. The higher one's own instinct is developed the better to see the truth.

James Gibb came in to see me at the casting director's house, and we connected immediately. He had obviously been working wherever he could as an actor living outside of Glasgow, and was working as an electrician to keep his family afloat. He responded with immense enthusiasm to the project, and said that he really wanted to play the part no matter the money, and as a bonus he could ride well. He certainly had a face that was able to transform to a knight's and his eyes were powerful. My idea was to have the knights like Kurosawa's, with longer unkempt hair and unshaven or bearded so they looked more natural. I decided on James for the role and met with a lot of opposition from the casting director who just could not understand why I would even consider him, let alone choose him. I would have none of it, so I said my goodbyes and left with clear instructions as to who she was to contract. In fact James was so good I cast him in a major role in my next short film I made in Edinburgh, *The Dollar Bottom*, which won an Academy Award for best dramatic short film in 1981, so in a way it was an immense justification for following my instinct.

Back in London, Les was adamant about producing the film with me, but I was worried about his wife Mandy and how she would take it, so I drove to see him at home in Radlett in Hertfordshire. I explained the path I had taken and the sacrifice financially that it meant, which was serious. I was deprived of any income, but prepared myself for it and was prepared to stick it out to the end. So if Les was to start producing from nowhere, as a successful art director and in demand as he was all the time, it was to be a serious consideration. It takes a great deal of courage to jump ship, and the attitude in the UK, especially at that time, was very Calvinistic, who wrote if you were born in a village you stayed in that village, so there would be little support from peers. I was more than happy to have Les on board, and to have a loyal friend at my side would be really supportive for me as I was going out on a limb and jumping in at the deep end. This was the advice I had given to anyone who asked my advice on how to make films or get into movies: just go do it, don't talk about it, and I had no qualms at all about following my own advice.

I contacted John Beard and asked him if he wanted to design his first film. He came to the apartment in Earls Court and we looked at all my photos and reference material and at what we needed. I had written a moment in the film where a bat that was a design feature on the Black Angel's shield suddenly flies off the shield and right over our heads. So we had to figure that out with little to no money to spend. A model-making team who had just set up shop happily agreed to make one for us that we would fly over camera on a thin wire, and the speed would create the illusion that the wings were flapping. We went through the weapons needed, especially the ax for the Black Angel, and I showed John the painting of the Death Dealer by Frank Frazetta as an inspiration. I needed two horses, one for the Black Angel and one for Sir Maddox, and required two of the ancient breed of heavy horses with their mane and forelocks unclipped, as they would have been.

There were actually quite a few props and dressings to get together. For example, I needed a hovel built from old sacks and leaves, as near the ruined mansion when Maddox returns home he sees a family living in absolute poverty.

Roger Pratt was my chosen director of photography. I trusted my instincts as I felt Roger understood exactly what I was after. We had looked at Georges de La Tour's paintings together and Ingres and my amazing book by the greatest French DP, Henri Alekan.

I asked Charles Knode, the brilliant costume designer of *Life of Brian* and the other Python movies, if he would look after the costumes for me. He had offered when we were in Tunisia to do anything I needed and he agreed at once. We discussed the maiden's costume and the Black Angel's as they would be the most difficult to source or make with pretty much zero budget. The rest of the costumes like Maddox and Anselm and the other small parts were straightforward rentals once I had cast the roles. Charles also looked after the makeup for me and liked doing that as he felt he could assimilate the look with the costumes and we were after a realistic, natural look anyhow.

I asked Alan Strachan to edit for me. I knew Alan from as far back as *Randall and Hopkirk* and we were still friends. I needed an experienced editor to help me through the process and be our eyes in London, as we would be sending the film back for development and not seeing anything until we returned. Alan was excited to do it. We asked Michael Samuelson's brother Peter, who at that time ran a small studio called Production Village in Cricklewood Lane, for edit suites. He gave us two rooms for the production for a very special price to help out, which was a great help to us. Production Village was built around a village green with a duck pond and looked like a farmyard surrounded by studios and edit suites and offices. It had a cobbled courtyard and families of ducks and animals. Coming through the gates from the noisy traffic on Cricklewood Lane you entered the incongruous location of a country farmyard, which even had a pub, The Hog's Grunt. It was a great place to work for us, and in fact several important movies were made there like *Breaking Glass*, which was shooting when we were there, and where I re-met its leading actor Jon Finch.

Trevor Jones would compose all the music. I spent hours with Trevor going through my influences as music was going to play a major role in my movie to set evocative moods and give a soundscape to the film. I loved visionary movies and I wanted this to exactly represent what was in my mind and imagination. Another major influence on me was Tarkovsky, the great Russian director who made all his films to connect to the subconscious, not the conscious mind. As I was making a myth, I wanted to connect at a more spiritual level, the way *Star Wars* was written by George based on the hero's journey. Music plays a tremendous role in connecting an audience to a deeper level of emotions, so I spent a great deal of time working on musical influences. *Black Angel* was limited in its narrative because of budget restraints, so I had to tell the story visually. I had Trevor watch *Seven Samurai* and *Ran*. I played Trevor a track by Stomu Yamashta called 'Wind Words'; the violin was played by his classical violinist wife, who was rated sixth in the world at the time. It is a really beautiful piece of music and was a very big influence to me on how I needed to evoke mood. I had seen Stomu perform with his Red Buddha Theatre at the Roundhouse in Chalk Farm, and was staggered at the emotional impact of this journey through Hiroshima, all told through music, dance, and mime. I saw him live once, and when he played drums he moved so fast sometimes he literally became a blur. A staggering composer, he disappeared to become a Buddhist monk in Tibet and still lives in Japan in relative seclusion.

I played Trevor the great Celtic composer from Breton, Alan Stivell, famous in France yet unknown in the UK. His music, like the 'Suite Irlandaise', was Celtic-influenced and made medieval romantic music contemporary with flute and harp and mixing in modern band elements.

There was also one song that I kept playing over and over and had Trevor listen to. Something in it caught my imagination and it had both sweetness and deep sadness. Francis Cabrel wrote a song when he was living in Paris and yearning for his life in the country called 'Carte Postale'. Something in it influenced me with its feeling so Trevor listened to this as well. I was training him to understand the emotional commitment the film had to have, to evoke a deep haunting sadness as it was a sad story but also spiritual in a relationship to myth. I also had Trevor watch *Death in Venice*; the use of Mahler's 'Fifth Symphony' was superb. The end scene as he dies on the beach is memorable, and Visconti's fusion of Venice and the story, supported by Mahler, is a wonderful use of cinema.

Again the music is so evocative. This was my goal, and Trevor I knew could understand what I was after, although still young and relatively inexperienced.

VANGELIS

Then I had Trevor sit down and absorb Vangelis. He was unknown in the UK at the time. I discovered him in France. I was watching television one day at the family home in Argeles Gazost and Frédéric Rossif's documentary was broadcast about the great sailing ships in the South China Sea. I was mesmerized. His images were absolutely stunning, often shot in slow motion against sunsets—totally breathtaking. The music was something the like of which I had never heard before, yet somehow was what I had played in my head. The composer was Vangelis Papathanassiou. Well, I had never heard of him, or ever seen such amazing documentaries on television in the UK. The music was sweet yet mystical and deep, and hauntingly evocative, exactly what I wanted for a movie. The next day I insisted on tracking this composer down, so we went straight to the record shop in Tarbes, the local big town half an hour away.

In my broken French I asked the owner if he knew Vangelis. He replied in English, as he was fluent. He said, "Yes, I have several of his tapes here. He's well known in France, his tapes and records sell in huge amounts." And he said, "He's not known at all in the UK, is he?" I acknowledged that I had never heard of him. The record shop owner laughed. He showed me the Sex Pistols tapes. "This is what we get from England; no one wants to listen to it, yet this man Vangelis makes such beautiful music. I don't understand the UK at all." I agreed with him. I bought all his tapes, as I wanted to listen to everything Vangelis had composed. The man laughed again. "Do you know the biggest irony? He lives in London." I could hardly believe it!" I asked, "For sure?" "Yes, for sure," he told me. I drove home, playing Vangelis all the way. *L'Apocalypse des Animaux* was so brilliant. Then *Opera Sauvage* confirmed my belief in what an amazing composer this was. One day I would track him down.

My cast and crew were almost complete now. I met with Sandy Lieberson and we transferred the government funds to my Painted Lady account. It was real! I was making a film. Roger Pratt and I spent a lot of time together planning the shoot and the look. We went to see Michael Samuelson, who owned the largest camera-hire facility in the UK at the time. Michael was another deeply committed and kind man. He looked at Roger and my meager list: one Arri, a few lenses, a couple of lights, and the rest were the accessories needed for the Arri, like tripod and fluid heads, etc. We needed a large zoom as I needed to pull back from Sir Maddox riding home to reveal a vast mountainous wilderness, and it was the only way to do it. I think our budget was seven hundred pounds. Michael added more lenses for us gratis, and despite our pleas that we couldn't afford it he insisted.

"Now how are you going to move the camera?" he asked us. Well we both fumbled. "We'll somehow hand-hold it and we have a wheelchair booked, the cheap way of tracking."

"You have to have some track and a dolly," he insisted. "Don't worry about it. I'll invest in you now and then when you make your first feature you'll come back to me and we will rent you all the equipment." He got us a length of track and a half-circle of track so we could curve, and a dolly. It was fantastic of him and really kind as it did make all the difference to us. We even had a viewfinder thrown in so we could set up shots. Roger chose a light for the underwater sequence and the underwater housing for the Arri. We also got a few pieces of black velvet for the swimming pool sequence and some weights. We had our equipment. I hired a sound recordist and now all we had to do was to go see Reg Dent and secure the exact horses. I'd saved around two thousand pounds for these, as I knew they would be expensive.

I went to Elstree to see Robert Watts and Gary Kurtz, and collected all the cans of leftover film. Bruce Sharman the production co-ordinator gave me all the wet gear left over, thin plastic suits to help keep out the rain. Bruce helped me a lot with the setting up of the production; I used to go to his house near Kew and Twickenham and go through all the production logistics, insurance and accounting and things like that.

Roger chose the crew we had used for filming Brian in the alien craft sequence in *Life of Brian*, shot in Terry Gilliam's Neal's Yard studios. Tony

Andrews was to be our grip. The advantage for Roger Pratt choosing the crew he had worked with and knew was that Tony Andrews had a Volkswagen van, so he could take all our equipment up to Scotland with him. Mike Todd was also hired as the clapper loader and Brian Herlihy was the focus puller.

We needed a lab on board with us to develop the film and do the grading and finishing work, which was another large expense in the budget. We went to see Mike Todd, the customer relations chief at Rank Laboratories in Denham and met with them to sort out an 'all in' deal. Everyone was willing to support me in the making of the film and giving me special rates for everything made it all possible. They promised me their top grader would do the end color timing as they could see from my explanation of what I was doing and my passion that I was intent on making something special. I think as well knowing the film would go out with *The Empire Strikes Back* helped. They knew they would get to make about 400 prints for the UK alone, so that was where they would make their money back. In fact my color grader was the best there, and was working on Stanley Kubrick's film *The Shining* at the same time. Companies like Rank and Samuelson's helped support emerging filmmakers. The rewards are that the filmmakers return when their careers gather momentum, and relationships are formed. Mike was great at this and recognized my ambitions. He really helped Alan and Roger and me; Rank bent over backwards to treat me as well as any top director. They are sorely missed from the UK scene now.

So we had it all in place. I just needed my two large heavy horses.

GIANT HEAVY HORSES

I went to the country, to the farm where Reg Dent kept all his horses, which was not too far from Pinewood Studios. We looked at a magnificent white horse that stood over seventeen hands tall. One of the ancient breeds of heavy horses with all its hair left unclipped, it was perfect for Sir Maddox. Then we decided on another giant, a black heavy horse about the same size, for the Black Angel. With all its hair, it looked very similar to the Death Dealer painting, and would look auspicious in profile as I imagined the first shot of the Black Angel would be. Shooting on the edge of winter had its advantages, as the horse's hair had grown. I did a deal with Reg to transport them to Scotland and use them for the seven days of filming. I remember settling a deal at about the two thousand pounds that I'd allowed in my budget. We would need a horse for Anselm, but that was okay to be a little smaller, and we would find one locally. It was a really special price for me as they had to rent me two horses, drive them all the way to the north of Scotland for the seven days of shooting, feed them and house them. A trainer and handler would be with them as well, to make sure they were able to do all I required for the shooting. We worked out the logistics of when we needed the horses there and exactly how many days it would take them to organize and get them to Scotland and settled.

The only other element I needed to put in place was a co-ordinator for the fight between Sir Maddox and the Black Angel. I wanted a battle on horseback first and then a fight on foot with Sir Maddox and the Black Angel fighting to the death with axes. I used to hang out a lot at Parsons in the Fulham Road. The manager Des Ward Smith was a highly trained martial artist, and kept offering to do the stunt work for me. I could not afford a stunt co-ordinator; it meant serious training and equipment and stunt doubles, all the usual requirements. I wanted the Black Angel to fight and the way I envisioned filming it handheld, I needed Tony Vogel to do his own work, and he wanted to. Being stage trained, especially with Shakespeare and other projects for classical theater, he was a well-trained swordsman. So Des agreed to come and do it, and didn't charge me much as it was his first film work. As he was to play the Black Angel I had Charles Knode fit him out with a strange black costume created from found elements, and we also had him go to the specialist opticians who made contact lenses for film work. I needed the Black Angel to have yellowish eyes, definitely not human.

All was set.

Alan Strachan established himself at Production Village the day we left with assistant Michael Bateman. We were to send rushes back daily if we could. I had worked with assistant director Nick Laws a few times and he was eager to climb the ladder to being a first AD. Nick came on board as my first assistant director and he was the production head and runner—he was my production, basically. The team was complete. John Beard left ahead of the crew and me with Nick Laws to set up and to establish the locations. Once everything was prepared in London and everybody's travel was organized, we headed up to Glasgow with Roger Pratt. Tony the grip loaded his Volkswagen bus, the type that was so popular in India with the hippies. He left London a few days early with the VW van loaded to the hilt with cameras and grip equipment and anything else we needed, including all the props. It was so heavy and overloaded that the wheels at the back were splayed out at an angle. We allowed a few extra days for travel so they could take it easy, as the van looked like it would only make forty miles an hour at max.

Les and I had decided to rent a camper wagon in Glasgow and drive on up to Dornie. The wagon was like a small caravan on wheels and was to serve as a mobile production office and dressing room for the actors. It also meant we had a much-needed toilet and a place to make tea and sandwiches, as all the locations were far from any civilization or facilities. It gave us a place for hair and makeup, as well as a changing area for the assistant to change the mags and load them with film. So it was a mobile base and small enough to get into the locations.

Roger and I had bought some fast stock as well as the short ends Gary had given us, because we needed to cope with some fairly low-light situations as it was the end of September and winter comes early to Scotland, especially the north. I had taken a gamble with the weather after studying winter patterns—I was worried a little but willing to risk it, as it was the amazing stormy skies that would create the mood for the film. I needed these really dramatic skies and light, and at the end of September and the beginning of October Scotland is at its most beautiful; you get constantly shifting cloud formations and sunlight streaking through like the fingers of God. There were no simple programs then for changing skies in post so what you filmed was what you got, and to make *Black Angel* into a surreal fantasy world I really needed those skies to be different. The gamble was winter and snow. When it comes to Scotland it comes with a fury, and who knows when, so I relied on my intuition and set the first day of the shoot as 29th September and we were to return home on the 10th October after the last day of shooting in Dunoon on the 9th.

Pat Carr, who was Robert Watts' right-hand woman, gave me lots of advice and printed out artist's waivers and sample crew contract letters for me. All had to be correctly handled and submitted to Twentieth

Century Fox as the film would get a wide release in cinemas and the lawyers are very strict about all elements being correctly handled and all personnel on a movie being correctly contracted so there is no comeback afterwards.

The signed documents for a film are called the chain of title and are the one aspect all distributors and film companies worry most about. Everyone working on a film, all equipment used and facilities have to have a signed contract.

Roger Pratt, Les, Patricia and I flew to Glasgow on the cheapest tickets available and rented the camper van. We drove Roger to Dunoon to look at the swimming pool we had got permission to use on the way. Roger could then think about how we were going to film the sequence. We had rented an underwater camera housing for the Arri and Roger had a few lights on the truck. The underwater housing was one of the more expensive pieces of equipment we had allowed ourselves, but was the only way to make the shot. Driving round the harbor I stopped to show Roger the Polaris base. We stood and watched the nuclear subs docked at the floating harbor in the middle and watched a nuclear sub as it silently exited the harbor. We were lucky to witness this again; I told Roger about my fantasy that there were Russian spies disguised as local fishermen watching the subs' movements from the windows of one of the little cottages lining the harbor. This was still the era of the Cold War after all. We made up more stories about the spies and who they might be on our way to Dornie.

We arrived in Dornie later in the evening. Mr and Mrs Snowie's guesthouse was closed for the season, but was open for the crew. Being a day early meant Roger and I could see the locations and plan out our first two days' shooting in advance. The next morning at dawn, we looked at the Eilean Donan Castle and where we could shoot from for the most dramatic shots. Roger and I decided on a perfect shot of it from the rocky headland that we would shoot at sunset or dawn. So we decided to have a go as soon as the transport arrived with the camera equipment and see if we could grab a shot at sunset. We would pan around the loch and end on the castle. This would give me the time to have the evocative music at the beginning with the credits to set the emotion of the film.

We drove around and checked out the hillside for the opening shot as Sir Maddox returns home, which would begin the journey in the dark. We had rented an old lantern and that would be our only light source—we could hide the battery and the cables under Les's multi-layered costume made up of sackcloth and rags. Les was going to play a beggar who approaches Sir Maddox looking for food. I wrote him in to give the idea that the land was ruined and people were begging for food from travelers.

Roger Pratt and I spent a couple of hours going through the storyboards over and over again and watching the skies changing every minute from the glass conservatory looking out over Eilean Donan. They rendered us speechless; neither of us had ever seen anything like it. Scotland was putting on a show for us. Sometimes massive veins of light shone through the clouds from the hidden sun, almost like moving images from Blake's etchings. If we could get these on film, it would be extraordinary, we felt.

The next morning the horsebox arrived with the two horses driven by Reg and his assistant, his wife Shirley, and they got them settled and stabled. Reg went in search of another smaller horse for Anselm. In the afternoon the Volkswagen with all our equipment finally arrived. Roger and I were looking at an even more spectacular sunset than usual. Roger looked at me and I nodded silently, knowing exactly what he was thinking. Roger didn't give the crew time to relax, just got them to unpack the camera equipment and tripod. We rushed down to the shoreline and set up. The skies were truly dramatic, and they raced to get the magazines loaded and the lenses and filters correct. The sunsets in winter are short-lived and Les and I watched as the light started to disappear on us. Roger was furiously working, but the moment he was able to shoot and take a look at the sweeping pan around the shoreline to the castle, darkness descended.

He checked his exposure meter and there wasn't even a reading. We'd missed it. But depressed as Roger was at not getting it, I said we could try in the morning for sunrise and tomorrow evening again, we had the time. We'd get to film another one during the next few days; I had allotted time for that in my schedule.

The next day, the first task on my schedule was to film the opening shot of Sir Maddox coming over the hill in the darkness, so we got up really early before dawn and made porridge to sustain us as it would be a long cold day. Turned out Tony Vogel was a secret porridge-making nut, so he made a vast vat of it with cream and sugar, which we all relished and ate in the darkness of very early dawn and drove in convoy to the location, which was right by the road to make it easier to get to in the dark. Whilst Tony Vogel and Les got dressed, Roger and I set up the shot and prepared the battery-operated lantern. We wanted it really dark with just the lantern as a light source so Les as the beggar would appear from nowhere. Reg's team got Richard (Sir Maddox's horse) prepared, and Tony practiced riding it for the shot. He was a very accomplished rider, so there was relief all round! Richard was a huge horse, but a very gentle one, and Tony was revealed to be very skilled at getting him exactly in the right place for the shots, which made our lives much easier.

We got the shot fairly quickly before dawn. The first shot is always the most nerve-wracking on a movie for me. I do anything to get one in the can so that take one is over. Usually I haven't slept much through analyzing every bit of the preparations and worrying that everything is ready. Once filming starts there is little time for anything other than getting through the day, and preparing for the next. Certainly normal life falls out the window; there becomes nothing else in one's head than getting the movie made and every shot the best it can be, and the restriction is always the same—the budget and the schedule. The lower the budget the less time there is, and so you have to compromise every minute trying to get the shots as you imagine. It's a virgin slate on a virgin film, and to me it's like being bloodied once that first one is in the can—it means the movie is finally being born. I got rid of take one on the first take of Sir Maddox sleeping on his horse as he walks through the hillside pass. We placed the lantern so that the yellow light gently reflected on his sleeping face. The intention was to show that he was on a long journey home, and that there was an unspoken trust between man and horse.

This explained without dialogue or narrative that they had come a long way together. This was the first reveal of the knight in the movie and I wanted the beggar to suddenly be there in the dark. Just a momentary glance from Sir Maddox and then he'd carry on sleeping. Having got all the shots in before dawn, the first daylight arrived and we were all freezing. It was so cold and damp, but everyone got stuck in to the next shots.

We continued on all day and filmed the sequence of Sir Maddox arriving home from the wars in the Holy Lands. The magnificent locations we had chosen and the light that kept changing during the day inspired everyone, and the cold and damp was quickly forgotten as I think everyone was exhilarated by what we had filmed and were eager to carry on and see more. With our small and ragged crew of about nine of us it was easy to move around and keep going.

It very lightly drizzled on and off, but mostly stayed dry. We had a very quick break for a sandwich at midday around our camper wagon. Patricia had kindly gone there to make us tea, as it was really cold. Roger Pratt was the first to take a large gulp from the plastic cups, which were all we had, and his automatic reject system caused an instant response and the tea shot back out of Roger's mouth as fast as it had gone in. "Cor," he said, with an expressive grimace on his face, "that's tire tea!" as he stared down into the cup. I tasted mine—sure enough it tasted of old Dunlop tires. Everyone else on the crew did the same and spat it out, exclaiming, "It's old tires!" Patricia, highly embarrassed, explained that as we had no water on board, and were miles from any shop, she had found a load of old tires in the woods next to our camp, and as they had a lot of rainwater in them, she had used that. As she was boiling it up she thought it would be safe. Everyone laughed, and I don't think there was a moment within the rest of the shoot when Roger didn't rib her about her tire tea!

We went back to Eilean Donan in time to catch the sunset and set up the shots. We weren't sure it would be as spectacular as the previous evening as the sky was overcast. Suddenly the skies opened up, more dramatic than the day before. Roger shot a pan around the shore, and it looked awesome. It was a great opening shot for the film, epic indeed.

Roger was staring at his meter, and said we should see if we could get another go at it on another day. He was unsure about being a stop under and if the negative would hold up on the big screen, so for safety thought we should keep trying, maybe at dawn on one of the days when we could schedule it again. Nick Laws and I looked at possible days. Then as the dusk began to turn into night, suddenly massive fingers of light beamed dustily through the breaking storm clouds and we filmed it. There was the dream in my head. As the light held up we had time to move position and get another shot, so that I could build a sequence. The light then disappeared and went too low to get any reading at all, so we packed up for the night and retired, exhausted.

The next day we set up for the journey through the first of the locations with the strange trees in the swamp. Sir Maddox was riding the first part and then leading Richard through the more mushy ground where the trees had lichen hanging from them due to the constantly damp air. We set up the shots, and now we all made use of the plastic rain gear Bruce had given us from *The Empire Strikes Back* shoot. Despite this we were already soaked before we got the first shot in the can. The drizzle certainly helped the look of the scene as Sir Maddox went through this strange and eerie landscape, so the weather was actually helping me get what I wanted. I could see Roger Pratt was puzzling over his trusted exposure meter, and shaking his head. The shot looked great through the camera, but he was playing around with F-stops. When I went across after getting Tony Vogel ready, Roger looked at me and told me the light was so low he couldn't get a reading. "What do we do, then?" I asked, suddenly feeling my stomach tighten, as this is a producer and director's nightmare, not being able to shoot, and not having enough money to cope with any delays. Roger had me look through the lens. "It looks fantastic, but I'm at least two stops under, so sod it," he said, and threw his exposure meter away onto the wet grass, "I guess I'll go by instinct." Which he did for virtually the rest of the shoot. We were on minimum F-stops a lot of the time, and gambled that we had enough light to give the negative the correct density and exposure.

Every shot when we looked at the rushes back in London was staggeringly beautiful. The depth of the image on the negative is truly a testament to Kodak film stock and the latitude we have. At the time, though, without being able to see anything for a few days, we were going on a wing and a prayer. This is why Roger has gone on to be one of the greatest directors of photography, and at the time who knows, if I had hired a much more experienced one they might have pulled the plug on me and refused to shoot until the light got better. Roger has a love of film and movies and he long admired Sven Nykvist as a mentor. Sven used to work in a way with Bergman much as we were working: with a tiny crew and natural light, relying on the Swedish light to donate a beauty or starkness to the images in Bergman's mind.

We certainly had no means of seeing anything, being in the wilds where we were. Nick Laws was driving the rushes each night to Stirling, the nearest city, where he could send them safely to London. Then Alan Strachan would get them two days later after they were developed. We had no means of seeing anything, so Roger and I had set up a system where we would call Alan after a few days and he would go through the shots with us by phone. If there was a serious problem anywhere, I could retake whatever was needed whilst still on location. Not ideal, but beggars can't be choosers.

I filmed Sir Maddox going between the trees, sometimes hanging more lichen on the branches. They reminded me of the trees covered in lichen in Don Siegel's film *The Beguiled*, a creepy thriller set in the Louisiana swamps. I thought it was a really good film, extremely different to anything he had done before and highly acclaimed in France. The setting in the strange trees in the swampland was unusual, and here I was in the wilds of Scotland finding a similar landscape.

We had a quick, wet sandwich break at lunch, this time with tea made from water we had carried with us. Roger pretended to spit his out as he took a sip—he couldn't resist the joke and was met with Patricia's sighs of "Enough already!" In fact the requests for tea continued through the day as it was really cold and being soaked to the skin didn't help. However, no one complained at all, as the crews were all very dedicated and seeing the shots we were getting one after the other inspired everyone to ignore the conditions. The forest setting and swamp were really unusual, perfect for the different world between the lake and the Black Angel.

In the afternoon I filmed Sir Maddox racing away from his ruined castle towards the riverbank. He was riding hard, trying to avoid his emotions boiling to the surface, after finding his wife and children dead from the plague and his home in ruins.

There was nothing left in this desperate plague-ridden land for him, so he was going to go back to the Holy Lands. Also in his mind was the thought that this was punishment for fleeing the battlegrounds and not obeying the Knights' Code.

John Young arrived that afternoon and Charles Knode got him and Patricia prepared for the following day. John was fairly easy as he was playing another old mystic in a simple medieval cloth cloak, and that way we could hide his face sometimes under the hood. Patricia had brought an antique white dress she and Charles had chosen back in London and a white shawl to cover her head. It became an ethereal look quite easily and Charles spent some time preparing her makeup, as she had to look ghostly white.

Next up was the waterfall sequence. John and Patricia got ready in our multi-purpose camper vehicle whilst Roger and I clambered over the rocks next to the small river to find the perfect shots for the sequence. We would place John's character on the opposite bank and the maiden too. Sir Maddox would follow the old man up the river to the waterfall, and there see the maiden again. We composed some shots using the waterfall; the wind was driving the mist from it into the air in swirling patterns like fog and gave a beauty to the shot with the maiden, like another painting. It was misty as hell, but a gorgeous light, perfect for the scene. It reminded me of Caspar David Friedrich's work, one of my other influences. In my mind, as well, thinking of how the maiden should be, was the wonderful painting, *The Lady of Shalott*, by another romantic painter favorite of mine, John William Waterhouse.

We filmed that scene and completed it and then tried Sir Maddox approaching the waterfall upriver. Again the swirling wind and rain made the misty river and trees look exactly like a Pre-Raphaelite painting. I was wet and cold but excited for Roger and myself, as the weather was creating added layers to the photography that I could only dream about. We had Sir Maddox ride as far as he could on Richard and then dismount and climb over the rocks to get to the maiden. As Sir Maddox climbs urgently towards where he last saw her, suddenly the old man appears and Sir Maddox calls loudly across the raging waters asking, "Where is the maiden?" We kept adding to John's costume, layer on layer of rags so that he looked like an ancient wandering mystic, and I kept his face pretty obscured to add to the mystery. He warns Sir Maddox of the dangers but agrees to lead him to the Black Angel. I planned on cutting away so the mystic had moved really fast in the landscape when Sir Maddox looked up again. We placed him way higher up the waterfall away from Sir Maddox. This was planned as an added layer of mystery, to illustrate that this was not an ordinary land Sir Maddox was in.

It took all day to complete the sequence. This ended with Sir Maddox calling for Richard, who galloped towards him on the opposite bank. Reg Dent's wife, Shirley, was looking after the horses and filming requirements, and everything she asked the horses to do, they did on cue. They were superbly trained, and looked magnificent in the wild Scottish landscape. I felt justified in spending so much of my budget on the two main horses for Sir Maddox and the Black Angel, as any hold-ups were just not possible with my schedule.

We raced back to the castle and set up again on the headland between the three lochs, as the arriving dusk looked more spectacular than any we had seen. Roger got set up really fast and we did another sweeping pan around the headland and this was the shot I used in the end to open the film.

On day four, we continued shooting the sequence of Sir Maddox following the old man through the rocky landscape. Today was a major day as John Beard had found a location where I could place the Black Angel for a first sighting. I wanted him sitting on his horse with the ax as a dramatic side shot, the first glimpse of this dark knight. Charles Knode built up the costume on Des Ward Smith and layered it in with pieces of dark chainmail and cloth. He had constructed a facemask with hanging pieces, which he slowly pieced together until it looked ominous and strange. With the contact lenses giving a yellowish color to the eyes it looked powerful when he had finished. Charles is a genius at putting costumes together and was well practiced in making them with little to no money for the Pythons, and making them look very real, which is what I was after.

There was little precedent at this time to refer to, so Charles and I had to rely on each other's instincts, and Charles understood the genre really well. We had Frazetta's painting to fall back on, but that wasn't exactly how I wanted the Black Angel, who represented death. With a form of chainmail cloak and black tights and boots, with specially prepared rubber-like gloves, he looked like I'd envisioned him as I wrote his character. John Beard had the shield with the bat insignia at its center brought to the location, and also a huge ax which was similar in shape to Frazetta's and to the great battle axes used in ancient times. And there he was. Death.

I was truly blessed by the weather. I needed a really dramatic background for the Black Angel when we first saw him, and had talked to Alan Strachan about it before I left. I had mentioned that it would be perfect to have a rainbow around the Black Angel, but we couldn't afford to matte one in on the budget I had. It would mean doing costly optical print work, and adding in animation at an effects house meant using a pin-registered camera for the plate. This was far beyond the reach of my meager funds. We decided to film the sequence in Dunoon, as the location was way better.

I finished the sequence—when Sir Maddox moves forward towards the Black Angel he simply disappears—and I would add a laugh from the old mystic and then show him disappearing into the woods, Sir Maddox leading Richard in pursuit. We filmed all the scenes next with Sir Maddox walking up through an interesting first location following the old mystic.

Nick Laws dashed off from the location with the next batch of film, and we went back to the guesthouse as daylight suddenly disappeared on us. James Gibb had arrived to play Anselm, and had a chance to ride his horse and for Charles to fit his costume and hair.

We had brought some longer wigs with us to match his hair and make him more warrior-like. As soon as we added these, James's great eyes and sculpted face took on the look of a worn knight from times past. It was thrilling to see the transformation and confirmed my reliance on my instinct in casting him.

John Beard had built flags on poles for me, which we fixed behind the saddles. These were inspired by the Japanese warriors in Kurosawa's movies, and planted on purpose by me as I didn't want the audience to think this was a classic medieval piece or Crusaders-era film, but more of an epic ancient fantasy that was totally reality-based, gritty and earthy. These little touches were visually exciting as the wind caused the flags to vibrate and make a great sound, and again gave the impression of a lonely wilderness. Also they threw out the notion of the purity of period and helped me try to make the film as a visual fantasy like an epic comic strip or graphic novel.

I continued the sequence for the title, filming in a magnificent valley we had found. The mountains and valley beyond where we were shooting formed a massive vista. I wanted to see this as a wide shot and then tighten in to the arriving dawn over the crest of the two mountains. To do this we had a massive zoom lens on the camera and used a tracking shot. I found extraordinary the attitude of many directors of photography who I had worked with towards zooms—they simply refused to use one. They somehow deemed them as equivalent to television. Thank goodness Roger Pratt was of the emerging new generation of directors of photography who threw away the traditions and regulations of the past and looked forward. Whatever it takes to get the shot, that's what you do—Roger and I were well versed in Sergio Leone and Kurosawa, two giants of the epic who used zooms to get what they wanted and shot some stunning film. Roger agreed instantly with me that to achieve the shot I wanted, we'd zoom in. Moving in really slowly, the shot inched its way to the two peaks, where I would place the title *Black Angel*. Music would create the mood, eerie and rather sad and beautiful. We again lucked out here. As we were ready to shoot, a black formation of clouds appeared right where we needed them, at the crest of the two valleys we were zooming in to. As a dawn light it was superb, and we quickly did several takes to get the zoom right—it's not easy for the operator and focus puller to get a steady, imperceptible move by hand. We could not, of course, afford the more sophisticated electric zoom motor attachment.

I think by now the small crew was blown away by what they were seeing. A director and the crew have the luxury of seeing rushes daily as that is what we see as we film, but none of them had seen the stunning images we were getting before, and like these shots on this day in such a massive scale.

Having got the opening shot we proceeded with Sir Maddox riding home later after the reveal at dawn, riding alone through these vast empty landscapes unique to Scotland. We set up all the track we had to film Sir Maddox riding and do another reveal of where he was. Again the bleak landscape was used to show his loneliness and that the land was empty of people, in preparation for the scenes to come when it was explained by his servant, the knight Anselm. This time we set up a small track on the ridge of a valley, and had Sir Maddox ride across the ridge. At the right moment the camera, which was slowly tracking, zoomed out to its widest and revealed a vast landscape of hills and mountains across the massive valley beyond. With the storm clouds in the sky it was pretty overwhelming on the day, and all I could hope was that we had captured the emotion on film.

As soon as we had finished we shifted locations again to lower in the valley. I had found another great landscape where we could place Sir Maddox's meeting with Anselm. I had hired a couple more local riders to be with Anselm. I wanted to see the riders pounding towards us over the vast landscape Kurosawa-like; only the ruins of a house betrayed any form of previous civilization. It looked like a lonely, abandoned, windswept valley. They meet, the horses panting from the hard ride, Anselm speaks to Sir Maddox and the first dialogue in the film describes the desperation they have found. He tells Sir Maddox that his family is dead, his home is in ruins, and the plague has killed everything. They are going back to the wars. Sir Maddox tells them to go and starts back towards his home to see for himself.

We quickly shifted locations and filmed the next shot of Sir Maddox arriving home. I had him ride through the extraordinary ancient valley I had found, the hillsides covered as far as the eye could see with rocky wall-like structures. These looked very ancient, now crumbled and broken, and instantly gave the impression of a land abandoned and destroyed. I used the vistas to my advantage and created epic landscapes, with Sir Maddox and Richard tiny in the frame at times, much as Kurosawa used his frames. Each of these shots cut together so I had to get each segment filmed exactly as I had storyboarded it. I did not have the luxury of spare takes or cover footage—we simply didn't have the film stock. I would have just enough to cut together each single shot in a sequence to get his journey onto film. We finished the day and completed all the riding through different vistas, and all I had left to film in these locations was Sir Maddox falling into the river, which I had left to last for the actor's sake.

On the last day there I filmed the river scene where Sir Maddox falls into the deep water. John Beard had been searching and searching for a suitable spot where Tony could actually ride Richard to the water's edge in a shallow part, but there was no location suitable to be found. The only place had a barbed-wire fence strongly constructed along the entire length and we did not have time or funds to remove it and replace it. John Beard had found one spot that worked for the action required, and we set up there.

I had Tony Vogel ride to the river knowing he would have to cross it. He dismounted from Richard to test the water, how deep it might be and how fast the flow was. The action was that as he tried this wearing heavy armor, he slipped on the muddy bank and fell into the water. I'd cut to underwater in the pool in Dunoon and continue the sequence. Being Scotland on the edge of winter the water was really cold, but Tony was game for anything. We had a basic wetsuit for him that Charles Knode had brought with us in preparation for the scene. I got the take in a couple of goes. Tony was so good, and he really made it work for me. He walked to the edge of the river and walked in as if testing it out, suddenly let his feet slip away from under him and down he went into the water. As he fell he went under and I cut. He clambered out, shaking but happy. We wrapped the last shot of the sequence here in Dornie and the Kyle of Lochalsh and returned to the Snowies' to pack up ready to travel on Sunday to Dunoon. John Beard left before us to find the exact locations for me.

Early Monday morning after we had settled into Dunoon we all left to find the location through the forestry trails for the area for the battle scenes between the Black Angel and Sir Maddox. We were following the maps that John Beard had created and at one junction stopped, unsure which way to go. These were logging roads cut through the forested areas of planted pines that Scotland had vast areas of. Suddenly John Beard arrived, running and red in the face and out of breath. He said he had lost his way, and his van had slipped off the road into a ditch, so he had run back to get us. This is the kind of dedication that I was taught and many other British crews had. John has since continued and risen very quickly whilst young as a major film designer, without going through the usual long traditional road through assisting and drawing, and he's all the better for it as he has a creative ability that was encouraged and developed whilst still young. This was my path too. John had worked for me on several films as assistant and was introduced to Terry Gilliam on *Life of Brian* as I took John with us to Tunisia. He has since gone on designing for Terry, and that has given him a massive design knowledge, as Terry always pushes the limits and the budget to visual heights not many other people attain. John jumped in my vehicle and we sped through rough roads until we found the location. With no signs and every road looking exactly the same, it was like being in a maze. This location was the small river leading to the fight area.

I was shooting a section of the scene where Sir Maddox climbs past the river, seeing the maiden, led by the old mystic who disappears. To get the shot we had the camera set up in the middle of the river on a small rocky area where the water dropped a few feet. I was directing the actors where to go while Roger Pratt was checking the skies and the light for the right moment to turn over, and Brian Herlihy was getting focus marks. We were all standing boot-deep in the freezing water. I turned and asked Roger, "What sign are you?" "Pisces," he answered. Being a Pisces myself I asked what date. "26th," he said. "I'm the 25th," I responded. Brian looked at us both with that curious look of 'here we go again'—turns out he was a Pisces too and within a couple of days of us. Well here we are again standing in water, getting soaked under the Scottish misty rain and loving it. No wonder.

We moved onto the Black Angel sequence. Sir Maddox had found the maiden, and in my sequence the Black Angel appeared and disappeared. Suddenly he was there again, sitting astride the charger, ax held ready for battle. A powerful image framed by a forest of trees around the clearing we had found. I had placed the maiden standing by the water framed by strange trees; again with the light rain and mist swirling it was another shot that transformed her ethereal quality into a painting. It was images like this I needed to turn this script into an epic and romantic legend, so I was deeply thrilled at every shot we managed to get despite the rain and damp. Once again the sunlight poured down in beams through the trees and the smoke that John and the grip laid into the trees created those cathedral-like shafts. As we turned over really fast to get the shots, I knew the crew was by now thinking I had sold my soul to the devil, or had some mystical connection to the powers above, as everything I asked for in the weather happened as we filmed. To me it was simply wishful thinking.

We began the sequence of the fight on horseback. I had carefully constructed the sequence in my simple storyboards, as again I could only film exactly what I needed and film stock was getting really tight now. When Sir Maddox arrives in the clearing, he leads Richard and looks around. Suddenly the Black Angel as a silhouetted figure is charging down on him. It roars past camera, blacking it out, and Sir Maddox crashes to the ground on his back with the wind blasting his hair. He rises quickly and grabs his ax from the tree where it had landed.

In the film I now cut to the Frazetta shot of the Black Angel as a fully arresting and classic image like a fantasy graphic. The knight gets his stave and charges down on Sir Maddox. As they clash there's another blur as the Black Angel crashes past Sir Maddox. We see the Black Angel again in silhouette, the ax hanging over the edge of the Black Angel's stave, held out like a jousting pole.

The background of trees for the Black Angel was pretty interesting, so we set up the shot with him side on riding the magnificent stallion and holding his ax. I had a smoke machine with us and John Beard was running around with the grip, laying smoke in amongst the trees. Then as we set the camera ready, the sun broke through the rain and thick clouds and suddenly veined down behind the Black Angel. We turned over and grabbed the moment. Roger Pratt couldn't contain his excitement as we filmed everything we needed as fast as we could before the clouds covered the skies again. I zoomed into a huge close-up, and it was here that the greatest miracle happened.

We called Alan Strachan after two days, so the film had been developed. He was stunned at the images we were getting, and cutting them together they fitted exactly as my storyboard. Roger and I were again relieved. Then Alan said something that surprised me, and I immediately thought he was winding me up.

He asked how I had created the rainbow, as I had talked about having one, but couldn't afford it. I laughed and said, "Very funny, Alan," but he insisted that there was a rainbow circling the Black Knight, exactly as I had described to him. Now I knew Alan was winding me up, but his sincerity seemed to be without question. Roger and I went back to work bemused.

Later when we were back at the edit room, on film, to my enormous surprise, we had a rainbow encircling the Black Angel, like a perfect arch around him. This only showed up on film later, it was never there looking through the camera. I couldn't believe it. Roger Pratt and I carefully analyzed the film, both in shock. I had always wanted the rainbow here, and there it was, as if we had planned it. We analyzed that a drop of rain was hanging on the end of the stave, and when the sun came out and backlit the knight it hit the drop of water and refracted into a rainbow. Whatever had caused it, there it was forever on film, and had created the perfect image for me.

I jump-cut to the ax suddenly midway between the Black Angel and Sir Maddox, again setting up an uneasy and strange feeling, and adding to the tension and danger. It all takes time to set up and rehearse with horses and the action, so we filmed the sequence piece by piece, trying to get the best light for each shot.

Then the demon Black Angel charges down again, all thundering hooves, filmed on the longest lens we had with us. We completed those scenes by the time the light disappeared on us. To watch and film these massive horses thundering at each other as if in a medieval joust and the clashing of shields and weapons was awesome. I began to experience what it must have been like in the Crusades as armies battled against each other on horseback. It's a kind of insanity: the smell of blood, the testosterone-fueled soldiers fighting for their lives in viscous heat, often exhausted from travel across tough landscapes in many different countries. It took a good part of a knight's lifetime to go to the Holy Lands and fight and return, if they were granted the ability to return. All this weighed heavily in Sir Maddox's mind, I imagined, as Tony created his character.

I filmed the sequence until Sir Maddox crashed from his horse and the Black Angel disappeared again. After the next day at the lake, I would carry on with the fight on foot all that day.

BLACK ANGEL: DAY 8

We arrived at the lakeside location the next day to film Sir Maddox emerging from the lake. I had allowed all day to complete this sequence, as it was not so easy. Tony Vogel had to get soaked yet again, and I had to get him under water at the beginning of the shot. Having tried this a few times, I had found it wasn't easy to get him completely under as a body is full of air and naturally floats. However, with the weight of his chainmail and Tony's reassurance, we tried. Charles got Tony back into a wetsuit to protect him as much as we could from the cold. He was once again absolutely game to try anything and everything to make it better.

I knew Tony couldn't actually disappear completely below the water and we began the day's shooting. Tony really concentrated and managed to get himself as far under as he could and I yelled "Action!" For the reverse shot that he sees as he emerges from the lake I set Richard the horse on the left side of the strange bank, and the maiden on the right side. With the 2.35 CinemaScope aspect ratio, positions were vitally important. This was to be like a classic painting and once again we had the backlit trees and the maiden standing in amongst them with a thin mist coming off the lake. Augmented by John Beard with his smoke machine, this softened the atmosphere and created a really perfect shot. Roger and I were soaked as we had to be in the lake to get the shots looking back at the land as Sir Maddox waded up from under the lake.

William Golding's novel, *Pincher Martin*, was of course in my mind as an inspiration, and using this location I was able to create a mystical land, that though different, was not enough for an audience to question it consciously. That was important—I did not want to create a fantasy land, as the journey from here to the end would only be understood at the last shot. This section of the film was a dream-like circle of life transformed into a knight's last quest.

It's very curious how themes and experiences repeat themselves. In my first feature film to come, *The Sender*, the lead character, John Doe, played so brilliantly by Željko Ivanek, tries to kill himself by filling his pockets full of water and walking into a lake in an attempt to drown himself, partly filmed as an underwater sequence. As I wrote earlier this is a journey into the subconscious, which water represents. In one of my long-form music videos I filmed in Croatia in the former Yugoslavia I had Tim Wheater, the new-age flutist, emerge from a lake as if being reborn; his song was called 'White Lake'.

I mention all this as I was making an epic fantasy with *Black Angel*, but it was to be a connection to the subconscious part of the mind so that the story through image would relate to a deeper level in us and touch the heart. That was my intention, anyhow, and to make it in a more accessible way than Tarkovsky, the genius of filmmakers, who made an entire film, *The Mirror*, to relate to our subconscious and not all on a conscious level. He did the same in one of my favorite films, *Stalker*. This is the power of myth.

Watching this scene through the camera as Sir Maddox approached this strange mythical land with banyan-type trees, and a maiden dressed all in white like a ghost in the mist, it was exactly what I imagined and it touched me deeply just watching the scene unfold. I was that knight wading from the water, walking out of my conscious mind into an amazing dream world.

When Sir Maddox makes it to the land and asks the maiden why she wants to die, she says, "I am bound to the Black Angel." People still seem to remember that line today; it is quoted on the blogs and Peter Briggs, the writer of the film *Hellboy*, told me he has that line in his brain still to this day. Strange how things get attached to us, but again that's the power of myth and image as they burn into our subconscious. This is the purpose of fairy stories and myths, and those keys are vital to us. I wanted to try to attempt to create a drama that achieved this connection on film, knowing it would get released into hundreds of cinemas with *The Empire Strikes Back*.

I filmed the old mystic who suddenly appears on the bank, and tells Sir Maddox to follow him. I jump-cut him up away into the trees, to start the journey in this land with a bit of strangeness, as if he could time-shift.

Now that I had completed the first part of the battle on horseback, I had the largest part of the fight on foot to complete. We got the Black Angel ready (his costume took by far the longest), and also I worked out wider shots first as the contact lenses for his eyes were not easy to handle. I blocked out the fight, as I wanted to film a lot of the action handheld, right in there with the characters. We had to carefully construct each section because there were no stunt doubles and they were fighting with axes and staves. I also had to work out exactly where to place the bat flying from the Black Angel's shield as John Beard had to think about setting this up and where to hide the fishing-line mechanism we pulled it on.

My largest concern was stock. We had put one roll aside for the underwater sequence on the last day. I had short ends left and different stocks so Roger had to balance out what time of day we shot with which type of stock, and we made a rough calculation of how much each section would take—there was enough for one take per shot in some areas. It's like measuring out a length of film and equating it to a piece of action, but the rule is make it work, or go home! I had the fight in sections and broken by cuts when the Black Angel was suddenly not there, creating more and more strange and eerie moments for Sir Maddox to cope with.

Having blocked out the first section we tried to set up the shot, but something was missing for me. We wanted to film in slow motion as this really helps to create more power visually for a fight. I wondered if we could put something in the air like the seeds flying in a forest that would give a magical feel. Charles Knode and John Beard had several cans of the spray material we used to create spider webs left over. We used it to spray the rubber on the Black Angel's costume to age it and blend the materials together, and Charles suggested we spray it in the air. We did an experiment and it looked fantastic, like strange webbing or seeds floating. So we filmed the scene from various wide angles and then with closer handheld shooting, which looked great. I have used this technique ever since. With the camera on Roger's shoulder he was able to be right in there, close to the actors and the weapons, and it looks extremely powerful. I filmed just enough to make the sequence cut together and work. We broke for a moment to let Des rest, and I filmed the bat flying from the Black Angel's shield. We set up the shield and the rubber bat on its wires so that John Beard could make it fly. It's amazing to me still how one can make something work on camera, with the right angle and lens, the right speed to film it at and cutting carefully to hide wires and any moment that looks unreal.

I needed the fantasy element to help the drama and also make the fight eerie and strange. To add to the scene, a bat is a symbol for the devil and darkness, so it helps the symbolic layering. We filmed it successfully, and I could see on our tiny monitor on the camera that we had got it. I filmed one more section of the fight and we broke as the light had gone.

All I had left to accomplish was to finish the fight and shoot the end sequence with the maiden and the death scene. We cleaned up all the missing shots from the fight and as the light was spectacular again, I filmed the wide shot of the maiden standing on the river bank and Sir Maddox defeated, kneeling before the Black Angel and begging him to take his life and spare the maiden's. I composed the framing with Roger and used the mist and wind again, with the rain softening the look to get some more rather beautiful images, as Roger still had no measurement on his exposure meter and was again working by instinct and by what he could see. I had a few feet left so we filmed a master of the final scene as a wide shot, and then a closer shot to sell the idea of Sir Maddox dying, defeated by Death, the core story at the heart of every human's journey on this planet, and at the center of every myth and legend. I was watching my simple version of it playing out in front of me, and my only wish was more time and more film stock to amplify the moment.

We started the last full day in rainy, windy, depressing weather, just what I needed to emphasize the sadness and loneliness of Sir Maddox's coming home. John Beard had been dressing the day before and created a rough sackcloth hovel where several children were hiding. We placed a metal plate with a crest on it in the dirt, where Sir Maddox would come across it in front of the castle. I had Sir Maddox gallop up to the front and dismount. It was raining and he was soaked, but it did really help the scene. The crew was soaked to the skin, too. Our plastic raingear had now completely vanished, torn to shreds and ripped by the rigors of shooting in wild places, so my old army coat and hat merely served to soak up more rain and keep me thoroughly soaked to the bone.

Sir Maddox looked at the ruins of his castle as he walked forward, and spotted the plate on the ground. He picked it up. All the memories of his family life and the sadness of loss I was able to convey in that simple moment. He walked into the castle and I filmed him looking around the debris of his life as he remembered it. We filmed him upstairs and I was able to pan around the ruin to show what he was seeing. I needed the moment for later as a poignant reminder of Maddox's life and loss. Later I would place some really haunting music over the pans around the house and create an atmosphere; it was all in my mind as we filmed each segment carefully. It was really raining cats and dogs at this stage and that helped a lot; rain is very evocative and creates a metaphor like tears from heaven.

I awoke somewhat relieved on the final day that I had got most of what I wanted in the can, yet with a slight dawning depression that this was the last day, and the shoot was almost done.

The horses were already on their way home and all we had to achieve was the underwater sequence.

We arrived at the Riverside swimming pool in Dunoon, supplied by the manager Jim Anderson, and the camera assistants began assembling the underwater housing and testing it out. Roger and I decided to hang a black velvet cloth in the water to give us an infinity background and we tied camera weights to the bottom and sunk it down, tying the top across the pool with ropes. Once the camera was in, tested and deemed to be watertight, Roger jumped into the pool in swimming trunks and we began to set up. Tony had an actual changing room to get ready in, a heady luxury after the last few days, and we were actually warm and dry all day for the first time in a long time. Tony and I discussed exactly what he had to achieve, as once under the water he was on his own and could act until he felt his breath was gone. We would film it in pieces, and using real time in cutting in the edit room would make it feel like he was drowning, as the time is longer than we can normally hold our breath. Roger would follow Tony and keep him in focus, as there was no way to communicate.

As Tony turned in the water, sinking, he had to attempt to wrestle the helmet off his head, eventually do it, and shoot to the surface. Having the armor and helmet on and a wetsuit under the weight when it was all soaked meant Tony could sink in the water. It's somewhat easier in swimming-pool water than fresh water outside for some reason. Salt water is impossible—it's way too buoyant. Once we had Tony in the water, Roger needed more light to look like sunlight from above. All he had was a single hand lamp, the exact same lamp that I had used in Ridley Scott's *Alien* on the bridge set behind each crew member, so we had to make do. Holding it above the water at the right angle made it look like a beam of sunlight penetrating the depths. John Beard threw a few reeds and plants in the bottom and we began filming.

Tony turned and turned in the water as if struggling and was pulling at his helmet to yank it from his head. We did several takes, as it was difficult for Roger to get it all. Brian Herlihy was also in the water in trunks and as usual was able to pull focus really accurately wherever Roger moved. It's doubly difficult in water as communication is so hard, but the shots seemed to work, never betraying that we were not under the stream, but filming in a swimming pool. In fact it looked really like stream water, slightly hazy with plankton and small pieces of plant life.

Then on a cue from me, Tony reacted to where the maiden's voice called out to him, and with a last desperate effort he pulled the heavy helmet from his head and pushed to the surface. After a couple of takes we got it. That was it, the last shot in the can.

We sat around somewhat relieved and a bit dazed. Had I pulled it off? Did I have enough footage? These are always the worries that go through a director's mind.

Later, as I was driving to the airport to return the camper, snowflakes fell heavily enough to make me turn on the windscreen wipers. The weather broke and it had started snowing heavily. Winter had descended with a vengeance, and I can't imagine what I would have done if it had come a few days earlier. I had taken a gamble to get the superb light at the end of the season, and been lucky. The crew determined now that I had definitely sold my soul to the devil, and in return was given amazing luck with the weather. We dropped off the van and headed for the airport and home.

The next morning Roger and I met at Rank Laboratories in Denham to look at rushes of what we had shot. Alan Strachan was there to join us, and praised the images no end. We looked at the film, and realized that what we had shot looked very different to anything we had seen before. Very rich and deep, the images were like paintings. We looked at the

Black Angel shot with the rainbow, and sure enough there it was, circling the Black Angel like a halo. This was luck indeed, to get that image exactly as I had prayed for.

Afterwards I drove to Production Village to look at what Alan had already assembled as a cut. He had followed my storyboards and we went through the sequences exactly as I had determined they'd be from shooting. We were already a little worried that I'd be short of material—as we finished shooting on the last day we literally ran out of film. I was down to the last reel and had just made it.

Most of the assembly was fairly easy, and we went to work daily to make the story credible and work as a drama. Trevor Jones came to work with me and brought some themes along. One was really haunting, that is the only word for it, and I placed it over the opening to help set the mood. Alan and I like cutting to rhythms sometimes and it helps to temp in tracks that create the emotions, especially in a visually structured film.

This was a visual poem after all.

Trevor Jones and I spent hours together getting the music feeling right. We decided we needed some electronic sounds, so we met and worked with Paddy Kingsland, who was working at the BBC. His music was more like sound layering and had to be integrated with Trevor Jones's music. These were still the early days of synth sound and Paddy was experimenting as an early pioneer with *Doctor Who*.

Alan Strachan walked across one day to my office, and asked me to go and see the fight as he had linked all the segments together.

I watched the ensuing battle straight through, and then we went back and analyzed it. It was going to work, which was the immediate relief. The bat seemed real, and created the right strangeness to cut away from the Black Angel. We both felt the fight wasn't long enough and also that it needed something to add to the power of it. Sound I knew would really make the atmosphere work; sound effects and music enhance fights on film when synced with the action, but we needed something more. I had wanted to film in slow motion, as that adds weight to a fight, but could not afford the film stock. Alan suggested a technique he knew called step printing. This process was done in the laboratory and they duplicated each frame two, three or four times and cut them in, effectively giving a slightly strange slow-motion effect. Alan then showed me what moments of the fight scene were like slowed down. I jumped out of my chair with excitement. It added power to each blow, which added huge weight to the scene, and also the spider's web flotsam in the air just became magical. This was what I had seen in my mind. So we agreed to try a test on one sequence, adding one frame, two frames and three frames so that we had three different speeds to look at. The bonus was added length. Alan had calculated that if we slowed each shot of the fight down three frames we could reach the twenty-five minute length I had agreed on for the film. Without these slowed-down sections we were light, I just hadn't had enough stock to film quite enough footage, and having discarded anything weak or that slowed the story down, we were under length.

We sent them off to Rank in Denham and waited impatiently for the tests to return. In the meantime we did a fine cut on the rest of the film with temp music to really fine-tune everything and use what I had to the maximum. Michael Bateman split out the dialogue and we switched around takes to use the best for the voiceover when Sir Maddox was under water. The tests came back and we chose the three-times-slower version. It was a huge bonus; the fights took on a power and a different physical force. With sound effects and music these scenes would work and we'd realize the potential of what I had managed to film. We locked the cut and Alan began neg-cutting to make a print from for Roger to do a final grading at Rank Laboratories. I was in the final stretch now, there was no going back once we locked the cut.

When Alan and I had assembled all the footage to a fine cut and added in sound effects and music, we went to the EMI sound-mixing theater at Elstree. We screened it on the big screen for Bill Rowe and Ray Merrin, his assistant. At the end Bill sat there, stunned. He turned to me and said it was epic and the images were so beautiful. "I'm sorry but you have to do a stereo mix, it would be a crime not to," he said. "It has to be in Dolby." We had budgeted for a mono mix, as I just didn't have the funds. He sat there and wouldn't give up. In the end, he offered to do it for a thousand pounds, that's all. Now this for Bill is like doing it for free. The costs of high-end mixing theaters like EMI are expensive.

Bill wouldn't take no for an answer so I agreed and said, "Leave it to me." I had a meeting with the labs and got a fixed price to finish the film, including grading. Again when they saw the footage, they gave me their top grader who was working at the time with Stanley Kubrick. He looked at what I had shot and said he had to grade it for me. I was allowed three prints to get the grading correct, that's all, but the grader said not to worry. Roger was very clear on what we needed and the shots were already pretty close to what we filmed.

Trevor and I went to CTS in Wembley to record the music with the players. John Richardson, the number-one recording engineer and mixer at CTS, kindly agreed to do the music record and mix down for us. CTS was the best studio in Britain to record film music and John was really the hero there, so it was an honor for me to be with the best again.

I can still remember the goosebumps, sitting in the recording booth behind John, as the first scenes of the movie were projected on the big screen and the musicians played the opening section of the movie as we panned around the skies to Eilean Donan castle. The music was a perfect complement to the film, and really made the atmosphere work for setting the tone for the movie. Sad, epic, and haunting are the best words to describe it, although words are always hard to find to match the way music affects the soul. I had played Trevor Andrei Tarkovsky's movies to show him how music truly gave a sense of spiritual depth to the images and we sought the same experience. Trevor had got it. People still tell me this is some of the finest music he ever composed, and we had worked with so little, but with so much passion.

We spent a few hours recording the music—we had three hours of musician studio recording time booked, so Trevor was highly stressed to get each section recorded as quickly as possible. The British session musicians were true masters at this. They arrived, rehearsed and got it, so fast. The composer conducted the sessions and John lay it down in components onto different recorders for each instrument so he could balance it out with Trevor into a mix-down.

This was then synced up for the final sound mix with Bill Rowe into about six components on separate tracks so that Bill could still mix down in the final runs through. Sometimes when it's mixed in with dialogue or sound effects in the final mix some instrument or drum, for instance, might be too loud or sharp, so you have the ability in the final mix to adjust all the levels. The music integrates into the sound effects as well; everything together has to serve the film.

We got it all done, and then I left Trevor with John to do all the technical laying-down work. It was amazing to see the entire movie, albeit in pieces, with music, and it all worked beautifully. Sometimes directors switch sections of music around and remove or cut others to get a scene to work, but in the end it comes down to whatever feels right, is right. Music is so important. It is equal to the vision and the dialogue and the drama; it tells an audience exactly where the emotions are going.

In music I include silence—this is of equal importance as a sound. Silence was used to enormous effect by Bergman and Tarkovsky as a means of making a scene really powerful, and these are two great masters I studied for techniques in how to structure music into scenes. In *Stalker* there is a scene in the swamplands where the lead character describes how music is the one emotion that touches the soul like nothing else, and Tarkovsky carefully layers in a note of music that comes so slowly out of the wind rustling the marshes that its arrival is imperceptible. It's a masterclass in drama.

Time was running out, as *The Empire Strikes Back* was soon to be released. Alan and I met in EMI at the mix studio for the final mix. Bill had given us two days in between his busy schedule and determined it was more than enough to make it a full-on mix. Watching Bill assemble the sound effects and dialogue with Ray Merrin, his associate, was like watching a magician at work preparing his tricks. They read the sheets prepared by Michael Bateman and Alan and assembled the sounds while watching the film by instinct and experience. They are so quick at it, and before you know where you are Bill is layering in the sounds, correcting as he goes. I sat next to Bill and hardly had to say a word about what I wanted. Long experience with some of the best directors in the world had given him a vast canvas of knowledge when it came to sound, and the film flowed like a river in sections as he put it all together. There was an occasional question or choice and then the music went in, and I watched in awe as the film came alive before my eyes. We went through the film like this on the first day and completed the majority of the work.

The second day we carried on to the end. Bill had left a half-day for all the technical requirements we call deliverables to be done, an essential part of our delivery of a film to a distributor. The voice is on a separate track so that foreign countries can easily dub them into their own language using our sound effects and music mix.

We broke for lunch and had a run-through of the film complete right after. Having done many movies now, I know that this is the best way to see a movie if you have a print.

This is truly the only opportunity to watch the movie hearing the sound the way it should be heard. Thank goodness Bill had persuaded me to make the stereo mix. Seeing that 2.35 widescreen and the images that big with stereo sound, it was really amazing the difference it made. It was kind of epic as I intended, and now I had to let it go, as I owned it no more—it had to be let loose on an audience. Pretty scary thought for me as I drove home, wondering what people would think of this first effort.

Roger and Alan and I went back to Rank in Denham to make the final combined prints. The grader screened the first one for us, and again it was great to see the film come alive in these final moments, but Roger and I were concentrating on the color-matching and densities of each shot, as we only had two more prints allowed, so we had to get it correct. Alan concentrated on the sound, and made notes of pops on the tracks, which used to happen in those days, and could have simply been a small piece of dirt on the track.

We had a few grading notes, and went through them carefully with him after on the grader, winding the film through shot by shot, as he adjusted the contrast and color levels to match them together. We wanted the opening shots really dark, just the lantern illuminating Sir Maddox's face, and we got this where we wanted it to be.

They made another print and we repeated the same viewing and notes session, and then the third day, the last print. The grader had told us not to worry, that it would be perfect, and indeed it was really smooth and as we wanted it.

All that work had come down to this, twenty-five minutes of celluloid, and now it would be exposed to people to see and judge and comment. There were many things I would have changed given more money and time, but it's the artist's curse, I think, to go back over every moment, and think of better ways to do things.

We had arranged for George to see the film whilst he was over in the UK when they were finishing the music for *The Empire Strikes Back*, and the release was imminent. We arranged the screening at Pinewood's Theatre 7. It was a big theater set up like a cinema, and was the largest screen around for a private showing.

I became more nervous when I saw who showed up—it was not just George and Gary. Marcia Lucas, Irvin Kershner the director of *The Empire Strikes Back*, Robert Watts, Sandy Lieberson, and Peter Beale were all there. I looked at Roger Pratt, who was as nervous as I was—this was a moment of truth, a reality check. I mumbled to Irvin and George that we had done our best with the short ends and the theater went dark as the lights went out. My stomach went into a knot that almost doubled me over. We watched in silence, and at least no one left. Or laughed. Then the credits rolled, and I thought to myself, *I am in this hallowed company of filmmakers, and Irvin is a seasoned Hollywood director with an independent spirit, and very smart.* I absolutely panicked, looking at what I had done. Suddenly it all seemed to be not good enough, and I quietly hid under the projection console where I had been sitting. Roger Pratt had rushed out to the toilet.

The lights came up. Irvin had seen me duck under and he walked over and gently took my arm and led me out. He looked at me and smiled. "Get used to it," he said. "It gets worse. Don't worry, it's really good." George came and congratulated me with Gary and Marcia and that was such a relief, I think it stopped me from going out and throwing up. I was shaking. George really liked the film and what it said, and they were all praising my vision, not really sure how I had achieved such breathtaking shots. Certainly the music had impressed everyone greatly. Sandy and Peter Beale congratulated me and saw that I had delivered what I had promised George. This was my baptism into the role of filmmaking, and the realization that there are no excuses, you just do your best every time whatever the means or budget you are given to try to make the vision in your head real, and stick to your guns. There will always be criticism and doubters and failures, but in my head there are no failures if you learn from your mistakes, and actually the mistakes are usually where you learn the most.

At least I had made a film, not just talked about it, and had put passion into it. I love myth and legend and had made my own version of it. Also I loved the integration of powerful and stunning visuals with drama, and that was my focus here, to put scenes on screen that would touch the soul. I wanted at that moment to go back and remake the film, and get it right as I saw it, but this seems to be the bane of filmmakers.

George and Sandy Lieberson endorsed the film enough to continue with the plan to release it with *The Empire Strikes Back*, and so about four hundred prints were struck.

On the morning *The Empire Strikes Back* was released I drove down to Leicester Square and went to the Odeon to watch the first screening of *Black Angel*, and check that the print was okay. Watching a film I had made being screened, those first images as the lights went out and the cinema screen lit up in the darkness with my pan around the loch and that beautiful music, was awe-inspiring, and equally scary. I sat at the back watching, hoping that no one would comment badly or shout, or worse walk out. The cinema remained quiet and it seemed to me the audience was moved by the film.

Jeremy Thomas, who I regard as one of the great producers of the UK, really liked the film. He became the rock for me in helping me forward and encouraging me. I was getting some negative comments from high people in the British film industry while at the same time I was getting letters sent to me from people all over the country who were telling me that my film had touched them deeply. That was what I had intended, and people were explaining how I had somehow touched their soul and their heart and how the film had really moved them and affected them. I had made the film on purpose as powerful meditation. I was influenced greatly by the great Russian director Tarkovsky, who made all his films to connect to the subconscious as myths are supposed to do, so these letters were deeply rewarding and fulfilling to me.

Then one day I received a call from John Boorman. He asked me if I would go to Theatre 7 in Pinewood and show *Black Angel* to his creative team, who were starting work on *Excalibur*. I was in great admiration of John Boorman; I considered him one of the few British filmmakers with real balls. He seemed unafraid to explore different genres and had made another of my favorite films, *Deliverance*.

Roger Pratt and I met John and his producer Michael Dryhurst. The creative team were all there: Alex Thomson the director of photography, Tony Pratt his designer and costume designer Bob Ringwood. There were also various other members of John's team, and Roger and I found ourselves once again screening this little film to some industry heavyweights. When the lights went up, John turned to his team and said, "You see, that's exactly what I want. The photography and the locations, the screen value and the drama."

I apologized to Tony Pratt who I knew well, and said we had had no money. I explained to John that because we had a crew and cast of thirteen people, and equipment comprising a camper van, a Volkswagen van and a couple of cars, I could get into remote locations where we could film amazing vistas. He would have no chance with a crew of one hundred or more that made up a big epic like his. He agreed and so did Tony and Alex.

We went through how I had gambled on the weather as well, and the gamble had paid off as I got some of the most dramatic skies I had ever seen. We talked about technical details and then John asked if I minded if he added an underwater scene like mine. I was flattered that a great filmmaker like John had even liked what I had done, let alone asked to use it as an inspiration. John remained a loyal supporter for me, and between him and Jeremy Thomas and George Lucas I gained enough confidence to continue.

One print had gone back with George Lucas to be archived and I remember George telling me he had shown it to Steven Spielberg, who said at the time it was the most enigmatic film he had ever seen.

I had attempted to make a Kurosawa-style epic in Scotland for a budget of twenty-five thousand pounds and somehow pulled it off despite the rain and lack of film. It proved very popular with the audiences wherever it was shown in different countries and led to some amazing encounters and controversies. Even to this day Internet sites ask about this film, as it has stayed in people's memories. The Internet Movie Database site (IMDb) still has blogs about it. A Swedish video company owner, Charles Aperia of VTC, loved the film so much he bought it to distribute in Scandinavia and took me to Sweden to see if we could make a film together. His entire family was very passionate about it, and Charles released it to great acclaim in Sweden. I think the Bergman type of images appealed. I even got to go and stand on the stages where Bergman had filmed *Fanny and Alexander*, another one of my very favorite movies. Again they felt it touched their soul deeply inside, and I was very humbled at their sincerity.

An amazing thing happened to me because of *Black Angel*. I was picked up by American agent Harry Ufland. Harry had screened movies at Twentieth Century Fox looking for new British directors and had fallen in love with *Black Angel*. Now let me put this in perspective: Harry owned a boutique agency called the Ufland Agency, and he was agent to Martin Scorsese, Robert De Niro, Jodie Foster, Harvey Keitel, Ridley Scott, Tony Scott, Bertrand Tavernier, Adrian Lyne, Martin Brest, et al. So when he called me in London and wanted to meet, I was pretty nervous.

Harry turned out to be really great and smart and friendly, and praised my film no end. He suggested we talk further and I mistakenly asked him if there was anywhere he wanted to go. He asked if we could have lunch at the Waterside Inn in Bray. I agreed immediately, and we fixed Sunday lunch for him and his wife Mary at the The Waterside Inn, owned by the Roux brothers, which has climbed from one Michelin star to two and is now one of the few three-star restaurants. It is sited on the River Thames in spectacular surroundings and the food is absolutely exquisite. We had lunch and a wonderful time with them, and by the end Harry had taken me on, though it was never stated that day. All I remember is paying as we had offered to take him there, and it cost me about three months' mortgage. However, the meal was memorable and well worth ten times that for the wonderful time we had. Thank goodness for credit cards and friendly bank managers—we used to have those, and mine, David Palmer at NatWest, was a friend who I'd have lunch with. Sadly now we are all numbers and speak to call centers. It is not an improvement.

And so I found myself with an agent in Los Angeles. I was so bewildered and unsure of being in such illustrious company that I wrote a card to Harry asking if it was real, was he really, truly now my agent? He sent me a message back saying: I AM YOUR AGENT. BELIEVE IT.

Harry arranged for me to go to Los Angeles for meetings, and to meet the team at the agency. Bill Unger was assigned to look after me on a day-to-day basis, and it was a pleasure to deal with such a smart and dedicated person. I felt in really good hands.

My highlight of this trip was when I went to meet Francis Ford Coppola and Fred Roos at his newly formed Zoetrope Studios. This was where the idea of making *Joan of Arc* was conceived, and we discussed another wonderful book I had been reading and thinking about, which I also wanted to make. I was given a deal with them to develop a film and to think seriously about what to make. Harry loved the idea of *Joan of Arc* and wanted Jodie Foster to play her. Jodie was fluent in French and in Paris at the time, so he tried to set up a meeting with her for when I returned. She would have been a wonderful Joan of Arc, and I was pushing hard to make this happen. At the studios when I was looking around the sets and meeting with the executives for more talks, I was invited to go to sit with Francis Ford Coppola in his mobile trailer on the backlot. Francis, who was always ahead of the game technically, had an instant system of recording and editing set up, where he could direct from his caravan by remote.

He was making *One from the Heart* at the time with Frederic Forrest and Nastassja Kinski. Francis had a portable edit system and mixing console and as he made each take he edited it straight in to see how it worked. He then called Frederic on a red phone in the corner of the studio and instructed him like that for take two. I sat fascinated by this wonderful master at work, and how he was really making young and vibrant movies at Zoetrope, experimenting with each one. I went onto the set to see Dean Tavoularis, the designer, and meet Frederic Forrest. I asked him how it was being directed by remote like that, and he said it was a bit strange, however he'd gotten used to it and if he really needed anything more he went to see Francis or Francis came to the set.

I was then honored to meet the legendary Michael Powell. He was working as an assistant to Francis, and was just relishing being back on a film set. Later he was hoping to make his film there and return to directing. He was in his late seventies and running around like a young man. I was so touched to see his enthusiasm and the heart he was putting into being there; here was one of the filmmaking masters of the world, who had so impressed me growing up, and I found it heartbreaking that he was not being given funding to make more movies. He said he was just grateful to be working. He was full of ideas and stories and god bless Francis Ford Coppola for giving him this chance, and Martin Scorsese who was going to produce a movie for him to direct afterwards. It's a cruel industry really that thwarted such a talent from continuing to do what he should have been doing after such an illustrious career. And why? Because the establishment proclaimed that *Peeping Tom* was a bad film, and had a shocking influence. Powell himself always defended it, saying that he was trying to explore what the future held, when violence in cinema became pronounced. He was exploring the dangers of showing violence and how it could influence someone unstable. It's a powerful film, which I think is among his best work, but it destroyed his career, he was so lambasted by the critics. He was never ever able to get funding again.

So here I was on hallowed ground and researching a movie to make at the studio with arguably one of the best directors of the era. I felt truly blessed.

STAR WARS: RETURN OF THE JEDI

Whilst waiting for my first feature film, *The Sender*, to officially start pre-production. I had a call from Robert Watts on George Lucas's behalf asking what I was doing. I told them that I was waiting on Paramount to begin casting on *The Sender*, and they asked me to go that day to EMI Studios and see George, who was at Elstree shooting *Return of the Jedi*. Richard Marquand was directing it and George was directing the second-unit work and pickups. George felt he wanted to spend more time on the main unit with Richard to keep the *Star Wars* vision exactly where he wanted it, so they asked if I would take over the second unit as director and work for about five to six weeks. They couldn't actually give me a credit at that stage as they had promised it to first assistant director David Tomblin. George was like family to me, and having helped me launch my career as a director so thoughtfully, the credit was unimportant. I would do anything to help him.

George and Robert needed me urgently to start that same day. He was in trouble over stage availability and the first unit had to move on from the huge battle scene they were shooting. I walked onto a stage where there were about five cameras setting up a huge stunt scene requiring twenty or more stuntmen and many extras for the ship's crew. George and the main unit just walked away and I took over after a deep discussion with George and the stunt co-ordinator about exactly what he wanted.

A rig had been set up in front of a massive blue screen to launch a huge piece of a spaceship's engine onto the set, as the ship was hit and the engine piece flew at the camera. In the finished scene it would smash through the cockpit window and onto the deck, plunging down onto the lower deck below as the crew threw themselves to safety. It was a huge stunt and action scene. I just got on with it and started orchestrating the actors and stunt players with my first assistant director. At one moment I looked around the stage and saw boxes of camera gear and very expensive lenses piled up on the set. I asked the camera boys to move them back for safety. They said they had talked to Kit West the special-effects head, who had assured them they were safe. I had a flash of instinct to move them, so I ordered them to move the boxes to the back beyond the set, just for safety. The grips and camera assistants moved everything, and we set up the shot. After much rehearsal and practice, as safety is always the main concern with stuntmen involved, the stunt co-ordinator Peter Diamond was happy and gave me the go-ahead.

We rolled cameras and I shouted "Action!" The crew went to work and looked like they were manning the ship in the middle of a heated battle, and then on a countdown of three the massive piece of junk engine was fired. It blasted into the air straight at the cameras, sailed through the window, and smashed into the deck, right where all the camera boxes were before I had moved them, breaking part of the set with the force of its trajectory.

Robert Watts walked over to me after I said cut and we had made sure everyone was okay. Robert gave me a hug and looked at the camera boxes. "You just earned your entire five weeks' salary," he said to me and left to see George. The camera assistant thanked me profusely, and we went back to work to shoot some cuts for the scene and complete the sequence as time, as always, was at a premium.

I spent ten days shooting Ewoks and begged George to let me stop and shoot something else. He just loved the scenes we were making up of Ewoks partying and wanted more and more. Jim Henson had baby puppet Ewoks dancing in their nests, moving to the beat of the music for the end of the movie. I also did a lot of shooting with Warwick Davis, who would later take over as Wicket in Crescent City when Kenny Baker fell ill. George liked the way Warwick played the little Ewok, so wanted me to shoot more and more footage of him. I knew then that George was planning an Ewok movie somewhere in his mind. I just kept begging to go back onto action scenes and was rewarded when given the task of filming the close-up of Harrison Ford being freed from being carbonized. They scheduled Harrison into makeup in-between first-unit shooting and we shot him waking from the carbon freeze and falling forward. Another iconic moment for me and the crew, a rewarding piece of cinema history captured.

FINAL WORDS

STAR WARS

This is a very tough industry that we are in, where resilience and patience, and for me having great mentors like designers John Box and John Barry, and filmmakers like George Lucas, Ridley Scott, Alan Pakula, George Miller, and John Boorman, enable an artist to keep the faith and not get disillusioned. The story of what George Lucas went through as a young filmmaker made him determined to succeed on his own terms, and stands as a testament to resilience. I am proud to have helped him achieve such phenomenal success with *Star Wars*, and connecting people back to the roots of myth and legend. Having practiced Buddhism and been engrossed in myths and legends from an early age, I immediately understood *Star Wars* and the underlying power of George's script. Finally cinema audiences were served a classic tale for the modern man that teenagers could relate to. They could enjoy the ride, as it were, but without even realizing that they were absorbing the keys embedded in all the classical myths and legends to help us grow into balanced adults, and actually engage us onto the spiritual journey. Joseph Campbell in his series of lectures on myth said that George was the only true modern mythmaker working today and he was right.

Now with the phenomenal success of J.J. Abrams continuing the *Star Wars* series with *The Force Awakens*, it does not surprise me at all that a new generation of children and adults is embracing *Star Wars*, finding it as exhilarating and exciting as when *A New Hope* was first released. J.J. Abrams has so reverently respected George Lucas's first *Star Wars* movie and brought back to a whole new audience what everyone loved about that first experience. He has done a masterful work in returning the true spirit of George's creation to a new audience. More and more people are asking about the making of the first film and how we achieved what we did, especially my role in creating Luke's lightsaber that plays such a prominent role in *The Force Awakens*. This simple prop that I made out of scrap and superglue for about twelve dollars has become the most iconic image of *Star Wars*. What a privilege to be a part of the enduring legacy of George's vision, and proving that George did hit the spot as a mythmaker. I hope that this book sheds light on many of the unanswered questions surrounding the making of the first film.

What is vitally important to remember as Disney, J.J. Abrams, and Kathleen Kennedy bring the *Star Wars* universe to a new and enthusiastic audience is that George Lucas single-handedly created this enduring world for children and adults, and managed to connect to a global audience. As religions and spirituality wane in the Western world, *Star Wars* has, in its way, created a new tale of optimism for people to believe in. A world where light triumphs over dark and where good conquers evil. It is a world full of hope.

ALIEN

It's the same with *Alien*. I am equally proud to have been at the core of the making of another enduring classic. Standing by Ridley's side on what was an incredibly tough shoot for him, it was as artistically rewarding as anything I have worked on as far as getting the look of the sets right in a science-fiction film. *Alien*'s look has influenced almost every science-fiction film since and still retains the power to entertain it had when first released.

BLACK ANGEL

When I looked for a story that had the hero's journey at its core as a central theme, *Nostradamus* came to me like a destined arrow from the dark. The story of a man out of time with the era he was born in who stood by his principles, and eventually succeeded with a humanitarian approach to everything against all odds, and threats of death. This has been the film I made that connected to audiences, once again enforcing the power of myth told through the eyes of one of the most famous seers in history. I was careful to include how he remained a committed family man, the most important element in his life that saw him hiding from the world that embraced him as a hero and yet criticized him heavily at times. George Lucas is the perfect example of a modern mythmaker, and despite his massive success still remains to this day a family-oriented man.

In the end this is the real hero's journey that each of us are destined to travel. *Lord of the Rings*, *Gladiator*, *Star Wars*, *Mad Max*, *Avatar*—all these films use the hero's journey at their core, and represent new cinematic ways of retelling these important myths. As human beings we need them. They contain keys to help us find our place in the world and help us grow through stages in life from child to adult. As reading and literature gives way to television and games, it is vitally important these myths are told and retold. The massive success these films have garnered with audiences worldwide is no accident.

They connect to the subconscious and whether consciously or subconsciously realized, their power to inform us of our true journey as human beings cannot be underestimated.

My first feature movie, *The Sender*, was a true baptism of fire, and the experience may be worthy to put down in words one day to help aspiring filmmakers. The realities of making a movie for an old-time TV studio producer and the amazing rollercoaster results and conflicts that went on with its release were daunting.

When I found out by accident that *The Sender* had been chosen as the opening film for the highly prestigious Avoriaz Fantastic Film Festival in France, an entirely new perspective on life as a film director was given to me. Avoriaz was the largest festival then for science fiction, fantasy, and horror films and attended by some of the most elite filmmakers. The hugely positive reaction to my film at the festival from incredibly talented peers like George Miller, Jean-Jacques Annaud, Claude Chabrol, Jim Henson, Gary Kurtz, and one of America's finest directors Alan Pakula, it began dawning on me that I had actually made a film that resonated with people. Alan Pakula loved the film and took me to lunch to talk about it. I began to understand what it took to be a movie director as Alan and George Miller gave me incredibly kind advice and encouraged me to go on. Alan Pakula told me something at lunch that day in Avoriaz that deeply connected to me, and his words of pure wisdom I have passed on since to many aspiring filmmakers.

"When you first start as an artist in any field you have this burning flame like a beacon inside you. Then as you progress you have to protect that flame from the pressures around you if you enter the world of Hollywood or any big business. To protect the flame you have to build thick concrete walls around it. The problem is that many artists build the walls so thick that the flame goes out."

I think the great Alan Pakula's words to me stand testament to everything and are a fitting epitaph to this book. Alan Pakula told me he long wanted to start Directors Anonymous, where fledgling directors could call seasoned veterans for advice and encouragement.

Alan's tragic and senseless death far too early is a huge loss to American and world cinema. I found out many years later that Quentin Tarantino admired *The Sender* and regarded it as the best film released in 1982.

As I write, *Black Angel* has had a resurrection beyond my wildest dreams. I had been hunting for the negative or a print for many years. Whilst I was filming *Nostradamus* in Transylvania a year after the revolution, with no phones and little contact with the outside world, my print that was in the vault with my masters at Richard Edlund's Boss Film Studios was thrown in the garbage when Boss went into the hands of the receivers. The only other print was one George Lucas had archived, but somehow, maybe with the transfer from the Egg Factory to Skywalker, the archivist could not track it down. The Twentieth Century Fox archivist in London tried searching as well, but turned up nothing.

After contacting me, writer Nathan Mattise wrote an article on *Black Angel* for *Wired* magazine in a series called 'Forgotten Relics'. Its influence at the time on *Excalibur* and the use of step-printing a scene in *The Empire Strikes Back* amongst other films, and the images of Scotland in 2.35 CinemaScope, seemed to have resonated widely.

Around the same time as the article I received a phone call from a Bob O'Neil, who announced he was the archivist at Universal Studios in Los Angeles and he had the negative and several tins of elements of *Black Angel*. I was, to put it mildly, shocked.

For many years I have been requested to release *Black Angel* again; Peter Briggs actually quoted lines from the film he remembered from thirty years ago on a call to me. It seems that people who saw it retained a memory of the images, even after all this time. As I was influenced by Tarkovsky's method of making his films to connect to the subconscious, not the conscious part of the brain, it seems to have worked. A Scottish fan, Guy Veale, actually came to its US premier screening in Mill Valley Film Festival in 2013. He traveled all the way from Glasgow, to prove that the images he had retained in his mind at five years old after seeing the film in the North Star Cinema in Lerwick, Shetland Islands, were real. His father had taken him to see *The Empire Strikes Back*, and *Black Angel* was therefore the first film he had ever seen—the images had haunted him for over thirty years.

What I kept pondering was that thirty years after I had made the film, times had changed so much; maybe it was best to let the film remain in people's memories. My fear was that the film would not stand the test of time. It seems the universe was conspiring against me when another random call came out of the blue from David Tanaka and Brice Parker. They were part of a film restoration society in Mill Valley, California; Brice worked for Athena, who had done some work on the restoration for one of the *Star Wars* movies, and David for Pixar. They had been tracking *Black Angel* from all the publicity surrounding the film as a lost piece of *Star Wars* history. *Wired* magazine had done an article about its important place in film culture and its influence on other movies. When the story broke online of the negative being lost for thirty years and miraculously found in Universal Studios, it was widely covered in the press; Steven McKenzie for the BBC online and Richard Verrier for the *Los Angeles Times* wrote extensive stories about it. The lost and recently restored film being commissioned by George Lucas to release with *The Empire Strikes Back* made the story very prominent globally. David and Brice called to offer to digitally restore the film as they felt it had an important place in film history because it had been so widely publicized as a part of the *Star*

Wars family. Knowing that George had step-printed a Yoda fight scene in *The Empire Strikes Back* after seeing my fight scenes and its influence on John Boorman's *Excalibur* they felt it should be restored and claim its place for everyone to see. Sensing both my enthusiasm and my reticence for the above reason, they said, "Let's get the neg out and digitized," and they would restore a frame and let me see what it looked like.

When I saw the result, looking exactly as I had filmed in Scotland in full 2.35 aspect ratio, and every detail and color exactly as Roger Pratt and I had filmed it, I couldn't say no. David's son Mitchell did a summer work experience digitally restoring the film frame by frame with a truly dedicated team at Athena Studios under Jon Peters and Colorflow, masterfully cared for at every process by producers David and Brice.

It was chosen for the closing film at the Mill Valley Film Festival and screened to a packed cinema. I felt nervous to attend, but Lina, my wife, insisted we go. It was a golden opportunity to watch it with an audience after thirty-five years and as she said my *Black Angel* is my legacy. It was also a chance to meet up with Jon Rinzler and George and I wanted Lina to meet Lynn Hale and Jane Bay. However nervous I was to watch it with an audience, David and Brice and the teams had done so much for the film I had to comment on their work and judge if we needed to restore the sound. After the screening a Q&A with the audience went on for almost two hours. Jane Bay was almost reduced to tears having not seen the film since I made it.

Most important was my questioning a group of young film students as to the pace and images and the way I told the story. I had stood before the audience before the screening and said, "Please set your clocks back thirty-five years," and these students were not even born then! And they all agreed one thing. They loved the film, and the pacing—it allowed them to enjoy the images. One said, "It's true—if I handed this in as my thesis work, I'd most likely be told to cut and pace it up, but they'd be wrong." Now I felt less nervous about letting the film out to be seen again. We also decided that Skywalker Sound should restore the soundtrack to match the picture.

David and I went to the ranch and showed their sound mixer Brandon Proctor the film. He was wise and said, "Don't do too much or the digitally restored sound won't match the original picture." They had to make the same decisions restoring the *Star Wars* films to the digital format. He was also aware of Bill Rowe and his legendary place in the history of film sound, and noted how well the film's sound had been mixed. So all they did was expand out the music and effects into surround 5:1 and clean up a few areas of dirt. Skywalker Sound are the best, and the soundtrack to *Black Angel* was very important to me as music is the one art that can truly touch the soul, as Tarkovsky illustrates in *Stalker*. After catching up over a long three-hour lunch with George, who happened to be at Skywalker Sound, and getting his advice on making *Black Angel* as a feature, we returned home.

Guy Veale was the happiest man I had known: what he thought was a dream but believed was real proved him to be right at the screening. He was so enthusiastic he offered to produce a small tour of *Black Angel* in Scotland and get the Glasgow Film Festival to host a new premiere.

Glasgow Film Festival had us booked in a small theater for the festival but as the days passed, more and more tickets got sold until we ended up in the main four-hundred-seat theater. The film was made entirely in Scotland and it was the first time ever that stunning images of Scotland in full CinemaScope were shown in the cinema. Also *The Dollar Bottom* had been the first film to win Scotland an Academy Award, so the reception for the film and me was like a returning hero.

The Q&A monitored by Guy Veale went on for over two hours. The digitally restored master looked and sounded amazing, I was so impressed with what David and Brice and the teams had achieved. A producer stood up in the audience who had produced the pilot for *Game of Thrones*, claiming that I had started it all many years ago. I was humbled and flattered.

We toured three other cities: Edinburgh, Dundee, and Inverness. I had cast three children in the film as plague victims, and they all turned up at the screening, and we spent a good deal of time after, talking and taking pictures. They told me that I had gone to the school to cast the roles, and they were the only children who didn't laugh during the casting, so they got the roles. Also, of course, their faces were right as well.

The only sad part of the journey was that James Gibb had just passed away, literally a few weeks before the screening. His wife and sister came and were thrilled with my stories about James and how I had cast him, and also given him a large role in the Academy Award-winning *Dollar Bottom*. I would love to have seen James; he was clearly not only a wonderful actor but also a great human being.

After the screening in Glasgow the BBC online article by Steven McKenzie garnered five hundred thousand hits in a week, and spawned a crescendo of articles. An *Esquire* online article by Jeremy Singer went viral—it is estimated we had millions of online press. Amazing after thirty years.

After a release on iTunes the film was posted on YouTube for a limited run to create a buzz for the announcement of the feature. With an introduction by me we garnered well over three hundred thousand hits in two days and much encouragement, as viewers seem to enjoy being able to savor the drama and landscapes and connect to the myth of it. With around six hundred and thirty thousand hits on iTunes I feel I caught a moment as a tide had turned and my original intention of connecting to the subconscious might have succeeded.

The result of all this is that the original story, a reality-based sword-and-sorcery epic, is being made—thirty-five years late, but the genre was just not acceptable at that time. Now *Lord of the Rings* and *Game of Thrones* have made the genre hot, and finally I am able to make a film that has been burning a hole in my soul all these years.

Black Angel is finally being made as the epic feature I always imagined and, coming full circle, I am returning to the cinema I love best of all: fantasy that is real and believable, and follows the classic hero's journey.

I have written this chapter because my last words to anyone aspiring to follow their dreams are truly more pertinent than ever. Do not let anyone tell you you can't—you can. Just have a dogged determination, and never, ever give up…

ACKNOWLEDGMENTS

I would like to express my deep gratitude to the following individuals who gave their support during the time I wrote down the memories of such an auspicious time in my career, and their recent help in creating a global awareness of my role in making *Star Wars*, *Alien* and *Black Angel*. This book would not be the same without their unending enthusiasm and help.

A special thanks to my wife, Lina Dhingra, whose love knows no bounds. Her help during the year and more I took off to write the first drafts of Cinema Alchemist made it all possible.

David Kennedy
John Rinzler
Lynn Hale
Jonathan Wilkins
Robert Lee
Stella Zhamkochian
Guy Veale
Jane Bay

This work is dedicated to Thomas, Camille, and Arjun.
And all the children in the world,
The Force is with you.

For more fantastic non-fiction, fiction, author events,
competitions, limited editions and more:

VISIT OUR WEBSITE
titanbooks.com

LIKE US ON FACEBOOK
facebook.com/titanbooks

FOLLOW US ON TWITTER
@TitanBooks

EMAIL US
readerfeedback@titanemail.com